Women in the Weimar Republic

Manchester University Press

Women in the Weimar Republic

Helen Boak

Manchester University Press
Manchester and New York
distributed in the United States exclusively by Palgrave Macmillan

Copyright © Helen Boak 2013

The right of Helen Boak to be identified as the author of this work has been asserted by her in accordance with the Copyright, Designs and Patents Act 1988.

Published by Manchester University Press
Oxford Road, Manchester M13 9NR, UK
and Room 400, 175 Fifth Avenue, New York, NY 10010, USA
www.manchesteruniversitypress.co.uk

Distributed in the United States exclusively by
Palgrave Macmillan, 175 Fifth Avenue, New York,
NY 10010, USA

Distributed in Canada exclusively by
UBC Press, University of British Columbia, 2029 West Mall,
Vancouver, BC, Canada V6T 1Z2

British Library Cataloguing-in-Publication Data
A catalogue record for this book is available from the British Library

Library of Congress Cataloging-in-Publication Data applied for

ISBN   978 0 7190 8818 6   hardback
ISBN   978 0 7190 8819 3   paperback

First published 2013

The publisher has no responsibility for the persistence or accuracy of URLs for any external or third-party internet websites referred to in this book, and does not guarantee that any content on such websites is, or will remain, accurate or appropriate.

Typeset in Sabon
by Servis Filmsetting Ltd, Stockport, Cheshire
Printed in Great Britain
by Bell & Bain Ltd, Glasgow

Contents

List of figures	vii
List of tables	ix
List of abbreviations	xi
Introduction	1
1 Women in the First World War	13
2 Women and politics	63
3 Women and work	134
4 Women, the family and sexuality	200
5 Women in the public realm	254
Conclusion	292
Bibliography	300
Index	345

Figures

2.1 'Your children need peace and bread; for that reason, women, cast your vote!' (December 1918). Bundesarchiv, Plak 002-004-017/Martha Jaeger 68
2.2 'German Women, German Loyalty. We are voting German National' (October 1932). Bundesarchiv, Plak 002-029-087 72
2.3 'Women – for peace and freedom! Vote Social Democrat List 2' (October 1932). Bundesarchiv, Plak 002-020-092 73
2.4 'Women. Only in the Soviet Union is there protection for mother and child! In Germany children are dying and women suffering! Fight with the Communists List 6' (Bavarian Landtag election poster, April 1932). Bundesarchiv, Plak 002-019-064 74
2.5 'Women! Take care of housing, prosperity, knowledge. Vote List 6 German Democrats!' (May 1928). Bundesarchiv, Plak 002-027-031/Theo Matejko 75
2.6 'Mothers, working women. We are voting National Socialist List 8' (April 1932). Bundesarchiv, Plak 002-040-011/Felix Albrecht 77
2.7 'Only a strong Germany can give the Germans work'. National Socialist demonstration in Berlin (1931). IMAGNO/Austrian Archives (s) 84
2.8 Weimar 1919: elected female representatives (1919). Landesarchiv Berlin, F Rep. 290, Nr. 58719 90
3.1 Homework in the Weimar Republic: an old woman carries huge crates and baskets of toys over the mountains to the distributors (1925). Archiv der Sozialen Demokratie der Friedrich Ebert Stiftung 149

3.2	The typing pool of a Berlin business (c. 1925). IMAGNO/Austrian Archives	151
3.3	Registrar: a young woman with a *Bubikopf* placing files in a cabinet (Berlin 1925). IMAGNO/Austrian Archives Photograph by Becker & Maass	151
3.4	Window dresser: a Berlin department store employee dresses the leg of a shop window mannequin (c. 1925). IMAGNO/Austrian Archives	152
4.1	Inflation: Germany is being liquidated. The Berlin Housewives' Associations' facility for the sale of private property (1923). bpk/Kunstbibliothek, SMB, Phototek Willy Römer/Willy Römer (20039006)	204
4.2	Women's dormitory in a Berlin homeless shelter (December 1930). Bundesarchiv, Bild 102-10840/ Georg Pahl	205
5.1	Young woman alone in the Romanisches Cafe, Berlin (1924). bpk	254
5.2	The radio provides the entertainment on a Berlin roof-top in summer (1926). bpk	260
5.3	A lone female driver defends herself against a would-be attacker (July 1931). Bundesarchiv, Bild 102-11988/ Georg Pahl	262
5.4	Eight young people on an excursion into the Berlin countryside (1928). bpk	264
5.5	'What do you say about Fräulein Mia?', *Berliner Illustrirte Zeitung* (13 November 1927). bpk/ Kunstbibliothek, SMB/Dietmar Katz	270
5.6	'The change in women's fashions: the fashionable woman of today and from our grandfathers' time', *Berliner Illustrirte Zeitung* (6 September 1925). bpk/ Kunstbibliothek, SMB/Dietmar Katz	271

Tables

2.1	The impact of female suffrage on the number of seats won by the major parties in the 1928 Reichstag election	79
2.2	The percentages of the total male (m) and female (f) votes cast for the NSDAP in selected areas in Reichstag elections, 1930–33	82
2.3	Female delegates to the state assemblies by party, 1919–33	91
2.4	Seats in the Prussian Landtag, 1919–32	92
2.5	Representatives in the National Assembly and the Reichstag, 1919–33	94
3.1	Women in the workforce according to each area of employment, 1907, 1925 and 1933	139
3.2	Working women in the female population, 1907, 1925 and 1933	140
3.3	The marital status of the female workforce, 1907, 1925 and 1933	140
3.4	The marital status of the female population, 1907, 1925 and 1933	140
3.5	The number of working women according to their marital status and occupational category, 1925 and 1933	141
3.6	The number of working women according to occupational classifications, 1925 and 1933	142
3.7	The percentages of the male and female workforce in each area of employment, 1907, 1925 and 1933	142
4.1	The marital status of the population, 1910, 1925 and 1933	202
4.2	Marriages and live births in selected years, 1885–1933	207
4.3	The divorce rate, 1910–33	223

Abbreviations

ADEF	Archive of the German Protestant Women's League, Archive of the German Women's Movement, Kassel
ADLV	General German Women Teachers' Association
AKDFB	Archive of the German Catholic Women's League, Cologne
BAB	Federal Archives Berlin
BAK	Federal Archives Koblenz
BdÄ	Federation of German Female Physicians
BdF	Federation of German Women's Associations
BfM	League for the Protection of Mothers
BKL	Queen Luise League
BVP	Bavarian People's Party
DAB	German Federation of Female Academics
DDP	German Democratic Party
DEF	German Protestant Women's League
DFBK	German Women's Committee to Combat the War Guilt Lie
DFK	German Women's Fighting League
DFO	German Women's Order
DNHV	German National Commercial Employees' Association
DNVP	German National People's Party
DStP	German State Party
DVP	German People's Party
GdA	Trade Union of White-Collar Workers
GLA	Generallandesarchiv, Karlsruhe
HLA	Helene Lange Archive, Berlin (in LAB)
ICW	International Council of Women
IFFF	International Women's League for Peace and Freedom, German branch

IWSA	International Women's Suffrage Alliance
KdF	Strength through Joy
KFB	Catholic Women's League
KPD	German Communist Party
LAB	State Archives, Berlin
NFD	National Women's Service
NLB	New Land Movement
NSDAP	National Socialist German Workers' Party
NSF	National Socialist Women's Organisation
RFMB	Red Women's and Girls' League
RNF	Ring of National Women
SdR	Statistisches Reichsamt, *Statistik des Deutschen Reiches*
SPD	German Social Democratic Party
StAH	Staatsarchiv Hamburg
StJhb	*Statistisches Jahrbuch für das Deutsche Reich*
USPD	German Independent Social Democratic Party
VEFD	Union of German Protestant Women's Organisations
VRT	Association of German Female Reich Postal and Telegraph Civil Servants
Z	The German Centre Party
ZdA	Central Union of White-Collar Workers
ZStA	Zentrales Staatsarchiv Potsdam

Introduction

The Weimar Republic, fourteen years of turbulent political, economic, social and cultural change, has attracted significant attention from historians, primarily because they are seeking to explain the Nazis' accession to power in 1933. In their search for continuities in German history, German historians in the 1960s and 1970s espoused the view that Germany had followed a special path, a *Sonderweg*, in which, following the failure of bourgeois liberals to unify Germany in 1848, the German nation-state created by Prussian military might in 1871 remained a politically and socially backward country with an authoritarian monarch and influential pre-industrial elites as the country underwent rapid economic and industrial development.[1] The late Detlev Peukert challenged this view and emphasised Germany's modernity, rather than its backwardness. He portrayed the Weimar Republic as 'a critical phase in the era of "classical modernity"' which began in the 1890s, and as 'a crisis-racked, modernising society'.[2] As Edward Ross Dickinson has noted, 'Germany appears here not as a nation having trouble modernising, but as a nation of troubling modernity.'[3] Peukert's interpretation stimulated further historical engagement with the semantics and notions of crisis and, to a lesser extent, modernity, and as a corollary encouraged historians to explore the Weimar Republic for its own sake, rather than as a precursor to the Third Reich.[4] In 2005 German historians noted that the word 'crisis', which featured in the titles of more than 370 books published during the Republic, was understood by contemporaries to mean a 'time of decision', with a choice between possible outcomes, and this openness about the future was, according to Rüdiger Graf, fundamental to the Republic which he describes as 'an open space of multiple developmental opportunities'.[5] Peukert himself noted that 'in a mere fourteen years nearly all the possibilities of modern existence were played out', and Peter Fritzsche has also referred to the Republic as 'a series of bold experiments' and as a time when 'nothing was certain and everything possible'.[6] This book seeks to explore the opportunities and possibilities that the Weimar Republic offered women.

Since the early 1970s, stimulated by the second-wave feminism of the 1960s, there has been a considerable increase in the number of works exploring women's experiences in the Weimar Republic, and many them have focused on the 'new woman'. For many, during the Republic and subsequently, the 'new woman' was a potent symbol of both Weimar's modernity and its crisis.[7] For some, she symbolised the opportunities offered by the Republic, for others its degeneracy, indicative of the contradictions inherent in modernity. Sporting a page-boy haircut, known in German as a *Bubikopf*, and a short skirt over her androgynous figure, she was economically independent and sexually emancipated. Her image featured prominently in popular culture, leading some to question to what extent the image reflected the actuality of women's lives during the Republic. Atina Grossmann is adamant: 'This New Woman was not merely a media myth or a demographer's paranoid fantasy, but a social reality that can be researched and documented.'[8] But who, precisely, was this 'new woman'? For Eric Weitz she was 'a class-bound image of middle- and upper-class women who had the independence and the means to pursue their interests and desires', while Grossmann comments: 'The "new woman" was not only the intellectual with masculine haircut and unisex suit or the young white-collar worker in flapper outfit so familiar to us from 1920s movies. She was also the young married factory worker who now cooked only one meal a day, no longer baked or canned, cut her hair short into a practical *Bubikopf*, and tried by all available means and at any price to keep her family small.'[9] Elizabeth Harvey has noted that 'any and every facet of "modern womanhood" became incorporated into the "new woman": "she" was both a devouring femme fatale and a cross-dressing lesbian, a sportswoman and an efficient housewife, a movie-going typist and a bluestocking student.'[10] Grossmann has seen in the 'new woman' a challenge to the 'old woman', who was the mother of several children, or the single feminist.[11] Cornelie Usborne, too, has emphasised the fundamental differences in the values and behaviour of women of different generations during the Republic.[12]

The proliferation and multiplicity of images of the 'new woman' in the middle years of the Weimar Republic attest to the increasing visibility of women in the workplace, outside the home, in the media, films, newspapers, illustrated magazines and political posters and on advertising hoardings. These images are more accessible to the historian than is the actuality of women's lives during the Republic, and this is one reason why there has been such a focus on the 'new woman' in the historiography and why cultural and art history studies of the representation and construction of women in popular culture abound, stimulated by Patrice Petro's exploration of the German cinema's attempt to address women as spectators.[13] The 'new woman', made flesh in the images of young, independent women working as shop assistants or typists and enjoying a myriad of leisure pursuits while being targeted by the advertising industry, was an urban phenomenon particularly prevalent in Berlin, a city which provides a wealth of resources for the historian. Julia Sneeringer's study of party-political propaganda aimed at women is based on Berlin, and Weitz has claimed in his history of Weimar Germany that 'Weimar was Berlin, Berlin Weimar.'[14] A concentration on Berlin downplays the significance of regionalism and religion in German history, and this book attempts to go beyond the boundaries of Berlin to seek evidence of the variety of women's experiences during the Weimar Republic, which were influenced not just by location, religion and age, but also by class, employment and marital status.

The 'new woman' is emblematic of a generation of young women who were able to take advantage of a range of opportunities and the relaxed social mores of the Weimar Republic to pursue the career of their choosing, to benefit from improved access to birth control so that they could control their fertility and plan their families, to venture unchaperoned outside the home, perhaps to partake of a range of recreational activities, to enjoy platonic friendships with members of the opposite sex, to talk openly about sexual matters with their partners and to participate fully in political life. The concept of the 'new woman' was a convenient target for those concerned about the continuing challenges to the pre-war gender order, which had first been undermined during the First World War, and in Birthe Kundrus's view, these challenges were perceived as 'an attack on male power and male identity'.[15] Other historians have alluded to a 'crisis of masculinity' brought about by the humiliation of the defeat in the war, the physical and psychological scars caused by the war and fears and anxieties about the changes in the relationship between the sexes, in the home, the workplace and society at large.[16] The 'new woman' was also the target for nationalists who believed that her selfish reluctance to have children endangered the future of the German race.

Historians disagree on the extent to which the Weimar Republic was an emancipatory experience for women. 'Emancipation' is here understood to mean the setting free of women from all legal, moral and intellectual restraints which barred them from total equality with men. The early years of the Republic, 1918 and 1919, have been portrayed as a period of opportunity and great optimism for women, who now enjoyed full suffrage rights and whose equality with men was, in principle, enshrined in Article 109 of the Constitution of the German Reich of 11 August 1919.[17] This has been contrasted with both the 'intense unrelenting attack on women' towards the end of the Republic and the move to the right of the middle-class women's movement and the liberal parties.[18] With regard to employment, Renate Bridenthal believes that '"progress" for women in this era was dubious indeed', and that women were pushed 'even further toward the bottom of the skills-and-pay pyramid than before'.[19] She sees in the myth of women's economic emancipation a reason why women voted for conservative parties that promoted women's traditional role within the home. Elizabeth Bright Jones has linked women's economic exploitation to voting behaviour. In her exploration of female farm labour in Saxony she has noted how the government's failure to address the overburdening of farm wives was exploited by right-wing agrarian parties.[20] Jill Stephenson, Ursula Nienhaus and Doris Kampmann have explored the difficulties encountered by women wishing to pursue professional careers.[21] Historians who have researched population policy, abortion, contraception and sex reform have, however, highlighted the improvements in women's access to birth control and in their reproductive rights during the Republic.[22] Weitz regards the promotion of a responsible and pleasurable sex life for all as one of the Republic's radical accomplishments, though Grossmann has emphasised that most sex reformers were concerned primarily with improving the sex lives of married couples, attempting 'to reconcile the New Woman to marriage and motherhood by improving her sex life'.[23] They wished to stave off the crisis in marriage and the family, as 'satisfying sex produced a better quality of offspring'.[24] Grossmann believes that 'birth control, abortion and sex education were first and foremost class and health issues, not women's issues'.[25] Julia Roos has, however, seen in the 1927 Law for Combating Venereal Diseases significant improvements in prostitutes' and women's rights.[26]

It is perhaps in the area of politics that most studies of women in the Weimar Republic are to be found. For many years Gabriele Bremme's 1956 study remained the only exploration of women's political role in the Weimar Republic.[27] In the 1970s historians began exploring the role of female politicians in the national parliament, the Reichstag, women's role in the German Social Democratic Party (Sozialdemokratische Partei Deutschlands, SPD), the German Communist Party (Kommunistische Partei Deutschlands, KPD) and the pre-1933 Nazi movement, and the female vote, principally from the perspective of women's electoral contribution to the rise of the Nazis.[28] It was to be the 1990s before historians began investigating the role of women in the other major parties, the liberal German Democratic Party (Deutsche Demokratische Partei, DDP), the German People's Party (Deutsche Volkspartei, DVP) and the right-wing German National People's Party (Deutschnationale Volkspartei, DNVP).[29] In the 2000s several studies by female German historians focused on conservative women within the political parties and in nationalist organisations, and in his 2004 study of women within the DVP and DNVP, the American Raffael Scheck highlighted the differing responses of right-wing women to the rise of the Nazis, but noted that 'the efforts of DVP and DNVP women to mobilise conservative women for the nation and, in particular, the DNVP women's demonstrations that racial hygienic thought and Christianity were compatible may well have eased many women's decision to vote for the Nazis'.[30] In 2002 Sneeringer's study of party-political propaganda revealed how the parties constructed women as political actors, and Thomas Mergel explored the impact on Weimar's political culture of women's entry into parliament.[31] It is one of the aims of this book to provide a synthesis of recent research in German and to make it accessible to an English-speaking audience.

This book aims to build upon the existing scholarship to produce a comprehensive survey of women in the economy, politics and society of the Weimar Republic.[32] Eve Rosenhaft has suggested that 'women *are* invisible unless we are looking straight at them',[33] and this book seeks to explore the diversity and multiplicity of women's experiences in Weimar Germany. The Republic was a post-war society, and an understanding of the significant impact that the First World War had on women and their roles in the economy and society is crucial for any interpretation of women in the Weimar Republic; this book, therefore, begins with a chapter on women and the First World War. It then seeks to explore to what extent the Weimar Republic was 'an open space of multiple developmental opportunities' for women and to consider the changes in women's roles, status and behaviour during the Republic and how these impacted on the gender order. Richard McCormick has argued that it was 'the blurring of traditionally gendered roles and behaviour' that 'was most emancipatory about Weimar culture', for women as well as men.[34] How accurate is Bridenthal's thesis that women actually made no progress, indeed went backwards, in the field of employment? What use did women make of their newly granted political rights? To what extent was the 'new woman' representative of women's experiences in the Weimar Republic? At its end, did German women experience the Nazi accession to power in 1933 as a rupture in their lives, as the outbreak of war in 1914 or its end and the revolution of 1918 had been? These are some of the questions to which this book hopes to provide the answers.

The archival material for this book has been collected over a number of years, principally from the Federal Archives in Koblenz and Berlin, the Zentrales Staatsarchiv Potsdam in the former German Democratic Republic, the Helene-Lange-Archiv, now housed in the Landesarchiv Berlin, the archives of the German Protestant Women's League, now housed in the Archiv der Deutschen Frauenbewegung in Kassel, the archives of the German Catholic Women's League in Cologne and a variety of smaller archives.[35] Historians of modern Germany are fortunate to have a range of official statistical publications at their disposal, and during the Weimar Republic several surveys, by professional organisations, trade unions and social scientists, were conducted into the lives of working women. In addition, numerous women's magazines give information about women's position in society, the activities of various women's organisations and issues of topical interest. These primary sources, together with the considerable number of second-

Introduction 7

ary studies that have appeared since 1970, form the basis for this interpretation of women in the Weimar Republic.

Notes

1 The key text is H.-U. Wehler, *The German Empire 1871–1918* (Leamington Spa: Berg, 1985). The German edition appeared in 1973. Wehler's thesis attracted criticism from British and American historians: R. J. Evans (ed.), *Society and Politics in Wilhelmine Germany* (London: Croom Helm, 1978); D. Blackbourn and G. Eley, *The Peculiarities of German History: Bourgeois Society and Politics in Nineteenth-Century Germany* (Oxford: Oxford University Press, 1984).

2 Detlev Peukert, *The Weimar Republic: The Crisis of Classical Modernity*, trans. R. Deveson (London: Allen Lane, 1991), p. xiii. For Peukert the Third Reich was 'one of the pathological development forms of modernity': Detlev Peukert, *Inside Nazi Germany: Conformity, Opposition, and Racism in Everyday Life*, trans. R. Deveson (London: Yale University Press, 1987), p. 249.

3 E. R. Dickinson, 'Biopolitics, Fascism, Democracy: Some Reflections on our Discourse about "Modernity"', *Central European History*, 37:1 (2004), 5.

4 For the ambiguities of modernity see A. McElligott (ed.), *Weimar Germany* (Oxford: Oxford University Press, 2009). See also P. Fritzsche, 'Did Weimar Fail?', *Journal of Modern History*, 68:3 (1996), 629–56.

5 M. Föllmer and R. Graf (eds), *Die 'Krise' der Weimarer Republik: Zur Kritik eines Deutungsmusters* (Frankfurt: Campus Verlag, 2005), p. 10; R. Graf, 'Either-Or: The Narrative of "Crisis" in Weimar Germany and its Historiography', *Central European History*, 43 (2010), 593.

6 D. Peukert, 'The Weimar Republic – Old and New Perspectives', *German History*, 6:2 (1988), 139; Fritzsche, 'Did Weimar Fail?', 633, 647.

7 A. Grossmann, *Reforming Sex: The German Movement for Birth Control and Abortion Reform, 1920–1950* (Oxford: Oxford University Press, 1995), p. 5.

8 A. Grossmann, 'Girlkultur or Thoroughly Rationalised Female: A New Woman in Weimar Germany?', in J. Friedlander, B. W. Cook, A. Kessler-Harris and C. Smith-Rosenberg (eds), *Women in Culture and Politics: A Century of Change* (Bloomington: Indiana University Press, 1986), p. 64.

9 E. D. Weitz, *Weimar Germany: Promise and Tragedy* (Princeton: Princeton University Press, 2007), p. 307; A. Grossmann, 'Crisis, Reaction, and Resistance: Women in Germany in the 1920s and 1930s',

in A. Swerdlow and H. Lessinger (eds), *Class, Race, and Sex: The Dynamics of Control* (Boston: G. K. Hall & Co., 1983), p.61.
10 E. Harvey, 'Culture and Society in Weimar Germany: The Impact of Modernism and Mass Culture', in M. Fulbrook (ed.), *German History since 1800* (London: Arnold, 1997), p.282.
11 Grossmann, '*Girlkultur*', p.67.
12 C. Usborne, 'The New Woman and Generational Conflict: Perceptions of Young Women's Sexual Mores in the Weimar Republic', in M. Roseman (ed.), *Generations in Conflict: Youth Revolt and Generation Formation in Germany 1770–1968* (Cambridge: Cambridge University Press, 1995), pp.137–63.
13 P. Petro, *Joyless Streets: Women and Melodramatic Representation in Weimar Germany* (Princeton: Princeton University Press, 1989); K. von Ankum (ed.), *Women in the Metropolis: Gender and Modernity in Weimar Culture* (Berkeley: University of California Press, 1997); R. W. McCormick, *Gender and Sexuality in Weimar Modernity: Film, Literature, and New Objectivity* (Basingstoke: Palgrave, 2001); V. R. Petersen, *Women and Modernity in Weimar Germany: Reality and its Representation in Popular Fiction* (Oxford: Berghahn, 2001). Studies of women writers and artists include: M. Meskimmon and S. West, *Visions of the Neue Frau: Women and the Visual Arts in Weimar Germany* (Aldershot: Ashgate, 1995) and M. Meskimmon, *We Weren't Modern Enough: Women Artists and the Limits of German Modernism* (Berkeley: University of California Press, 1999).
14 J. Sneeringer, *Winning Women's Votes: Propaganda and Politics in Weimar Germany* (Chapel Hill: University of North Carolina Press, 2002); Weitz, *Weimar Germany*, p.41. This claim has most recently been refuted by Benjamin Ziemann: B. Ziemann, 'Weimar was Weimar: Politics, Culture and the Emplotment of the German Republic', *German History*, 28:4 (2010), 545–7.
15 B. Kundrus, 'Gender Wars: The First World War and the Construction of Gender Relations in the Weimar Republic', in K. Hagemann and S. Schüler-Springorum (eds), *Home/Front: The Military, War and Gender in Twentieth-Century Germany* (Oxford and New York: Berg, 2002), p.169.
16 Petro, *Joyless Streets*, p.109; Graf questions the scale of the 'crisis of masculinity': R. Graf, 'Anticipating the Future in the Present: "New Women" and Other Beings of the Future in Weimar Germany', *Central European History*, 42 (2009), 648–9.
17 K. Canning, *Gender History in Practice: Historical Perspectives on Bodies, Class and Citizenship* (Ithaca, NY: Cornell University Press, 2006.

18 Weitz, *Weimar Germany*, p. 328; R. J. Evans, *The Feminist Movement in Germany, 1894–1933* (London: Sage, 1976).
19 R. Bridenthal, A. Grossmann and M. Kaplan (eds), *When Biology Became Destiny: Women in Weimar and Nazi Germany* (New York: Monthly Review Press, 1984), pp. 10–11.
20 E. B. Jones, *Gender and Rural Modernity: Farm Women and the Politics of Labour in Germany, 1871–1933* (Farnham: Ashgate, 2009).
21 J. Stephenson, 'Women and the Professions in Germany, 1900–1945', in G. Cocks and K. H. Jarausch (eds), *German Professions, 1800–1950* (Oxford: Oxford University Press, 1990), pp. 270–88; U. Nienhaus, *Vater Staat und seine Gehilfinnen: Die Politik mit der Frauenarbeit bei der deutschen Post (1864–1945)* (Frankfurt am Main: Campus Verlag, 1995); U. Nienhaus, *Nicht für eine Führungsposition geeignet: Josephine Erkens und die Anfänge weiblicher Polizei in Deutschland, 1923–1933* (Münster: Westphälisches Dampfboot, 1999); D. Kampmann, '"Zölibat – ohne uns!" – die soziale Situation und politische Einstellung der Lehrerinnen in der Weimarer Republik', in Frauengruppe Faschismusforschung (ed.), *Mutterkreuz und Arbeitsbuch: Zur Geschichte der Frauen in der Weimarer Republik und im Nationalsozialismus* (Frankfurt am Main: Fischer, 1988), pp. 79–104.
22 Grossmann, *Reforming Sex*; C. Usborne, *The Politics of the Body in Weimar Germany* (Basingstoke: Macmillan, 1992) and, especially, C. Usborne, *Cultures of Abortion in Weimar Germany* (Oxford: Berghahn, 2007).
23 Weitz, *Weimar Germany*, pp. 297–330; A. Grossmann, 'The New Woman and the Rationalization of Sexuality in Weimar Germany', in A. Snitow, C. Stansell and S. Thompson (eds), *Desire: The Politics of Sexuality* (London: Virago Press, 1984), p. 194.
24 *Ibid.*, p. 200.
25 Grossmann, 'Crisis, Reaction, and Resistance', p. 72.
26 J. Roos, *Weimar through the Lens of Gender: Prostitution Reform, Woman's Emancipation, and German Democracy, 1919–33* (Ann Arbor: University of Michigan Press, 2010).
27 G. Bremme, *Die politische Rolle der Frau in Deutschland* (Göttingen: Vandenhoeck & Ruprecht, 1956).
28 W. Phillips Shively, 'Party Identification, Party Choice, and Voting Stability: The Weimar Case', *American Political Science Review*, 66:4 (December 1972), 1203–25; J. Falter, T. Lindenberger and S. Schumann, *Wahlen und Abstimmungen in der Weimarer Republik: Materialien zum Wahlverhalten 1919–1933* (Munich: Beck, 1986), pp. 81–5; H. L. Boak, '"Our last hope": Women's Votes for Hitler – a Reappraisal', *German Studies Review*, 12:2 (May 1989), 289–310;

J. Falter, *Hitlers Wähler* (Munich: Beck, 1991), pp.136–46. Brian Peterson explored working-class women's politics through a study of the December 1924 Reichstag election: B. Peterson, 'The Politics of Working-Class Women in the Weimar Republic', *Central European History*, 10:2 (1977), 87–111. Two Americans investigated the women in the Reichstag: C. Koonz, 'Conflicting Allegiances: Political Ideology and Women Legislators in Weimar Germany', *Signs: Journal of Women in Culture and Society*, 1:3 (1976), 663–83, and P. L. Fessenden, 'The Role of Women Deputies in the German National Constituent Assembly and the Reichstag, 1919–1933' (PhD dissertation, Ohio State University, 1976). H. Boak, 'Women in Weimar Politics', *European History Quarterly*, 20:3 (1990), 369–99, explores women's role as elected representatives at all levels and in the political parties; see also H. M. Lauterer, *Parlamentarierinnen in Deutschland 1918/19– 1949* (Königstein: Ulrike Helmer Verlag, 2002). In the 1980s three books exploring German Social Democratic, Liberal and Christian Democratic women in the twentieth century touched on women politicians in the Reichstag: A. Huber (ed.), *Die Sozialdemokratinnen: Verdient die Nachtigall Lob, wenn sie singt?* (Stuttgart: Seewald Verlag 1984); L. Funke (ed.), *Die Liberalen: Frei sein, um andere frei zu machen* (Stuttgart: Seewald Verlag, 1984); and R. Hellwig (ed.), *Die Christdemokratinnen: Unterwegs zur Partnerschaft* (Stuttgart: Seewald Verlag, 1984). Women in the SPD were investigated by W. Thönnessen, *The Emancipation of Women: Germany 1863–1933* (London: Pluto Press, 1973) and R. Pore, *A Conflict of Interest: Women in German Social Democracy 1919–1933* (London: Greenwood Press, 1981). For women in the KPD see S. Kontos, *Die Partei kämpft wie ein Mann* (Frankfurt am Main: Stroemfeld Verlag, 1979) and a series of articles from East Germany including H.-J. Arendt, 'Weibliche Mitglieder der KPD in der Weimarer Republik – zahlenmässige Stärke und soziale Stellung', *Beiträge zur Geschichte der Arbeiterbewegung*, 19 (1977), 652–60; and D. Götze, 'Die organisatorische Vorbereitung für die Schaffung der kommunistischen Frauenbewegung 1919–1921', *Zeitschrift für Geschichtswissenschaft*, 23 (1975), 1165–76. For women in the pre-1933 Nazi women's movement see C. Koonz, 'Nazi Women before 1933: Rebels against Emancipation', *Social Science Quarterly*, 56:4 (1976), 553–63; J. Stephenson, *The Nazi Organisation of Women* (London: Croom Helm, 1981); M. H. Kater, 'Frauen in der NS-Bewegung', *Vierteljahrshefte für Zeitgeschichte*, 31:2 (1983), 202–41; C. Koonz, *Mothers in the Fatherland: Women, the Family and Nazi Politics* (London: Jonathan Cape, 1987).

29 A. Schaser, 'Bürgerliche Frauen auf dem Weg in die linksliberalen Parteien (1908–1933)', *Historische Zeitschrift*, 263:3 (1996), 641–80;

R. Scheck, 'German Conservatism and Female Political Activism in the early Weimar Republic', *German History*, 15:1 (1997), 34–55; R. Scheck, 'Women against Versailles: Maternalism and Nationalism of Female Bourgeois Politicians in the Early Weimar Republic', *German Studies Review*, 2:1 (February 1999), 21–42; E. Harvey, 'Pilgrimages to the "Bleeding Border": Gender and Rituals of Nationalist Protest in Germany, 1919–39', *Women's History Review*, 9:2 (2000), 201–29; R. Scheck, 'Women on the Weimar Right: The Role of Female Politicians in the Deutschnationale Volkspartei (DNVP)', *Journal of Contemporary History*, 36:4 (2001), 547–60.

30 A. Süchting-Hänger, *Das 'Gewissen der Nation': Nationales Engagement und politisches Handeln konservativer Frauenorganisationen 1900 bis 1937* (Düsseldorf: Droste Verlag, 2002); C. Streubel, *Radikale Nationalistinnen: Agitation und Programmatik rechter Frauen in der Weimarer Republik* (Frankfurt am Main: Campus Verlag, 2006); E. Schöck-Quinteros and C. Streubel (eds), *Ihrem Volk verantwortlich: Frauen der politischen Rechten (1890–1933): Organisationen – Agitationen – Ideologien* (Berlin: Trafo-Verlag, 2007); K. Heinsohn, *Konservative Parteien in Deutschland 1912 bis 1933* (Düsseldorf: Droste Verlag, 2010). For an excellent overview of literature on women on the political right see C. Streubel, 'Frauen der politischen Rechten in Kaiserreich und Republik', *Historical Social Research*, 28:4 (2003),103–66; R. Scheck, *Mothers of the Nation: Right-Wing Women in Weimar Germany* (Oxford: Berg, 2004), pp. 184–5.

31 Sneeringer, *Winning Women's Votes*; T. Mergel, *Parlamentarische Kultur in der Weimarer Republik: Politische Kommunikation, symbolische Politik und Öffentlichkeit im Reichstag* (Düsseldorf: Droste Verlag, 2002).

32 A useful overview is to be found in U. Frevert, *Women in German History: From Bourgeois Emancipation to Sexual Liberation* (Oxford: Berg, 1989); K. Hagemann, *Frauenalltag und Männerpolitik: Alltagsleben und gesellschaftliches Handeln von Arbeiterfrauen in der Weimarer Republik* (Bonn: J. H. W. Dietz, 1990) provides a magisterial account of the lives of working-class women in Hamburg's social democratic milieu.

33 Italics in the original: E. Rosenhaft, 'Women, Gender, and the Limits of Political History in the Age of "Mass" Politics', in L. E. Jones and J. Retallack (eds), *Elections, Mass Politics, and Social Change in Modern Germany* (Cambridge: Cambridge University Press, 1992), p. 160.

34 McCormick, *Gender and Sexuality in Weimar Modernity*, p. 3.

35 With the unification of Germany, the archival resources of East and West Germany are being reorganised, and those pertaining to the

Weimar Republic are now housed in Berlin and are undergoing reclassification. However, to maintain consistency, I have retained the original archival information in the format obtaining at the time when the material was collected.

1
Women in the First World War

> The German people's capacity for suffering must certainly be above the average. They proved it during the war years of starvation and sacrifice.[1]

'The war', claims Angelika Schaser, 'was a great mobiliser of women.'[2] As millions of men went off to war, women mobilised themselves out of economic necessity or patriotism, replacing men on local transport, volunteering for nursing training and organising welfare as they sought, in the words of Empress Auguste Victoria, 'to help', 'to lighten the struggle for our husbands, sons and brothers' and 'to dedicate all our energies to the Fatherland in its decisive struggle'.[3] Germany was rapidly transformed into a nation at war as spy fever raged, patriotism was displayed in shoe laces and hair ribbons and the German language was militarised while French and English words were banned and early victories were celebrated with holidays. Trains took troops to the front and brought refugees from East Prussia, prisoners of war and wounded soldiers. In schools, girls knitted socks and gloves to send to the front, and children followed the German advance on maps, began to collect metals for the war effort and encouraged their parents to subscribe to the first war loan.[4] All believed that the war would soon be over. Instead, it lasted four long years, during which women's relationship with the state and the gender order was transformed in the world of work, in the family and in society. Women were granted opportunities and faced challenges in both the public and the private spheres, and they had to endure enormous hardships and sacrifices. Inequalities were exacerbated and women's confidence in the state's administration was severely dented. Kathleen Canning has lamented the lack of scholarship exploring the significance for the post-war gender order of the transformations in women's lives wrought by the war, though Benjamin Ziemann has challenged the appropriateness of the word 'transformation', an indication that the war's legacy for women in the Weimar Republic is contested.[5] In general, historians divide into three schools of thought over the impact and legacy of the First World War on women's role in German society: some see the Great War as a catalyst for change, some believe it merely accelerated social, economic and cultural trends already underway before 1914, and others contend that any changes wrought during the war were purely temporary, 'emancipation on loan' as Ute Daniel has claimed.[6] This chapter will explore women's role in the economy and society during the First World War, in an attempt to ascertain which of these schools of thought is most appropriate and to assess the war's significance for the roles and perceptions of women in the Weimar Republic.

Women's contribution to the war effort

The First World War affected individual German women, as it did women in all the warring countries, in different ways, depending on their age, class, employment status, education, marital status and place of domicile, and on whether a male family member served at the front and if so, whether he was wounded, taken prisoner or killed. German women's reaction to the outbreak of war varied, too. The leader of the moderate middle-class women's umbrella organisation, the Federation of German Women's Associations (Bund Deutscher Frauenvereine, BdF), Dr Gertrud Bäumer, pre-empted the outbreak of war in her plans to mobilise German women on the home front, while the Women's League of the German Peace Society sent a telegram to the Kaiser asking him, in the name of all Germany's mothers, to maintain peace. Social democratic women took to the streets in 163 towns across Germany in demonstrations for peace.[7] Many women, particularly from the middle class, were, however, carried along on the wave of patriotic fervour that swept across Germany in early August 1914, accompanying loved ones to call-up offices or handing out chocolates, food, flowers and cigars to soldiers in transit at railway stations.[8] Middle- and upper-class women, some 40,000 in Berlin alone, rushed to volunteer for first-aid courses offered by the Red Cross, while aristocratic women donated buildings for hospitals.[9]

The German government had not planned for women's participation in the war effort, nor for the impact of a long war or a blockade on Germany's economy, industry and civilian society. The initial impact was, of course, the removal of men to the front, resulting in what Richard Bessel has termed the 'feminisation of German society'.[10] Women began to replace men as counter clerks on Berlin's underground and as conductors on its trams, and in Brunswick, the Duchess assumed control as regent.[11] They were to be the first of many in an overturning of the sexual division of labour which, according to Barbara Franzoi, was 'the fundamental condition of women's work in Imperial Germany', with gender-segmented industries and tasks ensuring that women did not compete with men.[12] The war was to offer women unprecedented opportunities to enter jobs and industries previously closed to them, and even to attain positions of responsibility within agencies of the state. While working-class women sustained the German war effort in factories, middle-class women, marshalled by the women's movement, took responsibility for welfare. Initially, however, the impact of the outbreak of war for many working women was unemployment, caused by the dislocation to German industry and transport networks brought about by the mobilisation, the reduction in production in the consumer industries where women's industrial work was concentrated, and the dismissal of domestic servants as middle-class families' incomes fell with the call-up of the male heads of household.[13] Contemporary perceptions were of large numbers of women, following a brief period of unemployment or coming onto the labour market for the first time, replacing conscripted male workers for the duration of the war. Marie-Elisabeth Lüders, for example, wrote in 1918 of an additional two million women joining the workforce since 1914.[14] Historians disagree over the increase in the numbers of women working during the war, according to the sources they use.[15] All agree, however, that women unable to find work in the textile and clothing industries, which dominated female industrial employment, found it in war-related industries, once industrialists' initial reluctance to employ them had been overcome. Between 1913 and 1918 the numbers of women working in textile concerns overseen by the factory inspectorate fell by 42 per cent and in clothing concerns by 20 per cent, while those employed in engineering firms rose by 544 per cent.[16] These former workers in the consumer industries were joined in the armaments industry by young women entering the labour market for the first time, by former domestic servants and agricultural workers, and by working-class soldiers' wives and widows, the last of whom constituted an untapped reservoir of labour and could not manage financially on their war allowance (see below).[17] In December 1916 70 per cent of married women working in the Bavarian armaments industry were soldiers' wives.[18] One chemical factory in Leverkusen reported that it had employed no married women before the war but that by 1917 half of its female workforce was married.[19] Soldiers' wives often had the first refusal of a job, and some took on their husband's jobs for the duration of the war. In mining, where the number of women employed rose from 15,969 in 1913 to 109,622 in 1918, some wives of conscripted miners were forced to work in order to keep their mine housing.[20]

More conspicuous were the many women who took over jobs as varied as chimney-sweeping, window-cleaning, road-sweeping and construction work, digging the new Berlin underground, for example, and those who joined the transport sector as tram, train and coach conductors and drivers, stokers and signal operators, though they received less training than the men they replaced.[21] On the Prussian-Hessian railway, for example, some 9,167 women were employed in 1914, mainly as cleaners, though a few held white-collar positions. This figure rose to 22,700 in 1915, 36,000 in 1916 and 107,000 in March 1918.[22] There were concerns about the visual masculinisation of women, in both musculature and dress. Women began to wear uniform and trousers.[23] Speaking in a Reichstag committee in March 1917 Dr Helfferich, at the time the State Secretary of the Interior and Deputy Chancellor, noted: 'When one looks at the women who are so active in all these heavy services, women in munitions, driving vans, cleansing the streets, one sometimes has to gaze hard to know whether it is a man or a woman.'[24] Robert Nelson notes the attempts to counterbalance the visible physical masculinisation of working women in pictures in soldiers' newspapers with photographs of them, attractively and femininely dressed when not at work.[25]

The public sector's attitudes towards the employment of women, both single and married, had to change in order to ensure an adequate workforce. The Imperial Post and Telegraph Service and regional education authorities allowed women civil servants who married during the war to stay in post, and those who had been forced to leave their posts on marriage but who had been widowed during the war were allowed to return.[26] To replace men from the public sector who had been called up, women entered branches previously closed to them. Berlin appointed its first female registrar, albeit in a deputising capacity, in 1916, while female architects were commissioned to design municipal buildings and structures.[27] During the war those women with a degree in medicine were allowed to take over the practices of male medical practitioners working at the front, apparently enhancing women's reputation with both patients and medical authorities.[28] For the first time women were allowed to teach in boys' junior and grammar schools, while in the Imperial Post and Telegraph Service women were now employed in senior positions as postal secretaries and head secretaries and in post offices of the third class, serving behind the counter, as well as collecting and delivering the post, jobs which made them far more conspicuous to the public than those in the telegraph and telephone service which had previously been their domain.[29] By July 1918 the Imperial Post and Telegraph Service had taken on 86,926 female war-time assistants.[30]

In the first years of the war, the mobilisation of women for the war effort tended to be independent of government planning, but the manpower and materiel demands of the battles of Verdun and the Somme on the Western Front and the entry of Romania into the war led to the call by the Third Supreme Army Command, established on 29 August 1916 under Field Marshal von Hindenburg and General Ludendorff, for all Germany's economic and social resources to be mobilised behind the war effort.[31] Hindenburg believed that there were 'thousands of women and girls ... running around who do not do anything, or at most practise some useless trade. The principle "who does not work, shall not eat" is, in our situation, more than justified, also with regard to women.'[32] However, the Auxiliary Service Law of 5 December 1916 did not include conscription for women, as it was believed that there was a reserve of female labour.[33] The newly created War Office set up a Women's Section to encourage women to take up employment and release men for the front, and appointed as its head a well-known social worker, Dr Marie-Elisabeth Lüders, recently returned from her post within the civilian administration in Brussels.[34] Lüders believed that a consideration of family and welfare policy was crucial to any mobilisation of women and so a Central Office for

Women's Work, also headed by Lüders, was set up within the War Office to oversee the implementation of all welfare measures deemed necessary to remove any obstacles to women's willingness to work. Ann Taylor Allen claims that had Lüders's guidelines been implemented they 'would have almost completely socialised child-care'.[35] The replication of the women's sections and offices for women's work in the War Office branches across Germany gave senior administrative positions to many prominent members of the middle-class women's movement who had considerable experience in social and welfare work, including Dr Gertrud Bäumer in Hamburg, Dr Elisabeth Altmann-Gottheiner in Karlsruhe, Dr Alice Salomon in Berlin and Dorothee von Velsen in Breslau.[36] The mantra became 'the mobilisation of women by women'.

Bessel has noted that the 'explicit attempts to mobilise German society essentially failed', in contrast to the more successful self-mobilisation that took place in the early years of the war.[37] In keeping with the aims of the so-called Hindenburg Programme, a decree of 6 March 1917 permitted the withdrawal of a soldier's wife's war allowance if she refused to work. Although the aim of the decree was supposedly to increase the number of soldiers' wives doing war work, it proved counter-productive, and in at least one area, Stettin, soldiers' wives who were working in agriculture continued to receive their full war allowance.[38] Attempts by what Bright Jones has called 'the only compulsory labour laws that included women' to forbid young women already working in agriculture from leaving and to ensure that country girls leaving school entered only agriculture were unsuccessful.[39] With the push for increased female participation in the workforce in order both to maximise the numbers of men at the front and to help implement the total mobilisation of all Germany's resources behind the war effort, the demand for female labour outweighed the supply from the beginning of May 1917 until the end of October 1918, and employers in the munitions industries increased women's wages in an attempt to win more women workers. While men's wages increased on average by 241 per cent between March 1914 and September 1918, women's wages rose by 263 per cent.[40] Seipp reports that at the powder and munition factory constructed in 1915 in Dachau outside Munich, women earned 60 per cent less than their male colleagues in 1916 and 40 per cent less in January 1918.[41] Even as late as early November 1918 the War Office was calling for all women in the districts of Münster, Hanover, Magdeburg, Kassel and Altona who were not engaged in war work, without distinction of class, to come and help in the war industry.[42]

Under the Hindenburg Programme, of 101,178 men freed for military service by July 1917 in Prussia, 64,142 were replaced by women.[43] From spring 1917, in an attempt to free more men for front-line duty, women volunteers aged between twenty and forty could be selected for employment as war auxiliaries serving behind the lines on the Western and Eastern Fronts, replacing men in orderly rooms and cash offices, and undertaking jobs as typists, telephonists, telegraphers, field librarians and postal censors among others.[44] Within weeks 4,784 women were to be found as auxiliaries behind the lines, their numbers increasing by September 1918 to 17,397.[45] They joined many women working as civilians, particularly in social welfare, in the occupation administrations in Belgium and Poland, but their presence was not universally welcomed. Soldiers, fearful of being replaced and sent to the front, saw their presence as lengthening the war. Many held the women auxiliaries in low regard because they came primarily from the lower middle classes and were thought to have undertaken the jobs for monetary gain; they earned considerably more than soldiers and the other women to be found at the front, nurses. Some auxiliaries also earned a reputation for loose morals.[46]

Of the 92,000 nurses employed by the military during the war, some 28,000 served in hospitals near the front line. Over 19,000 came from the Red Cross, where professional nurses were soon outnumbered by volunteer nursing auxiliaries who came from the upper and middle classes, and the others came from religious nursing orders.[47] On the whole nurses enjoyed a good reputation for being patriotic and willing to make sacrifices, though some were rumoured to be husband-hunting.[48] A report in the BdF's journal *Die Frau* in March 1915 claimed that thirty-eight women had been awarded the Iron Cross, primarily nurses, though some female drivers had also shown courage in the face of the enemy.[49] Women at the front line faced the same dangers as men; the first nurse to be killed by an aerial bomb was reputed to be Marga von Falkenhausen of the Sissone field hospital, and the same issue of *Jus Suffragii* reports the capture of Catholic nurses when the French took the hospital at Le Breuil.[50]

There were few women in military uniform. A few female

doctors were placed in charge of military hospitals in Germany and were accorded the relevant rank and uniform, though Despina Stratigakos claims that Elisabeth von Knobelsdorff, an architect, was the first woman soldier and officer, appointed in September 1914 to design military buildings, initially in Germany and then in occupied France.[51] It was not until June 1918 that the Supreme Command decided to set up a female communications corps, in order to release some 40,000 soldiers for the front by 1 January 1919, but the armistice of 11 November 1918 meant that the women training to join the communications corps never saw service.[52] However, perhaps the most senior woman behind the lines was Dr Elisabeth Schragmüller, a woman of initiative and intelligence who, like many wanting to work at the front, got a pass to Brussels, where she was initially employed scrutinising letters taken from Belgian prisoners of war. She so impressed her employers that she was sent to Lille for intelligence training and was subsequently appointed head of the section organising military intelligence against France. Based at the war-time Intelligence Service's headquarters in Antwerp, she was known by the French and British as 'Mademoiselle Doktor'.[53]

Elisabeth Schragmüller was one of the first generation of women to graduate with a doctorate from a German university. The numbers of women studying at Germany's universities rose by 77 per cent between the summer terms of 1914 and 1918, leading to claims that the universities were being feminised and to some demands, from Hindenburg for example, that they should be closed.[54] Attempts to mobilise female students for work in the munitions industry were, for the most part, unsuccessful.[55] Patriotic work in the munitions industry was, however, attractive to young girls working in agriculture, the traditional bastion of female labour and an area of enormous significance for the war economy; since the mid-1870s they had sought to better themselves and avoid the fate of their mothers.[56] Farmers' wives, however, could not leave the land, and as male family members were called up they became responsible for their farms, having to take over the male tasks such as ploughing as well as their traditional duties of animal husbandry and helping out at harvest time. Reports suggest that 44 per cent of farms in war-time Bavaria were run by women, considerably fewer than the 80 per cent of farms in Baden headed by women in 1917.[57] Soldiers coming home on leave at key points in the farming year, such as ploughing and harvest times, were shocked at their wives' poor health and loss of weight as the hard physical work took its toll on these women.[58] As one woman wrote to her husband, a prisoner of war: '3 years of working alone like a huge brute, people can't take it any more. We've already done a lot for God, and no end in sight. We had enough work to do before the war but no human being would have believed it would get as bad as this.' As Ziemann notes, 'towards the end of the war, their capacity to work declined rapidly'.[59]

The exhaustion felt by women working in the countryside was also experienced by those working in the munitions industry, along with malnutrition as the push to mobilise women workers coincided with deteriorating food supplies when the failure of the potato harvest in 1916–17 saw the turnip become the staple ingredient of German foods. According to the Bavarian War Minister in May 1918, 'a great part of the female labour force will soon be totally incapable of work if they continue to overexert themselves as they are doing at the present time'.[60] Worker protection laws, forbidding women to work for more than ten hours daily and eight hours on Sunday or to work at night, had been relaxed on 4 August 1914. Women could now perform heavy, dangerous and physically demanding work. Reports of women working fifteen hours a day and twelve hours at night in factories became common.[61] Such was the exploitation of women working in war-related industries that the Chancellor was compelled to issue warnings to employers, but these were little heeded unless a lack of raw materials or energy permitted a reduction in working hours.[62] The numbers of cases of sickness among working women rose sharply from 1917, in part because no regard was paid to a woman's ability to meet the physical demands of a job at recruitment and also because of the accumulated impact of exhaustion and malnutrition and work-related illnesses caused by poisoning.[63] The number of industrial accidents rose, too. Catherine Boyd reports that 310 women were killed during a fire at a grenade factory in eastern Germany on 17 July 1918.[64] Bajohr reports that in spite of extended working hours, industrial productivity fell by 20 per cent during the war, and Lüders noted that women's productivity fell markedly in the last two years of the war.[65]

Jürgen Kuczynski has claimed that 'never in the whole history of capitalism in Germany was the position of the female manual worker so bad as it was in the last year of the war', and Helene

Lange, the *grande dame* of the middle-class women's movement, wrote in 1924 that it was perhaps fortunate that women's employment had been so radically reduced during the demobilisation, as the form it had taken in the war economy constituted a 'ruinous pillaging of women's health'.[66] Women's work during the war had always been regarded as a temporary phenomenon, with some women even signing contracts that terminated at the war's end. Of paramount importance to the authorities in November 1918 was the smooth re-integration of the seven million returning troops into the economy, which was itself undergoing a transition to a peacetime one. The soldiers were to return to the jobs they had had before the war, replacing foreigners, prisoners of war and women.[67] The War Ministry issued guidelines on women's employment during the transition period which reflected discussions with various women's organisations and employers' representatives. The authorities were keen to see a return to the *status quo ante*, with everyone returning to where they had been and what they had been doing in 1914.[68] Mass unemployment of women was avoided through staggered dismissals, for fear of public disorder and a rise in prostitution. The speedy re-introduction of worker protection laws on 7 November 1918 curbed female employment, and many large employers offered voluntary severance payments as inducements for women to leave, while the introduction of the eight-hour day increased demand for male workers.[69] Employers acted quickly to dismiss women: Bosch fired 3,500 women at the end of November 1918 to make way for some 1,714 returning troops, while Krupp had dismissed 24,022 of its 26,587-strong female workforce by the end of December 1918.[70] Many women willingly gave up work on the return home of the family male breadwinner or on marriage as they, too, desired a return to normality, and so mass unemployment was avoided in what Bessel has described as 'not all that large a concern for the labour market'.[71] Some authorities, too, tried to return to the pre-war situation in higher education, restricting the numbers of new female entrants to the universities of Heidelberg and Tübingen and those in Prussia, in order to give preference to returning troops, for whom a career was a life-long matter rather than the temporary phase before marriage which it constituted for women. However, women found places at universities with no restrictions.[72]

Contemporaries were aware of the enormous contribution that women's work made to the German war effort. As early as 13

June 1915 churches gave thanks for women's efforts, and a hymn celebrating women's work was circulated to all women's, church and municipal organisations.[73] Speaking in a Reichstag debate about suffrage on 6 July 1917, the socialist deputy Dr Gradnauer commented, 'If the country issues well out of the war it will be largely due to women.' He noted, 'Not only in light trades but in heavy trades, in transport, behind the plough, women have proved their worth, as also in all branches of war relief. In all this they have shown great organising ability and a capacity to work for the general good.' [74] Welfare work expanded rapidly during the war (see below), and with it the need for professional social workers. During the war, the number of social work schools for women almost doubled, from fourteen to twenty-seven.[75]

Women and welfare

Much welfare work was undertaken voluntarily by middle- and upper-class women. While the Red Cross and the Patriotic Women's Association in many cities across Germany devoted themselves to caring for troops en route to the front or in hospital, other women's groups, including those affiliated to the BdF, women from the Catholic Women's League (Katholischer Frauenbund Deutschlands, KFB) and social democratic women came together under the banner of the National Women's Service (Nationaler Frauendienst, NFD) to become a major provider of social welfare.[76] The NFD was the brainchild of Dr Gertrud Bäumer, the leader of the BdF, which at the outbreak of the war claimed to have some half a million members. Bäumer believed that 'social welfare is women's war service' and was keen to place the middle-class women's movement in the service of the nation.[77] The NFD set itself four tasks: co-operation in maintaining regular food supplies; welfare for families whose breadwinners had been called up or had been made unemployed by the war; help in finding work for women who were forced to earn their own living because their breadwinner was absent, who were willing and able to fill jobs left vacant by men or who volunteered to work; and providing advice and information.[78] By 1917 there were NFD branches in sixty-four cities across Germany. Their priorities varied with location and over time. In Berlin the NFD, financed by the city, set up twenty-three district welfare commissions on 10 August 1914, each headed jointly by a middle-class and a Social Democratic woman.[79] This co-operation between bourgeois and Social Democratic women at a national level was groundbreaking, reversing the decision taken at the SPD's 1896 congress in Gotha which had declared that 'what class opposition divided, common sex cannot join'.[80] During the war women in twenty-nine of the SPD's thirty-five party districts worked together with middle-class women or the local authorities.[81] In September 1914 alone, the twenty-three welfare commissions in Berlin dealt with 119,716 cases; by 31 July 1917 the figure had risen to 1,730,346, and during this time they had also helped 244,368 families.[82] In the early months of the war the Berlin NFD helped the needy and the unemployed, distributing milk to schoolchildren and bread and other food coupons to the poor and setting up four work rooms, in each of which some 200 unemployed women were taught to sew and knit for the military in exchange for a weekly wage and luncheon vouchers. It offered advice on entitlements to benefits, producing detailed tabular information, and its members visited benefit claimants on behalf of the local authorities in order to ascertain need.[83] Depots were set up to collect unwanted clothing and bedding, which were transformed into items for distribution among the needy.[84] Other NFD branches set up kindergartens and crèches for children of conscripted soldiers' wives whose mothers had to go out to work, organised holidays in the country for women in need of a break and their children, or provided accommodation, medical care and employment for professional women who had fallen on hard times.[85] Hindenburg noted that the NFD's achievements were outstanding.[86]

Members of the NFD also played key roles within the war welfare offices which communities set up to cater for all those affected economically by the war. These welfare offices saw very close co-operation between private and communal providers of welfare, and in Hamburg, for example, women's welfare activities were totally integrated into the city's war welfare organisation (*Kriegshilfe*) in January 1916, at which time some 1,055 women worked voluntarily in war welfare.[87] Many cities co-opted women onto welfare-related committees in a consultative capacity.[88] From 1915 NFD members served as consumer representatives on local price-control commissions and took over the offices distributing ration cards.[89] The NFD was instrumental in educating women in the importance of household consumption for the national economy. Before the war

Germany had been dependent on foreign imports for approximately one-third of its food supply, as well as for fertiliser and animal feed, and no preparations had been made for a long war. 'Wasted food is the same as lost ammunition' became one motto.[90] Initially the NFD produced leaflets and regional recipes, which were reprinted in local newspapers, and ran cookery courses, encouraging women to use seasonal fruits and vegetables in their cooking. Over time the advice changed to reflect current shortages, suggesting for example cooking without fat, washing without soap, using straw to repair shoes or cooking inventive recipes with turnips.[91] What the NFD could not do, however, was to control the food supply, which was within the remit of the deputy commanding generals, who headed the twenty-four army corps districts across Germany and who, with the invocation of the 1851 Prussian Law of Siege at the beginning of the war, took over responsibility for the civilian administration. Bessel notes: 'The result was not the smooth running of the civilian administration by an efficient military, but, ultimately, the discrediting of the military in civilian eyes amidst mounting chaos.'[92]

Women and hardships

German estimates claimed that some 763,000 died during the war because of the Allied blockade, though historians have subsequently refuted this figure.[93] Lummel notes that 'civilians starved to ensure that the soldiers ate': the army was prioritised in the allocation of food supplies, with a soldier's daily allowance of fat and meat in the winter of 1916–17 being the equivalent of one week's rations for a city-dweller.[94] Belinda Davis believes that while 'government measures to combat the effects of economic war won widespread popular approval for the state over and over again during the course of World War I', the authorities' failure to ensure an adequate food supply ultimately 'undermined the authority and legitimacy of the state'.[95] Keith Allen, however, believes that 'local governments ... largely met the unprecedented administrative challenges presented by the wartime scarcity of foodstuffs' and writes of 'the relative success of Berlin's bread rationing programme'.[96] Bread shortages became apparent as early as October 1914, and authorities tried to deal with food shortages and inflation by setting maximum prices and introducing rationing, but this merely led to a thriving black market, tensions between rural producers and urban consumers, claims of war profiteering and demands from women of lesser means for a more equitable food distribution. People of 'lesser means', whose income fell below the official poverty line, were entitled to receive subsidised items of goods, whose prices were regulated.[97]

Nearly all of Germany's major cities experienced disturbances by women over food shortages during the war. In Berlin, police reported over fifty disturbances in one week in October 1915, all in working-class districts, and in the following month there were reports of disturbances in Aachen, Cologne, Leipzig and Münster. In Nuremberg in July 1916 women threw horse manure and cobblestones at policemen, while in Hamburg in the following month shop windows were smashed and fifty-seven foodshops plundered.[98] Davis claims that by early 1916 women protesting at food shortages also called for 'peace at any price', a demand that grew stronger after the privations of the turnip winter of 1916–17.[99] She believes that 'food shortages were central to the popular toleration of the war', with, as Anke Sawahn reports, two-thirds of foodstuffs going to the military.[100] By June 1916 most staple foodstuffs were subject to rationing, though this did not mean that they were available. As Toni Sender, a pacifist socialist who was a founder member of the Independent Social Democratic Party in April 1917, wrote, 'more often than not the word "butter" on the ticket was all one saw of butter'.[101] Working-class women would queue for hours outside shops to obtain their rations in what became known as 'polonaises'; these queues became fertile ground for the spreading of rumour, or 'subversive communication' as Daniel calls it, much to the authorities' disquiet, and some authorities introduced methods to prevent the queues from forming.[102] Ethel Cooper, an Australian musician who spent the war in Leipzig, noted on 5 March 1915 that food 'costs such a lot of time, trouble and money, that you have always to be thinking about it'.[103] One report in April 1916 claimed that over the preceding winter women in Berlin had queued for 100,000 hours in all, hours they could have spent working in the war industries.[104] Urban women also spent time on Sundays 'hamstering' for food in the countryside, for payment or barter, or even stealing it, and then had to run the risk of having the food confiscated by the police waiting to check passengers at the railway station on their way home.[105] A survey in 1916 revealed that many Germans living in towns were eating 40 per cent of the food intake they had eaten before the war.[106] By summer 1917 German rations amounted to 1,000 calories per day, compared with the official pre-war minimum of 2,280.[107] But only the urban poor depended on the ration allocation. The wealthy were able to purchase food on the black market and to send servants to queue for it, and those who lived in the countryside likewise had access to a wider variety and more plentiful supply of foodstuffs.[108] Sawahn notes that the week's menus suggested by a rural housewives' magazine for a Berlin family of five bore absolutely no semblance to reality, containing as it did meat, fish, cheese, sugar and cake.[109] But as the war went on, many in the middle class also went hungry, and even resorted to eating crow.[110] In order to ensure that inhabitants had access to at least one meal a day and to reduce the impact of food shortages and the time taken queuing for food, many authorities opened kitchens to provide lunchtime meals. Some areas even introduced kitchens for the middle classes, with tablecloths and table service, but across Germany the take-up was variable, with many people shunning them because of the social stigma attached to them and the feelings of humiliation and loss of social status at being seen at one of the kitchens.[111] Such were the food shortages on the home front that there were reports of soldiers sending home food parcels, a reversal of the many *Liebesgaben* (gifts of love) sent to the front in the early months of the war.

But food shortages were not the only privations that Germans had to suffer. The potato shortage coincided with one of the coldest winters in German history, and coal shortages led to a lack of heating and light. Clothes were rationed in August 1916, shoes in December 1916.[112] From the earliest days of the war, women were the targets for propaganda, which encouraged them to support the war by surrendering their gold and precious jewellery under the motto of 'I gave gold for iron', or subscribing to war bonds. Piete Kuhr noted in 1918, 'our parents and relatives have become poor because they have given up all their money, jewellery and valuables for the war-loan'.[113] Red Cross posters encouraged women to cut their hair so that it could be used in the war industries.[114] The greatest sacrifice of all, that of a mother of her son, was portrayed as 'the purest, most selfless, and most final of all', with the nation's survival dependent on maternal sacrifice.[115] However, even in sacrifice there was inequality. Matthew Stibbe notes that 'younger working-class conscripts from the big cities were more likely to be killed in action than their rural or older counterparts'.[116] Princess Blücher commented that whereas at the beginning of the war the Empress, with six sons and a son-in-law at the front, was perceived 'as an ideal for German women, willing to offer everything and without complaint for the weal of the Fatherland', towards the war's end she faced criticism that none had been killed or mutilated.[117]

Inequalities were perceived, too, in the disparity of benefits available to soldiers' wives and families. The government acknowledged that the conscription of men meant the loss of a breadwinner to many families, and so on 4 August 1914 it amended the Family War Benefit Law of 28 February 1888 to increase separation allowances to 9 Reichsmark (RM) a month in summer and twelve in winter for a serving soldier's wife, with 6 RM a month for each dependent child. The sums were fixed, irrespective of the soldier's previous wage, and were not paid to officers' wives.[118] Family War Benefit was an entitlement, bearing none of the stigma and civic consequences of poor relief, but the claimant had to apply for it, and in January 1915 it became means-tested. Married women's interaction with state agencies was no longer mediated by men. Class differences were exacerbated by the perceived intrusiveness of the interviews conducted by middle-class women, working within local welfare offices, in order to ascertain need.[119] By the end of 1915 some 4 million families, with a total of 11 million members, or one-sixth of the German population, were in receipt of Family War Benefit. In some areas such as Neukölln, a suburb of Berlin, half of the households were dependent on Family War Benefit.[120] Although the amount of benefit was increased throughout the war, historians are divided over the extent to which Family War Benefit was sufficient for a family to live on.[121] Many communities provided additional support to families to 'alleviate their need', but these benefits, paid in cash, coupons and kind, varied considerably, with some rural areas paying nothing and cities such as Berlin matching the Reich benefit. As the war went on these locally funded allowances were reduced.[122] Some soldiers' wives dependent on Family War Benefit felt great bitterness that the wives of civil servants and local authority white-collar workers continued to receive their husband's full wage. On the other hand, middle-class women believed that Family War Benefit enabled working-class soldiers' wives to spend their afternoons 'consuming quantities of cake and whipped cream with their children'.[123] Feelings of inequality were to grow as the war progressed.

Women under scrutiny

Women's behaviour became increasingly the object of public scrutiny and debate. Working women's lack of supervision was blamed for the perceived increase in unruly behaviour among adolescents, especially young men.[124] Accepted pre-war standards of behaviour were challenged, and one report from a Saxon village in May 1916 noted the unacceptable behaviour of 'young people under 18 years old, *especially girls from better circles*', who 'have been roaming around the streets after 9:00 at night without chaperones'.[125] The behaviour of soldiers' wives was closely monitored. As letters became the primary means of contact between husband and wife, women were admonished in 1916 to stop sending their husbands demoralising letters of woe complaining about the time spent queuing for scarce food resources. Rather they should write letters more worthy of true German women, letters depicting empathy, comradeship in battle and holding out on the home front.[126] Seipp notes that early propaganda stressing the closeness of victory was replaced in 1917 by exhortations to 'hold on', to endure the many material privations in the expectations of a more equal society and a better future after the war.[127]

It was in their private lives, however, that the behaviour of soldiers' wives was most closely scrutinised. Some communities employed watchmen to 'ensure morality and order', frequently relying on denunciations from local residents.[128] A soldier's wife's infidelity was seen as immoral, as a betrayal of the troops risking their lives for their country and, when a prisoner of war was involved, as an affront to patriotic feeling and even treason. Todd writes of twenty-five women being charged with treason in Leipzig in 1917 for having affairs with prisoners of war.[129] Already in 1914 the attention paid by German women to French prisoners of war who arrived in transports at German stations, giving them food, cigarettes and flowers, earned widespread criticism as 'base and un-German' behaviour, and steps were taken to prevent it.[130] Some army corps districts, using the 1851 Law of Siege, forbade any contact between prisoners of war and women that 'offends good morals', and women found to have been in a relationship with a prisoner of war, or even merely to have exchanged letters with a prisoner of war, faced at best having their names listed on church doors or public shaming in the local press, and at worst a prison sentence of up to one year.[131]

The increasing evidence of German women's sexual activity offended middle-class notions of sexual propriety, as it was seen as both unnatural and a danger to the moral and social order. However, the military accepted the need for male sexual desires to be met and introduced brothels at the front; it adopted the German system of regulation of prostitution in the occupied countries in order to try and prevent the spread of sexually transmitted diseases.[132] Concerns quickly grew in garrison towns about the number of conscripted soldiers' wives and unemployed women who, driven by economic necessity, were swelling the numbers of prostitutes, not merely because of the inappropriateness of their behaviour but also out of the fear of an increase in sexually transmitted diseases.[133] While the BdF and KFB petitioned the Prussian War Minister in December 1914 to ban extra-marital sex for all soldiers, as they were concerned not only about the consequences of venereal disease for the birth rate and the creation of healthy families but also about the loss of manpower to the army while infected men were being treated, the various military authorities at the front introduced a variety of measures aimed at reducing the incidence of venereal disease.[134] Some required the infected soldier to name the woman he believed had infected him: women continued to be blamed for the spread of sexually transmitted diseases, in spite of evidence that some soldiers preferred to contract venereal disease rather than face death at the front.[135]

Several deputy commanding generals within Germany issued decrees in 1916 which gave the police extensive powers to place the following under the supervision of the morals police: any woman found to have a sexually transmitted disease even if it could not be proven that she was a prostitute; any woman who was not found to have a sexually transmitted disease but who had slept with one man for money; and any woman who had slept with several men, with no money involved.[136] As Lisa Todd notes, German police forces tended to characterise as prostitutes all promiscuous women and conscripted soldiers' wives who took a lover.[137] The BdF feared not only that innocent women could become the victims of malicious denunciations but also that women, infected by husbands or fiancés, could be made subject to police supervision. It regarded many of the measures as anti-woman, and continued to call for a change in attitudes, away from women prostitutes being blamed for the spread of venereal disease and dealt with by the police and towards to a system of medical supervision for all infected men and women.[138]

The concern about the spread of venereal disease among the military was, to a large extent, unfounded. Bessel has shown that the proportion of servicemen with sexually transmitted diseases was probably lower in 1918 than it had been in 1914.[139] But it is indicative of the growing paranoia about the need for a comprehensive population policy, driven by the anxiety at the falling birth rate which was exacerbated by the war. Usborne notes that during the war the number of pro-natalist organisations doubled. Most had links to political parties and the churches, indicating that the birth rate, which had fallen from 39.0 live births per 1,000 inhabitants in 1891 to 29.8 in 1910, was regarded as a political and moral problem.[140] The sharp decline in births, first noticeable in April 1915, and the first recorded surplus of deaths over births that year provided the impetus for several conferences and commissions.[141] The Reichstag set up a Select Committee on Population Policy in May 1916 to propose legislation, and this led to the drafting of three laws aimed at combating venereal disease, suppressing abortifacients and contraceptives other than condoms and prohibiting sterilisation and abortion except when the mother's life was in danger.[142] Auguste Kirchhoff of the Bund für Mutterschutz (League for the Protection of Mothers, BfM) protested that the proposed law on contraceptives was 'the most inconceivably discriminatory law ever passed against women in the civilised world, a law that allows contraceptive devices to men but places contraceptive services intended for women as well as abortion under heavy controls'.[143] Historians, too, believe that this repressive draft legislation, driven by a desire to increase the birth rate, clearly targeted women. The BdF and other women's organisations protested against the draft, but the laws could not be enacted before the revolution of November 1918.[144]

For officials, increasing the birth rate was paramount, and so, in some districts, steps were taken to reduce women's access to birth control. In 1915 some military authorities banned the sale of contraceptives, while from 1916 attempts were made to cut the number of abortions, which was reckoned to be between 200,000 and 400,000 performed annually by doctors and between 30,000 and half a million performed illegally. Abortions could now be performed only by registered practitioners on women whose life was in danger.[145] Judges were urged to deal harshly with women found guilty of having an abortion, and Heinemann tells of a woman worker in Berlin receiving a sentence of two years, instead of the one year demanded by the state prosecutor, because her actions were deemed a danger to the public, undermining the nation's health and well-being.[146]

Usborne notes that most welfare proposals aimed at increasing the birth rate, such as the reform of midwifery, the creation of more children's hospitals, infant and maternity clinics, or special allowances for families with many children, were not implemented, perhaps because a lack of resources. The one exception was the extension in December 1914 of maternity benefits to soldiers' wives, which included a one-off payment to cover the cost of childbirth and an allowance paid for eight weeks. These were extended again in early 1915 to include unmarried women where a serviceman acknowledged paternity.[147] Nursing mothers were also entitled to benefit for twelve weeks, but their claims brought them under the supervision of the local welfare office, leading to complaints that they were being monitored.[148]

The war was estimated to have cost Germany some 2.2 million births.[149] The birth rate almost halved between 1914, when it stood at 26.8 per 1,000 inhabitants, and 1917, when it was 13.9.[150] The main reason for the fall in the birth rate was, of course, the absence of men at the front, with lucky soldiers being granted two weeks' leave every year, though prisoners of war did not return home.[151] Couples, many of whom regarded children as a financial burden and an impediment to social mobility, were reluctant to bring children into such a world, and the most widely practised form of contraception, *coitus interruptus*, was not only free but also immune to any repressive official measures.[152] As the war went on, malnutrition and exhaustion took their toll on women's health, and some women suffered from amenorrhoea.[153] Stokes notes a dramatic increase in deaths from childbed fever, resulting perhaps from exhaustion, poor nutrition or the increased risk of infection due to the lack of soap.[154] Some communities gave additional rations to pregnant women, usually on the condition that they attended a local welfare office and came under the supervision of a welfare worker.[155] Davis notes the ambivalent attitudes to pregnant women, claiming that there was 'no societal consensus on the virtues of "producing children for the nation"'. Women experienced suspicion about the identity of the father and resentment at the increased demands on the food supply. Davis claims that pregnant women frequently had difficulty obtaining extra milk, a policy halted in 1917 in recognition of public opinion, and that not only was pregnancy seen as a 'selfish' act by poorer women because it created another mouth to feed, but it also removed the woman from the workforce.[156]

The organised women's movement

Claudia Siebrecht has claimed that 'bourgeois German women, and members of the women's movement in particular, were among the most fervent and consistent supporters of the German war effort'.[157] This support was revealed not just in organisations such as the NFD but also in most middle-class women's organisations' uncritical acceptance of their government's stance. They campaigned to raise money for the families of fallen or wounded soldiers and sailors, and the 'War Donation: German Women's Thanks 1915' raised some 4.25 million RM.[158] They also encouraged women to buy war bonds, and the BdF called for Saturday 13 April 1918 to become the 'National Day of German Women', exhorting women to donate their day's earnings or expenditure to the eighth war bond, thereby fighting the heroic fight with their brave brothers at the front.[159]

In September 1914, led by the BdF, some well-known German women signed an appeal which was sent to over 4,000 women abroad, repudiating claims that Germany had started a war of conquest, attesting to Germany's love of peace and her reputation as one of the leading cultural nations in the world, lamenting the unspeakable cruelties of the misguided Belgians against German troops and the suffering of East Prussian villages and towns under a barbaric enemy, and calling upon them to help rebut the tissue of lies propounded by an unscrupulous foreign press.[160] In early 1915 Bäumer, on behalf of the BdF, declined an invitation to attend an international women's congress to be held in The Hague in late April 1915. Women's greatest responsibility, in Bäumer's eyes, was to support national resistance: 'It is obvious to us that during a national struggle for existence, we women belong to our people and only to them.'[161] In September 1917 the BdF and other women's organisations repudiated President Wilson's response of 27 August 1917 to Pope Benedict's peace proposal, which the BdF had welcomed 'in gratitude and hope'.[162] Their protests were welcomed by both Hindenburg and the Empress Auguste Victoria. Hindenburg, noting that 'German women were making a stand alongside men against foreign presumptuousness, just as they had borne sorrow and joy with us, proudly and self-sacrificingly', attested, 'We German men bow our heads in reverence before German women.'[163]

Just over a year later, at a request from the Berlin authorities, the BdF called upon local women's organisations to arrange demonstrations and declarations in the local press to strengthen the home front's resolve.[164] Scheck states that although the BdF withdrew the request following the German government's request for armistice negotiations on 4 October 1918, several demonstrations did take place.[165] In Hanover, for example, the women's organisations placed a proclamation in six newspapers, professing their gratitude to and trust in the men who had protected them and their home from a hard fate: 'And so at this hour we German women vow to you, the defenders of German freedom, that we shall fight shoulder to shoulder with you and hold out with you until the end.'[166] On 22 October 1918 the BdF published a declaration claiming that it could have no faith in a League of Nations built on trampled German honour:

> German women consider it a requirement of national self-respect and a duty towards those who have died of their own free will for the honour of the fatherland that the German people will accept no measures that have the character of 'punishment'. Before the German people accepts conditions which deny the memory of its dead and attach to its name an indelible stigma, women will also be ready to use their strength in a defensive struggle to the last.[167]

It is, however, doubtful whether working-class women, who as early as autumn 1915 were calling for an end to the war, shared these sentiments.[168] Nor did middle-class feminist pacifists and socialist activists, who were counted among the estimated 300 to 500 women actively opposed to the war. Among middle-class women it was to be primarily women from the Women's Suffrage League who espoused the cause of pacifism, earning Bäumer's thinly veiled criticism of undermining the solidarity of the women's movement.[169] Twenty-eight of the 1,136 delegates who attended the Hague congress from 28 April to 1 May 1915 were German, including Anita Augspurg, Lida Gustava Heymann, Constanze Hallgarten, Gertrude Baer and Auguste Kirchhoff of the Women's Suffrage League and Helene Stöcker, leader of the BfM, who was banned from public speaking in 1918 for criticising the Treaty of Brest-Litovsk.[170] Throughout the war Augspurg and Heymann sent petitions to the German Chancellor, calling for the self-determination of nations and for a peace without annexations or reparations. Their attempts to have leaflets printed, including one calling for 'war on war', were blocked, their letters censored, telephones tapped, houses searched and movements restricted. In February 1917 they were expelled from Bavaria and Baden, but they still maintained links with people in twenty-nine towns, even holding meetings of delegates in Frankfurt am Main on 30 April 1917 and 25 May 1918.[171] The strength of their links with female social democratic opponents of the war who were led by Clara Zetkin is not known, though Lilli Jannasch, who had attended the Hague congress and who was to write in their magazine after the war, did have contacts with anti-war members of the SPD.[172] Zetkin called an international socialist women's meeting in Berne, Switzerland, from 26 to 28 March 1915, and it was attended by some seventy women from eight countries. Women of the working classes were told that the only beneficiaries of the war were capitalists and were asked to work for a peace without annexations. Some 200,000 copies of the manifesto were distributed illegally in Germany. Zetkin's post was censored and her house searched before her arrest for treason on 29 July 1915. She was released from prison on 12 October 1915 owing to ill-health. Marginalised by the Majority Socialists, an ailing Zetkin was unable to mobilise masses of working women against the war.[173] The extent to which women participated in the wave of strikes that hit Germany's industrial centres in April 1917 and in greater numbers in January 1918, with their demands not just for better food distribution, but also for higher wages and a rapid peace settlement, is not known. Stibbe reports that more than half of the strikers in some munitions plants in January 1918 were women.[174]

Feminist pacifists frequently called for the democratisation of the state and for women's influence to be felt within it. They were appalled when in January 1918 seven women, the best-known of whom was a former feminist and founder member of the extreme nationalist German Fatherland Party, Dr Käthe Schirmacher, formed the Home Army of German Women (Heimatheer Deutscher Frauen) in Berlin. The Home Army of German Women called upon women not only to rebut any defeatist comment overheard on the street, on public transport, at the theatre or in the soup kitchens but also to denounce anyone complaining or spreading rumours which might impact negatively on the public mood. By June 1918 it had branches across Germany and its events regularly attracted several hundred women. It was reportedly set up in response to a request from the military command in Brandenburg in an attempt to monitor public opinion and control defeatism. It is not known how many Germans were denounced by its followers.[175] The army had previously sought, in spring 1917, to mobilise women's groups in support of its propaganda campaign to unite all Germans behind the war effort, a clear recognition by some in the military not only of the need to re-energise continuing support for the war on the home front following the privations of the turnip winter of 1916–17 but also of the significant role that women could play in mobilising that support. Stibbe has argued that in the second half of the war nationalist men expended considerable effort in trying to mobilise patriotic women for their cause, and the German Fatherland Party, founded on 2 September 1917 in response to a Reichstag resolution for a peace without annexations, could boast a one-third share of female members, the highest proportion of any German political party.[176] This is a clear sign of the impact that women's increased participation in public life had, even among those who had been opposed to it before the war.[177] The German Fatherland Party wished to mobilise patriotic female support behind a drive for a victory with annexations rather than improve women's right to participate in public life, and few women attained senior positions within the party which refused to discuss female suffrage.[178]

The mainstream women's movement suspended any feminist campaigns at the beginning of the war. It is clear that BdF leaders hoped that women's contribution to municipal welfare would lead to a re-appraisal of their participation in Germany's public and political life. Indeed, the League against Women's Emancipation accused women of being unscrupulous in exploiting the fatherland's hour of need for their own benefit and to further their own ends.[179] With the Kaiser failing to mention women in his Easter address of 1917 in which he encouraged greater participation of all the nation's forces in political life, and female suffrage at communal level and within public welfare administration being discussed in provincial parliaments, the BdF at its annual general meeting in September 1917 produced a statement on women's place in the socio-political reorganisation of Germany. It noted the absence of any reference to women in the Kaiser's comments and called, *inter alia*, for both active and passive suffrage for women. This call led to the decision of the German Protestant Women's League (Deutsch-Evangelischer Frauenbund, DEF), concerned about the democratisation of German society implicit in the granting of female suffrage, to leave the BdF in March 1918.[180]

During 1917 Social Democratic women, whose party was the only one to support female suffrage, began to work with the BdF and Germany's two suffrage organisations to campaign for the vote for women.[181] They faced resolute conservative opposition to female suffrage at all levels. On 20 January 1917 in a debate in the Prussian Diet on granting the municipal suffrage to women, one delegate claimed that 'If Germany gave votes to married women it would break up the German family. The political women's movement is an assault on the family.'[182] The appointment of Max von Baden as Chancellor gave new hope to the campaign for female suffrage, and leading women from the social democrats, trade unions, BdF and suffrage organisations wrote to him on 25 October 1918, calling for female suffrage and requesting a meeting.[183] On 4 November 1918 a joint rally of socialist and bourgeois women, attended by over 2,000 women, was held in Berlin to call for the vote along with similar rallies in Munich and Hamburg.[184] In the Reichstag the inter-party discussions on franchise reform between the Social Democrats, the Liberals and the Catholic Centre Party (Die Deutsche Zentruspartei (Zentrum), Z) ultimately led to an agreement to support female suffrage on 8 November 1918, driven perhaps by the declaration of universal suffrage by Kurt Eisner, the leader of the revolution in Munich, on 7 November 1918.[185] Female suffrage, proclaimed by the Council of People's Delegates on 12 November 1918, was a gift of the revolution, not granted in response to women's lobbying nor as a reward for women's work during the war.[186]

Middle-class women had always been sensitive to accusations that women were benefiting from the war while men were dying, hence their determination not to demand female suffrage as a reward for women's work.[187] Attitudes towards women's role in the war effort were ambivalent, with some recognising the enormous contribution that women had made, while as the war progressed others blamed women's work in munitions and as auxiliaries behind the lines, and women's purchasing of war loans, for continuing the war. Ultimately, some blamed women for the loss of the war.[188] While the 'stab-in-the back' myth placed the blame for Germany's defeat on the shortcomings of politicians and failures on the home front, some in nationalist circles singled women out for particular opprobrium. In his memoirs Colonel Max Bauer criticised women's extensive self-adulation and their moral failings, which could be seen in the spread of venereal disease and the fall in the birth rate as they exploited their husbands' absence for sexual excesses, and he judged their total contribution to the war effort as inadequate. The real work had been done only by men. Even some women, like the DEF leader Paula Mueller-Otfried, claimed that it was not the war front but the home front that had failed. She criticised working-class women's grumbling letters and moaning and groaning, which, she argued, undermined soldiers' morale, and later believed that women's fight against the Treaty of Versailles and for national recovery compensated for women's shortcomings during the war.[189]

Conclusion

At the beginning of this chapter we noted the three historiographical interpretations of the First World War's impact on and legacy for women's role in German society. Many of the changes wrought by the war were intended to be only temporary, and few could be termed emancipatory, and hence Daniel's description of them as 'emancipation on loan' seems inappropriate.[190] Given the lack of accurate statistical data, it is impossible to determine the extent to which the war might have accelerated structural trends such as the increase in the numbers of married women working or the increase in the number of women in white-collar employment. The First World War was a catalyst of change for German women. They had mobilised themselves into the public sphere in the world of work, in welfare and in protest at the authorities' inability to ensure sufficient food supplies. In the world of work, they had replaced men, entering jobs and positions previously closed to them and thus overturning both the sexual division of labour and gender-segregated industries. Middle-class women were appointed to positions in local authorities and national agencies to help organise women's contribution to the war effort and to ensure the smooth running of the home front. Women's relationship to the state changed as middle-class women assumed responsibility for welfare and women came into direct contact with the agents of the state to receive their Family War Benefit or welfare payments. The state addressed women directly as targets of propaganda, urging them to hold out or to subscribe to war bonds, and it realised the significance of household consumption, determined and delivered by housewives, for the national economy. Women also had to experience the state's attempted interference in their private lives: their behaviour, in public and private, was closely monitored as the authorities attempted to ensure that they were upholding their womanly role as the guardians of German homes, values and culture, which German men were fighting to protect, and maintaining their motherly role as the guarantors of the survival of the German nation.[191] Women had to endure enormous hardships and privations, to varying degrees depending on their class and wealth, and class differences were exacerbated during the war. However, in post-war Germany, women's war-time sacrifices and suffering were overshadowed in public discourse by the sacrifice of the 'fallen soldiers'.[192] The war had fundamentally transformed the gender order, and Nelson has noted that 'the crisis of gender order' was 'a crisis of masculinity'.[193] During the war male anxieties about the increasing independence of women grew as they entered employment and replaced male breadwinners, took responsibility for their families' existence in very difficult circumstances and became independent agents in their interaction with agencies of the state. The authorities hoped to ease these anxieties by a return to the pre-war gender order in employment, the family and society in general. At the war's end many women welcomed the speedy return of their menfolk and their resumption of their responsibilities as the family breadwinner and head of the household. Ziemann has written of the 'utterly conservative consequences' of the war on gender relations within the family, for traditional family values held sway and traditional gender roles within the family resumed as couples sought a return to normality.[194] However, the spread of knowledge among soldiers about contraceptive methods ensured that couples would continue to restrict the size of their families, though the most popular methods, *coitus interruptus* and the use of condoms, meant that women were dependent on the co-operation of their husbands.[195] For some women, a return to the pre-war situation was impossible. Over two million German soldiers died during the war, leaving some 600,000 women widowed and 1,192,000 children fatherless.[196] Young women's marriage prospects were reduced, thus creating a surplus of women who would have to earn their own living. The changes in women's lives and their relationship with the state wrought by the war, the granting of political equality to women by the revolution in November 1918 and the rights enshrined in the new constitution made possible new opportunities for women's independence and agency in the Weimar Republic. The tensions created between these new opportunities and the desire held by many for a return to a pre-war gender order in society at large were to form the backdrop to women's lives during the Weimar Republic.

Notes

1 T. Sender, *The Autobiography of a German Rebel* (London: Labour Book Service, 1940), p. 81.
2 A. Schaser, 'Women in a Nation of Men: The Politics of the League of German Women's Associations (BDF) in Imperial Germany', in I. Blom, K. Hagemann and C. Hall (eds), *Gendered Nations: Nationalisms and Gender Order in the Long Nineteenth Century* (Oxford: Berg, 2000), pp. 249–68.
3 The Empress's call of 6 August 1914 became a propaganda poster and also a postcard: see J. H. Quataert, *Staging Philanthropy: Patriotic Women and the National Imagination in Dynastic Germany, 1813–1916* (Ann Arbor: University of Michigan Press, 2001), p. 279 and D. Welch, *Germany, Propaganda and Total War 1914–1918* (London: Athlone Press, 2000), p. 19.
4 Piete Kuhr, *There We'll Meet Again: The First World War Diary of a Young German Girl*, trans. W. Wright (Gloucester: Walter Wright, 1998), *passim*. Kuhr was a schoolgirl who later danced as Jo Mihaly. Evelyn, Princess Blücher, *An English Wife in Berlin* (New York: E. P. Dutton & Company, 1920), pp. 5–7, 9–10, 13, 16.
5 Canning, *Gender History in Practice*, pp. 220–1; Ziemann, 'Weimar was Weimar', p. 549.

6 Ute Daniel, *The War from Within: German Working-Class Women in the First World War*, trans. Margaret Ries (Oxford and New York: Berg, 1997), p. 283. For war as a catalyst, see S. Bajohr, *Die Hälfte der Fabrik: Geschichte der Frauenarbeit in Deutschland 1914 bis 1945* (Marburg: Verlag Arbeiterbewegung und Gesellschaftswissenschaft, 1979), p. 101, and Y.-S. Hong, 'The Contradictions of Modernisation in the German Welfare State: Gender and the Politics of Welfare Reform in First World War Germany', *Social History*, 17:2 (1992), 251–70. Birthe Kundrus believes that 'there is considerable evidence that the First World War did not constitute a turning point in gender relations and identity': Kundrus, 'Gender Wars', p. 172.

7 S. Hering, *Die Kriegsgewinnlerinnen: Praxis und Ideologie der deutschen Frauenbewegung im Ersten Weltkrieg* (Pfaffenweiler: Centaurus,1990), p. 86; H. Hagenlücke, 'The Home Front in Germany', in J. Bourne, P. Liddle and I. Whitehead (eds), *The Great World War, 1914–1945: Who Won? Who Lost?* (London: HarperCollins, 2001), pp. 57–73.

8 J. Verhey, *The Spirit of 1914: Militarism, Myth and Mobilization in Germany* (Cambridge: Cambridge University Press, 2000), pp. 68, 78, 97, 102. Verhey was one of the first to challenge the totality of patriotic fervour in Germany in 1914.

9 Only 3,000 could be accepted: G. Bäumer, 'Heimatchronik', *Die Frau*, 21:12 (September 1914), 750, entry for 12 August 1914; Verhey, *The Spirit of 1914*, pp. 47–50. Countess Blücher, an English woman married to a German aristocrat, joined a Red Cross nursing course in August 1914. Her husband inherited the title and estates in 1916: Blücher, *An English Wife in Berlin*, pp. 15, 17, 20, 144.

10 R. Bessel, 'Mobilizing German Society for War', in R. Chickering and S. Förster (eds), *Great War, Total War: Combat and Mobilization on the Western Front, 1914–1918* (Cambridge: Cambridge University Press, 2000), p. 447.

11 Baümer, 'Heimatchronik', p. 749, entry for Wednesday, 5 August 1914; 'Women as Rulers', *Jus suffragii*, 9:2 (1 November 1914), 183. The Duke of Brunswick had gone to the front; his wife was one of the Emperor's daughters.

12 B. Franzoi, *At the Very Least She Pays the Rent: Women and German Industrialisation, 1871–1914* (London: Greenwood Press, 1985), p. 6.

13 Bajohr, *Die Hälfte der Fabrik*, 102; C. Lorenz, 'Die gewerbliche Frauenarbeit während des Krieges', in J. T. Shotwell (ed.), *Der Krieg und die Arbeitsverhältnisse* (Stuttgart: Deutsche Verlagsanstalt, 1928), pp. 311–91; Daniel, *The War from Within*, p. 25. For unemployment in general at the beginning of the war see R. Bessel, *Germany after the First World War* (Oxford: Clarendon Press, 1993), pp. 11–12.

14 Lüders quoted in Hering, *Kriegsgewinnlerinnen*, p. 76. Hering herself claims that an additional 5 million women joined the workforce during the war: *ibid.*, p. 143. Renate Wurms claims that 10.8 million women were working in 1913, and 16 million in 1918: R. Wurms, '"Krieg dem Krieg" – "Dienst am Vaterland": Frauenbewegung im Ersten Weltkrieg', in F. Herve (ed.), *Geschichte der deutschen Frauenbewegung* (Bonn: Pahl-Rugenstein, 1982), pp. 84–118.

15 Some use factory inspectors' reports for industrial concerns with more than ten employees, which show that there was a 52.2 per cent increase in the female industrial workforce: R. Meerwarth, A. Günther and W. Zimmermann, *Die Einwirkung des Krieges auf Bevölkerungsbewegung, Einkommen und Lebenshaltung in Deutschland* (Stuttgart: Deutsche Verlagsanstalt, 1932), pp. 350–1; Bessel, *Germany after the First World War*, p. 38. Daniel, however, basing her findings on returns to the compulsory sickness insurance funds, claims that there was merely a 17 per cent increase in the number of women working during the war. She notes that not all employers reported consistently: U. Daniel, 'Women's Work in Industry and Family: Germany, 1914–18', in R. Wall and J. Winter (eds), *The Upheaval of War: Family, Work and Welfare in Europe, 1914–1918* (Cambridge: Cambridge University Press, 1988), pp. 268–9; Daniel, *The War from Within*, pp. 40–7, 276; U. Daniel, 'Fiktionen, Friktionen und Fakten – Frauenlohnarbeit im Ersten Weltkrieg', in G. Mai (ed.), *Arbeiterschaft 1914–1918 in Deutschland* (Düsseldorf: Droste, 1985), pp. 277–323. The compulsory sickness insurance funds covered factory workers, white-collar workers earning less than 2,500 RM a year, domestic servants, agricultural labourers and public sector workers.

16 The chemical industry saw an increase of 681 per cent: calculated from figures in Meerwarth, Günther and Zimmermann, *Die Einwirkung des Krieges auf Bevölkerungsbewegung*, pp. 350–1. Reich Labour Ministry statistics show even more spectacular gains – of 3,637 per cent in engineering between September 1914 and September 1918, for example: Bajohr, *Die Hälfte der Fabrik*, p. 125. For government restrictions on the textile industry see Daniel, *The War from Within*, pp. 59–60.

17 Daniel, *The War from Within*, p. 47; R. Bessel, '"Eine nicht allzu grosse Beunruhigung des Arbeitsmarktes": Frauenarbeit und Demobilmachung in Deutschland nach dem Ersten Weltkrieg', *Geschichte und Gesellschaft*, 9 (1983), 215.

18 Bessel, *Germany after the First World War*, p. 20.

19 A. Karbe, *Die Frauenlohnfrage und ihre Entwicklung in der Kriegs- und Nachkriegszeit* (Rostock: C. Hinstorffs, 1928), p. 75.

20 Bajohr, *Die Hälfte der Fabrik*, p. 131; Wurms, '"Krieg dem Krieg"', p. 86.
  A Transport Workers' Union report in October 1915 revealed that 2,799 of 13,954 women working for seventy tram operators were wives of conscripted former workers: *Gewerkschaftliche Frauenzeitung*, 1:3 (2 February 1916), 18. See also Daniel, *The War from Within*, pp. 54–5.
21 'Die Strassenbahnschaffnerin', *Gewerkschaftliche Frauenzeitung*, 1:3 (2 February 1916), 18–20; 'Frauen im Eisenbahndienst', *Gewerkschaftliche Frauenzeitung*, 1:23 (8 November 1916), 184.
22 In 1914 1,504 of these women were civil servants, and in 1918 1,754, indicating that the vast majority were employed as assistants. Figures found in A. Kunz, *Civil Servants and the Politics of Inflation in Germany, 1914–1924* (Berlin and New York: De Gruyter, 1986), p. 51, and *Unter dem Reichsadler*, 9:9 (10 May 1917), 143; Bajohr, *Die Hälfte der Fabrik*, p. 121.
23 *Jus suffragii*, 10:11 (1 August 1916), 168; 'Frauen in Uniform', *Die christliche Frau*, 14:6 (June 1916).
24 'Increase of Women in Industry', *Jus suffragii*, 12:6 (1 March 1918), 89.
25 R. L. Nelson, 'German Comrades – Slavic Whores: Gender Images in the German Soldier Newspapers of the First World War', in Hagemann and Schüler-Springorum (eds), *Home/Front*, pp. 77–8. Brocks notes that the rare postcards of working women tended to depict them in uniform: C. Brocks, *Die bunte Welt des Krieges: Bildpostkarten aus dem Ersten Weltkrieg* (Essen: Klartext, 2008), p. 236.
26 The Union of Female Post and Telegraph Civil Servants wanted these widows to be given preferential treatment when appointments were being made to civil servants' posts, a desire shared by the education authorities: *Unter dem Reichsadler*, 7:7 (8 April 1915), 133; *Unter dem Reichsadler*, 8:2 (27 January 1916), 33; S. Habeth, 'Die Freiberuflerin und Beamtin (Ende 19. Jahrhundert bis 1945)', in H. Pohl and W. Treue (eds), *Die Frau in der deutschen Wirtschaft* (Wiesbaden: Franz Steiner Verlag, 1985), p. 164.
27 *Gewerkschaftliche Frauenzeitung*, 1:12 (7 June 1916); D. Stratigakos, 'The Professional Spoils of War: German Women Architects and World War 1', *Journal of the Society of Architectural Historians*, 66:4 (2007), 468–70.
28 Habeth, 'Die Freiberuflerin und Beamtin', pp. 158, 164. A report from February 1914 claimed that there were 196 women doctors practising in Germany, fifty-six of them in Berlin: *Die christliche Frau*, 12 (February 1914), 178.
29 J. Doerner, 'Neun Jahrzehnte Frauenbeschäftigung bei der Postverwaltung', *Jahrbuch des Postwesens*, 7 (1956–57), 377–42, 382–3; *Evangelische Frauenzeitung*, 15:6 (15 May 1915), 124–5.

30 U. Nienhaus, 'Frauen, Männer und Arbeitgeber Staat – das Beispiel der deutschen Post', *Sozialwissenschaftliche Informationen*, 4 (1989), 242; Nienhaus, *Vater Staat und seine Gehilfinnen*, p. 344.
31 Daniel has referred to it as 'self-mobilisation': Daniel, *The War from Within*, p. 50.
32 Quoted in *ibid.*, p. 66.
33 The Chancellor, Bethmann-Hollweg, and women's organisations were against the conscription of women: *ibid.*, p. 67; G. D. Feldman, *Army, Industry, and Labor in Germany 1914–1918* (Princeton: Princeton University Press, 1966), pp. 174–7. For the women's organisations see: Archiv des Katholischen Deutschen Frauenbundes (AKDFB), Collection 1-22-6, letter from the Catholic Women's League to the Interior Minister dated 24 November 1916; 1-22-1, confidential memo of the BdF to the Catholic Women's League of 21 November 1916; 1-22-1, 'Zur Organisation der Frauenarbeit durch das Kriegsamt', Berlin, 20 November 1916.
34 Lüders believed that her task was fivefold: to increase the number of women working in the war economy, particularly in munitions and agriculture; to find new and appropriate methods of advertising jobs and placing women in them; to train women workers; to improve the quantity and quality of goods produced by women and to reduce the frequency with which women changed jobs: M.-E. Lüders, 'Die Entwicklung der gewerblichen Frauenarbeit im Kriege', *Schmollers Jahrbuch für Gesetzgebung, Verwaltung und Volkswirtschaft im Deutschen Reiche*, 44 (1920), 241–75 and 569–93.
35 A. T. Allen, *Feminism and Motherhood in Western Europe, 1890–1970* (Basingstoke: Palgrave Macmillan, 2005), p. 199; U. von Gersdorff, *Frauen im Kriegsdienst, 1914–1945* (Stuttgart: Deutsche Verlagsanstalt, 1969), pp. 22–4, 128–34; Daniel, *The War from Within*, pp. 77–8. The Central Office merged with the Women's Section in June 1917.
36 Hering, *Kriegsgewinnlerinnen*, pp. 167–8.
37 Bessel, 'Mobilising German Society for War', p. 444.
38 Wurms, '"Krieg dem Krieg"', p. 86. The women's organisations believed that the decree was introduced for financial reasons and called for at least 50 per cent of a women's wage to be excluded in calculations for war allowance: Landesarchiv Berlin (LAB), BRep 235, Helene-Lange-Archiv (HLA) MF 2740, letter signed by several women's organisations to the Reich Office of the Interior dated 4 June 1917 and reply from the Reich Chancellery of 14 August 1917.
39 Jones, *Gender and Rural Modernity*, p. 94. Bavaria passed such laws in March 1915 and other areas in April 1917.

40 G. Bry, *Wages in Germany, 1871–1945* (Princeton: Princeton University Press, 1960), pp. 7, 93, 96.
41 A. R. Seipp, *The Ordeal of Peace: Demobilisation and the Urban Experience in Britain and Germany, 1917–1921* (Farnham: Ashgate, 2009), p. 97.
42 Bundesarchiv Berlin (BAB), R3901/2814, Kriegsministerium. Kriegsamt, 12 August 1918 and 1 November 1918.
43 Lorenz, 'Die gewerbliche Frauenarbeit', p. 329. A further 31,244 were replaced by men aged between seventeen and sixty who were conscripted under the Auxiliary Service Law, and 5,792 were replaced by men not included in the Auxiliary Service Law.
44 C. E. Boyd, '"Nationaler Frauendienst": German Middle-class Women in Service to the Fatherland, 1914–1918' (PhD dissertation, University of Georgia, 1979), pp. 177–8, 181; B. Schönberger, 'Motherly Heroines and Adventurous Girls: Red Cross Nurses and Women Army Auxiliaries in the First World War', in Hagemann and Schüler-Springorum (eds), *Home/Front*, p. 91. See also K. Hagemann, '"Jede Kraft wird gebraucht": Militäreinsatz von Frauen im Ersten und Zweiten Weltkrieg', in B. Thoss and H.-E. Volkmann (eds), *Erster Weltkrieg – Zweiter Weltkrieg: Ein Vergleich* (Paderborn: Schöningh, 2002), pp. 87–8.
45 Boyd, '"Nationaler Frauendienst"', pp. 178–82. Schönberger puts the figure at over 20,000: Schönberger, 'Motherly Heroines', p. 91.
46 Schönberger, 'Motherly Heroines', pp. 96–8; Boyd, '"Nationaler Frauendienst"', p. 180.
47 During the early months of the war regular reports from Lutheran nurses on the front line would appear in the *Evangelische Frauenzeitung*. A small number of nurses also came from the Professional Organisation of Nurses in Germany. Schulte puts the number of Red Cross nurses at 19,073: R. Schulte, 'The Sick Warrior's Sister: Nursing during the First World War', in L. Abrams and E. Harvey (eds), *Gender Relations in German History: Power, Agency and Experience from the Sixteenth Century to the Twentieth* (London: UCL Press, 1996), pp. 124–6; Schönberger, 'Motherly Heroines', p. 106.
48 On the differences between views of nurses and of auxiliaries see Schönberger, 'Motherly Heroines', pp. 92–6.
49 *Die Frau*, 22:6 (March 1915), 376; *Jus suffragii*, 9:4 (1 January 1915), 215. Women often received their medals from members of the royal houses or from Hindenburg: *Jus suffragii*, 9:5 (1 February 1915), 237; *Jus suffragii*, 9:7 (1 April 1915), 272.
50 *Jus suffragii*, 9:4 (1 January 1915), 222.
51 *Jus suffragii*, 9:5 (1 February 1915), 237. Koch notes that forty-six female medical practitioners had been called up at the start of the war

and dismissed in spring 1915: S. H. Koch, 'Militärpolitik im "Jahr der Frau"': Die Öffnung der Bundeswehr für weibliche Sanitätsoffiziere und ihre Folgen' (PhD dissertation, University of Brunswick, 2008), pp. 23–4. Knobelsdorff was given the rank of lieutenant: Stratigakos, 'The Professional Spoils of War', pp. 465–6.
52 Gersdorff, *Frauen im Kriegsdienst*, pp. 31–3, 247–51, 258–9; Boyd, '"Nationaler Frauendienst"', pp. 183–7.
53 H. Hieber, '"Mademoiselle Docteur": The Life and Service of Imperial Germany's only Female Intelligence Officer', *Journal of Intelligence History*, 5:2 (2005), 91–108.
54 Calculated from figures in Statistisches Reichsamt, *Statistisches Jahrbuch für 1921/22* (Berlin: Verlag für Politik und Wirtschaft, 1922), pp. 320–1 (volumes of this publication are hereafter cited as *StJhb*). For Hindenburg's calls for the closure of universities, with the exception of medical schools, see Feldman, *Army, Industry, and Labor*, pp. 173, 187. Hindenburg's letter to the Chancellor in October 1916 is found in S. R Grayzel, *Women and the First World War* (Harlow: Pearson, 2002), pp. 128–9.
55 Lüders, 'Die Entwicklung der gewerblichen Frauenarbeit', p. 263. Some students worked during the vacation; see the report by one of thirty students in Gersdorff, *Frauen im Kriegsdienst*, pp. 189–90. Medical students were apparently the most reluctant to work in munitions factories: Archiv des Deutsch-Evangelischen Frauenbundes, Kassel (ADEF), FF3, report of 17 October 1917.
56 The 1907 census revealed that 47.1 per cent of the female workforce was to be found in agriculture: calculated from figures in Statistisches Reichsamt, *Statistik des Deutschen Reiches* (*SdR*), vol. 402, p. 442; E. B. Jones, 'Pre- and Post-War Generations of Rural Female Youth and the Future of the German Nation, 1871–1933', *Continuity and Change*, 19:3 (2004), 354.
57 B. Ziemann, *War Experiences in Rural Germany, 1914–1923* (Oxford: Berg, 2007), p. 156; Bessel, *Germany after the First World War*, p. 15.
58 Ziemann, *War Experiences in Rural Germany*, pp. 48–9.
59 Letter of 7 June 1917, quoted in *ibid.*, p. 158.
60 Quoted in Boyd, '"Nationaler Frauendienst"', p. 151; Bajohr, *Die Hälfte der Fabrik*, p. 145.
61 Bajohr, *Die Hälfte der Fabrik*, pp. 134–5; Boyd, '"Nationaler Frauendienst"', p. 155. Night work also became common for women in the Imperial Post and Telegraph Service: E. Fisch, 'Der Einfluss des Krieges auf die Entwicklung der Frauenarbeit', *Unter dem Reichsadler*, 8:6 (March 1916), 111–14.
62 Warnings were issued on 11 December 1916, 11 August 1917

and 9 January 1918: Lüders, 'Die Entwicklung der gewerblichen Frauenarbeit', p. 264; Bajohr, *Die Hälfte der Fabrik*, pp. 137–40.

63 Lüders reports that the sickness figures improved in the transport sector once strong girls replaced soldiers' wives: Lüders, 'Die Entwicklung der gewerblichen Frauenarbeit', pp. 271–2. See also Bajohr, *Die Hälfte der Fabrik*, pp. 141, 151, and C. Eifert, 'Frauenarbeit im Krieg: Die Berliner "Heimatfront" 1914–1918', *Internationale wissenschaftliche Korrespondenz zur Geschichte der Arbeiterbewegung*, 21:3 (1985), 282.

64 120 had been killed the previous year in a similar incident in Schleswig-Holstein: Boyd, '"Nationaler Frauendienst"', p. 157.

65 Bajohr, *Die Hälfte der Fabrik*, p. 146; Lüders, 'Die Entwicklung der gewerblichen Frauenarbeit', p. 267.

66 J. Kuczynski, *Studien zur Geschichte der Lage der Arbeiterin in Deutschland von 1700 bis zur Gegenwart* (Berlin: Akademie-Verlag, 2nd edn, 1965), p. 190; H. Lange, *Die Frauenbewegung in ihren gegenwärtigen Problemen* (Leipzig: Quelle & Meyer, 3rd edn, 1924), p. 55.

67 Büttner reports that there were 5.3 million soldiers in the field and 2.7 million within Germany at the beginning of November 1918; the total had been reduced to one million by the end of January 1919: U. Büttner, *Weimar: Die überforderte Republik 1918–1933* (Stuttgart: Klett-Cotta, 2008), p. 131. Bessel claims that there were 'nearly one million foreign workers and another million prisoners of war' working in Germany in summer 1918: Bessel, *Germany after the First World War*, p. 126.

68 Bundesarchiv Koblenz (BAK), Nachlass Lüders 157, Kriegsministerium, Kriegsamt. Anlagen 1 und 2 zu Nr. 40/11.18 A.Z.S.2.

69 'Verordnung über die wirtschaftliche Demobilmachung. Vom 7. November 1918', *Reichsgesetzblatt 1918*, no. 149 (8 November 1918), 1292–3; S. Rouette, '"Gleichberechtigung" ohne "Recht auf Arbeit": Demobilmachung der Frauenarbeit nach dem Ersten Weltkrieg', in C. Eifert and S. Rouette (eds), *Unter allen Umständen: Frauengeschichte(n) in Berlin* (Berlin: Rotation, 1986), pp. 171–2. For the demobilisation see Bessel, *Germany after the First World War*, chapters 4 and 5, and for a case study of Württemberg see G. Mai, 'Arbeitsmarktregulierung oder Sozialpolitik? Die personelle Demobilmachung in Deutschland 1918 bis 1920/24', in G. D. Feldman, C.-L. Holtfrerich, G. A. Ritter and P.-C. Witt (eds), *Die Anpassung an die Inflation* (Berlin and New York: De Gruyter, 1986), pp. 202–36.

70 Figures from Mai, 'Arbeitsmarktregulierung oder Sozialpolitik?', pp. 214–15.

71 Bessel, '"Eine nicht allzu grosse Beunruhigung des Arbeitsmarktes"' The marriage rate in 1918 was 5.4 per 1,000 inhabitants, rising from a low of 4.1 in 1915 and 1916 and peaking at 14.5 in 1920: *StJhb 1935*, p. 36. On the desire for a return to normality see Rouette, '"Gleichberechtigung"', p. 179. For the impact of the demobilisation on women's work in the Republic see Chapter 3 below.

72 Reasons cited for the restriction of places for women included the shortage of accommodation and spaces in lecture halls: Generallandesarchiv, Karlsruhe (GLA), 231/4547, letter of Education Minister no. A13874 of 6 December 1918 to the senate of Heidelberg University; *Sozialistische Monatshefte*, 25:1 (1919), 571. In Baden, the proportion of female students rose from 4.7 per cent in summer 1918 at the University of Freiburg to 11 per cent a year later, whereas at Heidelberg the proportion fell from 17.7 per cent to 11.5 per cent: calculated from figures in Badisches Statistisches Landesamt, *Statistisches Jahrbuch für das Land Baden 1925* (Karlsruhe: Macklot, 1925), p. 51.

73 M. Walle, 'Die Heimatchronik Gertrud Bäumers als weibliches Nationalepos', *Ariadne*, 24 (1993), 21. For the hymn see Welch, *Germany, Propaganda and Total War*, pp. 156–7 and p. 294.

74 'Women's Suffrage in the Reichstag', *Jus suffragii*, 11:12 (1 October 1917), 8. See also L. Kuntze, 'The Extension of German Women's Work in War Time', *Jus suffragii*, 11:4 (1 February 1917), 66–7.

75 Wurms, '"Krieg dem Krieg"', p. 85; C. Sachsse, 'Social Mothers: The Bourgeois Women's Movement and German Welfare-State Formation, 1890–1929', in S. Koven and S. Michel (eds), *Mothers of a New World: Maternalist Politics and the Origins of Welfare States* (London: Routledge,1993), pp. 136–58.

76 In Magdeburg, for example, it was the Red Cross that led fifty-four women's associations in providing welfare: *Evangelische Frauenzeitung*, 15:7 (1 January 1915), 52. In Schneidemühl Piete Kuhr's grandmother was in charge of the Red Cross depot at the railway station that catered for soldiers passing through: Kuhr, *There We'll Meet Again*, pp. 13, 128, 142. Streubel claims that the Patriotic Women's Association had over 590,000 members in 1914: Streubel, 'Frauen der politischen Rechten', p. 110. For women in the Red Cross see J. H. Quataert, 'Women's Wartime Services under the Cross: Patriotic Communities in Germany, 1912–1918', in Chickering and Förster (eds), *Great War, Total War*, pp. 453–83, and for the Patriotic Women's Association see Quataert, *Staging Philanthropy*.

77 Evans notes the BdF's habit of double-counting its member organisations and puts the actual membership figure at around 250,000: Evans, *The Feminist Movement*, pp. 193–4. Streubel puts the figure

in 1913 at 470,000: Streubel, 'Frauen der politischen Rechten', p. 110. Bäumer had circulated her plans on 31 July 1914, receiving approval for them from the Prussian Interior Ministry the following day: LAB, BRep 235, HLA MF 2744, 'Protokoll einer Besprechung von Vorstandsmitgliedern des Bundes deutscher Frauenvereine am Freitag, dem 31. Juli 1914 vormittags 10 Uhr in Berlin, Deutsches Lyceum Club, Karlsbad12/3' and 'Protokoll der 2. Besprechung von Vorstandsmitgliedern des Bundes deutscher Frauenvereine am Sonnabend 1. August 1914 4 Uhr in Berlin, Deutsches Lyceum Club, Karlsbad12/3'.
78 LAB, BRep 235, HLA MF 2743, 'Nationaler Frauendienst', *Die Frau*, 21:12 (September 1914), 757.
79 Nationaler Frauendienst, *Der Nationale Frauendienst in Berlin,1914–17* (Berlin: Vaterländische Verlags- und Kunstanstalt, 1917) pp. 8, 47; Eifert, 'Frauenarbeit im Krieg', pp. 285–6; Hagemann, *Frauenalltag und Männerpolitik*, p. 423. However, from 1916 this policy had to be shelved as the number of Social Democratic women able to undertake regular voluntary work dwindled.
80 J. H. Quataert, 'The German Socialist Women's Movement 1890–1918: Issues, Internal Conflicts, and the Main Personages' (PhD dissertation, University of California, Los Angeles, 1974), pp. 77–8; K. Honeycutt, 'Clara Zetkin: A Left-Wing Socialist and Feminist in Wilhelmian Germany' (PhD dissertation, Columbia University, 1975), pp. 193–8; R. J. Evans, *The Feminists* (London: Croom Helm, 1977) pp. 149, 159–61. Frevert notes that from 1900 individual Social Democratic women were permitted 'to co-operate occasionally and temporarily with women's rights advocates and other bourgeois elements': U. Frevert, 'Women Workers, Workers' Wives and Social Democracy in Imperial Germany', in R. Fletcher (ed.), *Bernstein to Brandt: A Short History of German Social Democracy* (London: Edward Arnold, 1987), p. 44.
81 Berliner Geschichtswerkstatt e.v. (ed.), *August 1914: Ein Volk zieht in den Krieg* (Berlin: Nishen, 1989), p. 106. Hanover had no socialist women's organisation, hence socialist women played no role in the Hanover NFD, which incorporated some thirty women's organisations: N. R. Reagin, *A German Women's Movement: Class and Gender in Hanover, 1880–1933* (Chapel Hill and London: University of North Carolina Press, 1995), p. 191.
82 Nationaler Frauendienst, *Der Nationale Frauendienst in Berlin*, p. 41; A. Pappritz, 'Nationaler Frauendienst', in E. Altmann-Gottheiner (ed.), *Kriegsjahrbuch des Bundes Deutscher Frauenvereine 1915* (Leipzig and Berlin: Teubner, 1915), p. 30.
83 Tables of entitlement and documentary evidence required found in AKDFB, Collection 1-22-7.

84 *Die Frau*, 21:12 (September 1914), 758–9.
85 'Nationaler Frauendienst Heidelberg', *Die Frau*, 22:3 (December 1914), 167–8.
   In Munich the NFD helped 1,061 women, funding language and music classes for children from poor families for at least three years: A. Wack, 'Frauenarbeit in der Kriegsfürsorge in München' (PhD dissertation, University of Munich, 1918).
86 ADEF, FF1, Hanover NFD circular to members dated 25 October 1917. See also the complimentary remarks of the American Ambassador: J. W. Gerard, *My Four Years in Germany* (London: Hodder and Stoughton, 1917), pp. 217–19.
87 Hagemann, *Frauenalltag und Männerpolitik*, p. 524.
88 'Women in Municipal Life' and 'Women in Town Administration', *Jus suffragii*, 11:6 (1 March 1917), 85. Wack claims that the five women on Munich's principal welfare committee had voting rights: Wack, 'Frauenarbeit in der Kriegsfürsorge in München'.
89 'Die Mitarbeit des Nationalen Frauendienstes in der Lebensmittelfürsorge', *Evangelische Frauenzeitung*, 16:9 (1 February 1916), 67.
90 B. Davis, *Home Fires Burning: Food, Politics, and Everyday Life in World War 1 Berlin* (Chapel Hill and London: University of North Carolina Press, 2000), p. 122. Hagenlücke claims that Germany imported about one quarter of its food, while Hardach claims that Germany had to import 10 per cent of her milk, 40 per cent of her eggs and fats, 60 per cent of her fish and one-third of her fertilisers and animal feed: Hagenlücke, 'The Home Front in Germany', p. 63; G. Hardach, *The First World War 1914–1918* (London: Allen Lane, 1997), p. 110. For the motto see E. Wex, *Staatsbürgerliche Arbeit deutscher Frauen 1865 bis 1928* (Berlin: Herbig, 1929), p. 90.
91 N. R. Reagin, *Sweeping the German Nation: Domesticity and National Identity, 1870–1945* (Cambridge: Cambridge University Press, 2007), p. 77. For leaflets produced by the Catholic Women's League see AKDFB, Collection 1-22-8.
92 Bessel, *Germany after the First World War*, pp. 4–5; Feldman, *Army, Industry, and Labor*, pp. 31–4.
93 *Gewerkschaftliche Frauenzeitung*, 4:3 (12 February 1919), 23. The blockade continued until 12 July 1919. Jay Winter puts the figure at 478,500: see A. Kramer, *Dynamics of Destruction: Culture and Mass Killing in the First World War* (Oxford: Oxford University Press, 2007), p. 154 for a discussion of the numbers of civilian deaths and the reason for them.
94 P. Lummel, 'Food Provisioning in the German Army in the First World War', in I. Zweiniger-Bargielowska, R. Duffett and A. Drouard (eds), *Food and War in Twentieth Century Europe* (Farnham: Ashgate,

2011), pp. 15, 23. Patients in psychiatric hospitals seem to have been particularly hard hit by malnutrition and neglect: Kramer, *Dynamics of Destruction*, p. 326.

95 Davis, *Home Fires Burning*, pp. 2, 22; T. Bonzon and B. Davis, 'Feeding the Cities', in J. Winter and J.-L. Robert (eds), *Capital Cities at War: Paris, London, Berlin 1914–1919* (Cambridge: Cambridge University Press, 1997), p. 339.

96 K. Allen, 'Food and the German Home Front: Evidence from Berlin', in G. Braybon (ed.), *Evidence, History, and the Great War: Historians and the Impact of 1914–18* (Oxford: Berghahn, 2003), pp. 180, 188.

97 Bread became the first food to be subject to rationing in Berlin in January 1915: Davis, *Home Fires Burning*, pp. 24–31; K. Allen, 'Sharing Scarcity: Bread Rationing and the First World War in Berlin, 1914–1923', *Journal of Social History*, 32:2 (1998), 373. Chickering refers to the blue cards permitting people of lesser means to purchase subsidised goods in Freiburg as the 'official badge of poverty': R. Chickering, *The Great War and Urban Life in Germany: Freiburg, 1914–1918* (Cambridge: Cambridge University Press, 2007), pp. 450–1.

98 Davis, *Home Fires Burning*, pp. 81–9; Wurms, '"Krieg dem Krieg"', pp. 88–9. For Freiburg in the summer and autumn of 1916 see Chickering, *The Great War and Urban Life in Germany*, p. 406.

99 B. Davis, 'Homefront: Food, Politics and Women's Everyday Life during the First World War', in Hagemann and Schüler-Springorum (eds), *Home/Front*, p. 123.

100 Davis, *Home Fires Burning*, p. 22; A. Sawahn, *Die Frauenlobby vom Land: Die Landfrauenbewegung in Deutschland und ihre Funktionärinnen 1898 bis 1948* (Frankfurt am Main: DLG Verlag, 2009), p. 115.

101 Sender, *Autobiography*, p. 81. Ethel Cooper noted in November 1915 that no fats were to be sold on Mondays and Thursdays, no meat on Tuesdays and Fridays and no flour at weekends, though the rich bought double the preceding day: C. E. Cooper, *Behind the Lines: One Woman's War 1914–18*, ed. D. Denholm (Sydney: Collins, 1982), letters of 7 and 30 November 1915. Teuteberg notes that only the bread ration card guaranteed the amount one would receive: H.-J. Teuteberg, 'Food Provisioning on the German Home Front, 1914–1918', in Zweiniger-Bargielowska, Duffett and Drouard (eds), *Food and War in Twentieth Century Europe*, p. 62.

102 U. Daniel, 'The Politics of Rationing versus the Politics of Subsistence: Working-Class Women in Germany, 1914–1918', in Fletcher (ed.), *Bernstein to Brandt*, pp. 93–4; for Freiburg, where in late 1916 the police introduced multiple distribution centres to try and scatter the

crowds, see Chickering, *The Great War and Urban Life in Germany*, pp. 405–7. In May 1917 police in Heilbronn issued a decree forbidding queuing outside shops before they opened: E. Koch, 'Jeder tut, was er kann fürs Vaterland: Frauen und Männer an der Heilbronner "Heimatfront"', in G. Hirschfeld, G. Krumeich, D. Langewiesche and H.-P. Ullmann (eds), *Kriegserfahrungen: Studien zur Sozial- und Mentalitätsgeschichte des Ersten Weltkriegs* (Essen: Klartext Verlagsgesellschaft, 1997), pp. 46–7.
103 Cooper, *Behind the Lines*, letter of 5 March 1916.
104 LAB, BRep 235, HLA MF 2749, *Verbrauchswirtschaft im Kriege*, 1:7 (14 April 1916).
105 Kuhr, *There We'll Meet Again*, p. 191; Daniel, 'The Politics of Rationing', p. 92.
106 Davis, *Homes Fires Burning*, p. 117; another official put the figure at one-third.
107 P. Loewenberg, 'Germany, the Home Front (1): The Physical and Psychological Consequences of Home Front Hardship', in H. Cecil and P. Liddle (eds), *Facing Armageddon: The First World War Experienced* (London: Pen & Sword Books Ltd, 1996), p. 556. Davis claims the minimum ration was 1,985 calories per day but munitions workers were granted 3,072: Davis, *Home Fires Burning*, p. 180. In Düsseldorf rations amounted to 7,900 weekly in 1917, compared with the allocation of 26,500 calories in the Hamburg poorhouse in 1900: E. H. Tobin, 'War and the Working Class: The Case of Düsseldorf 1914–1918', *Central European History*, 13:3–4 (1985), 257–98. The situation improved slightly in 1918.
108 Davis, *Home Fires Burning*, p. 191.
109 Sawahn, *Die Frauenlobby auf dem Land*, p. 115.
110 Kuhr, *There We'll Meet Again*, p. 200. Princess Blücher did not have to resort to slaughtering the family kangaroos until May 1918: Blücher, *An English Wife in Berlin*, p. 225.
111 Allen, 'Food and the German Home Front', pp. 174–9; Davis, *Home Fires Burning*, pp. 143–54. Davis notes that the Food War Office called upon all towns of over 10,000 inhabitants to create public kitchens. In Schöneberg, Berlin, there were nine public and two middle-class kitchens in 1917; a full portion in the public kitchen cost 50 Pfennig (Pf), in the middle-class kitchen 80 Pf: G. Wenzel, 'Schöneberg voran! An der Front der Tod, in der Heimat die Not', in Berliner Geschichtswerkstatt (ed.), *August 1914*, p. 167. Chickering notes that many people used public kitchens not for food but for warmth: Chickering, *The Great War and Urban Life in Germany*, pp. 277, 458.
112 Cooper, *Behind the Lines*, letter of 4 February 1917, tells of a temperature of minus 24°F. For the impact of the coal shortage in Freiburg see

Chickering, *The Great War and Urban Life in Germany*, pp. 217–18; Eifert, 'Frauenarbeit im Krieg', p. 289; Blücher, *An English Wife in Berlin*, pp. 134, 156, 184.

113 Kuhr, *There We'll Meet Again*, p. 261. Gold wedding rings were replaced with iron rings: Chickering, *The Great War and Urban Life in Germany*, p. 194. For the drives to obtain gold see Gerard, *My Four Years in Germany*, pp. 300–4. For the ninth war loan's poster 'To the German women and girls' see C. Siebrecht, 'The *Mater Dolorosa* on the Battlefield – Mourning Mothers in German Women's Art of the First World War', in H. Jones, C. O'Brien and C. Schmidt-Supprian (eds), *Untold War: New Perspectives in First World War Studies* (Leiden and Boston: Brill, 2008), pp. 262–3.

114 In transmission belts: Kuhr, *There We'll Meet Again*, p. 178; Chickering, *The Great War and Urban Life in Germany*, p. 190; B. Hamann, *Der Erste Weltkrieg: Wahrheit und Lüge in Bildern und Texten* (Munich: Piper Verlag, 2nd edn, 2008), p. 267; Quataert, 'Women's Wartime Services under the Cross', pp. 470–2.

115 Siebrecht, 'The *Mater Dolorosa* on the Battlefield', pp. 261–4.

116 M. Stibbe, *Germany 1914–1933: Politics, Society and Culture* (Harlow: Pearson, 2010), p. 46.

117 Blücher, *An English Wife in Berlin*, pp. 20, 309. A well-known British propaganda leaflet, 'One family which has not lost a single member', played on this inequality of sacrifice: Welch, *Germany, Propaganda and Total War*, p. 230.

118 During the war 13,123,011 German men served in the armed forces: Bessel, *Germany after the First World War*, p. 5. Daniel claims that by the end of 1915 over one-third of all German marriages at the time had a husband serving in the military: Daniel, *The War from Within*, p. 130.

119 For claimants' perceptions of the process see R. Chickering, *The Great War and Urban Life in Germany*, pp. 445–6. For a report from a visitor see 'Erlebnisse einer Recherchéurin', *Berliner Tageblatt*, 20 October 1914, reproduced in H.-U. Bussemer, '"Weit hinter den Schützengräben": Das Kriegserlebnis der bürgerlichen Frauenbewegung', in Berliner Geschichtswerkstatt e.V. (ed.), *August 1914*, pp. 144–5.

120 On Family War Benefit see L. Frohman, *Poor Relief and Welfare in Germany from the Reformation to World War 1* (Cambridge: Cambridge University Press, 2008), pp. 213–15; Davis, *Home Fires Burning*, pp. 37–46; Daniel, *The War from Within*, pp. 177–88; B. Kundrus, *Kriegerfrauen: Familienpolitik und Geschlechterverhältnisse im Ersten und Zweiten Weltkrieg* (Hamburg: Christians, 1995), pp. 52–3; Bessel, *Germany after the First World War*, pp. 30–1. During the war the

benefit was extended to soldiers' illegitimate children and to former wives who had been the innocent party in a divorce.

121 Daniel believes that Family War Benefit was 'adequate in most cases' in the countryside, where many families would still have had some land but, beyond the first few months of the war, not in towns and cities, whereas Christiane Eifert claims that the benefit, with rent supplements, amounted to just 30 per cent of a family's pre-war wage. Daniel, *The War from Within*, p. 188; Eifert, 'Frauenarbeit im Krieg', p. 281. See also Davis, *Home Fires Burning*, p. 37; Kundrus, *Kriegerfrauen*, p. 94.

122 The benefits included rent aid from the local community, allowances from the husband's former employer or trade union, meals for schoolchildren or a small piece of land to cultivate: Daniel, *The War from Within*, pp. 176-9; Kundrus, *Kriegerfrauen*, pp. 57, 94-5. In Göttingen, soldiers' families were given one-eighth of an acre: www.stadtarchiv.goettingen.de/chronik/1915 03htm, chronicle for 15 March 1915 (accessed 19 July 2007).

123 Kundrus, *Kriegerfrauen*, p. 85; Davis, *Home Fires Burning*, pp. 36-7. Davis explains that before the war the middle classes had prided themselves on their ability to afford afternoon cake, and saw it as a symbol of their middle-class status.

124 Chickering, *The Great War and Urban Life in Germany*, p. 501; R. Chickering, *Imperial Germany and the Great War, 1914–1918* (Cambridge: Cambridge University Press, 1998), pp. 122-3; E. Domansky, 'Militarization and Reproduction in World War 1 Germany', in G. Eley (ed.), *Society, Culture, and the State in Germany, 1870–1930* (Ann Arbor: University of Michigan Press, 1996), p. 445; Daniel, *The War from Within*, p. 163.

125 Italics in the original: Jones, *Gender and Rural Modernity*, pp. 106-7; Stibbe, *Germany 1914–1933*, p. 47.

126 Some 7 million letters were sent home from the front daily, so many that soldiers were encouraged to use postcards: Chickering, *Imperial Germany and the Great War*, p. 101; C. Hämmerle, '"Wirf ihnen alles hin und schau, dass du fort kommst": Die Feldpost eines Paares in der Geschlechter(un)ordnung des Ersten Weltkrieges', *Historische Anthropologie*, 6 (1998), 435. Teachers helping women to write letters to their husband at the front were given guidance by the Education Ministry to avoid any demoralising topics: E. Demm, 'German Teachers at War', in Cecil and Liddle (eds), *Facing Armageddon*, p. 714.

127 Seipp, *The Ordeal of Peace*, pp. 92, 105, 264.

128 L. M. Todd, 'Sexual Treason: State Surveillance of Immorality and Infidelity in World War One Germany' (PhD dissertation, University

of Toronto, 2005), pp. 139–42; L. M. Todd, '"The Soldier's Wife who Ran Away with the Russian": Sexual Infidelities in World War 1 Germany', *Central European History*, 44 (2011), 266. Harris tells of one divorcee in a monogamous relationship being denounced as a prostitute by a male middle-class neighbour: V. Harris, *Selling Sex in the Reich: Prostitutes in German Society, 1914–1945* (Oxford: Oxford University Press, 2010), p. 120.

129 Todd, 'Sexual Treason', p. 152. For the affairs of soldiers' wives see Ziemann, *War Experiences in Rural Germany*, pp. 123, 164; Chickering, *Imperial Germany and the Great War*, p. 120; Daniel, *The War from Within*, p. 144.

130 Todd, 'Sexual Treason', pp. 139–42; Verhey, *The Spirit of 1914*, pp. 80–2.

131 Ziemann, *War Experiences in Rural Germany*, p. 165; Daniel, *The War from Within*, 146; Chickering, *The Great War and Urban Life in Germany*, pp. 356–7.

132 A. François, 'From Street Walking to the Convent: Child Prostitution Cases Judged by the Juvenile Court of Brussels during World War One', in Jones, O'Brien and Schmidt-Supprian (eds), *Untold War*, p. 154; Todd, 'Sexual Treason', pp. 63–6.

133 J. Roos, ' Weimar's Crisis through the Lens of Gender: The Case of Prostitution' (PhD dissertation, Carnegie Mellon University, 2001), p. 36; for the rise in rates of prostitution and venereal disease see Chickering, *The Great War and Urban Life in Germany*, p. 358.

134 These measures included compulsory health checks for all soldiers. See P. Weindling, 'The Medical Profession, Social Hygiene and the Birth Rate in Germany, 1914–1918', in Wall and Winter (eds), *The Upheaval of War*, pp. 417–37; C. Usborne, 'Pregnancy is the Woman's Active Service: Pronatalism in Germany during the First World War', in Wall and Winter (eds), *The Upheaval of War*, pp. 389–416; S. Michl, *Im Dienste des 'Volkskörpers': Deutsche und französische Ärzte im Ersten Weltkrieg* (Göttingen: Vandenhoeck & Ruprecht, 2007), p. 129. For the BdF and KFB see LAB, BRep 235, HLA MF 2740, 'An die dem Bund angeschlossenen Verbände und Vereine', 3 December 1914. The NFD published leaflets urging soldiers to avoid prostitutes and careless sexual intercourse: LAB, BRep 235, HLA MF 2741, 'Deutsche Soldaten'.

135 Todd, 'Sexual Treason', pp. 95, 115–16; Usborne, 'Pregnancy is the Woman's Active Service', p. 391. For men preferring to contract venereal disease rather than fight see Daniel, *The War from Within*, p. 141; A. Watson, *Enduring the Great War: Combat, Morale and Collapse in the German and British Armies, 1914–1918* (Cambridge: Cambridge University Press, 2008), p. 39.

136 LAB, BRep235, HLA MF 2740, BdF petition to the Reichstag dated 30 October 1916; 'Bekanntmachung', Kolberg, 26 May 1916, for the Second Army Corps District; for the 20th Army Corps in Allenstein on 12 May 1916 see Daniel, *The War from Within*, p. 144.
137 Todd, 'Sexual Treason', p. 107; Daniel, *The War from Within*, p. 143.
138 LAB, BRep 235, HLA MF 1247, *Die Frauenfrage*, 20:9 (1 September 1918), 1–2. This was partially realised in emergency laws of 11 and 17 December 1918 which permitted the compulsory treatment of all infected men and women and imprisonment for up to three years for those who had sexual intercourse while knowing they had venereal disease: P. Weindling, *Health, Race and German Politics between National Unification and Nazism, 1870–1945* (Cambridge: Cambridge University Press, 1989), p. 357; Bessel, *Germany after the First World War*, p. 234.
139 Bessel, *Germany after the First World War*, pp. 236–7. Watson claims that rates of venereal disease were higher in 1918 when men attempted to escape the trenches: Watson, *Enduring the Great War*, p. 206.
140 Usborne, *The Politics of the Body*, p. 18. Perhaps the best-known association was the Society for Population Policy, founded on 19 October 1915: Weindling, *Health, Race and German Politics*, p. 295. Weindling claims that 'by 1916 the army supported the demand for a comprehensive population policy' and that the Kaiser, too, acknowledged this on 14 October 1916: Weindling, 'The Medical Profession', pp. 422–3, 426. Figures taken from *StJhb 1935*, p. 36.
141 For details see Weindling, *Health, Race and German Politics*, pp. 285, 290, 295–6; Usborne, *The Politics of the Body*, p. 17; Daniel, *The War from Within*, p. 134. The BdF devoted its 1916 war-time conference to population policy: A. T. Allen, 'Feminism and Eugenics in Germany and Britain, 1900–1940: A Comparative Perspective', *German Studies Review*, 23:3 (2000), 488.
142 A. T. Allen, 'Feminism, Venereal Diseases, and the State in Germany', *Journal of the History of Sexuality*, 4:1 (1993), 45–6; Usborne, *The Politics of the Body*, pp. 21–3; J. Woycke, *Birth Control in Germany 1871–1933* (London: Routledge, 1988), pp. 144–5. The law also envisaged the compulsory reporting of the patient's details following an abortion or sterilisation.
143 Quoted in Allen, 'Feminism, Venereal Diseases, and the State in Germany', p. 46. The law would have affected the most popular female contraceptive, post-coital douching: Usborne, *The Politics of the Body*, pp. 18, 24, 27.
144 Usborne, *The Politics of the Body*, p. 68.
145 Condoms, seen as a prophylactic against venereal disease, were not

banned: *Ibid.*, pp. 21–2, 28. Usborne believes that abortion was possibly the most significant factor in the decline in the birth rate.
146 Usborne, 'Pregnancy is the Woman's Active Service', p. 392; R. Heinemann, *Familie zwischen Tradition und Emanzipation: Katholische und sozialdemokratische Familienkonzeptionen in der Weimarer Republik* (Munich: Oldenbourg Wissenschaftliches Verlag, 2004), p. 53.
147 Usborne, *The Politics of the Body*, pp. 20–1; Weindling, *Health, Race and German Politics*, pp. 286–90; P. R. Stokes, 'Contested Conceptions: Experiences and Discourses of Pregnancy and Childbirth in Germany, 1914–1933' (PhD dissertation, Cornell University, 2003), pp. 174–6; 'Extension of Maternity Benefits', *Jus suffragii*, 9:12 (1 September 1915), 350. The benefit was an entitlement, yet had to be applied for. At least six of the eight weeks for which women could claim the allowance had to follow the birth.
148 Frohman, *Poor Relief and Welfare in Germany*, p. 209.
149 Some contemporary reports put the figure higher, at 3.3 million, but this did not take into account the decline in the birth rate before 1914: Daniel, *The War from Within*, pp. 134, 208; Usborne, *The Politics of the Body*, p. 31.
150 From 1,818,596 to 912,109: *StJhb 1935*, p. 36.
151 Ziemann tells of soldiers who had not had leave after two years, while farmers tended to be given leave three times a year to coincide with the agricultural calendar, which drew complaints from their less fortunate comrades: Ziemann, *War Experiences in Rural Germany*, pp. 45–8. Specialist workers were also brought home for longer periods.
152 Usborne, *The Politics of the Body*, pp. 26–9; Todd, 'Sexual Treason', p. 201; Weindling, *Health, Race and German Politics*, p. 247.
153 War amenorrhoea became a topic of medical discourse as increased numbers of cases were noted in the autumn of 1916 with the deterioration in the food supply: Michl, *Im Dienste des 'Volkskörpers'*, pp. 171–3; Stokes, 'Contested Conceptions', p. 173.
154 Stokes, 'Contested Conceptions', pp. 173–4. Weindling gives a figure of 65,000 deaths per year: Weindling, *Health, Race and German Politics*, p. 287. Winter and Cole also note a substantial increase in the number of women in Berlin dying in childbirth from 1915 onwards, a trend that reached its peak in 1923: J. Winter and J. Cole, 'Fluctuations in Infant Mortality Rates in Berlin During and After the First World War', *European Journal of Population*, 9 (1993), 251–2.
155 Stokes, 'Contested Conceptions', pp. 319–62.
156 Davis, *Home Fires Burning*, pp. 165–6; Davis, 'Homefront', p. 127.
157 C. Siebrecht, 'Martial Spirit and Mobilisation Myths: Bourgeois Women and the "Ideas of 1914" in Germany', in A. S. Fell and

58 Women in the Weimar Republic

I. Sharp (eds), *The Women's Movement in Wartime: International Perspectives, 1914–1919* (Basingstoke: Palgrave Macmillan, 2007), p. 47.

158 The BdF worked closely with the KFB: LAB, BRep 235, HLA MF 2751, letter of KFB to Gertrud Bäumer of 31 March 1915 notifying her of their decision taken on 16 December 1914 to hold a war donation campaign; HLA MF 2750, *Die Frauenfrage*, 17:6 (16 June 1915) reporting the BdF's approval for a 'Donation Fund of German Women for the German Army' on 16 April 1915. A meeting of the women's associations' leaders was held in Berlin on 5 July 1915 to finalise plans: HLA MF 2749. Proclamation found in HLA MF 2750; newspaper clipping giving the amount raised found in HLA MF 2749.

159 LAB, BRep 235, HLA MF 2742. The idea apparently came from the Leipzig branch of the Women Teachers' Association, which had already implemented such a campaign for the sixth and seventh war bonds. Women were encouraged to club together or to pay in instalments.

160 Signatories included the leaders of the BdF, KFB, German Protestant Women's League, artists such as Käthe Kollwitz, writers such as Ricarda Huch and well-known personalities such as Cosima Wagner: LAB, BRep 235, HLA MF 2741, BdF letter to its affiliates, 22 September 1914, seeking addresses for women abroad to whom the appeal could be sent. See also Siebrecht, 'Martial Spirit and Mobilisation Myths', pp. 43–4. It is clear that the women's movement believed German government propaganda with regard to atrocities: J. Horne, 'German Atrocities, 1914: Fact, Fantasy or Fabrication', *History Today*, 52:4 (April 2002), 47–53. The KFB produced a similar letter in December 1914: 'Denkschrift des Katholischen Frauenbundes an die Frauen und Frauenvereine der neutralen Staaten', *Die christliche Frau*, 13:1 (January 1915), 1–5.

161 LAB, BRep 235, HLA MF 2754, BdF press release dated 27 April 1915: 'Zum internationalen Frauenkongress im Haag'; see also L. Rupp, 'Constructing Internationalism: The Case of Transnational Women's Organisations, 1888–1945', *American Historical Review*, 99:5 (December 1994), 1589. Bäumer's letter appeared in translation in 'German Women and the Hague Congress', *Jus suffragii*, 9:9 (1 June 1915), 308–9.

162 The other protest had been drawn up by Berlin's Women's Protestant League leader, Countess von Schwerin-Löwitz, and was signed by over seventy women's organisations: 'Kundgebung deutscher Frauen gegen die Wilsonnote', dated 22 September 1917, found in ADEF, K-16-DEF-FF2; BdF text found in LAB, BRep 235, HLA MF 2742, Gertrud Bäumer to the BdF's executive committee, 9 October 1917, and in

HLA MF 1338, *Die Frauenfrage*, 19:19 (1 October 1917). For the BdF see also Scheck, 'Women against Versailles', 24; for Schwerin-Löwitz see M. Stibbe, 'Anti-Feminism, Nationalism and the German Right, 1914–1920: A Re-Appraisal', *German History*, 20:2 (2002), 199, and Süchting-Hänger, *Das 'Gewissen der Nation'*, pp. 115–16.

163 Hindenburg's telegram to Schwerin-Löwitz found in ADEF, K-16-DEF-FF2 and to Gertrud Bäumer, along with the Empress's telegram, in LAB, BRep 235, HLA MF 2742, Bäumer to the BdF's executive committee of 9 October 1917; Süchting-Hänger, *Das 'Gewissen der Nation'*, p. 116.

164 LAB, BRep 235, HLA MF 2742, Gertrud Bäumer and Alice Bensheimer to the BdF's executive committee members, 3 October 1918.

165 Scheck, 'Women against Versailles', p. 24.

166 ADEF, FF1, 6 October 1918.

167 LAB, BRep 235, HLA MF 2883, declaration found in G. Bäumer, *Die nationalpolitische Stellung des Bundes Deutscher Frauenvereine während des Krieges: Sonderabdruck aus dem Jahrbuch des Bundes Deutscher Frauenvereine*, (1920), p. 7. See also Evans, *The Feminist Movement*, p. 211; Scheck, 'Women against Versailles', p. 24. On 27 October 1918 the leaders of many of the major women's organisations in Berlin met to consider protests but came to no conclusion, as the path the German government was going to take – a defensive struggle or the continuation of peace negotiations – was not known. The speed of events then overtook them: ADEF, K-16-DEF-FF2, 'Protokoll der Sitzung betreffend Massnahmen, die sich aus der gegenwärtigen Lage ergeben, am Sonntag, dem 27. Oktober 1918, vormittags 10.30 Uhr'.

168 Davis, *Home Fires Burning*, pp. 96–7; Blücher, *An English Wife in Berlin*, pp. 90–1.

169 Hering, *Kriegsgewinnlerinnen*, p. 91. Bäumer's confidential notification to the BdF's associations was made public, much to her chagrin: G. Bäumer, 'Der Bund Deutscher Frauenvereine und der Haager Frauenkongress', *Die Frauenfrage* (1 September 1915), 1–3, found in BAK, Nachlass Lüders 2.

170 C. Wickert, B. Hamburger and M. Lienau, 'Helene Stöcker and the Bund für Mutterschutz', *Women's Studies International Forum*, 5:6 (1982), 615.

171 Frauenliga für Frieden und Freiheit (Deutsches Zweig), *Völkerversöhnende Frauenarbeit* (Munich: Heller, 1920), pp. 25–6, 38–9, 42–5, 48, 56–60; Evans, *The Feminist Movement*, p. 222.

172 E. Kuhlmann, 'The Rhineland Horror Campaign and the Aftermath of War', in I. Sharp and M. Stibbe (eds), *Aftermaths of War: Women's Movements and Female Activists, 1918–1923* (Leiden: Brill, 2011), p. 104.

173 Toni Sender, who attended the Berne conference, also had her post watched and house searched: Sender, *Autobiography*, pp. 62–72. For Zetkin see R. J. Evans, *Comrades and Sisters: Feminism, Socialism and Pacifism in Europe 1870–1945* (Brighton: Wheatsheaf, 1987), pp. 133–7.
174 M. Stibbe, *Germany 1914–1933*, pp. 51–3; U. Herrmann, 'Social Democratic Women in Germany and the Struggle for Peace Before and During the First World War', in R. R. Pierson (ed.), *Women and Peace* (Beckenham: Croom Helm,1987), pp. 95–7. It is reported that some 1,700 women workers at Berlin's Wittenau munitions factory went on strike from 17 to 22 August 1918: Wurms, '"Krieg dem Krieg"', p. 89. Military advisers heaped the blame on women and young people being led astray by unscrupulous, malicious agitators: Bajohr, *Die Hälfte der Fabrik*, pp. 151–2.
175 F. Altenhoner, 'Das "Heimatheer deutscher Frauen": Propaganda durch bürgerliche Frauen in Berlin 1918 zwischen Aufklärung und Denunziation', *Ariadne*, 47 (May 2005), 38–43; Frauenliga für Frieden und Freiheit (Deutsches Zweig), *Völkerversöhnende Frauenarbeit*, pp. 52–3.
176 There were some in the army who continued to believe that it was inappropriate to attempt to mobilise women in this way: Stibbe, 'Anti-Feminism, Nationalism and the German Right', pp. 197–201; U. Planert, *Antifeminismus im Kaiserreich: Diskurs, soziale Formation und politische Mentalität* (Göttingen: Vandenhoeck and Ruprecht, 1998), p. 235. The Pan-German League admitted women members from 1916.
177 Stibbe claims that this change in attitude amounted to the end of organised anti-feminism: Stibbe, 'Anti-Feminism, Nationalism and the German Right', p. 209.
178 Stibbe, 'Anti-Feminism, Nationalism and the German Right', p. 202. On right-wing mobilisation of women see also E. Harvey, 'Visions of the *Volk*: German Women and the Far Right from Kaiserreich to Third Reich', *Journal of Women's History*, 16:3 (2004), 153–6.
179 Kundrus, *Kriegerfrauen*, p. 101.
180 'Die Stellung der Frau in der politisch-sozialen Neugestaltung Deutschlands', found in Bayerisches Hauptstaatsarchiv, Munich, Abt. 1, MInn 73626. For a sample of discussions in local parliaments, see 'Suffrage Debate in Parliament', *Jus suffragii*, 11:6 (1 March 1917), 85; 'Woman suffrage in the Reichstag', *Jus suffragii*, 12:1 (1 October 1917), 5. Correspondence and documents relating to the DEF's decision to leave the BdF to be found in ADEF, A14e. See also Evans, *The Feminist Movement*, pp. 226–7.

181 Evans notes that Social Democratic women, the BdF, and the suffrage organisations agreed to work together on 22 September 1917 and that a joint public meeting planned for 10 December 1917 coinciding with the discussion of female suffrage in the Prussian Landtag was banned by the authorities: R. J. Evans, *Sozialdemokratie und Frauenemanzipation im deutschen Kaiserreich* (Berlin: Verlag J. H. W. Dietz, 1979), p. 303. See also A. K. Hackett, 'The Politics of Feminism in Wilhelmine Germany, 1890–1918' (PhD dissertation, Columbia University, 1976), pp. 985–90, and B. Clemens, *'Menschenrechte haben kein Geschlecht!' Zum Politikverständnis der bürgerlichen Frauenbewegung* (Pfaffenweiler: Centaurus, 1988), pp. 114, 179. A joint meeting was, however, held on 22 April 1918 in Berlin.

182 'Suffrage Debate in Parliament', *Jus suffragii*, 11:6 (1 March 1917), 85. See also Planert, *Antifeminismus im Kaiserreich*, pp. 180–1.

183 Women of the Independent Social Democratic Party refused to sign. The letter was printed in *Die Gleichheit*, 29:3 (8 November 1918), 17–18; Hering, *Kriegsgewinnlerinnen*, p. 79.

184 'Suffrage Demonstrations', *Jus suffragii*, 13:4 (1 January 1919), 48; Hackett, 'The Politics of Feminism', pp. 1013–15.

185 For the discussions see Hackett, 'The Politics of Feminism', pp. 1020–8; Evans, *Sozialdemokratie und Frauenemanzipation*, pp. 303–4. Canning believes that as late as 8 November 1918 the Reichstag rejected female suffrage: Canning, *Gender History in Practice*, p. 218.

186 *Reichsgesetzblatt 1918*, no. 153 (12 November 1918), 1304. See Chapter 2 below for reaction to the granting of female suffrage and women's subsequent role in political life.

187 'The Press and Women's Suffrage', *Jus suffragii*, 10:10 (1 July 1916), 145.

188 Ingrid Sharp has noted that 'resentment against women stretched to encompass blame for both the war itself and the fact that it was lost': I. Sharp, 'Blaming the Women: Women's "Responsibility" for the First World War', in Fell and Sharp (eds), *The Women's Movement in Wartime*, p. 82.

189 A. Süchting-Hänger, 'Die Anti-Versailles-Propaganda konservativer Frauen in der Weimarer Republik – eine weibliche Dankschuld?', in G. Krumeich (ed.), *Versailles 1919: Ziele – Wirkung – Wahrnehmung* (Essen: Klartext Verlag, 2001), p. 304; Süchting-Hänger, *Das "Gewissen der Nation"*, p. 234; Harvey, 'Visions of the Volk', p. 157. Watson notes the enduring cohesion of the German army as soldiers followed their officers into captivity, thus speeding the war's end: Watson, *Enduring the Great War*, pp. 230–1.

190 K. Canning, 'Women and the Politics of Gender', in McElligott (ed.), *Weimar Germany*, p. 147; Daniel, *The War from Within*, p. 283.

191 For women as 'bearers of German cultural values' see Siebrecht, 'Martial Spirit and Mobilisation Myths', pp. 46–7; Harvey, 'Visions of the Volk', p. 154.
192 Quataert, 'Women's Wartime Services under the Cross', p. 483. Siebrecht notes that it is only in women's art work that the mourning mother is a feature: Siebrecht, 'The *Mater Dolorosa* on the Battlefield', pp. 288–9.
193 Nelson, 'German Comrades – Slavic Whores', p. 80.
194 Ziemann believes that traditional gender roles within the family remained until the 1960s: B. Ziemann, 'Geschlechterbeziehungen in deutschen Feldpostbriefen des Ersten Weltkreiges', in C. Hämmerle and E. Saurer (eds), *Briefkulturen und ihr Geschlecht: Zur Geschichte der privaten Korrespondenz vom 16. Jahrhundert bis heute* (Vienna: Böhlau Verlag, 2003), p. 282. Hesther Vaizey has noted a similar pattern after the Second World War: H. Vaizey, *Surviving Hitler's War: Family Life in Germany, 1939–48* (London: Palgrave Macmillan, 2010), p. 122.
195 Ziemann, *War Experiences in Rural Germany*, p. 223.
196 Bessel, *Germany after the First World War*, p. 275; K. Hausen, 'The German Nation's Obligation to the Heroes' Widows of World War I', in M. R. Higonnet, J. Jenson, S. Michel and M. C. Weitz (eds), *Behind the Lines: Gender and the Two World Wars* (New Haven and London: Yale University Press, 1987), p. 128.

2

Women and politics

'In the storm of Revolution with one blow full citizen rights have fallen into our lap', wrote Marie Stritt, leader of the Imperial Union for Female Suffrage, in November 1918.[1] Female suffrage, the right of women aged twenty and over to vote and to be elected onto all legislative bodies, was an act of revolution enshrined in a proclamation of the Council of People's Delegates of 12 November 1918.[2] Barely ten years after all German women had been granted freedom of association they had gained political equality with men, becoming, according to the socialist women's magazine *Die Gleichheit*, 'the freest in the world'.[3] It was the realisation of a demand which had formed part of the SPD's programme since 1891, but it came as a complete shock to the few middle-class women who had campaigned for it.[4] Some have seen in the introduction of female suffrage an attempt to halt the spread of bolshevism, since women were thought to vote conservatively, or to persuade the Paris Peace Conference that Germany was now a liberal, democratic state.[5] Female suffrage was not, however, universally welcomed by either men or women, with Paula Mueller-Otfried referring to it as a 'two-edged sword' and 'a Greek gift', though she repudiated a petition for its abolition in February 1919.[6] This chapter seeks to explore women's participation in Weimar politics, as voters, elected representatives, members of political parties and targets of their propaganda, and as political activists outside the parliamentary arena. It will investigate the impact of female suffrage on German politics and political culture and will determine which parties, if any, benefited from female suffrage. Was it 'the women's vote that brought Hitler to triumph' as Hermann Rauschning claimed in 1939 or did the Nazis exert, in Richard Evans's words, 'no particular attraction for women at the polls'?[7] How did the political parties respond to women's political equality with men? What were the achievements of Weimar's female elected representatives, and did they succeed in creating 'a new atmosphere', as Alice Salomon had predicted in early 1919?[8]

Women and the revolution

Ziemann has noted that 'when the revolution came in 1918, its gender was male'.[9] This is hardly surprising, as the spark for the revolution was the sailors' mutiny in Wilhelmshaven and Kiel in late October 1918, which led to the setting-up of soldiers' and workers' councils; these spread spontaneously across Germany, reaching Berlin on 9 November 1918. Here the Majority Socialist Philipp Scheidemann proclaimed the new German Republic, and the government of a six-man Council of People's Delegates was set up, comprising three members from the SPD (now known as the Majority Socialists) and three from the German Independent Social Democratic Party (Unabhängige Sozialdemokratische Partei Deutschlands, USPD), which had split from the SPD over its support for the war. Women were clearly visible in the demonstrations and street processions that mushroomed in Germany's towns and cities, and some played a more active role; Helene Zirkel, for example, hoisted the red flag over Berlin's police headquarters on 9 November 1918.[10] The fears of the upper and middle classes that they and their property might be targeted in the revolution were to prove unfounded, and Princess Blücher expressed her admiration on 11 November 1918 for 'the disciplined and orderly way in which a revolution of such dimensions has been organized, with until now the least possible loss of life'.[11] It is not known how many women lost their lives during the revolutionary unrest which continued in various cities in the following months, but female bystanders were among those killed in the sporadic gunfire in Germany's cities in November 1918.[12] Some women were, however, to die because of their espousal of revolutionary ideals, the best-known being Rosa Luxemburg. A Marxist theorist imprisoned for her pacifism during the First World War, she was a leading member of the Spartacus League, alongside Karl Liebknecht. The Spartacus League formed an independent ideological grouping within the USPD and was highly critical of the USPD's participation in government. It wanted to push the revolution forward towards the dictatorship of the proletariat and the destruction of the capitalist system and demanded that the elections to the National Assembly be postponed and all power placed in the hands of the soldiers' and workers' councils. Its demands were rejected by a meeting of the Greater Berlin USPD on 15 December 1918, which led it to create its own party, the KPD, on 30 December 1918. Its attempt to turn a protest in Berlin in early January 1919 into an uprising to overthrow the government led to the arrest and murder in custody of both Liebknecht and Luxemburg. Their murder at the hands of the army and the *Freikorps* (paramilitary units made up of demobilised soldiers) not only robbed the KPD of its best-known leaders but also led to the KPD's implacable enmity towards the SPD.[13]

Rosa Luxemburg had not concerned herself with women's issues. Her friend Clara Zetkin had formulated the SPD's position on the women question. For Zetkin, the question of female emancipation was an economic one, and women's status in society was determined not by their sex but by their class. Women should, therefore, join with the men of their class to fight for the overthrow of the capitalist order and the end of its exploitation of the working class.[14] Zetkin and other prominent women within the SPD, including Luise Zietz and Käte Duncker, were opposed to the SPD's support for the war, and joined the USPD in 1917. This left the SPD women's movement in the hands of younger and less ideological women, such as Marie Juchacz, who placed more emphasis on practical welfare work than on the class struggle.[15] A more ideological understanding of women's position was to continue in the KPD while those women in the USPD who had not been affiliated to the Spartacus League were to prove less radical than men in the party. Fewer women than men favoured accepting the twenty-one conditions for the USPD to join the Communist International in October 1920. Robert Wheeler believes that 'women tended to be more moderate and passive in their politics than men', and this is reflected in women's share of party membership. In 1920 women made up 17.5 per cent of the SPD's membership, 15.2 per cent of the USPD and 9 per cent of the KPD.[16] Those women who did not leave the USPD after the larger part of it joined the KPD in December 1920, women such as Luise Zietz and Toni Sender, were to find their way back into the SPD in 1922.

Speaking at the USPD's women's conference in November 1919, Toni Sender bemoaned the fact that 'women have hardly played any role in the councils'.[17] The workers', soldiers' and peasants' councils assumed responsibility for local administration in November 1918, and thousands of women worked for them within the bureaucracy, ensuring food supplies, for example.[18] Few women were elected to the councils, however; only fifty women served on the councils in twenty-eight towns, and in Berlin five women were to be found on the 276-strong workers' councils, with no woman on the executive council.[19] At the first National Congress of Workers' and Soldiers' Councils meeting in Berlin in December 1918 only two women were to be found among the 496 delegates, one from the SPD and the other from the USPD.[20] The workers' councils were elected during the demobilisation when women were being dismissed, and only those gainfully employed could vote. This led to calls from socialist women for housewives' councils or for quotas for women on the councils, and there were reports of a housewives' council in Jena in spring 1919.[21] On the other hand, the radical feminists Anita Augspur and Lida Gustava Heymann, who served in the commission with responsibility for prisons and welfare institutions in Munich, called for independent women's councils with a central executive.[22]

No overall picture of women's participation in the councils emerges. Much depended on the political composition of the council and the nature of the revolution in the city. In general, it was to be women who had been politically active before or during the war who were chosen or elected to serve, if only for a short time. Grebing claims that women on the councils worked in areas responsible for food supplies, housing, education and welfare.[23] In Frankfurt, Toni Sender served as the general secretary on the executive to the workers' council, while in Brunswick the USPD's Minna Fasshauer was appointed the People's Commissioner for Education on 10 November 1918, losing her post on 22 February 1919 when the council was replaced by a coalition government.[24] The concern of left-wing women such as Zetkin and Sender about women's scant participation on the councils was not shared by many women, particularly among the middle and upper classes, who perhaps saw the councils as temporary local phenomena and considered them to be less significant than politics at the national level. They were keen to take advantage of the rights the revolution had granted them and to help determine the complexion of the national and state governments by casting their votes for the first time in elections to the National Assembly and to state legislatures.

Attracting the female vote

Marie Stritt noted that the women's movement faced two tasks in late 1918: persuading women of their duty to vote and persuading the political parties to place women high up on their election lists so that they had a good chance of being elected.[25] The Weimar Republic adopted a system of proportional representation, with Germany being divided from 1920 into thirty-five electoral districts; 60,000 votes were required to win a party a seat in the Reichstag, so the total of seats fluctuated with the turnout. Votes surplus to 60,000 were grouped together across several electoral districts to create another tier, and were added together at national level for the final distribution of seats.[26] Each political party produced a list of candidates for each electoral district and also a national list, and the place that a candidate occupied on these lists was crucial to the candidate's chances of being elected. In November 1918 the BdF led the way in trying to organise the political education of women. It created a special committee and issued guidelines to all of its affiliated associations on how to prepare women to join political parties and to cast their vote, producing explanatory leaflets on the voting procedures and the parties' programmes.[27] The Union of German Protestant Women's Organisations (Vereinigung der Evangelischen Frauenverbände Deutschlands, VEFD) opened an advisory office in Berlin, which ran training courses in public speaking for women and provided female speakers for many of the meetings held by the Protestant Church to educate women about the vote, as well as producing numerous leaflets and brochures.[28] In early December it agreed to work together with the Political Working Group of German Catholic Women's Associations to educate Christian women to vote in the forthcoming election.[29] The committee charged with the political education of women adopted the maxims 'The right to vote means a duty to vote' and 'Vote and canvass women to vote', and its publicity handouts became models for those published by other national and local committees, and also for those of the political parties. Mothers were encouraged to vote so that their children had bread, wives so that their husbands had work and professional women so that their rights could be represented (see Figure 2.1). German women were told that 'any woman who neglects her duty to vote harms herself and the Fatherland'.[30] The political parties also produced leaflets educating women about the

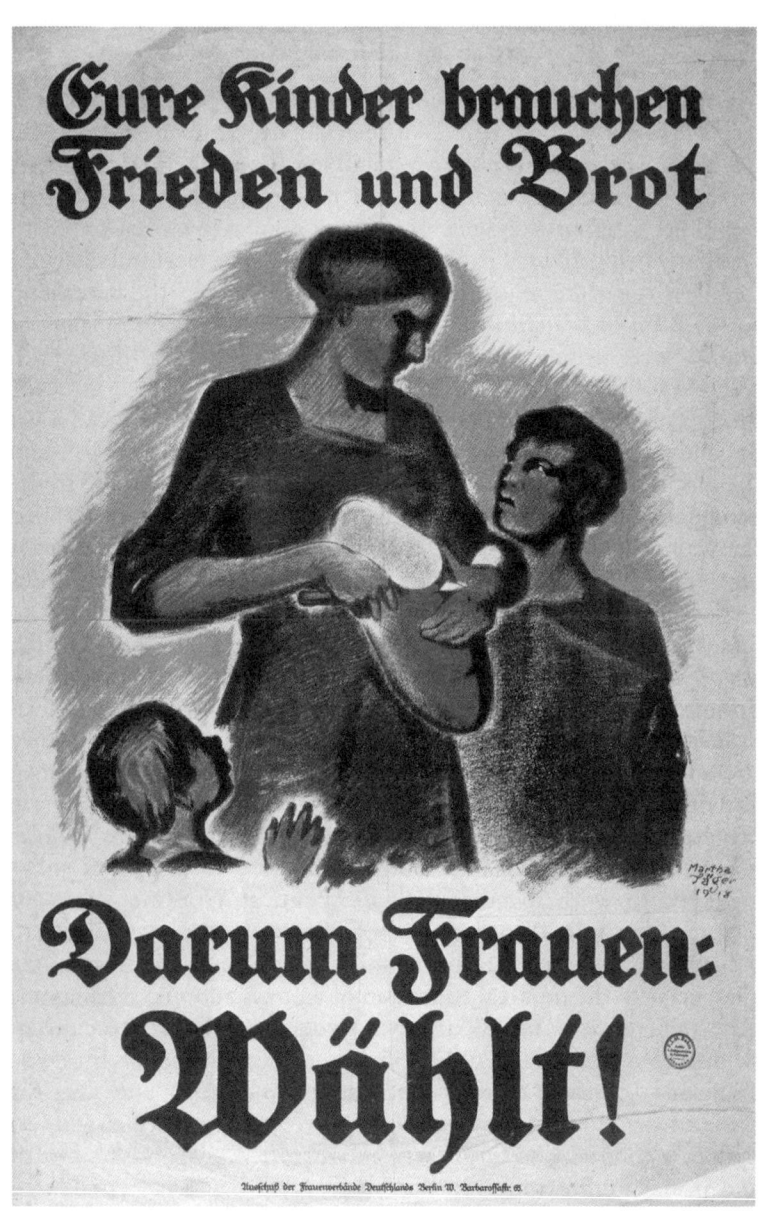

Figure 2.1 'Your children need peace and bread; for that reason, women, cast your vote!' (December 1918)

vote and voting procedures; the DDP, for example, advised women to take proof of identity to the polling station and to get there early; Sunday lunch should be cooked the day before.[31]

Whatever their position on female suffrage had been, the political parties moved quickly in late 1918 to try and win women's votes by targeting them with gender-specific propaganda and by placing women on their lists of candidates for election. Sneeringer has explored the parties' written electoral appeals to women in Berlin and has noted the 'sense of possibility and optimism' which pervaded the National Assembly campaign.[32] In late 1918 and early 1919 'Berlin's streets rioted in colour orgies' as 'every free space was relentlessly covered' with posters.[33] A minority of posters targeted women, who were inundated with leaflets, the volume of gender-specific written propaganda being greater in 1918–19 than at any other time in the Republic.

In addition to distributing posters and leaflets, the parties attempted to win women's votes through meetings: women speakers joined men at general meetings, and in late 1918 and early 1919 the leaders of the bourgeois and Social Democratic women's movement were kept busy with speaking engagements for their chosen party, Gertrud Bäumer giving three speeches a day.[34] The women had to overcome not just their inexperience in speaking before thousands of people, but also difficulties in obtaining permission to speak in occupied areas such as the Rhineland and the physical strains of electioneering.[35] During the Republic, women-only meetings, often including entertainment and refreshments, increasingly became favoured for attracting women to a party, and in the early 1930s the SPD began to hold women-only mass rallies to protect women from the impact of the increasing radicalisation and militarisation of politics.[36] Karen Hagemann has noted how women were excluded from participating in political events because of the location and content of party meetings in the Republic's early years, and then in the early 1930s by increasing political violence.[37] In the late 1920s the SPD, the KPD and the National Socialist German Workers' Party (Nationalsozialistische Deutsche Arbeiterpartei, NSDAP) began using the new mass media (slide shows and films) at meetings, but political parties were not allowed to use the radio, which, as Kate Lacey has argued, might have facilitated women's political education as it could reach them in their homes.[38] The majority of the female electorate consisted of housewives, whose use of public space was, in Hagemann's words, 'extraordinarily circumscribed'.[39] Housewives could be reached by the women's supplements in the parties' newspapers and the parties' women's magazines. As part of a new approach to attracting women voters, therefore, the SPD decided to downplay its ideological rhetoric, and in 1924 it introduced a twice-monthly women's magazine, *Die Frauenwelt* (*Women's World*), containing short stories, recipes and sewing patterns, which had a circulation of 100,000 in 1926; it was the basis for the KPD's *Der Weg der Frau* (*Women's Way*), launched in May 1931.[40] Women could also learn about the parties' stance on women's rights and on issues of interest to them in the brochures that the parties produced and in their petitions to and actions within the Reichstag or the regional state parliaments, the Landtage. The SPD and the KPD were the only parties that attempted to mobilise women in the workplace.[41]

Thomas Childers has noted how each political party, appropriating its own political language and imagery, targeted discrete occupational groups.[42] In 1918–19 the parties addressed leaflets to women *inter alia* as wives, mothers, countrywomen, and working women in a variety of jobs, detailing their stance on women's rights and on issues they believed were of interest to women. They quickly restricted the amount and variety of electoral propaganda aimed at women, perhaps because of financial constraints or because they had determined that such propaganda was not decisive in women's voting preferences. Sneeringer notes that 'by 1924 all parties assumed that women voted on the basis of cultural issues'.[43] Women's rights were to reappear in the parties' gender-specific propaganda in the early 1930s as they attempted to turn women away from the NSDAP by highlighting its attitudes to women's role in politics and the economy.[44] In attempting to persuade women not to vote for the NSDAP, the DNVP, for example, distinguished itself from the NSDAP by noting that it welcomed women's active participation in politics.[45] In their appeals to women as wives and mothers, roles which resonated with women's self-image, the Centre Party, DNVP and DVP emphasised women's duties to the nation, duties which, they stated, should be more highly regarded than any feminist demand, and they called for women's support to help them 'maintain and protect Christian, German family life' and 'the holiness of marriage', for marriage and family were the 'germ cells for the nation's life and power'. The danger to the

German institutions of the family, religion and education came, in these parties' propaganda, from socialism, though the DNVP also stressed the danger to them from the Jews.[46] The DNVP was openly anti-semitic, and Sneeringer believes that 'extreme nationalism distinguished the DNVP's propaganda message to women from that of other parties'.[47] Figure 2.2 shows a DNVP election poster from October 1932 aimed at women and bearing the words 'German women, German loyalty', lines from the national anthem, while a young and an older woman stand on either side of the imperial flag. While there are similarities with the written appeals to the female electorate from the Centre Party, DNVP and DVP, there are nuanced differences in language and style, and in policy. The DVP, for example, adopted a more liberal approach to women's rights; it supported the introduction of divorce on the basis of irreconcilable differences, whereas the Centre Party and DNVP were adamantly opposed to any change in the divorce laws.[48] Similarly, the parties of the left, the SPD, the USPD and the KPD, targeted the working woman, demanding the recognition of women's equal right to work, equal pay for equal work, equal unemployment benefits and equal educational opportunities. Figure 2.3 shows a SPD poster for the November 1932 Reichstag election campaign, showing a confident young working woman with her arm aloft and sporting an Iron Front emblem on her jacket, encouraging women to vote for freedom and peace. The USPD's rhetoric was staunchly Marxist, while the KPD's was militaristic and preached revolution. The KPD frequently depicted women as 'the passive objects of capitalist exploitation' and compared German women's experiences negatively with those of Russian women, as can be seen from Figure 2.4, an election poster for the 1932 Bavarian election.[49] Differences in the left-wing parties' policies relating to women can be seen in the issue of abortion, with the SPD seeking reform of the abortion laws and the KPD and USPD their abrogation.[50] The DDP was, according to Thomas Childers, the only party which sought to create 'a new language of democratic participation', and this was clearly evident in its appeals to women, which addressed women's rights, though from 1924 its posters appealed to women as mothers (see Figure 2.5, a poster from May 1928).[51] Sneeringer has noted that every party 'exhorted women to act politically on behalf of others – their children, the *Volk*, the working class – and only rarely for

Figure 2.2 'German Women, German Loyalty. We are voting German National' (October 1932)

Figure 2.3 'Women – for peace and freedom! Vote Social Democrat List 2' (October 1932)

Figure 2.4 'Women. Only in the Soviet Union is there protection for mother and child! In Germany children are dying and women suffering! Fight with the Communists List 6' (Bavarian Landtag election poster, April 1932)

Figure 2.5 'Women! Take care of housing, prosperity, knowledge. Vote List 6 German Democrats!' (May 1928)

themselves', and that the 'new woman' 'barely surfaced in the language of Weimar politics'.[52]

The importance of gender-specific propaganda in winning women's votes is unknown. The party which benefited most from female suffrage, the Centre Party, produced little gender-specific propaganda, though it knew that other Catholic organisations would mobilise its female constituency. The NSDAP, however, did not concentrate its efforts on targeting women as a discrete constituency until the early 1930s, by which time it had realised both the significance of women's votes for the party's chances of electoral success and the necessity of repudiating other parties' propaganda about its views on women's role in society and employment, articulated in the often contradictory statements of party luminaries.[53] Figure 2.6, a Nazi poster for the April 1932 Prussian Landtag election, is a recycled poster from the 1928 Reichstag election, asking mothers and working women to vote for the NSDAP.[54] The NSDAP did not have a coherent programme with regard to women's role in society; its opponents highlighted anti-feminist comments – such as Esser's promise to dismiss all women from public sector employment, Strasser's claim that housewives would have to learn to manage on their husbands' earnings, Hitler's statement that a woman became entitled to the rights of citizenship only on marriage, and Goebbels's belief that a woman's duty consisted of looking beautiful and having children – while also noting the party's repudiation of passive female suffrage and its bellicose intentions.[55] Women's voting choices were, however, not determined by a party's stance on women's rights, but by its position on a range of issues important to them, and electoral propaganda was merely one element in a variety of sources by which women could be informed of the parties' policies. They could also be influenced in their political choices by family, friends, work colleagues, fellow members of the organisations they joined, their local member of the clergy or local traditions.

The female vote

Hedwig Dransfeld, the leader of the KFB and a candidate for the Centre Party, wrote of women's tremendous enthusiasm for and interest in voting, which was to find expression in the high female turnout in the elections to the National Assembly on 19 January

Figure 2.6 'Mothers, working women. We are voting National Socialist List 8' (April 1932)

1919.[56] In thirty-four of the Reich's thirty-seven electoral districts the female turnout was 82.3 per cent, only slightly lower than the 82.4 per cent turnout of men.[57] Reasons for the smallness in the difference between the male and female turnouts, which was lower in 1919 than in any other national election in the Weimar Republic, might be found in women's great interest in voting for the first time, the wish to influence their country's future in the turbulent days at the war's end, or just the sheer novelty of casting their vote, but the reason more probably stems from the low turnout among men under twenty-five, many of whom might have been imprisoned abroad, still in uniform or on their way home from the front.[58] However, women's interest in voting quickly waned, and in the eighteen electoral districts which collated separate voting statistics for the 1920 Reichstag election 72.7 per cent of men and 63.3 per cent of women cast their ballots.[59] The difference between the percentages of women and men eligible to vote who actually did so narrowed in the crisis years of the early 1930s, a trend that continued into the Federal Republic.[60] Because women outnumbered men in the electorate, a lower female turnout did not necessarily mean that fewer women than men voted. On the contrary, such was the preponderance of women among the German electorate, with 21,025,998 women aged twenty and over in 1925 compared with 18,769,662 men, that it is more than likely that, even though the female turnout lagged behind the male, the actual number of women who voted exceeded that of men.[61]

The law of 30 November 1918 provided for men and women to vote separately, and throughout the Republic separate voting took place in a broad variety of cities, towns and country districts in both Protestant and Catholic areas; the results may, therefore, be considered relatively representative. The largest number of votes counted by gender was for the 1928 Reichstag election, amounting to 20.6 per cent of the total of valid votes cast.[62] Additional studies carried out in a variety of locations for various elections reveal that men and women regarded Reichstag elections as more important than Landtag elections, and considered local elections the least important. Town-dwellers made more use of their right to vote than did those living in the countryside, and this was especially true for women.[63] Married women were more likely to vote than single women, and female domestic servants were found to be the occupational group which made least use of their right to vote.[64]

Table 2.1 *The impact of female suffrage on the number of seats won by the major parties in the 1928 Reichstag election*

Party	Reichstag seats won	Reichstag seats without the female vote	Difference
Z	62	50	+12
DNVP	73	64	+9
DVP	45	43	+2
DDP	25	26	−1
SPD	153	157	−4
NSDAP	12	16	−4
KPD	54	62	−8

Source: H. Zurkuhlen, 'Wahlbeteiligung und Stimmabgabe der Frauen', *Die Frau*, 36:2 (November 1928), 79.

In the elections to the National Assembly, the SPD received 37.9 per cent of the vote, followed by the Centre Party with 19.7 per cent, the DDP with 18.5 per cent and the DNVP with 10.3 per cent. In the three districts where men and women voted separately and from which information is available, it is clear that a higher percentage of the female vote than of the male went to the Centre Party, and that the reverse was true for the SPD.[65] There were claims that female suffrage had cost the socialists a majority, but Jürgen Falter has pointed out that the results of the National Assembly election represented an aberration in the shares of the votes going to the three electoral blocs, with the bourgeois-Protestant bloc losing support compared with the 1912 election, the political left gaining support and the Catholic bloc remaining stable. However, by the 1920 Reichstag elections the balance of power between the blocs had returned to 1912 levels.[66] It is clear that the parties which benefited most from female suffrage throughout the Weimar Republic were the Centre Party and its Bavarian sister party, the Bavarian People's Party (Bayerische Volkspartei, BVP), while the party which gained the least was the KPD, as one contemporary observer's calculations, detailed in Table 2.1, illustrate.

On the whole the female vote behaved in much the same way as the male vote during the Republic, with any fall in the male vote for a particular party being reflected by a similar drop in the female vote. Yet far more women than men voted for religious parties. Dr Hartwig pointed out in 1928 that 'parties which do not respect religion are cutting their own throats'.[67] In none of the statistics available does the share of the male vote cast for the Centre Party exceed that of the female vote, with the difference being smallest in Protestant urban areas and largest in rural, unindustrialised Catholic districts.[68] Though the share of the female vote going to the Centre Party and BVP gradually waned during the life of the Republic – their share of the vote fell from 19.7 per cent in 1919 to 14 per cent in 1933 – these parties remained the ones for which more women in staunchly Catholic areas voted than any other party up to 1932, and in some cases March 1933.[69] Tingsten claimed that the Centre Party's 'key position in German politics ... was due to the support of women'.[70] In Protestant areas the right-wing DNVP and to a lesser extent the DVP received disproportionately more support from women than from men, though to a lesser degree than was the case with the Centre Party. In the 1928 and 1930 Reichstag elections in Berlin, for example, the DNVP received 17.5 per cent and 13.6 per cent of the total female vote respectively, and of the male vote 13.7 per cent and 9.6 per cent.[71] No other party, with one or two rare exceptions in certain elections, gained much from female suffrage. The DDP and its more conservative successor, the German State Party (Deutsche Staatspartei, DStP), received in the main a greater share of the male than of the female vote, though the difference between the two was small. Much larger was, on average, the difference in the shares of the male and female vote being given to the SPD, especially in the early years of the Republic. This difference narrowed during the Weimar Republic, and as the SPD's share of the total vote halved from January 1919 to March 1933, women were slower to leave the party than men, who transferred their votes to the KPD and the NSDAP. In the last few elections of the Republic the SPD gained a slightly higher share of the female than of the male vote in districts with a strong KPD vote.[72] Sneeringer notes that 'it was only after the SPD muted its anti-clericalism that its female vote rose', while Peterson believes that women were inclined 'to support a style of working-class politics which was respectable and parliamentary, and as the SPD grew increasingly conservative over the years of the Weimar Republic, they were able to attract a larger and larger women's vote'.[73] Other contemporary commentators believed that women were more loyal voters than men, and 'less inclined to change their vote'.[74] Working-class women were more reluctant than men to transfer their allegiance to the KPD, which they shunned. In none of the elections in which separate voting took place did the share of the female vote going to the KPD exceed that of the male vote.[75] Women's reluctance to vote for the KPD can also be seen in the lack of support that its candidate Ernst Thälmann received in the Reich presidential elections of 1932.[76] Writing in 1931, Dr Hartwig described the KPD and the NSDAP as 'out-and-out men's parties'.[77] With the exception of the elections to the Reichstag in May 1924, following the attempted Hitler putsch of November 1923, when the *völkisch* bloc had polled 26.3 per cent of the female and 25.7 per cent of the male vote in selected areas of Bavaria, the NSDAP had not received much electoral support from either men or women before 1930.[78] In those areas where men and women voted separately in the 1928 Reichstag election, the NSDAP polled 2.6 per cent of male and 1.8 per cent of female votes.[79] The Reichstag election of September 1930, which saw the NSDAP poll 18.3 per cent of the vote to become the second largest party after the SPD, witnessed the largest turnout since 1919, and separate voting statistics reveal a larger increase in the female than in the male turnout. In those districts where votes were counted separately, the NSDAP received 17.4 per cent of the male and 15.3 per cent of the female vote. In all areas except two the female vote for the Nazis was increasing at a faster rate than the male one, albeit from a small base.[80] This trend was to continue into the July 1932 Reichstag election, so that the difference in the shares of the male and female votes going to the NSDAP narrowed in Catholic areas while in Protestant areas the Nazis received almost equal shares of the vote from both sexes. By the Reichstag election of March 1933, which witnessed the highest turnout of the Republic, the NSDAP was receiving a larger share of the female than of the male vote, as Table 2.2 shows. If this pattern was repeated throughout Germany, then, according to Tingsten, 'it may be regarded as probable that the so-called national coalition (Nazi and German-national party) did not gain a majority among the men, their bare Reichstag majority being due to the strong support of women voters'.[81]

It is impossible to know why women cast their votes for the NSDAP, and historians have offered a variety of plausible reasons, which range from the material self-interest of single working women to a desire for the Republic's destruction.[82] The notion that Hitler held a charismatic appeal for women has been discounted by the separate voting returns for the 1932 Reich presidential election,

Table 2.2 *The percentages of the total male (m) and female (f) votes cast for the NSDAP in selected areas in Reichstag elections, 1930–33*

Place	1930		1932[a]		1932[b]		1933	
	m	f	m	f	m	f	m	f
Ansbach	34.6	33.3	–	–	47.6	50.0	51.2	55.6
Augsburg	14.9	10.4	25.2	21.1	24.5	21.6	33.4	31.4
Bavaria	18.9	14.2	29.2	25.6	27.4	24.7	36.2	34.4
Bremen	12.9	11.1	29.9	30.9	20.8	20.9	30.8	34.4
Cologne	19.8	15.5	26.4	22.8	21.8	19.2	33.9	32.9
Dinkelsbühl	33.2	31.9	–	–	54.4	56.1	58.6	61.5
Konstanz	–	–	32.0	26.0	26.1	21.8	35.9	32.8
Leipzig	14.6	13.1	–	–	–	–	34.1	38.8
Ludwigshafen	17.4	14.0	–	–	28.6	27.7	34.5	34.9
Magdeburg	19.8	18.7	36.3	38.9	31.1	34.0	38.1	43.3
Regensburg	19.7	13.1	23.3	17.3	20.0	14.9	33.1	28.9
Wiesbaden	29.1	26.0	43.0	43.7	36.1	36.8	44.9	47.3

Notes: [a] Election of 31 July 1932; [b] election of 6 November 1932.

Source: Stadtarchiv Konstanz, SII/12716, 12719, 12720; *Zeitschrift des bayerischen statistischen Landesamtes*, 63 (1931), 93–4; 65 (1933), 103–4, 328; Tingsten, *Political Behaviour*, pp. 52–5.

where Hindenburg would have won in the first round had only women voted.[83] It is clear that women who had a strong sense of voter identification with the Centre Party, the SPD or the KPD were able to resist the NSDAP's appeal, but once the NSDAP began to be perceived as the 'responsible guardian of the national interest' with respect for religion, it was able to attract the votes of primarily Protestant women of all classes.[84]

The organisation of women in the political parties

Winning women's votes for a party was primarily the task of its women's organisation, and the NSDAP's decision to target the female electorate was facilitated by its decision to create a unified women's organisation, the new National Socialist Women's Organisation (Nationalsozialistische Frauenschaft, NSF), with effect from 1 October 1931.[85] The lack of a unified Nazi women's organisation and a coherent programme on women's role in society is indicative of the scant regard paid by the party to women in its early years. The NSF's first leader was Elsbeth Zander, who had created the largest Nazi women's group, the German Women's Order (Deutscher Frauenorden, DFO), in Berlin in September 1923. It had been formally affiliated to the NDSAP since January 1928, and in August 1930 had some 160 branches with around 4,000 members. At all levels the NSF leader was to be appointed by the relevant male party leader; the NSF's tasks included providing practical assistance to the *Sturmabteilung* (the storm section, SA – the Nazis' paramilitary wing), social welfare, ideological training and instruction in the national economy, and winning women for the party as members and voters.[86] The NSF produced its own leaflets in the presidential and Reichstag elections of 1932.[87] All female party members, as well as the wives and daughters of impecunious male party members, were to be members of the NSF. On 14 September 1930 the NSDAP had 7,625 female members, who made up 5.6 per cent of the membership, and 56,386 women joined the party between then and 30 January 1933, with women constituting 7.8 per cent of the new members.[88] In December 1931 NSF membership stood at 19,382, and by December 1932 it had increased to 109,320; by spring 1933 the NSF had succeeded in setting up a branch in every town and larger community, though it encountered difficulties in staunchly Catholic districts.[89] The NSF's organ was to be Zander's *Opferdienst der deutschen Frau* (*Sacrificial Duty of the German Woman*). In their writings Nazi women condemned the middle-class women's movement for its liberalism, individualism, internationalism and pacifism; their purpose was to serve the German people and to help in the great struggle to free Germany: 'Emancipation from women's emancipation is the first demand of a generation of women who want to save the German people and race.'[90] Geraldine Horan has noted that Nazi women's language 'reflects the portrayal of themselves as helpers, supporters' and reveals their 'belief in their moral and spiritual superiority' and their portrayal of themselves as 'leaders of spiritual renewal'. Their language 'praises motherhood' and 'women's traditional roles' and 'marginalises women who do not conform to Nazi ideals'.[91] Nazi women, dressed in uniform and wearing insignia, would disrupt the meetings of other parties or those held by the women's movement, and hold marches of their own, as can be seen from Figure 2.7. On 31 January 1932, at a DStP meeting in Karlsruhe, Gertrud Klink, the Baden NSF women's leader who in 1934 was appointed the

Figure 2.7 'Only a strong Germany can give the Germans work'. National Socialist demonstration in Berlin (1931)

Reich Women's Leader, harangued Gertrud Bäumer, and she and her followers drowned out Bäumer's closing remarks by singing the *Horst-Wessel-Lied*. On another occasion in Berlin in a meeting before the November 1932 Reichstag election, one Nazi woman spat at Dorothee von Velsen, the chair of the German Women's Citizens' Association.[92]

Detailed membership figures for the Centre Party, DNVP, DVP and DDP are not available. In a speech given to the BdF's general assembly in 1929, Frances Magnus-Hausen claimed that women constituted about 25 per cent of the DDP's membership, between 35 and 60 per cent of the DVP's and 47 per cent of the DNVP's.[93] Each party institutionalised women's segregation in its *Reichsfrauenausschuss*, or Reich women's committee, whose tasks included winning women as voters and members, educating women politically and advising the party on all issues relating to women. The DNVP was the first party to set up its *Reichsfrauenausschuss*, in early December 1918, closely followed by the DVP. It was to be 1919 before a network of DNVP women's committees at local, district and state level began to be set up, with a system of

Vertrauensfrauen (women of trust) in places with no committee. At each level the party funded the women's committee, and its chair had a seat on the party executive, thus integrating the committee into the party structure.[94] Scheck claims that by the end of 1922 the DNVP had thirty-eight state women's committees, 1,900 other women's committees and 2,748 *Vertrauensfrauen*, while the DVP had committees in thirty-two electoral districts and 500 other committees across Germany.[95] The DNVP drew its female members from a range of existing organisations, such as the DEF, the VEFD, the housewives' associations and nationalist organisations such as the German Women's Naval League, as well as attracting individuals, and their political views ranged from traditional conservatism, often imbued with deeply felt religious convictions, to racist ultranationalism. Both Andrea Süchting-Hänger and Scheck believe women activists to have been the bearers of racist ideology in the party, and Scheck believes they may have prepared German women for the Nazis' racism.[96] Most women supported Hugenberg when he took over the leadership of the party in 1928 and moved the party to oppose parliamentary democracy, though this support might also have been attributable to the belief that the previous leadership had done little to support women's active participation in politics.[97]

In addition to winning women for the party, the women's groups also performed essential tasks such as fund-raising, distributing election materials and collecting party subscriptions as well as performing acts of charity for party members in need. One of the best-known initiatives was the DVP's 'Mother's Aid Wandering Basket' (*Mütterhilfe Wanderkorb*), a collection of all the items a new mother needed for the care of her baby.[98] Scheck has noted that women in the DNVP and DVP regarded the party as an extension of their family and invested heavily in it, performing motherly and housewifely tasks such as organising social events and providing the refreshments and, often with their husbands, the entertainment; they thus contributed to the creation of a thriving and convivial local party culture.[99] Scheck has noted that grassroots women's groups did not necessarily share the same concerns as the *Reichsfrauenausschüsse* and that their links were of variable quality, though the *Reichsfrauenausschüsse* tried to keep their groups informed by means of newsletters.[100] The DDP did not create its *Reichsfrauenausschuss* until the summer of 1919, and it had *Vertrauensfrauen* in local branches with a major representative (*Hauptvertrauensfrau*) in each electoral district. In 1921 the DDP had thirty-six *Hauptvertrauensfrauen* and 1,058 *Vertrauensfrauen*, though this number had fallen to some 700 women by 1926, and the women's groups appear to have been plagued by financial difficulties.[101] The Centre Party did not create its Women's Advisory Committee until June 1922, having relied heavily on the KFB to fulfil the functions of a *Reichsfrauenausschuss*. Advisory committees were set up at state, district and local levels; and the Women's Advisory Committee's newsletter did not appear until January 1926.[102]

The SPD already had in place a women's organisation which predated the Republic, though the party split in 1917 had serious repercussions for the social democratic women's movement. Of the eighty-five women present at the SPD's women's conference in Weimar in June 1919 only fourteen had attended pre-war conferences.[103] The new head of the SPD's women's organisation, Marie Juchacz, was pleased to report a significant increase in female party members since the war, with 206,354 women making up 20.4 per cent of the party's membership in 1919.[104] However, the number of women members fell steadily from 1920, with women's share of the membership almost halving by 1923; in 1924 the SPD adopted new tactics to win women members, and it succeeded in increasing women's share of the membership to 22.8 per cent in 1931.[105] The SPD, like the bourgeois parties, had difficulty in attracting young women; in 1930 women under the age of thirty made up less than 19 per cent of the SPD's female members.[106] As with all the parties, there were strong regional variations in women's share of the party membership; in 1930 women constituted 30 per cent of the membership in Magdeburg but only 12 per cent in Hessen-Offenbach.[107] In 1924 the SPD decided that women should be represented on all committees and in all delegations according to their share of the membership, and though women's share of seats on the party committee exceeded this share in 1927 and 1929, their share of party conference delegates and elected representatives was less favourable.[108] From June 1924 the party's female functionaries were catered for by the monthly *Die Genossin* (*The Female Comrade*), which by 1931 had a circulation of 40,000.[109] SPD women were, first and foremost, members of the party, and the women's movement was just a part of that party.[110] Within the party there was a separation of tasks and areas of interest along gender lines, which also found expression in the separate women's conferences which were held after the first six party conferences during the Weimar Republic. Only in 1929 did a woman, Marie Juchacz, deliver a paper to the main party conference, and in the ensuing discussion only women spoke.[111] One of the women's movement's key tasks was winning women voters and members for the party, a task that some men felt was beneath their dignity. SPD women were well aware of the anti-feminist views held by some of their male colleagues, some of whom believed that women had no place in politics.[112] Marie Juchacz believed that social welfare work among the working class, previously the domain of middle-class women, could win women for the movement, and in December 1919 the SPD set up its Workers' Welfare Organisation (*Arbeiterwohlfahrt*); by 1930 this had 2,300 local branches whose practical welfare work was carried out by 114,000 helpers, most of whom were voluntary and female.[113] Christiane Eifert believes that the *Arbeiterwohlfahrt* not only failed in its aim of providing a political training ground for women but also had little influence on social policy.[114] Welfare work was to become a niche for Social Democratic women, allowing men of the party free rein in what they considered to be more prestigious political areas.[115] Some SPD women were well aware of the dangers of restricting their activities to the welfare sphere. Juchacz, however, was unwilling to challenge the male party leadership in order to institute within the party the equality of the sexes in which it professed to believe.[116]

The KPD espoused the equality of the sexes. Its policy towards women in society and the party was drawn up by Clara Zetkin and approved at the unifying congress of KPD and left-wing USPD women in December 1920, where it was also decided to set up a Reich Women's Bureau. Zetkin envisaged local agitation committees to win women for the party.[117] However, by 1924 the party had deemed this policy a failure. Male party members were to be told repeatedly that winning women for the party was also their responsibility. The Reich Women's Bureau was closed and a women's department set up in the party's political bureau, while the delegate system of conferences became the favoured method of winning women for the party, with some 20,000 women attending the Reich congress in 1931.[118] In 1925 the party introduced the Red Women's and Girls' League (*Roter Frauen- und Mädchenbund*,

RFMB), a supra-political uniformed organisation aimed at mobilising proletarian women. Within two years it had attracted some 25,000 women, 80 per cent of whom were not members of the party.[119] The KPD was extremely successful in mobilising women in its campaign against Article 218, the abortion paragraph, but, hide-bound by ideology and concerned at spawning autonomous women's groups outside its control, it was unable to convert many of those mobilised into members.[120] Accurate membership figures are not available, though there are estimates of women's membership rising slowly from 9 per cent of members in December 1920 to 16.5 per cent in 1929 and then holding steady at 15 per cent in the early 1930s.[121] Women in the party were catered for from 1927 by the magazine *Die Kämpferin (The Female Fighter)*. Few women attained high party positions, only thirty-four (6.7 per cent) of the party's leading functionaries between 1924 and 1929 being women.[122]

Women politicians

In the first speech given by a woman to the National Assembly, on 19 February 1919, Marie Juchacz noted, 'we women now have the opportunity to develop our powers within the framework of our chosen ideology'.[123] With the relaxation of the laws of association, from 15 May 1908 women had been able to join the political party of their choosing, and many women active in the bourgeois women's movement joined the liberal parties which merged to create the Progressive People's Party in 1910, and they created their own women's working group within it. Conservative women were also proactive in creating their own Association of Conservative Women (Vereinigung Konservativer Frauen), independent of the German Conservative Party, in April 1913.[124] The right-wing, liberal and socialist parties, therefore, had women they could call upon to act as candidates in the elections to the National Assembly. The Centre Party relied on the KFB to provide it with candidates, while the DEF and housewives' associations furnished the DNVP and DVP with candidates. So many leading members of the BdF stood for election for the DDP, including Gertrud Bäumer, Helene Lange, Marie Stritt, Marianne Weber, Marie Baum and Marie-Elisabeth Lüders, that it labelled itself 'the women's party'. In late 1918 there were suggestions that the BdF should convert itself into a Women's Party, and like 'a ghost that keeps coming out of the grave' the idea resurfaced in 1924, following a fall in the number of women elected to the Reichstag, and in the early 1930s.[125] Its re-emergence was indicative of the powerlessness and frustration felt by some bourgeois Liberal women at their inability to exert more influence within their chosen party. While the leaders of the KFB initially embraced a political role, working closely with the Centre Party, the leaders of the BdF and other women's organisations such as the DEF decided that the women's movement still had a role to play outside parliamentary politics and determined to maintain a non-party-political stance, as they were aware of the range of political opinions held by members. Throughout the Republic the party-political neutrality of the BdF and the DEF was under constant scrutiny, the BdF being accused by Conservatives of being the mouthpiece of the DDP, and the DEF's leadership of increasingly instilling a DNVP perspective.[126]

In 1918–19 the mood among women candidates for the National Assembly was one of optimism. They hoped, as 'mothers of the nation' and the representatives of their parties and of the German people, to enrich Germany's political life culturally and morally.[127] Kirsten Heinsohn has noted that women on the left emphasised their role in the construction of democracy and political and social improvements, whereas women on the right wanted to rescue Germany from the abyss and restore national honour.[128] On 19 January 1919 thirty-seven of the 310 women candidates were elected to the National Assembly, their number later increasing to forty-one as women replaced men whose seats became vacant.[129] They thus constituted 9.6 per cent of delegates, an auspicious beginning to women's participation in Germany's political life.

In early 1919 women were also elected to the state parliaments and local councils (see Figure 2.8). Overall, 117 women made up 6.1 per cent of 1,918 delegates to state assemblies, though seven of the state assemblies contained no female delegate.[130] There are no comprehensive statistics on women's participation in local councils throughout the Republic, though some surveys and regional statistics shed some light. One 1919 survey of 529 towns with over 10,000 inhabitants revealed 1,396 female councillors, who made up about 11 per cent of all town councillors.[131] However, other surveys and the results from Bavaria and Baden indicate that the larger the community, the greater the proportion of women elected.[132] Surveys reveal

Figure 2.8 Weimar 1919: elected female representatives (1919)

that women served mainly on social welfare, youth and education committees, areas in which they may have gained some expertise, as women had been allowed to serve on such committees in some states from the turn of the century.[133] From the scant evidence available, it appears that the number of female town councillors gradually declined, though the decline was not uniform. In Baden, women held 12.3 per cent of council seats in sixteen towns with over 10,000 inhabitants in 1919, but this figure had fallen to 6.8 per cent by 1930.[134] However, in towns with strong support for the SPD or KPD, such as Mannheim, women's share of council seats increased.[135] The fall in women's share of seats in town councils, and in other legislatures, could be attributable to the increasing support for the NSDAP, which, in keeping with a decision taken on 21 January 1921, never allowed a woman to represent it; to the parties' reluctance to allocate seats to women once they were aware that female voters were not swayed in their voting choices by the presence of women on a party's election list; to the increasing jockeying for position of interest groups within the bourgeois political parties; or to the lack of suitable women candidates, as revealed in a 1929 survey.[136]

Table 2.3 *Female delegates to the state assemblies by party, 1919–33*

Party	Total delegates	Women	%women
KPD	503	50	9.9
SPD	1,825	113	6.2
Z	467	27	5.8
BVP	141	5	4.3
DDP	592	50	8.4
DVP	403	25	6.2
DNVP	615	35	5.9
Others	1,684	31	1.8
Total	6,230	336	5.4

Source: W. H. Schröder, W. Weege and M. Zech, *Kollektive Biographie der Landtagsabgeordneten der Weimarer Republik 1918–1933* (Cologne: Quantum, 2004), http://biosop.zhsf.uni-koeln.de/ParlamentarierPortal/bioweil.htm (accessed 5 August 2011).

At state level, no uniform picture of the level of women's representation emerges. Throughout the Republic some 336 women served in state legislatures, making up 5.4 per cent of all delegates (see Table 2.3). One-third of the women represented the SPD, and just under half (48.5 per cent) were concentrated in only three of the twenty-seven state legislatures: Prussia, Hamburg and Bremen. Five state legislatures had no female representative throughout the Republic.[137] Although some states, such as Baden and Hamburg, witnessed a fall in their numbers of women representatives, others such as Saxony saw an increase, which was attributable to the strength of the left-wing parties.[138] In Prussia, however, women's share of representatives remained strong thanks not only to the SPD's willingness to have women represent it but also because of the relatively high percentages of women among the DNVP and Centre Party delegations, as Table 2.4 shows. Scheck believes that the DNVP and DVP leadership promised to ensure that women were represented in the Prussian Landtag rather than in the Reichstag, as the Landtag was an assembly in which social and cultural legislation, women's area of expertise, played a considerable role, whereas the Reichstag was more concerned with foreign and military affairs, men's areas of expertise.[139]

Attention focused on women in the Reichstag, the national parliament, where women's share of seats fell to 6.1 per cent in May

Table 2.4 Seats in the Prussian Landtag, 1919–32

Party	1919			1921			1924			1928			1932		
	Total	Women	% Women	Total	Women	% Women	Total	Women	% Women	Total	Women	% Women	Total	Women	% Women
DNVP	50	2	4.0	75	5	6.6	109	8	7.3	82	8	9.8	31	2	6.4
DVP	21	2	9.5	58	6	10.3	45	3	6.6	40	3	7.5	7	1	14.3
DDP	65	2	3.0	26	2	7.6	27	2	7.4	21	1	4.8	2	0	0.0
Z	88	5	5.6	84	8	9.5	81	8	9.6	71	9	12.7	67	8	11.9
SPD	145	10	6.8	114	15	13.1	114	16	14.0	137	19	13.9	94	15	16.0
KPD	–	–	–	31	3	9.6	44	2	4.5	54	2	3.7	57	6	10.5
Others	32	2	6.7	40	3	7.5	30	0	0.0	45	0	0.0	164	0	0.0
Total	401	23	5.7	428	42	9.8	450	39	8.5	450	42	9.3	422	32	7.6

Source: E. Wolff (ed.), *Jahrbuch des Bundes Deutscher Frauenvereine 1932* (Berlin and Leipzig: Bensheimer, 1932), pp. 86–9.

1924 (see Table 2.5), causing concern in the BdF about women's perceived fall in influence in the legislature and leading to demands from women in all the parties, except the KPD, for women to be given more consideration on their parties' election lists.[140] During discussions on electoral reform, suggestions were made in 1926 that 8 per cent of all Reichstag seats, and in 1930 7.5 per cent, be reserved for women. Gertrud Bäumer was, however, opposed to 'sinecures for women' on the election lists.[141] Some women began to discuss drawing up separate women's lists at national level, but the BdF considered them to be feasible only at a local level, where they had enjoyed some limited success.[142] In the May 1924 Reichstag elections, 351 women made up 9.7 per cent of the electoral candidates, an identical percentage to that constituted by the 339 female candidates in December 1924, and in both elections the DDP had the highest percentage of women on its lists, 17.1 per cent and 14.5 per cent respectively.[143] By 1930 the number of women candidates had increased to 571, but as the number of parties standing for election had mushroomed, women's share of candidates fell to 10.4 per cent.[144] The Centre Party had decided in 1920 that in electoral districts with five candidates at least one should be a woman, preferably placed second on the list, but the other parties had not laid down any such directives. The BVP always placed a woman, Thusnelda Lang-Brumann, in either first or second place on its national list to ensure it had female representation in the Reichstag, and Gertrud Bäumer was also assured of at worst second place on the DDP/DStP national list. The other parties did not consistently allow women to head their national lists; in May 1924, for example, Margarete Behm headed the DNVP's national list, while the DVP and Centre Party each placed a woman in second place.[145] However, it would appear that the parties in many electoral districts were reluctant to place women on their lists at all. Walmsley notes that women were elected to serve in any numbers in the Reichstag from only eight electoral districts.[146]

Asked in 1928 why women had been pushed down the parties' election lists, the leaders of women's organisations and elected female representatives cited the demands made within parties by economic interest groups to have 'their' candidate elected, male fear of competition from women for election, women politicians' restrictions of their areas of interest and the apathy of the female electorate.[147] The BdF wrote to all the major parties before each

Table 2.5 Representatives in the National Assembly and the Reichstag, 1919–33

Party	19 January 1919			6 June 1920			4 May 1924			7 December 1924			20 May 1928		
	Total	Women	% Women	Total	Women	% Women	Total	Women	% Women	Total	Women	% Women	Total	Women	% Women
NSDAP[a]	–	–	–	–	–	–	32	0	0.0	10	0	0.0	12	0	0.0
DNVP	41	3	7.3	65	2	3.1	103	4	3.9	109	5	4.6	78	2	2.6
DVP	22	1	4.5	62	3	4.8	44	2	4.5	51	2	3.9	45	2	4.4
DDP[b]	74	5	6.8	44	4	9.1	28	2	7.1	32	2	6.3	25	2	8.0
Z/BVP	89	6	6.7	68	4	4.6	81	5	6.2	88	5	5.7	78	4	5.1
SPD	165	19	11.5	113	13	11.5	100	11	11.0	131	16	12.2	152	20	13.2
USPD	22	3	13.6	81	9	11.1	–	–	–	–	–	–	–	–	–
KPD	–	–	–	2	1	50.0	62	5	8.1	45	3	6.7	77	12	15.6
Others	10	0	0.0	12	0	0.0	22	0	0.0	55	0	0.0	46	0	0.0
Total	423	37	8.7	466	36	7.7	472	29	6.1	493	33	6.7	490	33	6.7

Party	14 September 1930			31 July 1932			6 November 1932			5 March 1933		
	Total	Women	% Women	Total	Women	% Women	Total	Women	% Women	Total	Women	% Women
NSDAP[a]	107	0	0.0	230	0	0.0	196	0	0.0	288	0	0.0
DNVP	41	3	7.3	40	3	7.5	52	3	5.8	50	2	4.0
DVP	30	1	3.3	7	1	14.3	11	1	9.1	2	0	0.0
Z/BVP	87	5	5.7	97	7	7.2	90	5	5.6	92	6	6.5
SPD	143	16	11.2	133	15	11.3	121	13	10.7	120	13	10.8
KPD	77	12	15.6	89	12	13.5	100	13	13	81	9	11.1
Others	78	1	1.3	8	0	0.0	12	0	0.0	14	0	0.0
Total	577	39	6.8	608	38	6.3	584	35	6.0	647	30	4.6

Note: [a] The völkisch bloc in 1924; [b] from 1930 the DStP.

Source: to maintain uniformity, all information is taken from the relevant handbooks: *Handbuch der verfassungsgebenden deutschen Nationalversammlung* (Berlin: Carl Heymanns Verlag, 1919), pp. 114–19; *Reichstags-Handbuch I. Wahlperiode* (Berlin: Julius Sittenfeld, 1920), pp. 375–80; *Reichstags-Handbuch II. Wahlperiode* (Berlin: Druck und Verlag der Reichsdruckerei, 1924), pp. 351–6; *Reichstags-Handbuch III. Wahlperiode* (Berlin: Druck und Verlag der Reichsdruckerei, 1925), pp. 171–6; *Reichstags-Handbuch IV. Wahlperiode* (Berlin: Reichsdruckerei, 1928), pp. 253–9; *Reichstags-Handbuch V. Wahlperiode* (Berlin: Reichsdruckerei, 1930), pp. 268–75; *Reichstags-Handbuch VI. Wahlperiode* (Berlin: Verlag der Reichsdruckerei, 1932), pp. 6–12; *Reichstags-Handbuch VII. Wahlperiode* (Berlin: Reichsdruckerei, 1933), pp. 195–201; *Reichstags-Handbuch VIII. Wahlperiode* (Berlin: Reichsdruckerei, 1933), pp. 65–71.

Reichstag election from December 1924, asking them to place women in secure positions on their election lists, and in 1930 it also called upon the female electorate to overcome voter apathy and vote for those parties committed to Germany's reconstruction, rather than destruction.[148] The Nazis' electoral success sent a shock wave through the organised bourgeois women's movement, and the BdF set up a National Political Working Group under Gertrud Bäumer to draw up a plan to combat the perceived fall in women's political influence.[149] By 1932 the BdF was concerned that women's very participation in politics was at stake, and in June 1932 it called for meetings to be held across Germany to promote women's civic rights and their right to work. On 2 July 1932 Emma Ender, a former BdF chair, set up 'Frauenfront 1932' (Women's Front 1932) in Hamburg, an organisation open to individual members to fight all attempts to suppress women from political and public life and the use of violence in political debates.[150] The BdF ceased its strict adherence to party-political neutrality and began to target the NSDAP's anti-feminism, producing from July 1932 a series of *Gelbe Blätter*, 'Yellow Pages – Material in Women's Struggle for Work and the Professions', in association with the German Female Academics' Association.[151] Ender's and the BdF's concerns do not seem to have resonated with female voters. In July 1932 women's share of Reichstag seats fell to 6.2 per cent as the Nazis became the largest party in the Reichstag. However, if the Nazis' share of seats is ignored, women's share of Reichstag seats was 8.3 per cent in 1930, 10.1 per cent in July 1932, 9 per cent in November 1932 and 8.4 per cent in March 1933. The BdF and bourgeois women were concerned about the fall in women's share of Reichstag seats in general because it affected the parties they supported in particular. In refusing to allow women to represent it, the NSDAP claimed to be protecting them from the 'dirty business of parliamentary politics'. One female DVP politician drily noted that the Nazis were in part responsible for politics becoming a brutish, dirty business.[152]

Writing in 1929, Thusnelda Lang-Brumann claimed, 'It's no game, no hobby and no pleasure being a delegate.'[153] Thomas Mergel has noted how women's entry into parliament impacted on Germany's political culture, and although parliamentarians effected the art of pragmatic compromise, abiding by procedural rules and realising the need to work together, the political in-fighting and manoeuvring for position, the 'cage' of party discipline, the often malicious, polemic speeches and the back-biting ripostes remained features of parliamentary life.[154] After 1930 the Nazis and Communists did not adhere to parliamentary procedural etiquette, and female parliamentarians faced verbal abuse and even physical violence.[155] Outside parliament, Toni Sender remembered the verbal abuse she suffered at election meetings from both Nazis and Communists in the early 1930s and the Nazi violence against her, from slashing her car tyres to throwing stones through her apartment windows.[156] In addition, the walk-out of NSDAP and DNVP Reichstag delegates in February 1931 and the increasing use of presidential decrees signalled the death throes of parliamentary democracy. Heinsohn has claimed that the diminution of the influence of the Reichstag and the use of presidential decrees to effect the Reichstag's business after 1930 led to a return to the pre-war system of political notables, from which women were excluded.[157]

Scheck has noted some female politicians' disillusionment with political life, from which they withdrew.[158] In early 1932 the DVP's women's newsletter was acknowledging that women were seeing much, if not all, that they had created as politically independent citizens falling apart.[159] Within the DStP, the heir to the self-proclaimed 'Women's Party' in 1919, Marie-Elisabeth Lüders wrote that 'in scarcely any party have women been so unscrupulously deceived and disappointed as in the German State Party in which every democratic principle is ignored', referring to the 'rape of female passive suffrage'.[160] Paula-Mueller Otfried, 'the fearless fighter for Protestant Christian ideology' who had represented the DNVP in the Reichstag from 1920, was obliged to give up her mandate in September 1932 because she did not fit in with Hugenberg's remodelled DNVP, and her colleagues in the DEF were forced to face the inescapable truth that women's influence in public life was becoming ever smaller.[161] Gertrud Bäumer, who had served in the national parliament since 1919, did not stand for re-election in 1932, and with parliamentary debate frequently disintegrating into violence, the only woman to speak in the Reichstag after the July 1932 election was Clara Zetkin, who, as the oldest member, opened the session on 30 August 1932.[162]

Christiane Streubel has investigated the speeches of the female delegates who served in the National Assembly and the Reichstag for the DNVP. It was customary for the parties to nominate speakers, but Margarete Behm, a well-respected, quick-witted parliamentarian who was capable of a speedy, amusing riposte, nominated herself on the list of speakers.[163] She was one of several highly regarded women in parliament, but others were, in Adele Schreiber-Krieger's words, 'nobodies'.[164] Women spoke 820 times on the floor of the national parliament, many of these speeches being made in the National Assembly, and some of the 111 women who served between 1919 and 1933 never gave a speech.[165] Women parliamentarians, many initially lacking confidence, concentrated their efforts on working in the parliamentary sub-committees.[166] Throughout the Republic the most women were to be found on the population policy sub-committee, which was headed in the National Assembly by the DNVP's Anna von Gierke, then in the first Reichstag by Adele Schreiber (SPD) and following the December 1924 election by Paula Mueller-Otfried (DNVP).[167] By 1931 forty-nine of the 616 members of twenty-two sub-committees were women (8 per cent), with eleven sitting on the population policy sub-committee and eight on the education sub-committee, though by this time productive work within the sub-committees was limited.[168] These sub-committees dealt with those areas in which women had experience and expertise. Not all women devoted their energies to the social policy sphere; Toni Sender became an expert on trade and sat on both the trade and foreign policy sub-committees at various times throughout the Republic.[169] Few women, such as Marie-Elisabeth Lüders and Luise Zietz, expressed concern that in limiting their interests to the social policy sphere women were concentrating their efforts in areas at the margins of power politics. Some historians claim that male politicians were happy to support women's concentration on areas of social policy (welfare and education) because not only did they not have confidence in women's ability to act in other areas, but also they were thereby able to maintain a stranglehold on real political power and influence.[170] Thusnelda Lang-Brumann noted that women were never allowed near 'high politics'.[171] During the Weimar Republic no woman held a cabinet post and none sat in the upper house, the Reichsrat. Elsewhere in Europe, Olga Rudel-Zeynek was the president of the Austrian upper house from 1927 until 1930 and from 1932 to 1934, and Nina Bang became the Danish Education Minister in 1924, while in Britain Margaret Bondfield became Labour Minister in 1929.[172]

In the early 1930s some contemporary observers expressed the belief that women had had little influence on Germany's political life. Both Bäumer and Sender disagreed, and as Janet Walmsley states, 'the role of women in creating socio-political legislation in the first ten years of the Republic was indispensable'.[173] The Reich Youth Welfare Law of 1922, the Law Combating Venereal Diseases of 1927 and the Law Concerning the Employment of Women before and after Childbirth of 1927 were all, according to Sender, due 'to the intelligent and assiduous work of women Reichstag members'.[174] One law to improve the working conditions of homeworkers, the Homework Law of 7 April 1922, was nicknamed 'Lex Behm' after Margarete Behm, who had been the driving force behind it.[175] Although the women of the Reichstag collaborated on legislation which improved women's lives without challenging patriarchal society, they had entered parliament as representatives of their party, not of women, and ideological differences held sway in their responses to proposed legislation relating to divorce reform, abortion, the status of illegitimate children, the Reich School Law and the Law to Protect Young People from Trashy and Smutty Literature in 1926, the last of which was supported by women from the DNVP, the DVP, the Centre Party and Gertrud Bäumer, while other DDP, SPD and KPD women voted against.[176] Women were reluctant to break party discipline, though in July 1919 two Centre Party delegates, Helene Weber and Marie Schmitz, voted against the law accepting the terms of the Treaty of Versailles, contrary to the party line, and in 1921 Paula Mueller-Otfried and Margarete Behm supported a KPD petition to permit women to serve on juries, much to their party's displeasure.[177] In the early years women would meet to discuss issues of interest to them all, but meetings of all women delegates became rarer as the parties' disapproval was felt. Marie Schmitz (Z), who served in the National Assembly, later expressed her disappointment that women had not worked more together.[178] The first joint petition of all the women in the National Assembly on 1 March 1919 called for the lifting of the Allied blockade and the return of German prisoners of war and was supported by their parties.[179] Within the National Assembly women fought against accepting the Treaty of Versailles for as long as possible; within the SPD, women believed that the Treaty carried the seeds of new wars, while non-socialist women were motivated more by nationalist concerns.[180] Women in the National Assembly voiced the nation's concern about the repercussions of Germany's defeat both within parliament and outside it, and it was to be outside the legislative arena that women were to be most active in their campaigns against the Treaty of Versailles, through existing and newly created organisations. These organisations initially included Social Democratic women, but as the foreign policy of the Republic developed they were to become the domain of nationalist women. Working-class women's activism centred on issues of welfare and population policy and was facilitated by the existing left-wing organisations, with links to the SPD and KPD.

Women's extra-parliamentary political activism

When the details of the Treaty of Versailles became known on 7 May 1919, the BdF and DEF issued a joint declaration stating that a peace that strangled the future of Germany's children, that ripped territory from the Fatherland and placed it under foreign rule and that ran contrary to the basic principles in Wilson's Fourteen Points was unacceptable; in full awareness of the consequences, they would support the government if it refused to sign the Treaty.[181] Women's organisations quickly arranged mass protest meetings, and protests were subsequently held following every dispute arising from the Allies' attempts to implement the Treaty, such as the demand to hand over suspected war criminals in February 1920 or to give 810,000 milk cows to France in October 1920.[182] Süchting-Hänger believes that those against the Treaty were aware not only that women could be more open in their criticism without fear of retribution but also that their 'honest outrage' could influence public opinion abroad.[183] This can be seen clearly in the campaigns against the 'black shame', France's deployment of colonial troops in the occupied Rhineland, in which women parliamentarians from all parties except the USPD and the KPD participated, both inside and outside parliament. The VEFD had protested about this deployment to women's organisations in Sweden, Norway, Denmark, Holland and Switzerland as early as December 1918, and the campaign came to a head in 1920.[184] In June 1920 the Reich Interior Ministry set up the League of Rhenish Women (Rhenische Frauenliga), headed by Margarete Gärtner, to co-ordinate protests against the 'black shame'. By April 1921 it had held thirty-four protest meetings across Germany, with speakers including Marie-Elisabeth Lüders and Helene Weber, and over thirty women's organisations including the BdF, the DEF, the KFB and the League of Jewish Women had become affiliated to it. In October 1920 a petition, signed by seventy-one women's organisations, including the *Reichsfrauenausschüsse* of the DNVP, DVP and DDP, the KFB, DEF, BdF, BfM and Jewish Women's League as well as organisations in Sweden, Holland and Austria, was presented to the League of Nations. The petition detailed claims of sexual assaults by colonial troops on German women and boys, and protested against German towns being forced by the French to set up brothels, staffed by German women, to 'offer white flesh to black beasts'.[185] The depiction of defenceless German women being defiled by primitive, sexually debauched colonial troops symbolised the humiliation of a disarmed, defenceless Germany, a highly civilised and cultured white race at the mercy of black savages.[186] The 'black shame campaign' was contentious and it had lost its vigour by 1922. The pacifist Lilli Jannasch believed it was both racialist and sexist, and she drew comparisons with German soldiers' behaviour and the creation of brothels for German troops during the First World War.[187] Hedwig Dransfeld, however, was more concerned about the way in which the campaign impugned the moral integrity of the women of the Rhineland.[188]

Women in the bourgeois parties and organisations concerned themselves with the fate and well-being of Germans in the occupied territories and in those lost under the Treaty of Versailles, and with the refugees from these areas. They raised funds for charitable purposes and organised children's holiday exchanges as well as trips to the 'bleeding borders'.[189] Following the division of Upper Silesia after the plebiscite in March 1921, the BdF, KFB, DEF, VEFD and Jewish Women's League and the *Reichsfrauenausschüsse* of the DNVP, DVP and DDP called upon German women to donate money, clothes and food to lessen the suffering of their Upper Silesian sisters.[190] Käthe Schirmacher, a DNVP delegate to the National Assembly and member of the Ring of National Women (Ring Nationaler Frauen, RNF; see below), proclaimed emotively, 'Upper Silesia is burning' and asked, 'What is happening daily in Upper Silesia? The most bare-faced robbery of German life and property, the destruction of the German presence and German work. The Pole robs and murders, the Frenchman lets it happen or helps.'[191] Women's organisations also protested strenuously against the occupation of the Ruhr by French and Belgian troops in January 1923, with some calling for a boycott of French and Belgian goods, and at the end of the occupation they demanded the release of those imprisoned and the speedy return of those who had been expelled.[192]

A German Women's Committee to Combat the War Guilt Lie (Deutscher Frauenausschuss zur Bekämpfung der Kriegsschuldlüge, DFBK), supported by the German Foreign Ministry, was founded in November 1921, and its preparatory committee included Gertrud Bäumer (DDP and BdF), Hedwig Dransfeld (Z and KFB), Paula Mueller-Otfried (DNVP and DEF) and Clara Mende (DVP and RNF), the last of whom went on to chair the committee until its dissolution in October 1933.[193] While some women, such as Gertrud Bäumer and Helene Lange, believed that Germany was not solely responsible for the outbreak of the war, others believed Germany to be totally innocent. In 1925 the BdF left the DFKB after the BdF had adopted a more conciliatory stance to Germany's former enemies in the wake of Foreign Minister Stresemann's new policy of reconciliation, which created tensions and differences of opinion between DVP and DNVP women. These tensions came to a head in 1929 with disagreements over the support for the demand for a referendum on the Young Plan, and several staunchly nationalist groups left the DFKB to set up the National Women's Committee to Combat Versailles.[194] Süchting-Hänger believes that the initial consensus of bourgeois women's organisations against the Treaty of Versailles broke down, so that by 1929 the campaign had become the domain of increasingly radical right-wing women, who used it as a cipher for their real aim of destroying the Republic.[195]

Women's new nationalist organisations

When the DEF left the BdF in March 1918 its leader, Paula Mueller-Otfried, bemoaned the lack of a Conservative women's organisation of the stature of the BdF. The Weimar Republic was, however, to witness the birth of several right-wing women's organisations, and DNVP women were to be instrumental in their development. The first to be set up was the RNF on 30 April 1920, by, among others, the DNVP women Ilse Hamel and Beda Prilipp, both journalists, and its main goal was to strengthen German *Volkstum*.[196] The creation of the RNF is indicative of the concern that Conservative women had about the BdF's influence on the women in its member organisations, which included professional, charitable and housewives' associations, and on young women, and about the way it was perceived as the representative of German women vis-à-vis the government and women's organisations overseas because Conservative women also believed it was the 'shock troops of the DDP'. The RNF was essentially a nationalist-*völkisch* umbrella organisation which worked through its six committees, though its major influence came through its twice-monthly magazine *Die deutsche Frau (The German Woman)*, which was a mouthpiece for eighteen right-wing women's groups and had a circulation of 10,000.[197]

The most successful right-wing women's organisation created during the Weimar Republic was the Queen Luise League (Bund Königin Luise, BKL), named after the Prussian queen who was revered as a wife and mother who had resisted Napoleon's occupation.[198] By 1933 the BKL had a reported total of 200,000 members.[199] Its foundation in Halle on 3 May 1923 is portrayed as either an attempt by six women, led by Else Sennewald, who was to be its deputy leader throughout its existence, 'to fight, suffer and conquer' shoulder-to-shoulder with German men in the wake of the Ruhr invasion, or as a sister organisation to the veterans' league, the Stahlhelm, which is how it was perceived by the authorities and the press throughout the Republic.[200] The BKL united all German women under purely national perspectives, exclusive of party politics, and its aims included the education of the female sex to help in the great work of freeing Germany from enemies at home and abroad.[201] Jews were not allowed to join. The BKL spread gradually throughout northern and eastern Germany, creating its own Sunday paper in April 1927; this had a circulation of 14,000 by 1931.[202] Later that year the Berlin Stahlhelm set up its own women's group, though elsewhere the link between the BKL and the Stahlhelm appears to have remained strong, with Stahlhelm leaders speaking and Stahlhelm bands playing at BKL gatherings, and the Stahlhelm providing first-aid courses for BKL members.[203] In 1929 some DVP women severed their links with the BKL over its support for the referendum on the Young Plan, and the BKL began to penetrate further into southern Germany, where it was, in places, shunned as a 'Prussian creation'.[204] Although it was supposed to appeal to women of all classes and to cultivate 'faith, hope and love', it was primarily attractive to the lower middle class, though in the early years many of its leaders came from the nobility or were married to officers in the Stahlhelm.²⁰⁵ Eva Schöck-Quinteros refers to the BKL's 'crude mixture of militarism and religiosity'.²⁰⁶ During their annual gatherings, often attended by their patron, Crown Princess Cecilie, BKL women would usually attend a church service, where their new pennants were consecrated.²⁰⁷ On 1 April 1932 Charlotte von Hadeln, leader of the DNVP women's group and the Protestant Women's Aid in Cottbus, became BKL leader; at her first meeting of national representatives she called for them to join in the fight against the 'war guilt lie' (the repudiation of Article of 231 of the Versailles Treaty which laid the blame for starting the war on Germany), for Germany's release from paying reparations and for the regaining of Germany's military strength.²⁰⁸ The BKL's links to the NSDAP appear to have varied from place to place. Reports from Neulussheim in Baden in 1926 reveal that its BKL members frequently attended Nazi meetings.²⁰⁹ In March 1932 the leader of the Silesian branch of the BKL, Freifrau von Buddenbrock, advised her members to vote for 'the only candidate on the right', and Crown Princess Cecilie made known her support for Hitler in the second round of the presidential elections.²¹⁰ Heinsohn claims that as early as May 1932 BKL leaders had placed their organisation unconditionally under Hitler's authority.²¹¹

The leader of the third right-wing women's organisation to be created during the Weimar Republic, Guida Diehl, transferred her allegiance from the DNVP to the NSDAP in 1930. During the war she had set up her New Land Movement (Neulandbewegung, NLB), a community of like-minded, educated young women whose aim was to create a new country of justice, purity, truth and love and to help in Germany's rebirth. Based in Eisenach, it had a reported total of 20,000 members in 1920, but Süchting-Hänger notes that as the organisation became more involved in politics, its membership fell.²¹² In October 1926 Diehl founded the German Women's Fighting League (Deutscher Frauenkampfbund, DFK) to combat degeneracy and to maintain German Christian womanhood. It was a loose federation which claimed to have some thirty-nine member organisations with a membership of 183,000 by 1928.²¹³ The DFK, like the RNF and BKL, was a member of the Reich committee calling for a referendum on the Young Plan, consolidating what Liz Harvey calls 'a bloc of national opposition against the Republic'.²¹⁴

Diehl's NLB adherents were young, Protestant, predominantly middle-class and from rural areas, typical of the kind of women whom the mainstream parties and the bourgeois women's movement had tried, and failed, to win. Only Catholic youth groups continued to attract female members in respectable numbers.[215] Liz Harvey notes the preference of young Protestant women for the co-educational youth movement, rather than the women's movement.[216] Those young women who did join the women's movement criticised its bureaucracy and the lack of any forum for debate. Most were indifferent to any women's rights agenda, perceiving feminism as anti-men and a product of discredited liberal democracy.[217] Contemporaries lamented young women's indifference to public affairs and their lack of appreciation of the rights the women's movement had fought for.[218] However, Liz Harvey notes the increasing awareness among young women in Protestant youth leagues of the social misery caused by the Depression from 1930 and of Germany's enslavement through the Treaty of Versailles, leading some to espouse Nazism.[219]

German women and the international scene

Young women's awareness of Germany's military situation might well have been raised by the campaign, initiated by the German Foreign Office and orchestrated by a range of women's groups with international links, to gather signatures for petitions to be placed before the Disarmament Conference which was due to begin in Geneva in February 1932.[220] German women's groups could not agree on a joint petition; the BdF, KFB and VEFD and a collection of sixteen nationalist women's organisations each submitted different petitions, and the German branch of the International Women's League for Peace and Freedom (Internationale Frauenliga für Frieden und Freiheit, IFFF) supported its parent organisation's petition. While the BdF and the KFB called for a general, equal disarmament of nations, the VEFD also demanded equality for Germany in all military matters. The nationalist women's groups, which included the *Reichsfrauenausschuss* of the DNVP, the RNF and the BKL, demanded Germany's right to military sovereignty, in keeping with her status as a nation.[221]

The IFFF was instrumental in attracting women's signatures for the petitions to the Disarmament Conference from around the world.

Its German branch was created in June 1919 out of the Women's Committee for a Lasting Peace. Its leaders, the Munich-based women Anita Augspurg and Lida Gustava Heymann, published the monthly magazine *Die Frau im Staat* (*Woman in the State*) from 1919 to 1933 to promote feminism, understanding between nations and a lasting peace.[222] Lifelong pacifists, Augspurg and Heymann were involved in the World Congress against War in Amsterdam in August 1932, alongside women from the KPD.[223] In December 1918 they had protested against the 'inhuman ceasefire conditions that seriously threaten our people's existence' and expressed 'a belief in justice and reconciliation among nations'.[224] They were among the first women at the war's end to pick up links with sister organisations abroad. The IFFF collected money for the reconstruction of Arras in northern France, and it also received money from its French sister organisation to alleviate German children's suffering, but some German women's organisations refused to accept it.[225] It called for world disarmament with the motto 'No more war', and its demand in 1920 for the Bavarian Education Ministry to revise all its schoolbooks to remove all chauvinist, militaristic and inflammatory passages earned the scorn of the DEF.[226] By 1928 the IFFF had representatives in eighty German towns, with members coming from the middle class and intellectual circles, and before the 1930 Reichstag election its eclectic demands included changing the Defence Ministry into a Peace Ministry, the lifting of the death penalty, the banning of carrying weapons and their production and sales, bringing the Civil Code into line with the Constitution, the end of protectionist trade measures, and guarantees against the misuse of Article 48 of the Constitution to implement legislation in breach of the Constitution. It held conferences throughout the Republic, which in 1929 and 1931 explored modern methods of warfare and the protection of the civilian population. However, the State Secretary in the Reich Chancellery claimed in 1931 that the IFFF had found little resonance within Germany.[227]

For years the Protestant and nationalist women's organisations had refuted the BdF's right to represent the voice of German women at home and abroad. In 1920 the BdF declined an offer to attend the conference of the International Council of Women (ICW) in Oslo, in part out of fear of the propaganda that German nationalist and conservative women would make out of its attendance, as they were always accusing the BdF of internationalism and pacifism.[228]

With government approval and financial support several women attended the conference of the International Women's Suffrage Alliance (IWSA), an organisation founded in 1904 by women who supported female suffrage, in Rome in 1923, with Gertrud Bäumer as the official German delegate. Clara Mende protested about the lack of representation from women of the right, and Dr Marx (Z) complained at the lack of a Catholic woman's voice.[229] When the IWSA's 1929 conference in Berlin coincided with the tenth anniversary of the signing of the Versailles Treaty, the DFBK organised a counter-demonstration, attended by 4,000, and Beda Prilipp accused the conference participants of degrading and besmirching the German people's unparalleled sacrifice in the war; she hoped that the demonstration had made them aware of another Germany, one that did not espouse international reconciliation.[230] German women attended the ICW's conferences in Washington in 1925 and Vienna in 1930, at the second of which Bäumer spoke on 'Women and the reconciliation of nations'. Clara Mende, while acknowledging Bäumer's and Alice Salomon's contribution to the conference, bemoaned the lack of German women in key posts in the international women's movement and the passivity of the German women's movement in its dealings with the international movement.[231] Gertrud Bäumer was held in high regard abroad; she had been the German delegate to the section of the League of Nations exploring social questions in 1926, when Germany first entered the League, and she was canvassed to stand for election as chair of the ICW in 1929, replacing Lady Aberdeen, and as the chair of the League of Nation's social questions section in 1930, replacing Dame Rachel Crowdy.[232] In Germany, however, she was vilified by the nationalist women's organisations over her reflections on a visit to Verdun in May 1927 in which she expressed her thoughts that the huge sacrifices made in the war, by both French and Germans, had been in vain and her doubts about the purpose of war in general. Bertha Hindenberg-Delbrück, a DNVP member and leader of the Housewives' Association in Hamburg, accused Bäumer of the lack a 'German heart' and, in her inference that the huge sacrifice of German soldiers had been in vain, of insulting those German women whose loved ones had died. Hindenberg-Delbrück's reaction was indicative of the sensitivities and the difficulties that many German women had in coming to terms with the war and its legacy and of the lack of any consensus on how the war was to be remembered, while Bäumer's espousal of reconciliation and international understanding reflected the changing attitudes of many democratic women towards Germany's relationship with its former enemies.[233]

Conclusion

'The great day of January 19, 1919, signified a world turning point for German women. Consciously or unconsciously we all felt that', wrote Marie Stritt after the elections to the National Assembly.[234] The mood was one of hope and optimism: 'the women of Germany are not entering political life to accept it as they find it, but are determined to create a new atmosphere'.[235] Women's aspirations may have been idealistic, and Thomas Mergel has noted German citizens' unrealistically high expectations of politicians and the political system at the beginning of the Republic.[236] Women ultimately failed to create a new atmosphere. Men held firmly onto the reins of political power within the political parties, the legislatures and the government, and a gender-specific division of roles, responsibilities and areas of interests became the norm within the elected assemblies and the political parties. This division reflected the notions of gender difference prevalent in the bourgeois women's movement in the late nineteenth century, which stressed women's distinctive qualities and the contribution they could make to the public sphere in the realms of maternal and social welfare.[237] By 1932 not only Germany's financial situation but also the mindset of all sections of society did not permit these areas to be regarded as priorities, though there had been some significant advances in the 1920s.[238] The increasing masculinisation of politics from 1928, which manifested itself in political violence and the militarisation of political culture, seen clearly in the NSDAP and the KPD, also marginalised women, and they were not immune to the violence.[239]

Already in 1919 Marie Stritt had noted that the parties had placed women on their election lists 'more from necessity than choice', and as the political system became increasingly mired in interest-group politics and fragmentation, women lacked a powerful lobby to ensure that their respective parties placed them in assured positions on the election lists. Women were dependent on the goodwill of their male colleagues for their active participation in political decision-making bodies, and some parties, in particular those on the left and the early DDP, appear to have been committed to allowing women to represent them, but the SPD's and DDP's losses at the polls impacted on the number of women elected, especially in the case of the DDP.[240] However, female participation was not evident in all legislative bodies, particularly in small rural communities, but also in some state legislatures, where women were concentrated in only a few. Even at the level of national politics, female delegates were elected from a small number of electoral districts.

Female suffrage benefited political parties that espoused religious values, in particular the Catholic Centre Party. Stephenson believes that 'Hitler's electoral chances would have been even better without female suffrage', and the results of the 1932 presidential election would confirm this to be the case.[241] It is clear that it was men's votes that brought the NSDAP to prominence. However, by 1932 primarily Protestant women of all classes who were not ideologically bound to another party were voting in similar proportions to men for the NSDAP, which had become the major party within the bourgeois-Protestant bloc. The female electorate did not appear to share bourgeois women's concern about the loss of bourgeois women's influence in the legislature or Nazi anti-feminism; these matters had been stressed by other parties in both their written propaganda and specially convened meetings, which, along with the campaigns of the BdF and KFB, brought the issue of women's rights into the political arena in the early 1930s for the first time since 1919.[242] Female voters shared the concerns of male voters about the economy, unemployment, Germany's foreign policy and corruption in local government.[243]

The SPD, the Centre Party, the Catholic organisations and the early DDP invested in the parliamentary democracy of the Republic. While the SPD mobilised working-class women in defence of the democratic Republic through the Iron Front, nationalist women's organisations rallied opposition to the Republic and called for a return to a strong Germany and an authoritarian empire under a strong leader, and were willing to use the mechanics of democracy to destroy it. They always intended to play a role in this new Germany, but had failed to grasp, in the pacifist Auguste Kirchhoff's words, that the main task of *völkisch* women was to be productive wombs of the Third Reich.[244] Others have, however, noted how politically reliable Aryan women did become people's comrades (*Volksgenossinnen*) in the Third Reich. These women acted as part of a 'women's community of action', combining the properties of both mother and fighter, particularly during the war, when there were 3.5 million female neighbourhood volunteers and millions more women in the civilian air defence organisation.[245] Adolf Hitler's assumption of the chancellorship on 30 January 1933 signalled the end of female passive suffrage in Germany. Within months all political parties other than the NSDAP were banned; this removed any possibility of women being elected onto political decision-making bodies, whose influence dwindled in any case. Women who had been politically active during the Weimar Republic, particularly for left-wing parties, were often subject to arrest and detention as the Nazis moved against their political enemies. Marcelline Hutton claims that approximately 3,000 female political prisoners were detained between 1933 and 1939.[246] Some women, like Toni Sender and Marie Juchacz, went into exile, where some continued their struggle against the Nazis, while others, like their colleague Toni Pfülf, committed suicide.[247] While some withdrew from political activism, others joined opposition and resistance movements. The Nazis also destroyed the bourgeois women's movement and the pacifist movement.[248] In the Third Reich, approved women's participation in the political sphere was to take place under the auspices of the Nazi women's organisations, and Sybille Steinbacher has emphasised the previously unknown opportunities for participation and advancement in public life which these gave to politically reliable Aryan women.[249] Women remained, however, far removed from the real nexus of power in the party and in the state.

Notes

1 M. Stritt, 'German Women have Got the Vote', *Jus suffragii*, 13:4 (January 1919), 44.
2 It was anchored in the law of 30 November 1918 relating to the elections for the National Assembly: *Reichsgesetzblatt 1918*, no. 153 (12 November 1918), 1304, and no. 167 (30 November 1918), 1353–8. The age at which women could be elected to legislative bodies was raised to twenty-five in the electoral reform prior to the first Reichstag election: *Reichsgesetzblatt 1920*, no. 87 (27 April 1920), 627–35.
3 *Die Gleichheit*, 29:5 (6 December 1918), 33. Prior to 15 May 1908 women had complete freedom of association in Baden, Württemberg, Hamburg and Bremen: Evans, *The Feminist Movement*, pp. 72–3.

4 H.-J. Arendt, J. Kirchner, J. Müller, E. Schotte and F. Staude (eds), *Dokumente der revolutionären deutschen Frauenbewegung zur Frauenfrage, 1848–1974* (Leipzig: Verlag für die Frau, 1975), pp. 32–4; Stritt, 'German Women have Got the Vote', p. 44; C. Jellinek, 'Die Frau im neuen Deutschland', *Die Frauenfrage*, 22:4 (16 December 1920), 188. See also K. Canning, 'Sexual Crisis and the Writing of Citizenship: Reflections on States of Exception in Germany, 1914–1920', in A. Lüdtke and M. Wildt (eds), *Ausnahmezustand und Polizeigewalt* (Göttingen: Wallstein Verlag, 2008), pp. 201–2. For the middle-class suffrage campaign see Evans, *The Feminist Movement*, pp. 71–113, and A. Hackett, 'The German Women's Movement and Suffrage, 1890–1914: A Study of National Feminism', in R. J. Bezucha (ed.), *Modern European Social History* (London: D. C. Heath & Co., 1972), pp. 356–86.

5 R. Bridenthal and C. Koonz, 'Beyond *Kinder, Küche, Kirche*: Weimar Women in Politics and Work', in B. A. Carroll (ed.), *Liberating Women's History* (Chicago: University of Illinois Press, 1976), p. 320.

6 The petition to the National Assembly came from two anonymous women: Heinsohn, *Konservative Parteien*, pp. 63–4. Planert identifies the initiator of the petition as Emma Witte, an executive member of the League for the Prevention of the Emancipation of Women: U. Planert, 'Mutter und Volk', in Schöck-Quinteros and Streubel (eds), *Ihrem Volk verantwortlich*, p. 124.

7 R. J. Evans, 'German Women and the Triumph of Hitler', *Journal of Modern History*, 48:1 (1976), on-demand supplement, pp. 1, 35; cf. Evans, *Comrades and Sisters*, pp. 157–95.

8 A. Salomon, 'Women's Hopes for the New Order', *Jus suffragii*, 13:5 (February 1919), 62.

9 B. Ziemann, 'Germany 1914–1918: Total War as a Catalyst of Change', in H. W. Smith (ed.), *The Oxford Handbook of Modern German History* (Oxford: Oxford University Press, 2011), p. 387.

10 H. Grebing, *Frauen in der deutschen Revolution 1918/19* (Heidelberg: Stiftung Reichspräsident-Friedrich-Ebert-Gedenkstätte, 1994), p. 6; P. Fritzsche, *Germans into Nazis* (Cambridge, MA: Harvard University Press, 1998), p. 86; Blücher, *An English Wife in Berlin*, pp. 280–1.

11 Blücher, *An English Wife in Berlin*, pp. 275, 287, 290.

12 Women were among the eight people killed and twenty-nine wounded in demonstrations in Kiel on 3 November 1918, and three women were killed in Berlin on 9 November 1918: H.-J. Arendt, 'Weibliche Opfer militaristischen Terrors in Deutschland (1918–1920)', *Beiträge zur Geschichte der Arbeiterbewegung*, 26:2 (1984), 229. On the different paths the revolution took across Germany see Stibbe, *Germany 1914–1933*, pp. 55–6.

13 J. P. Nettl, *Rosa Luxemburg* (Oxford: Oxford University Press, 1966), pp. 486–94.
14 For the development of Zetkin's ideas see Evans, *Comrades and Sisters*, pp. 15–36.
15 Quataert, 'The German Socialist Women's Movement', pp. 349–64.
16 Seven of nine female USPD Reichstag delegates opposed acceptance: R. F. Wheeler, 'German Women and the Communist International: The Case of the Independent Social Democrats', *Central European History*, 8:2 (1975), 136–7. Arendt quotes a figure of 7.5 per cent for female KPD membership in the autumn of 1920: Arendt, 'Weibliche Mitglieder der KPD', pp. 652–4.
17 Quoted in C. Weill, 'Women in the German Revolution: Rosa Luxemburg and the Workers' Councils', in C. Fauré (ed.), *Political and Historical Encyclopaedia of Women* (London: Fitzroy Dearborn, 2003), p. 413.
18 Forschungsgemeinschaft 'Geschichte des Kampfes der Arbeiterklasse um die Befreiung der Frau' (ed.), *Die Frau und die Gesellschaft* (Leipzig: Verlag für die Frau, 1974), p. 68; Grebing, *Frauen in der deutschen Revolution*, p. 6.
19 Grebing, *Frauen in der deutschen Revolution*, p. 11.
20 C. Sternsdorf-Hauck, *Brotmarken und rote Fahnen: Frauen in der bayerischen Revolution und Räterepublik 1918/19* (Cologne: Neuer ISP Verlag, 2008), p. 47.
21 *Ibid.*, pp. 50–5; G. Bölke, *Die Wandlung der Frauenemanzipationsbewegung von Marx bis zur Rätebewegung* (Hamburg: Verlag Association, 1975), p. 57.
22 Heymann and Augspurg also served among eight women as delegates to the Bavarian Congress of Workers', Peasants' and Soldiers' Councils in early spring 1919: Sternsdorf-Hauck, *Brotmarken und rote Fahnen*, pp. 26, 48.
23 Grebing, *Frauen in der deutschen Revolution*, p. 12.
24 Grebing refers to Fasshauer as Germany's first female minister: *ibid.*, p. 12; Sender, *Autobiography*, p. 103.
25 Stritt, 'German Women have Got the Vote', p. 47.
26 'Reichswahlgesetz vom 27. April 1920', *Reichsgesetzblatt 1920*, no. 87 (28 April 1920), 627–35. A different system had been used in the elections to the National Assembly, with initially thirty-eight states being allocated a given number of seats per 150,000 of population: 'Reichswahlgesetz vom 30. November 1918', *Reichsgesetzblatt 1918*, no. 167 (30 November 1918), 1345–52.
27 The committee was joined by representatives from most women's groups, with the exception of the KFB and the socialists: A. Salomon, 'Der Ausschuss zur Vorbereitung der Frauen für die Nationalversammlung', *Die Frauenfrage*, 21:1 (January 1919), 1.

For the attempts to educate Hamburg's women see K. Hagemann and J. Kolossa, *Gleiche Rechte – gleiche Pflichten?* (Hamburg, VSA-Verlag, 1990), pp. 60–1.
28 C. G. Woodfin, 'Reluctant Democrats: The Protestant Women's Auxiliary and the German National Assembly Election of 1919', *Journal of the Historical Society*, 4:1 (2004), 91–2.
29 This collaboration built upon the agreement in June 1918 between the DEF and KFB to work together in areas of common interest: ADEF, O9a; *Die christliche Frau*, 16:5–6 (May–June 1918), 104. Principles of the agreement of December found in ADEF, G2dn, and AKDFB, 1-17-4.
30 Leaflets found in LAB, HLA, Film 52-239[6], and AKDFB, 1-17-4. One of the committee's leaflets detailing the voting system was adopted by the German Democratic Party (Deutsche Demokratische Partei, DDP), with the final section being changed to encourage women to vote for it.
31 LAB, FRep 240/1024, 'Für den Wahltag'; Sneeringer, *Winning Women's Votes*, p. 29.
32 Sneeringer, *Winning Women's Votes*, pp. 23, 67.
33 I. K. Rigby, 'German Expressionist Political Posters 1918–1919 – Art and Politics: A Failed Alliance', *Art Journal*, 44:1 (1984), 33–9. Election posters had been banned in Prussia and some other states before 1918. As well as on hoardings and advertising columns, posters were displayed on election lorries and by men with sandwich boards: G. Paul, *Aufstand der Bilder: Die NS-Propaganda vor 1933* (Bonn: Dietz, 1990), pp. 96, 151; D. Janusch, *Die plakative Propaganda der Sozialdemokratischen Partei Deutschlands zu den Reichstagswahlen 1928 bis 1932* (Bochum: Brockmeyer, 1989), pp. 57–67.
34 Grebing, *Frauen in der deutschen Revolution*, p. 6.
35 *Ibid.*, pp. 5, 14; AKDFB, 1-17-4, Dransfeld's letter to Erzberger of 11 January 1919.
36 BAB, R8005/485, Bl. 87, letter of DNVP head office to the Reich women's committee of 21 December 1918; BAK, Z.Sg.I.44/8, 'Wahlkampfrichtlinien für Frauen'; K. Hagemann, '"Equal but not the same": The Social Democratic Women's Movement in the Weimar Republic', in Fletcher (ed.), *Bernstein to Brandt*, p. 139; A. Grossmann, 'German Communism and New Women: Dilemmas and Contradictions', in H. Gruber and P. Graves (eds), *Women and Socialism: Socialism and Women* (Oxford: Berghahn, 1998), p. 152; Sender, *Autobiography*, pp. 112–14.
37 K. Hagemann, 'Men's Demonstrations and Women's Protest: Gender in Collective Action in the Urban Working-Class Milieu in the Weimar Republic', *Gender and History*, 5 (1993), 103, 105, 107–9.

38 Hagemann, *Frauenalltag und Männerpolitik*, p.539; K. Lacey, 'From Plauderei to Propaganda: On Women's Radio in Germany, 1924–1935', *Media, Culture and Society*, 16 (1994), 591. The Brüning cabinet permitted party propaganda on the radio for the July 1932 election: Paul, *Aufstand der Bilder*, p.196.
39 Hagemann, 'Men's Demonstrations', p.107. Working-class women's public spaces were courtyards, markets and shops. In 1925 74.5 per cent of women of voting age were or had been married: *StJhb 1932*, pp.12–13.
40 A. von Saldern, 'Modernization as Challenge: Perceptions and Reactions of German Social Democratic Women', in Gruber and Graves (eds), *Women and Socialism*, pp.99–100; BAK, R134/62, eighth circular of the KPD central committee of 13 April 1931.
41 Hagemann, *Frauenalltag und Männerpolitik*, p.563; Grossmann, 'German Communism', p.137.
42 T. Childers, 'The Social Language of Politics in Germany: The Sociology of Political Discourse in the Weimar Republic', *American Historical Review*, 95:2 (1990), 331–58.
43 Sneeringer, *Winning Women's Votes*, p.75.
44 *Ibid.*, p.231.
45 Scheck, *Mothers of the Nation*, pp.165–6.
46 A range of propaganda leaflets are to be found in LAB, FRep 240 Zeitgeschichtliche Sammlung, FRep 260 Plakatsammlung; and BAK, Z.Sg.I.42/7 and 42/8 (DVP); Z.Sg.I.108/7 and 108/ 9 (Z); Z.Sg.I.44/7, 44/8 and 44/9 (DNVP).
47 J. Sneeringer, '"Frauen an die Front!" The Language of "Kampf" in DNVP Women's Propaganda 1918–33', in Schöck-Quinteros and Streubel (eds), *Ihrem Volk verantwortlich*, pp.183, 190.
48 M. Munk, *Recht und Rechtsverfolgung im Familienrecht* (Berlin: Liebmann, 1929), p.64.
49 E. D. Weitz, 'The Heroic Man and the Ever-Changing Woman: Gender and Politics in European Communism, 1917–1950', in L. L. Frader and S. O. Rose (eds), *Gender and Class in Modern Europe* (Ithaca: Cornell University Press, 1996), p.315.
50 Election materials found in BAK, Z.Sg.I.90/38 (SPD), Z.Sg.I.91/7 (USPD) and Z.Sg.I.65/77, 'Frauen im Kampf um Brot und Freiheit'; *Die Kommunistin*, 3:6 (25 March 1921), 41–2. See also H. Boak, 'Mobilising Women for Hitler: The Female Nazi Voter', in A. McElligott and T. Kirk (eds), *Working towards the Führer* (Manchester: Manchester University Press, 2003), pp.71–2. The Iron Front was set up in December 1931 by the SPD, trade unions and other social democratic organisations to defend the Republic against the NSDAP: see D. Harsch, 'The Iron Front: Weimar Social Democracy between

Tradition and Modernity', in D. E. Barclay and E. D. Weitz (eds), *Between Reform and Revolution: German Socialism and Communism from 1840 to 1990* (Oxford: Berghahn, 1998), pp. 251–73.

51 Childers, 'The Social Language of Politics in Germany', 326; Sneeringer notes the DDP's 'new language of citizenship': Sneeringer, *Winning Women's Votes*, pp. 187, 271.
52 Sneeringer, *Winning Women's Votes*, pp. 16, 278.
53 *Ibid.*, pp. 223–4; Boak, '"Our last hope"', pp. 301–2.
54 Sneeringer, *Winning Women's Votes*, p. 161, has the 1928 poster.
55 LAB, BRep 235 HLA MF 1373, 'Arbeiterinnen! Angestellte! Mütter! Frauen!'; Boak, 'Mobilising Women', pp. 76, 80.
56 AKDFB, Collection 1-17-4, Dransfeld's letter to Erzberger of 11 January 1919. She had spoken to an audience of 4,000 women in Düsseldorf and 6,000 in Essen, but was concerned that the Spartakist terror might keep women from the polls.
57 A total of 12,421,167 men and 14,572,345 women voted. Separate voter turnout figures are missing from East Prussia, Schleswig-Holstein and Thuringia: J. Hofmann-Göttig, *Emanzipation mit dem Stimmzettel: 70 Jahre Frauenwahlrecht in Deutschland* (Bonn: Verlag Neue Gesellschaft, 1986), pp. 27–8. In Nuremberg, Cologne, Bremen and Hamburg the female turnout exceeded the male: Dr Hartwig, 'Wie die Frauen im Deutschen Reich von ihrem politischen Wahlrecht Gebrauch machen', *Allgemeines statistisches Archiv*, 17 (1928), 500–1.
58 Hartwig, 'Wie die Frauen im Deutschen Reich', pp. 502–3.
59 *Ibid.*, p. 500.
60 Bremme, *Die politische Rolle der Frau*, pp. 35–7.
61 Population figures calculated from *StJhb 1932*, p. 12.
62 Falter, too, believes that such was the diversity of the samples that the separate voting statistics are representative of the differences in male and female voting behaviour: Falter, *Hitlers Wähler*, pp. 139–40. In May 1924 6.9 per cent of the total votes cast were collated into men's and women's votes, in December 1924 6.2 per cent and in 1930 16.8 per cent: Hofmann-Göttig, *Emanzipation mit dem Stimmzettel*, p. 32. The statistics were collated centrally only until the 1930 Reichstag election and for the 1932 presidential elections. They tend to underrepresent the vote going to the Centre Party, BVP and DNVP: see H. Boak, 'National Socialism and Working-Class Women before 1933', in C. Fischer (ed.), *The Rise of National Socialism and the Working Classes in Weimar Germany* (Oxford: Berghahn, 1996), pp. 165–6.
63 Dr Hartwig, 'Das Frauenwahlrecht in der Statistik', *Allgemeines statistisches Archiv*, 21 (1931), 169–7; Hartwig, 'Wie die Frauen im Deutschen Reich', pp. 500–4.

64 Hartwig, 'Wie die Frauen im Deutschen Reich', p. 505; H. Tingsten, *Political Behaviour: Studies in Election Statistics* (London: P. S. King & Son, 1937), pp. 137–43; F. Barfels, 'Die Frau als Wählerin', *Die schaffende Frau*, 11 (1929–30), 359–61.

65 In Cologne 47.6 per cent of the female vote went to the Centre Party and 32.2 per cent to the SPD. For men these figures were 32.9 per cent and 46.1 per cent respectively: Hartwig, 'Wie die Frauen im Deutschen Reich', pp. 506–9.

66 The balance was maintained until 1933: J. Falter, 'The Social Bases of Political Cleavages in the Weimar Republic', in Jones and Retallack (eds), *Elections, Mass Politics, and Social Change*, p. 376. Tingsten claims that the socialist parties would have received 55 per cent of the vote if only men had voted: Tingsten, *Political Behaviour*, p. 47. The claim that female suffrage had cost the SPD an absolute majority surfaced soon after the elections: BAB, R901/55222, Bl. 31, report in the *Weser Zeitung* of 2 February 1919.

67 Hartwig, 'Wie die Frauen im Deutschen Reich', p. 507.

68 Thus, in the 1928 Reichstag election the Centre Party received 0.6 per cent of the male vote and 0.8 per cent of the female vote in Leipzig, but in the Baden village of Kirrlach (98.9 per cent Catholic) the figures were 54.9 per cent and 93.5 per cent respectively. However, in another village, Gengenbach (96.3 per cent Catholic), which was a centre for quarrying and housed paper and tobacco industries, the Centre Party polled 27.9 per cent of men's votes and 60.4 per cent of women's: calculated from figures in *SdR*, vol. 372, part 3, pp. 24, 33.

69 Thus the Centre Party's share of the female vote cast in Cologne fell from 47.6 per cent in 1919 to 30.9 per cent in March 1933, with the male vote falling from 32.9 per cent to 19.3 per cent: Tingsten, *Political Behaviour*, p. 57. In Regensburg the BVP's share of the female vote fell from 59.5 per cent in the 1919 Landtag election to 46.9 per cent in March 1933, and its share of the male vote from 42.3 per cent to 31.1 per cent: *Zeitschrift des bayerischen statistischen Landesamtes*, vol. 51 (1919), 876, and vol. 65 (1933), 327.

70 Tingsten, *Political Behaviour*, p. 47.

71 In staunchly Catholic areas the DNVP sometimes received a higher share of the male than of the female vote. Calculated from figures in *SdR*, vol. 372, part 3, p. 11, and vol. 382, part 3, p. 16. Had only women voted, the DVP/DNVP candidate for the Reich presidency in 1925, Karl Jarres, would have won outright in the first round: *SdR*, vol. 321, pp. 48–9.

72 See Boak, 'National Socialism and Working-Class Women', Tables 7.2, 7.3 and 7.4, pp. 169–71.

73 Sneeringer, *Winning Women's Votes*, p. 274; Peterson, 'The Politics

of Working-Class Women', p. 109. For the SPD's realisation of the significance of religion in women's voting choices see Boak, '"Our last hope"', p. 291. The SPD lost five million votes from 1919 to 1920, but had regained three million by 1928, before its vote declined steadily. It is more accurate to say that women's share of the SPD's votes rose.
74 H. Beyer, *Die Frau in der politischen Entscheidung* (Stuttgart: Enke, 1933), p. 66; Tingsten, *Political Behaviour*, p. 60.
75 The difference was largest in rural Catholic areas and smallest in industrial cities with a politicised working-class. Bremme has the KPD receiving a higher share of the female vote (17.7 per cent) than the male vote (13.5 per cent) in the Prussian Landtag election; the latter is clearly a misprint for 23.5: Bremme, *Die politische Rolle der Frau*, p. 249; Boak, 'National Socialism and Working-Class Women', pp. 172–5.
76 In the twenty-one areas in which men and women voted separately, Thälmann received 19.7 per cent of the male vote and 14.0 per cent of the female, or 16.8 per cent of the total vote, in the first round. The figures in the second round were 15.4, 10.4 and 12.9. Throughout the Reich Thälmann received 13.2 per cent of the vote in the first round and 10.2 per cent in the second: *SdR*, vol. 427, pp. 74–7.
77 Hartwig, 'Das Frauenwahlrecht in der Statistik', p. 181.
78 In the April 1924 election to the Bavarian Landtag it had received 32 per cent of the male and 31.4 per cent of the female vote in those areas where votes were collated separately, and places where the *völkisch* bloc did well in 1924, such as Ansbach and Dinkelsbühl, became Nazi strongholds in the early 1930s. Figures taken from *Zeitschrift des bayerischen statistischen Landesamtes*, vol. 56 (1924), 236, 307.
79 This gives an average of 2.2 per cent for the NSDAP in these areas against a Reich average of 2.6 per cent: *SdR*, vol. 372, part 3, pp. 32–3.
80 This gave a total of 16.3 per cent: *ibid.*, vol. 362, part 3, p. 33.
81 Tingsten, *Political Behaviour*, p. 59. Falter ascribes the greater increase in women's votes going to the NSDAP in March 1933 to the numbers of previous non-voters: Falter, *Hitlers Wähler*, p. 140.
82 See Boak, 'Mobilising Women', pp. 84–5, for the range of reasons. For material self-interest, see M. A. Berntson and B. Ault, 'Gender and Nazism: Women Joiners of the Pre-1933 Nazi Party', *American Behavioral Scientist*, 41 (1998), 1211. For the Republic's destruction, see Evans, *Comrades and Sisters*, p. 185.
83 Boak, '"Our last hope"', pp. 300–1.
84 J. Stephenson, 'National Socialism and Women before 1933', in P. D. Stachura (ed.), *The Nazi Machtergreifung* (London: Allen and Unwin, 1983), pp. 38–9.
85 H.-J. Arendt, S. Hering and L. Wagner (eds), *Nationalsozialistische*

Frauenpolitik vor 1933 (Frankfurt am Main: Dipa Verlag, 1995), p. 48. For other reasons compelling the leadership to create a women's organisation see Stephenson, *Nazi Organisation*, pp. 33–50.
86 Stephenson, *Nazi Organisation*, pp. 30, 56, 75.
87 D. Mühlberger, *Hitler's Voice: The Völkischer Beobachter, 1920–1933*, vol. 2: *Nazi Ideology and Propaganda* (Oxford: Peter Lang, 2004), pp. 315, 341–56.
88 Reichsorganisationsleiter der NSDAP (ed.), *NSDAP Partei-Statistik* (Munich: Zentralverlag der NSDAP, 1935), pp. 28–30. The highest percentage of female party members in 1930 was in Franconia, and the lowest in Danzig, which recorded a 43.6 per cent increase over the next two years. Strasser, the party's Organisation Leader, decreed on 31 December 1931 that female party members could not belong to other women's organisations: Arendt, Hering and Wagner (eds), *Nationalsozialistische Frauenpolitik*, p. 351.
89 Arendt, Hering and Wagner (eds), *Nationalsozialistische Frauenpolitik*, pp. 50, 326; Stephenson, *Nazi Organisation*, p. 85.
90 S. Rabe, *Die Frau im nationalsozialistischen Staate* (Munich: Münchener Druck- und Verlagshaus, 1932), pp. 3–6.
91 G. Horan, *Mothers, Warriors, Guardians of the Soul: Female Discourse in National Socialism 1924–1934* (Berlin: Walter de Gruyter, 2003), pp. 8, 196–7, 319.
92 S. Hering, '"Ich ging meinen Weg" – Erinnerungen bürgerlicher Frauenrechtlerinnen an das Jahr 1933', *Ariadne*, 18 (November 1990), 11. For Bäumer, see interview with Frau Luise Riegger, Karlsruhe, 20 June 1975 (in author's possession), and report in *Karlsruher Zeitung* (1 February 1932).
93 F. Magnus-Hausen, *Zehn Jahre deutsche Staatsbürgerin* (Berlin: Herbig, 1930), p. 13. Süchting-Hänger, however, puts the female share of the DNVP's membership at the end of 1922 at 10 per cent, whereas Scheck's figures show that women made up 62.2 per cent of members joining the Berlin-North-West branch of the party between February 1919 and March 1920. Süchting-Hänger, Das *'Gewissen der Nation'*, p. 171; Scheck, *Mothers of the Nation*, p. 143. Beyer refers to a 'surprisingly large number of women' in the DNVP, with figures for Danzig in September 1921 (54 per cent), Hamburg in January 1925 (43.2 per cent) and Giessen at the end of 1928 (40.3 per cent): Beyer, *Die Frau*, p. 44.
94 The first meeting of the DNVP's *Reichsfrauenausschuss* was on 6 December 1918. The DVP's network was based on electoral districts, not states, though in some cases the two were identical: Scheck, *Mothers of the Nation*, pp. 24–5. The DVP's *Reichsfrauenausschuss* was initially self-financing but lack of funds led to its being integrated

into the party's head office: BAK, Nachlass Katharina von Kardorff 26, pp. 205–10, correspondence of 31 October 1922.
95 Scheck, *Mothers of the Nation*, pp. 32, 35. The distribution of committees was uneven across the country.
96 *Ibid.*, p. 7; R. Scheck, 'Women in the Non-Nazi Right during the Weimar Republic: The German Nationalist People's Party (DNVP)', in P. Bacchetta and M. Power (eds), *Right-Wing Women: From Conservatives to Extremists around the World* (London: Routledge, 2002), p. 152; Süchting-Hänger, *Das 'Gewissen der Nation'*, pp. 207, 271, points out that women's share of seats on the party's *völkisch* committee was the highest of all committees.
97 Süchting-Hänger, *Das 'Gewissen der Nation'*, pp. 319–20; Heinsohn, *Konservative Parteien*, p. 210.
98 BAK, Z.Sg.1 44/8, 'Wahlkampfrichtlinien für Frauen'; BAK, Nachlass Katharina von Kardorff 22, p. 40, letter of the Gelsenkirchen women's group dated 27 June 1924; BAB, R8005/485, Bl. 87, letter from the DNVP head office to the *Reichsfrauenausschuss* of 21 December 1918; Scheck, *Mothers of the Nation*, p. 149.
99 Scheck, *Mothers of the Nation*, pp. 85, 137–42, 150. See also R. Scheck, 'Die Partei als Heim und Familie. Frauen in den Ortsvereinen der Deutschnationalen Volkspartei und der Deutschen Volkspartei in der Weimarer Republik', in Schöck-Quinteros and Streubel (eds), *Ihrem Volk verantwortlich*, pp. 158–60, 168, 171–3.
100 Scheck notes that not every local women's group subscribed to the newsletter: Scheck, *Mothers of the Nation*, pp. 29, 34, 139, 150.
101 BAK, R45III/5, pp. 134–6, minutes of sixth party congress, 4–6 December 1925; BAK, R45III/6, p. 314, minutes of the women's congress in 1926. Scheck notes the lack of party funding for DDP women's groups: Scheck, *Mothers of the Nation*, p. 39. The DDP's *Reichsfrauenausschuss*, noting the financial problems of local women's groups, encouraged them to meet in private houses: BAK, R45III/30, pp. 132/3, circular letter from the *Reichsfrauenausschuss* to the *Hauptvertrauensfrauen* on 30 December 1922.
102 The party had set up a Department for Women's Questions on 1 May 1921: H. Weber, 'Der Reichsfrauenbeirat der Deutschen Zentrumspartei', *Die Frau*, 36:5 (February 1929), 258. For women's calls for a centralised committee and preparations for it see the papers in AKDFB, Collection 1-47-9. Sack notes that following the setting-up of the Women's Advisory Committee the KFB became a professional women's association, and following Hedwig Dransfeld's death in 1925 the officers of the KFB no longer represented the Centre Party in the Reichstag: B. Sack, 'Katholismus und Nation: Der katholische Frauenbund', in U. Planert (ed.), *Nation, Politik und Geschlecht:*

Frauenbewegungen und Nationalismus in der Moderne (Frankfurt am Main: Campus, 2000), p. 294.
103 Quataert, 'The German Socialist Women's Movement', pp. 350–1.
104 *Protokoll über die Verhandlungen des Parteitages der Sozialdemokratischen Partei Deutschlands abgehalten in Weimar vom 10. bis 15. Juni 1919* (Berlin: Buchhaltung Vorwärts Paul Singer, 1919), p. 459; Thönnessen, *The Emancipation of Women*, p. 116.
105 In 1923 130,000 women made up 10.3 per cent of the membership; in 1931 there were 230,331 female members: Thönnessen, *The Emancipation of Women*, p. 116. For the change in tactics see Hagemann, *Frauenalltag und Männerpolitik*, pp. 537–40. Hagemann claims the majority of new members were 'the wives of Social Democratic workers': Hagemann, '"Equal but not the same"', p. 137.
106 25 per cent were over sixty: Hagemann, '"Equal but not the same"', p. 137.
107 *Jahrbuch der deutschen Sozialdemokratie* (Berlin: J. H. W. Dietz, 1930), pp. 223–5.
108 In 1927 women made up 23.8 per cent of the party committee, in 1929 25 per cent: *Sozialdemokratischer Parteitag 1927 in Kiel* (Berlin: J. H. W. Dietz, 1927), p. 305; *Die Genossin*, 6:12 (December 1929).
109 Hagemann, *Frauenalltag und Männerpolitik*, p. 539; Thönnessen, *The Emancipation of Women*, pp. 119–21.
110 According to Karen Hagemann, 'only 21 per cent of the 9,844 SPD local branches had a women's group' in 1931: Hagemann, '"Equal but not the same"', p. 141.
111 The 1931 conference did not discuss women: Boak, 'Women in Weimar Politics', p. 382; Pore, *A Conflict of Interest*, p. 61.
112 Pore, *A Conflict of Interest*, pp. 57–9; *Sozialdemokratischer Parteitag 1927*, p. 59; *Sozialdemokratischer Parteitag 1925 in Heidelberg* (Berlin: J. H. W. Dietz, 1925), p. 347.
113 Hagemann, '"Equal but not the same"', p. 140. Von Saldern states that there were 1,919 branches with 150,000 helpers in 1926 and 2,600 branches with 135,000 helpers in 1933. She claims that half of the Berlin SPD women's membership was engaged in voluntary welfare work for the *Arbeiterwohlfahrt*, and that 60 per cent of its members were women: von Saldern, 'Modernization', p. 99.
114 C. Eifert, 'Coming to Terms with the State: Maternalist Politics and the Development of the Welfare State in Weimar Germany', *Central European History*, 30:1 (1997), 40–3.
115 Hagemann, '"Equal but not the same"', pp. 140–1.
116 *Sozialdemokratischer Parteitag 1927*, pp. 332, 337; W. Smaldone, *Confronting Hitler: German Social Democrats in Defense of the*

Weimar Republic, 1929–1933 (Lanham: Lexington Books, 2010), p. 115.
117 'Richtlinien für die Frauenagitation', in Arendt et al. (eds), Dokumente, pp. 88–95.
118 Ibid., pp. 99–100: 'Frauenarbeit ist nicht Arbeit der Frauen unter der Partei, sondern Arbeit der Partei unter den Frauen'; ZStA, St.12/83, Bl. 1-2, circular of the East Prussian women's section of 27 October 1921; Bl. 71–2, circular of the KPD political office of 17 June 1924.
119 H.-J. Arendt and W. Freigang, 'Der Rote Frauen- und Mädchenbund – die revolutionäre deutsche Frauenorganisation in der Weimarer Republik', Beiträge zur Geschichte der Arbeiterbewegung, 21 (1979), 249–58; E. D. Weitz, Creating German Communism, 1890–1990: From Popular Protests to Socialist State (Princeton: Princeton University Press, 1996), pp. 215–17. The RFMB was created when women were banned from the militaristic Red Fighters' League.
120 Weitz, Creating German Communism, p. 230; Grossmann, 'German Communism', pp. 144–5, 152; Weitz, 'The Heroic Man', pp. 350–1.
121 Arendt, 'Weibliche Mitglieder der KPD', p. 654.
122 H. Weber, Die Wandlung des deutschen Kommunismus (Frankfurt am Main: Europäische Verlagsanstalt, 1969), vol. 2, p. 26.
123 'Die erste Parlamentsrede einer Frau in Deutschland', Die Gleichheit, 29:12 (14 March 1919), 89–91.
124 Schaser, 'Bürgerliche Frauen', pp. 658–60; Heinsohn, Konservative Parteien, p. 41.
125 G. Bäumer, 'Die Frau und die Nationalversammlung', Die Frauenfrage, 21:1 (January 1919), 3–4. There were reports that a women's party had been founded in June 1920 by a Frau Denera: BAB, R8034 II/7973, Bl. 46–7, 59, 80; 'Appell an die Frauen!', Die Frau im Staat, 13:8–9 (August–September 1931), 31. Adele Schreiber's remark is found in A. Blos (ed.), Die Frauenfrage im Lichte des Sozialismus (Dresden: Kadan, 1930), p. 111.
126 Boak, 'Women in Weimar Politics', pp. 372–3; BAB, R8034II/7973, Bl. 25, I. Hamel, 'Zusammenschluss der nationalgesinnten Frauenvereine', Die Post (8 October 1919); ADEF, G2d1, letter of Paula Mueller to M. Von Tiling, 26 November 1918; ADEF, B1a, letter from the Württemberg branch of the DEF of 17 July 1926 and the declaration of the Ulm group who were democrats; ADEF, B1a, letter from Cologne members to M. von Tiling and P. Mueller-Otfried in December 1931 against the DNVP/DVP leanings of the DEF; Süchting-Hänger, Das 'Gewissen der Nation', pp. 150–1.
127 'Mothers of the Nation', in M. Stritt, 'Germany', Jus suffragii, 13:6 (March 1919), 76; Schaser, 'Bürgerliche Frauen', pp. 641–3.
128 Heinsohn, Konservative Parteien, p. 249.

129 Marie-Elisabeth Lüders (DDP) replaced the late Friedrich Naumann on 30 September 1919. The other three seats were taken by two SPD and one USPD woman: M. Schwarz, *MdR biographisches Handbuch der Reichstage* (Hanover: Verlag für Literatur und Zeitgeschehen, 1965), p. 708.

130 The most favourable share was to be found in Reuss jüngerer Linie, where women held three of the twenty-one seats (14.3 per cent): 'Die Frauen in den Parlamenten', *Deutsche Allgemeine Zeitung*, 24 September 1919, found in BAB, R901/55222, Bl. 2. The party breakdown of the 117 was as follows: SPD 44, USPD 10, KPD 2, DDP 31, Z 17, DNVP 6, DVP 5: D. von Velsen, 'Die Frau und die Volksvertretung: Eine statistische Studie', in E. Altmann-Gottheimer (ed.), *Jahrbuch des Bundes Deutscher Frauenvereine 1920* (Berlin: Teubner, 1920), p. 27.

131 Magnus-Hausen, *Zehn Jahre*, p. 10. The women were distributed among the major parties as follows: SPD 484, USPD 179, DDP 276, Z 215, DVP 69, DNVP 77.

132 A 1925 survey revealed that in Prussia 12 per cent of council seats in cities with over 500,000 inhabitants were filled by women, with women's share of council seats falling incrementally to 2 per cent in villages with between 10,000 and 5,000 inhabitants. In Saxony these figures were 11.5 per cent and 2.2 per cent respectively, and in Bavaria 10 per cent and 1.4 per cent: calculated from figures in *Nachrichtenblatt des Bundes Deutscher Frauenvereine* (*Nachrichtenblatt des BdF*), 6:4 (15 April 1926) and *Mitteilungen des deutschen Städtetages*, 1 (1 January 1926), 13–18, found in BAK, Z.Sg.1 41/4. Fifty-two women constituted less than 0.1 per cent of the 62,836 councillors in Bavaria's villages in 1919 whereas ninety-one women were to be found among 423 councillors in fifteen district towns (6.4 per cent): *Zeitschrift des bayerischen statistischen Landesamts*, 53 (1921), 405–8.

133 G. Bäumer, *Die Frau im deutschen Staat* (Berlin: Junker und Dünnhaupt, 1932), p. 34.

134 Badisches Statistisches Landesamt, *Über die deutschen Nationalversammlungswahlen in Baden, die badischen Gemeinde-, Bezirksrats- und Kreisabgeordnetenwahl und das Frauenwahlrecht* (Karlsruhe: C. F. Müller, 1921), pp. 76–8; *Karlsruher Zeitung* (22 December 1930).

135 Women's share increased from 8.3 per cent in 1919 to 11.9 per cent in 1930: E. Hoffmann, *Die Gemeindewahlen in Mannheim 1911–1930* (Mannheim: Gengenbach & Hahn, 1932), pp. 69–70.

136 Arendt, Hering and Wagner (eds), *Nationalsozialistische Frauenpolitik*, p. 346. Nearly half of the 238 women who answered the survey had served since 1919: E. Wex, 'Erfahrungen und Wünsche der

Stadtverordneten', *Die Frau*, 37:11 (August 1930), 649–57, and 37:12 (September 1930), 701–6.
137 Prussia had eighty-three female delegates throughout the Republic, Hamburg forty-five and Bremen thirty-five, followed by Danzig and Lübeck with twenty-three each: http://hsr-trans.zhsf.uni-koeln.de/volumes/vol1contents.htm (accessed 14 July 2011).
138 Boak, 'Women in Weimar Politics', pp. 375–7.
139 Scheck, *Mothers of the Nation*, pp. 52, 55.
140 For the Centre Party see AKDFB, Collection 1-47-10, letter from the Reich Women's Advisory Committee to the parliamentary executive committee of 13 November 1924 and letter of the Düsseldorf women's advisory committee of 16 November 1924 threatening to withdraw from all election work; for the DVP see BAK, Nachlass Katharina von Kardorff 22, p. 19, letter to DVP *Reichsfrauenausschuss* of 11 November 1924; DVP Reich women's conference resolution in Stadtarchiv Mannheim, S2/1201-3, *General-Anzeiger* (20 March 1924); for the DDP see BAK, Nachlass Lüders 109, letter from DDP *Reichsfrauenausschuss* to Oskar Meyer of 24 October 1929; for the SPD see *Sozialdemokratischer Parteitag 1924* (Berlin: J. H. W. Dietz, 1924), pp. 224, 231, 237–43; for the DNVP see Heinsohn, *Konservative Parteien*, pp. 85–91.
141 BAK, R43I/999, pp. 818–24, suggestions by Dr Klöcker to Reich Minister on 26 August 1926; R43I/1000, pp. 275–311, printed paper dated 26 August 1930 from the Reich Interior Minister to the Reichsrat; R45III/22, p. 57, DDP executive committee meeting of 19 July 1930.
142 Boak, 'Women in Weimar Politics', p. 386–7.
143 For the six major parties, women made up 12.6 per cent of candidates in May 1924 and 12.2 per cent in December 1924: *SdR*, vol. 315, part 3, p. 11.
144 Women made up 14.7 per cent of the candidates for the six major parties, their highest share being 20.6 per cent in the KPD: *SdR*, vol. 382, part 3, p. 11. Swett notes that a 1929 KPD directive that one-third of its electoral candidates should be women applied only to local elections: P. Swett, *Neighbors and Enemies: The Culture of Radicalism in Berlin, 1929–1933* (Cambridge: Cambridge University Press, 2004), p. 92.
145 Boak, 'Women in Weimar Politics', pp. 384–5; *Die Frau*, 32:4 (January 1925), 121; R. Deutsch, *Parlamentarische Frauenarbeit II: Aus den Reichstagen von 1924–1928* (Berlin: Herbig, 1928), p. 7. For the positions on the election lists of elected DNVP women see Heinsohn, *Konservative Parteien*, pp. 87–8.
146 These districts were Berlin, East Prussia, Potsdam (both districts),

Thuringia, Westphalia-South, Cologne-Aachen and Dresden-Bautzen: J. Walmsley, 'The Political Role of Catholic Women during the Weimar Republic, 1918–1933' (PhD dissertation, University of California Riverside, 2000), p. 73. Walmsley notes that women were elected to represent the Centre Party from three districts, and Heinsohn has noted that women were elected to represent the DNVP from five districts: Heinsohn, *Konservative Parteien*, p. 88.

147 'Frauenkandidaturen und die Parteien: Zu unserer Umfrage', *Frau und Gegenwart*, 5:18 (1928), 2–3, and 5:21 (1928), 7–8.

148 BdF letter sent on 3 November 1924, found in *Die Frau*, 32:3 (December 1924), 91; 'Reichstagswahl 1930', *Nachrichtenblatt des BdF*, 10:8 (August 1930), 70.

149 On 22 July 1931, in association with other organisations including the KFB and the Jewish Women's League, it published an exhortation to women to support peace at home and national steadfastness in foreign affairs. The VEFD refused to sign: *Nachrichtenblatt des BdF*, 10:11 (October 1931), 77; 'Kundgebung deutscher Frauenvereine', *Die christliche Frau*, 29:8 (August 1931), 226.

150 'Frauenfront 1932', *Nachrichtenblatt des BdF*, 12:8 (August 1932), 65–6.

151 LAB, BRep 235 HLA MF 2906, MF 2907, MF 3632, letter of June 1932 detailing meetings of women's organisations on 6 May 1932. Evans notes the limited readership of the 'Yellow Pages': Evans, *The Feminist Movement*, p. 255. The DEF and KFB also became concerned about Nazi antifeminism: Süchting-Hänger, *Das 'Gewissen der Nation'*, p. 349; U. Baumann, 'Religion, Emancipation, and Politics in the Confessional Women's Movement in Germany, 1900–1933', in B. Melman (ed.), *Borderlines: Genders and Identities in War and Peace, 1870–1930* (London: Routledge, 1998), pp. 300–1.

152 *Die Frau*, 40:6 (March 1933), 382; R. Scheck, 'Zwischen Volksgemeinschaft und Frauenrechten: Das Verhältnis rechtsbürgerlicher Politikerinnen zur NSDAP 1930–1933', in Planert (ed.), *Nation, Politik und Geschlecht*, p. 238.

153 T. Lang-Brumann, 'Streiflichter auf zehn bewegte Jahre', *Die christliche Frau*, 27:3 (March 1929), 73. Sender likewise thought that it was not a highly desirable job: Sender, *Autobiography*, p. 152.

154 Mergel, *Parlamentarische Kultur in der Weimarer Republik*, pp. 104–8; M. Zettler, 'Von der ersten Schulung im Parlament', *Die christliche Frau*, 27:3 (March 1929), 69; G. Bäumer, 'Eindrücke von der Nationalversammlung', *Die Frau*, 26:6 (March 1919), 165–6; Koonz, 'Conflicting Allegiances', p. 666.

155 Helene Weber (Z) was the target for younger KPD women, though

Clara Zetkin tended to abide by parliamentary rules: Walmsley, 'The Political Role', pp. 175–6.
156 Her attempts to sue the Nazis for slander for calling her a prostitute failed: Sender, *Autobiography*, pp. 267–9, 280–3. A socialist woman councillor was also called a prostitute by Nazis during a Leipzig council meeting: LAB, BRep 235 HLA MF 1374, *Korrespondenz Frauenpresse* (23 April 1931).
157 Heinsohn, *Konservative Parteien*, pp. 252–3.
158 Scheck, *Mothers of the Nation*, p. 159. On the disillusionment of women within the DDP see Boak, 'Women in Weimar Politics', pp. 385–6.
159 BAK, R45II/64, p. 1094, *Frauenrundschau* (5 January 1932).
160 BAK, Nachlass Lüders 100, letter to Johanna Waescher of 27 October 1932; Nachlass Dietrich 223, pp. 203–4, letter from Lüders to Dietrich of 15 July 1932.
161 'An die Mitglieder des Deutsch-Evangelischen Frauenbundes', *Evangelische Frauenzeitung*, 34:11 (November 1932), 17–18; Süchting-Hänger, *Das 'Gewissen der Nation'*, p. 325; Harvey, 'Visions of the *Volk*', p. 160.
162 Fessenden, 'The Role of Women Deputies', pp. 9, 183.
163 C. Streubel, '"Meine Herren und Damen!" Rednerinnen der deutschnationalen Fraktion im Parlament der Weimarer Republik', in D. Boschoff and M. Wanger-Egelhaaf (eds), *Mitsprache, Rederecht, Stimmgewalt: Genderkritische Strategien und Transformationen der Rhetorik* (Heidelberg: Universitätsverlag Winter, 2006), pp. 131–4.
164 BAK, Nachlass Schreiber 15, article entitled 'Women in German Politics'.
165 Streubel, '"Meine Herren"', pp. 119–20. According to Streubel, the 820 speeches were divided among the parties as follows: SPD 252, USPD 110, KPD 112, Z/BVP 119, DDP/DStP 90, DVP 68 and DNVP 56. Koonz says that women in the National Assembly made 340 speeches and comments, with Luise Zietz (USPD) speaking 104 times: Koonz, 'Conflicting Allegiances', p. 671.
166 Between 1920 and 1924 thirteen women sat on the Reich youth welfare sub-committee, eleven on the population policy sub-committee, eight on the education sub-committee and five on the social policy sub-committee: 'Rundschau', *Die christliche Frau*, 22:4 (April 1924), 63. The sub-committees usually had twenty-eight members.
167 'Rundschau', *Die christliche Frau*, 27:3 (March 1929), 87; Fessenden, 'The Role of Women Deputies', p. 69; Heinsohn, *Konservative Parteien*, p. 86.
168 Bäumer, *Die Frau im deutschen Staat*, pp. 50–1.
169 Sender, *Autobiography*, p. 231.

170 Pore, *A Conflict of Interest*, pp. 42, 66; Streubel, '"Meine Herren"', p. 142; Schaser, 'Bürgerliche Frauen', p. 642; B. B. Frye, *Liberal Democrats in the Weimar Republic: The History of the German Democratic Party and the German State Party* (Carbondale: Southern Illinois University Press, 1985), pp. 95–6, 201.
171 BAK, Kl.Erw. 65-4, Nachlass Lang-Brumann, 'Sind die Frauen zur politischen Tätigkeit geeignet?'
172 Boak, 'Women in Weimar Politics', p. 378; *Heidelberger Tageblatt* (5 January 1928), *Frauenzeitung*.
173 Scheck, *Mothers of the Nation*, p. 159; C. Teusch, 'Soziale Hilfsbereitschaft für Volk und Nation', *Die christliche Frau*, 27:3 (March 1929), 75–8; Walmsley, 'The Political Role', p. 120; G. Bäumer, *Die Frau im neuen Lebensraum* (Berlin: Herbig, 1931), p. 98.
174 Bäumer, *Die Frau in neuen Lebensraum*, p. 98; Sender, *Autobiography*, p. 231.
175 Behm was the chair of the Union of Female Homeworkers, and the law included women in the national insurance scheme: Koonz, 'Conflicting Allegiances', p. 676; Scheck, *Mothers of the Nation*, p. 73. Half of Behm's twenty-two speeches in parliament related to homeworkers: Streubel, '"Meine Herren"', p. 121.
176 Scheck, *Mothers of the Nation*, p. 97; Frye, *Liberal Democrats*, p. 151; Schaser, 'Bürgerliche Frauen', p. 678.
177 *Stenographische Berichte über die Verhandlungen des Reichstages*, vol. 327, pp. 1421–3; Scheck, *Mothers*, p. 70. Some women would absent themselves from voting if they did not agree with their party's stance on an issue: Fessenden, 'The Role of Women Deputies', pp. 48–9.
178 M. Schmitz, 'Erinnerungen an die deutsche Nationalversammlung', *Die christliche Frau*, 27:3 (March 1929), 79.
179 Magnus-Hausen, *Zehn Jahre*, p. 4; H.-M. Lauterer, 'Republikanerinnen des Herzens: Sozialdemokratinnen und Nation 1914–1933', in Planert (ed.), *Nation, Politik und Geschlecht*, p. 282. In the first Reichstag, from 1920 to 1924, only six petitions were put forward jointly by women, and Bäumer claimed that the women were unwilling to seem disloyal to their parties: G. Bäumer, *Lebensweg durch eine Zeitwende* (Tübingen: Rainer Wunderlich Verlag, 1933), p. 383; 'Rundschau', *Die christliche Frau*, 22:4 (April 1924), 64.
180 C. Bohm-Schuch, 'Friede', *Die Gleichheit*, 29:20 (5 July 1919), 153.
181 'Frauenkundgebung zu den Friedensverhandlungen', *Evangelische Frauenzeitung*, 19:15–16 (May 1919), 57.
182 Scheck, 'Women against Versailles', p. 25; Süchting-Hänger, *Das 'Gewissen der Natio'*, pp. 218–19.
183 Süchting-Hänger, *Das 'Gewissen der Nation'* p. 218. In addition,

Christiane Streubel believes that women's espousal of nationalist causes allowed men holding more moderate views to be portrayed as lacking patriotism: C. Streubel, 'Forschungen zur politischen Rechten', in Schöck-Quinteros and Streubel (eds), *Ihrem Volk verantwortlich*, p. 16. See also C. Streubel, 'Raps across the Knuckles: The Extension of War Culture by Radical Nationalist Women Journalists in post-1918 Germany', in Sharp and Stibbe (eds), *Aftermaths of War*, p. 75.

184 ADEF, G2d1.
185 For the parliamentary debates on 20 May 1920 see LAB, BRep 235, HLA MF 2752, Deutscher Volksbund, 'Rettet die Ehre'; HLA MF 2892, 'Die schwarzen Truppen am Rhein', *Deutsche Frau in schwerer Zeit*, 2:30 (30 July 1920); S. Mass, 'Von der "schwarzen Schmach" zur "deutschen Heimat"', *WerkstattGeschichte*, 32 (2002), 47–8. For Gärtner see J. Roos, 'Women's Rights, Nationalist Anxiety and the "Moral" Agenda in the Early Weimar Republic: Revisiting the "Black Horror" Campaign against France's African Occupation Troops', *Central European History*, 42:3 (2009), 479–80; J. Roos, 'Nationalism, Racism and Propaganda in Early Weimar Germany: Contradictions in the Campaign against the "Black Horror on the Rhine"', *German History*, 30:1 (2012), 52–3.
186 I. Wigger, '"Black Shame" – the Campaign against "Racial Degeneration" and Female Degradation in Interwar Europe', *Race and Class*, 51:3 (2010), 33–46. See also E. Kuhlman, 'The Rhineland Horror Campaign and the Aftermath of War', in Sharp and Stibbe (eds), *Aftermaths of War*, p. 92; Roos, 'Women's Rights', pp. 476–81.
187 Kuhlman, 'The Rhineland Horror Campaign', pp. 97, 104–6. For the reasons for the campaign's decline by 1922 see Roos, 'Nationalism, Racism and Propaganda', pp. 55–74.
188 Roos, 'Nationalism, Racism and Propaganda', pp. 67–8. Within nationalist circles, German women who fraternised with colonial troops were perceived as immoral traitors: Roos, 'Women's Rights', pp. 486–8.
189 Scheck, 'Women against Versailles', p. 27; Harvey, 'Pilgrimages', pp. 207–9, 213–14.
190 LAB, BRep 235 HLA MF 2751, 'An die deutschen Frauen!' (Oberschlesier-Hilfswerk); ADEF, Q12, 'Gerechtigkeit für Oberschlesien'.
191 LAB, BRep 235 HLA MF 1338, 'Brennende Herzen'; Scheck, *Mothers of the Nation*, p. 123.
192 ADEF, G2d, calls of 15 February 1923 and 5 November 1923; Scheck, 'Women against Versailles', p. 26.
193 The German Protective League for Germans on the Borders and Abroad instigated the foundation of the DFBK. Other women on the

preparatory committee included Katharina von Oheimb (DVP), Else Frobenius (DVP, the chair of the Protective League's women's group), Margarete Gärtner and right-wing women such as Beda Prilipp (DNVP and RNF) and Amelie Roth: ADEF, EE1, 'Zur Beurteiligung der deutschen Frauen an der Schuldfragearbeit', November 1921. The women's committee met for the first time on 3 November 1921 and represented fifty-two women's organisations: Süchting-Hänger, *Das 'Gewissen der Nation'*, pp. 225–6.

194 ADEF, EE1, letter from Paula Mueller-Otfried to Clara Mende of 6 February 1932; Streubel, *Radikale Nationalistinnen*, p. 144; R. Scheck, 'Wahrung des Burgfriedens: Die Wirkung des Ersten Weltkrieges auf die bürgerliche Frauenbewegung der Weimarer Republik', in J. Dülffer and G. Krumeich (eds), *Der verlorene Frieden: Politik und Kriegskultur nach 1918* (Essen: Klartext, 2002), pp. 225–6. The National Women's Committee transformed into the Ring of National Women's Associations in March 1932, and one of its first acts was to recommend a vote for Hitler as President: ADEF, O2, letter from K. Hertwig to P. Mueller-Otfried dated 18 March 1932; LAB, BRep 235 HLA MF 1367, 'Ring nationaler Frauenbünde' in *Der Jungdeutsche*.

195 Süchting-Hänger, *Das 'Gewissen der Nation'*, p. 310.

196 BAB, R8034II/7973, Bl. 25, I. Hamel, 'Zusammenschluss der nationalgesinnten Frauenvereine', *Die Post* (8 October 1919); B. Prilipp, 'Zusammenschluss nationaler Frauenvereine', *Die Post* (7 January 1920); ADEF, Q12, Ring nationaler Frauen. For Mueller-Otfried's attempts to create a Conservative women's organisation see ADEF, O12, meetings of 13 January and 19 February 1920; G2d, meetings of 21 October and 10 November 1919; A. Hänger, 'Politisch oder vaterländisch? Der vaterländische Frauenverein zwischen Kaiserreich und Weimarer Republik', in Schöck-Quinteros and Streubel (eds), *Ihrem Volk verantwortlich*, pp. 77–8.

197 BAB, R1501/125984, Bl. 14a-18, 'Aus den Mitteilungen des Landeskriminalpolizeiamts. Nr. 15 vom 1.8.30'; Süchting-Hänger, *Das 'Gewissen der Nation'*, pp. 166, 188.

198 For the development of mythology around Queen Luise see B. Förster, *Der Königin Luise-Mythos: Mediengeschichte des 'Idealbilds deutscher Weiblichkeit'* (Göttingen: Vandenhoeck & Ruprecht, 2011).

199 Süchting-Hänger, *Das 'Gewissen der Nation'*, p. 165.

200 E. Schöck-Quinteros, 'Der Bund Königin Luise: "Unser Kampfplatz ist die Familie"', in Schöck-Quinteros and Streubel (eds), *Ihrem Volk verantwortlich*, p. 234. Its leader from August 1923 was Marie Netz, a member of the DNVP and the leader of the DNVP women's group in Halle, and its members wore a cornflower blue dress; their emblem was a four-centimetre silver oval wreath, with the letter 'L'

under a crown in the centre: BAB, R1507/395, Bl. 3, 'Abschrift aus Lagebericht L.I.A. Dresden vom 10.12.24'. The BKL also had a youth group for girls aged between fourteen and seventeen.
201 BAB, R1507/395, Bl. 31, 'Satzungen des "Königin Luise" Bund Deutscher Frauen und Mädchen. Landesverband Schlesien'. The Bremen group's statutes can be found in Schöck-Quinteros and Streubel (eds), *Ihrem Volk verantwortlich*, p. 322.
202 Schöck-Quinteros, 'Der Bund Königin Luise', p. 254.
203 BAB, R1501/125982, report in *Die Welt am Abend* (5 June 1930). The Berlin BKL had refused to be subordinate to the Stahlhelm: BAB, R1507/395, Bl. 56, 'Abschrift aus Lagebericht des Pol. Präs. Berlin vom Ende Januar 1928'.
204 Schöck-Quinteros, 'Der Bund Königin Luise', p. 251. The Berlin branch sent a telegram to President Hindenburg asking him not to sign the Young Plan: BAB, R1501/125982, report in *Deutsche Zeitung* (20 February 1930).
205 Süchting-Hänger, *Das 'Gewissen der Nation'*, p. 167. In 1924 a third out of nineteen Gau executives were from the nobility and in 1925 eight out of thirty: BAB, R1507/395, Bl. 5, 'Aus der Reichshauptstadt: Zum Geburtstag der Königin Luise', *Deutsche Tageszeitung* (10 March 1925); p. 9, 'Königin-Luise-Bund', *Der Stahlhelm*, 6 September 1925. The DFO also had the motto 'faith, hope and love'.
206 Schöck-Quinteros, 'Der Bund Königin Luise', p. 253.
207 BAB, R1507/395, Bl. 74, 'In Stahlhelmuniform auf der Kanzel', *Volkswille* (12 July 1929), report of second BKL state assembly in Potsdam.
208 Schöck-Quinteros, 'Der Bund Königin Luise', p. 245; BAB, R1501/125982, Bl. 20, 'Tagung des Bundes Königin Luise', 22 May 1932. In 1930 von Hadeln had led a group of thirty BKL women on a study trip to Italy, where they were greeted by Mussolini and met members of the fascist women's organisations, at whose achievements she marvelled: BAB, R1501/125982, Bl. 5, Abschrift Deutsche Botschaft Rom 18 Juni 1930; for Hadeln's letter of thanks see Schöck-Quinteros and Streubel (eds), *Ihrem Volk verantwortlich*, pp. 326–9.
209 BAB, R1507/395, Bl. 41, report from Karlsruhe dated 1 December 1926.
210 The Stahlhelm and DNVP, which had supported Duesterberg in the first round, had expressed no preference in the second: BAB, R1501/125982, Bl. 18; 'Der schlesische Königin-Luise Bund für Adolf Hitler', *Völkischer Beobachter*, in Arendt, Hering and Wagner (eds), *Nationalsozialistische Frauenpolitik*, p. 64; Süchting-Hänger, *Das 'Gewissen der Nation'*, p. 354.

211 K. Heinsohn, 'Germany', in K. Passmore (ed.), *Women, Gender and Fascism in Europe, 1919–45* (Manchester: Manchester University Press, 2003), pp. 50–1.
212 *Ibid.*, pp. 46–7; Süchting-Hänger, *Das 'Gewissen der Nation'*, pp. 341–2, gives the membership in 1932 at 2,000. For the NLB see G. Diehl, *Was wir wollen: Frage und Antwort über den Neulandbund* (Eisenach: Neulandverlag, 1918).
213 Heinsohn, 'Germany', p. 47; see BAB, R1501/125019, IAN1377/27.7.31, 'Deutscher Frauenkampfbund', which claims that this figure is undoubtedly exaggerated.
214 Süchting-Hänger, *Das 'Gewissen der Nation'*, p. 313; Harvey, 'Visions of the *Volk*', p. 159.
215 Silvia Lange, quoted in Streubel, 'Frauen der politischen Rechten', p. 47; L. E. Jones, 'Generational Conflict and the Problem of Political Mobilisation in the Weimar Republic', in Jones and Retallack (eds), *Elections, Mass Politics, and Social Change*, p. 355. For the DDP see M. Dönhoff, 'Die Frau in der DDP', *Die Frau*, 36:5 (February 1929), 268–70; for the DVP see BAK R45II/31, p. 416, DVP party congress in Mannheim, 21–4 March 1930.
216 E. Harvey, 'The Failure of Feminism? Young Women and the Bourgeois Feminist Movement in Weimar Germany 1918–1933', *Central European History*, 28:1 (1995), 15–17.
217 *Ibid.*, pp. 13–14, 25–6.
218 G. Bäumer, 'Die Stellung der weiblichen Jugend zum politischen Leben', *Die Frau*, 37:11 (August 1930), 640; E. Harvey, 'Serving the Volk, Saving the Nation: Women in the Youth Movement and Public Sphere in Weimar Germany', in Jones and Retallack (eds), *Elections, Mass Politics, and Social Change*, pp. 201–21.
219 E. Harvey, 'Gender, Generation and Politics: Young Protestant Women in the Final Years of the Weimar Republic', in Roseman (ed.), *Generations in Conflict*, pp. 195–205.
220 BAK, Nachlass Lüders 4, 'Anwesenheitsliste der Frauenverbände bei der im Auswärtigen Amt am 5. August 1931 stattgehabten Besprechung über Abrüstungsfragen'; P. Mueller-Otfried, 'Abrüstung', *Evangelische Frauenzeitung*, 33:12 (December 1931), 34. The BdF's stance led ostensibly to the housewives' associations leaving it.
221 Mueller-Otfried, 'Abrüstung', pp. 35–6; G. Krabbel, 'Katholische Frauen zur Abrüstung', *Die christliche Frau*, 30:1 (January 1932), 2–3; BAB, R1501/125982, Bl. 17, 'Sechzehn nationale Frauenverbände fordern für Deutschland Wehrhoheit', *Deutsche Zeitung* (14 January 1932).
222 'Was will "die Frau im Staat"?', *Die Frau im Staat*, 1:1 (February 1919), 1.

Women and politics 131

223 W. Greiling, 'Internationale Frauenliga für Frieden und Freiheit – Deutscher Zweig (IFFF-DZ) 1915–1933', in D. Fricke, W. Fritsch, H. Gottwald, S. Schmidt and M. Weißbecker (eds), *Lexikon zur Parteiengeschichte: Die bürgerlichen und kleinbürgerlichen Parteien und Verbände in Deutschland (1789–1945)*, vol. 3 (Leipzig: Bibliographisches Institut, 1985), p. 134; BAK, R134/73, pp. 104–10, IAN 2162.c7/6.12, 14 December 1932, Betrifft: Weltkongress gegen den imperialistischen Krieg (Frauenkonferenz).
224 BAB, R901/56107, Bl. 12, report in *Vorwärts* (19 December 1918).
225 LAB, BRep 235 HLA MF 2737, letter of IFFF to BdF of 29 January 1921; letter of refusal from Verein Frauenwohl dated 3 March 1921; N. Gabriel, '"Nichts von diesem Kleinmut, nichts von dieser Angst": Feminismus, Internationalismus und Pazifismus bei Anita Augspurg und Lida Gustava Heymann', *Ariadne*, 24 (November 1993), 64. For the IFFF after the First World War see E. Kuhlman, 'The "Women's International League for Peace and Freedom" and Reconciliation after the Great War', in Fell and Sharp (eds), *The Women's Movement in Wartime*, pp. 227–40.
226 Proclamation in *Die Frau im Staat*, 3:11 (November 1921), 3. The DEF noted that such schoolbooks were only to be found in France: *Evangelische Frauenzeitung*, 10:7–8 (July–August 1920), 82.
227 *Die Frau im Staat*, 12:9–10 (September–October 1930), 1; BAB, R901/32873, Bl. 102, 6 May 1931. The IFFF held conferences in 1919, 1920, 1922, 1924, 1925, 1927: L. G. Heymann and A. Augspurg, *Erlebtes – Erschautes* (Bodenheim: Athenaeum Verlag, 1987), pp. 192–3; Greiling, 'Internationale Frauenliga für Frieden und Freiheit', pp. 128–36.
228 B. Greven-Aschoff, *Die bürgerliche Frauenbewegung in Deutschland 1894–1933* (Göttingen: Vandenhoeck & Ruprecht, 1981), p. 113; Scheck, 'Women against Versailles', p. 31. There was also criticism from the right that one of the BdF delegates would be a Jew, Alice Salomon.
229 BAB, R901/32872, Bl. 12, 19. Marie Stritt had attended the IWSA conference in Geneva in June 1920, but with the dissolution of the German suffrage organisations, the Foreign Office asked Bäumer, Lüders and Juchacz to attend. German women also attended the IWSA conferences in Paris in 1926, in Berlin in 1929 and in Belgrade in 1931. For right-wing women journalists' criticisms see Streubel, 'Raps across the Knuckles', pp. 81–2.
230 B. Prilipp, 'Internationaler Kongress für Frauenstimmrecht in Berlin', *Evangelische Frauenzeitung*, 30:8 (August 1929), 201–3; Süchting-Hänger, *Das 'Gewissen der Nation'*, pp. 310–11.
231 BAB, R901/32873, Bl. 33-5.

232 Bäumer was reluctant to give up her post in the Interior Ministry and declined nomination: BAB, R901/32873, Bl. 6f.f, 38.
233 G. Bäumer, 'Wofür die Millionen fielen: Eine offene Antwort', found in LAB, BRep 235 HLA MF 1359; Scheck, 'Wahrung des Burgfriedens', pp. 226–7; Süchting-Hänger, *Das 'Gewissen der Nation'*, pp. 254–6; 'Wandlungen der gemässigten Frauenbewegung', *Die Frau im Staat*, 9:11 (November 1927), 5. One reason given for the failure of some DDP women to join the DStP was their pacifism: BAK, Nachlass Lüders 257, pp. 1–6, report of the *Reichsfrauenausschuss* for Dr Dietrich, 28 February 1931.
234 Stritt, 'Germany', p. 76.
235 Salomon, 'Women's Hopes for the New Order', p. 62.
236 T. Mergel, 'High Expectations – Deep Disappointments: Structures of the Public Perception of Politics in the Weimar Republic', in K. Canning, K. Barndt and K. McGuire (eds), *Weimar Publics/Weimar Subjects: Rethinking the Political Culture of Germany in the 1920s* (Oxford: Berghahn, 2010), pp. 193–4.
237 A. T. Allen, *Feminism and Motherhood in Germany 1800–1914* (New Brunswick: Rutgers University Press, 1991).
238 BAK, R45II/64 p. 1094, *Frauenrundschau* (5 January 1932).
239 Heinsohn, *Konservative Parteien*, pp. 255–6; D. Schumann, 'Political Violence, Contested Public Space, and Reasserted Masculinity in Weimar Germany', in Canning, Barndt and McGuire (eds), *Weimar Publics*, pp. 236, 247–9.
240 Stritt, 'Germany', p. 76. Of the fifty DDP women who were elected to a state parliament throughout the Republic, twelve served only in the first assembly in 1919. Five of the twelve had sat in the Bremen legislature, which reduced its number of seats from 200 to 120 in 1920, and the DDP's number of seats fell from 39 to 18: Calculated from information in http://hsr-trans.zhsf.uni-koeln.de/volumes/bioweil/frauen.htm (accessed 14 July 2011).
241 Stephenson, 'National Socialism and Women before 1933'.
242 Sneeringer, *Winning Women's Votes*, p. 231; Boak, 'Mobilising Women', pp. 75–80.
243 K. Heinsohn, 'Kampf um die Wählerinnen: Die Idee der "Volksgemeinschaft" am Ende der Weimarer Republik', in S. Steinbacher (ed.), *Volksgenossinnen: Frauen in der NS-Volksgemeinschaft* (Göttingen: Hubert & Co., 2007), p. 43. For the Sklarek scandal see D. Harsch, *German Social Democracy and the Rise of Nazism* (Chapel Hill: University of North Carolina Press, 1993), p. 69.
244 Kirchhoff's 1931 remark quoted in Schöck-Quinteros, 'Der Bund Königin Luise', p. 231.

245 Kramer claims that women made up 70 per cent of the civilian air defence organisation: N. Kramer, *Volksgenossinnen an der Heimatfront: Mobilisierung, Verhalten, Erinnerung* (Göttingen: Vandenhoeck & Ruprecht, 2011), pp. 342–4.
246 M. Stibbe, *Women in the Third Reich* (London: Arnold, 2003), pp. 134–5; M.-E. Lüders, *Fürchte dich nicht: Persönliches und Politisches aus mehr als achtzig Jahren, 1878–1962* (Cologne: Westdeutscher Verlag, 1963), pp. 130–8; M. J. Hutton, *Russian and West European Women, 1860–1939: Dreams, Struggles and Nightmares* (Oxford: Rowman and Littlefield, 2001), p. 376.
247 Smaldone, *Confronting Hitler*, pp. 114–15, 144. Pfülf committed suicide on 8 June 1933, distraught at the SPD's failure to defend itself against Nazism.
248 The IFFF leaders, Lida Gustava Heymann and Anita Augspur, who had been on the Nazi 'hit list' in 1923, were abroad in Italy when Hitler became Chancellor, and they never returned to Germany. Their property was confiscated and their archive destroyed: Gabriel, '"Nichts von diesem Kleinmut"', p. 61. For the BdF see A. von Zahn-Harnack, 'Schlussbericht über die Arbeit des Bundes Deutscher Frauenvereine', *Die Frau*, 40:9 (June 1933), 551.
249 S. Steinbacher, 'Differenz der Geschlechter? Chancen und Schranken für die "Volksgenossinnen"', in F. Bajohr and M. Wildt (eds), *Volksgemeinschaft: Neue Forschungen zur Gesellschaft des Nationalsozialismus* (Frankfurt am Main: S. Fischer Verlag, 2009), pp. 95–6. Föllmer notes these opportunities in the Labour Service, and Reese in the League of German Girls: M. Föllmer, 'Was Nazism Collectivistic? Redefining the Individual in Berlin, 1930–1945', *Journal of Modern History*, 82:1 (2010), 77–8; D. Reese, *Growing up Female in Nazi Germany* (Ann Arbor: University of Michigan Press, 2006), pp. 73–88.

3
Women and work

Fundamental to the image of the 'new woman' in the 1920s was her economic emancipation. David Schoenbaum writes of 'the economic liberation of thousands of women sales clerks ... an ever increasing contingent of women doctors, lawyers, judges and social workers ... social forces that had brought thousands of women into shops, offices, and professions in competition with men'.[1] However, work is of itself not emancipatory for women; only when it provides them with the means to live independently of any other financial support can it be deemed emancipatory. Bridenthal sees in the myth of women's economic emancipation in the Weimar Republic a reason why women voted for right-wing parties which praised the traditional role of wife and mother. She believes that 'in some important ways, women actually fell back' and argues that rather than advance in the Weimar Republic, women 'pressed more and more into unskilled work with lessened responsibility or out of the economy altogether ... lost status and relative independence and, quite probably, a corresponding sense of competence and self-worth'.[2] This chapter will explore women's participation in the world of work during the Weimar Republic to ascertain the opportunities available to women and assess the extent of their economic liberation. It will investigate the impact, if any, on women's employment of the two major economic crises of the Republic, the hyperinflation of 1922–23 and the Depression in the early 1930s, and of the post-war demobilisation, the stabilisation of the German economy and the rationalisation of German industry from 1924. Attitudes towards female employment fluctuated with the state of the economy and varied with the type of employment. In times of prosperity, little criticism was heard, but in times of economic difficulties, demands for the dismissal of women, particularly married women, grew louder, and the more professionally esteemed the type of employment, the more vociferous the demands.

The period of demobilisation, 1919–23

We have already noted the relatively smooth re-integration of the returning troops into the workforce at the war's end and the desire for a return to normality, thought to be the pre-war gender order. On 8 November 1918 the War Ministry issued guidelines for female employment during the demobilisation, acknowledging that some women would have to work but stating that this should be in areas where they had worked previously or had proved themselves, in areas where there were labour shortages (agriculture and domestic service) and in areas corresponding to their nature, which did not endanger their health and in which they did not compete with men. Women with no economic necessity to work should return to family life, and women who had left their home town in search of work should return, with fares being paid to facilitate this.[3] Leaflets advised female manual and white-collar workers to return to their families or their previous employment or to take the opportunity to improve their qualifications. They were told: 'Be thrifty! Protect your honour and your health! Act sensibly and calmly!'[4] For some women, however, it was to prove impossible to return to their pre-war employment. In Berlin there were reports that seamstresses' hands had become too coarse and lacking in dexterity through factory work, while those who had worked at night or in munitions factories suffered from failing eyesight.[5]

Immediate post-war unemployment peaked in early 1919, coinciding with the severest raw materials shortages, and was of short duration.[6] Female employment fell below its June 1914 level between February and May 1919, a fall which may have been attributable to the demobilisation decree of 28 March 1919. This decree enshrined in law that only those who were forced to work out of economic necessity should do so, and permitted the dismissal of those who had moved to find employment during the war, or who had worked in agriculture or domestic service at the start of war or during it, a decree which was gender-neutral in language but impacted disproportionately on women.[7] The rise in female unemployment may also have been attributable to the wave of mass dismissals of women in some areas, such as Hanover, Erfurt, Detmold and Darmstadt, as each district's demobilisation committee, which was made up of local employers and workers' representatives, implemented national framework legislation.[8] The committees came under considerable pressure from male professional organisations and workers' committees to dismiss women. Especially vociferous in its demands for women's dismissal was the German National Commercial Employees' Association (Deutschnationaler Handlungsgehilfenverband, DNHV), as office work was one area where women were thought to be in direct competition with men and where job opportunities were sparse. Some employers were reluctant to dismiss female employees, who were not only cheaper to employ than men, but also more obedient.[9] It appears that, in the demobilisation, female white-collar workers had a better chance of keeping their jobs than industrial workers; Bosch dismissed 37.5 per cent of its female white-collar workers and 70 per cent of its female manual workers between the armistice and 1 March 1919.[10] Richard Bessel has argued that demobilisation committees resisted pressure for the wholesale dismissal of women; they acted as 'local representatives of the public good' and were sensitive to an individual's personal circumstances, as the law required them to be.[11] Many contemporary observers, however, noted a fundamental rejection of women's employment in some sections of society during the demobilisation, which espoused the motto 'Die Frau gehört ins Haus' ('Women belong in the home').[12] In many places meetings, often organised by women's associations, were held to protest against the wholesale, indiscriminate dismissal of women workers, and on 1 August 1919 thirty-four female delegates to the National Assembly, representing all the major parties, submitted an interpellation protesting against the actions of the demobilisation committees and calling for greater female participation in any decision-making relating to women's employment.[13] Legislation from 13 November 1918 also decreed that only those women forced to work through economic necessity were eligible to receive unemployment benefit, and the authorities did everything possible to exclude even these women from receiving anything.[14] While women made up about one-third of unemployment benefit recipients in Baden in April 1919, this share had fallen to one-eighth by August 1920, with only war widows who had children, and infirm elderly women, receiving benefit.[15] Across Germany women who refused domestic service positions, or who failed to attend the domestic service training courses that the authorites put on, had their benefits withdrawn.[16] Rouette reports, however, that the withholding of benefit forced women in Berlin to take up domestic service positions out of economic necessity and that, just as at the start of the war, emergency work rooms were set up for unemployed women, for tasks such as repairing clothing.[17]

Bessel notes that the mass dismissals were only a temporary phenonomen as the inflation-fuelled economy quickly began to improve, but female unemployment remained higher than male unemployment throughout the early years of the Republic.[18] Only in agriculture and domestic service did demand for female workers exceed supply throughout 1919, as women consciously shunned these areas of employment.[19] Women were reluctant to return to these traditional, more restrictive and more physically demanding areas, in spite of the revocation of the *Gesindeordnung* (servants' order) on 12 November 1918.[20] Bessel tells of young girls informing employment exchanges that 'farmers should do their dirty work themselves', and Bright Jones writes of 'the abysmal failure of the 1919 demobilisation regulations' in keeping young people in agriculture.[21] Women's shunning of work in domestic service and agriculture was to be part of several general trends in women's employment during the twentieth century, and before exploring women's employment in these areas during the Weimar Republic in more detail, it is necessary to survey these general trends.

Working women

During the early years of the twentieth century the female workforce was relatively stable. The important changes which did occur were not in the numbers of women working but in the types and sectors of employment in which women were engaged and the marital status of working women. Any investigation into women's employment in the Weimar Republic is greatly facilitated by the comprehensive census data of 1925 and 1933, which break down into five occupational categories – independent workers, family helpers, white-collar workers and civil servants, manual workers and domestic servants – and five employment sectors: agriculture, industry, trade and commerce, the civil service and the professions, and domestic service. Working women not only made up about one-third of the total workforce, but also constituted about one-third of the total female population, as can be seen from Tables 3.1 and 3.2.[22] Other women were independently wealthy or dependent on their families. Girls between eighteen and twenty were more likely to work than any other age group, 77.4 per cent of women in this age group being classed as working in 1925 and 78.6 per cent in 1933. From 1907 the age at which girls first went into employment was raised: girls either stayed at home to help in the family, benefited from compulsory further education prescribed in Article 145 of the Weimar Constitution or were affected by unemployment during the Depression.[23] Although more than half of working women were single and were forced to earn their own living or contribute to the family's finances, single women's share of the female workforce fell from 1907 to 1933, as did their share of the female population, illustrating the fall in the birth rate and the higher frequency of marriage (see Tables 3.3 and 3.4.). Indeed, the most noticeable increase was in the number of married women in employment as women stayed on at work after marriage, which was possible only if both partners worked and, making use of better contraceptive information, planned their family.[24] This trend continued, with married women making up 41 per cent of the female workforce in 1939, and 59.8 per cent in West Germany in 1980.[25] However, during the Weimar Republic over two-thirds of all married working women were classed as 'family helper' (see Table 3.5), which meant working in one's husband's or another relative's business, usually for no formal payment. Although under Article 1358 of the Civil Code of 1900 a wife could not go out to work without her husband's permission, under Article 1356 a married woman was obliged to work without payment in her husband's business 'insofar as such an activity is customary, according to the circumstances in which the couple lives'.[26] Between 1925 and 1933 the number of married female family helpers increased as the economic crisis forced shopkeepers and other independent tradesmen to dismiss employees and rely on their wives' unpaid assistance.[27] Some 70 per cent of married women, however, were housewives, dependent upon the earnings of their husbands and children.[28] Another trend from 1907 was the decreasing share of widowed and divorced women within the female workforce, an indication that many widows and divorcees received financial support in some form from an earlier marriage or from Weimar's welfare state.[29]

Table 3.1 Women in the workforce according to each area of employment, 1907, 1925 and 1933

Area of employment	1907			1925			1933		
	Total	Women	% women	Total	Women	% women	Total	Women	% women
Agriculture	8,556,219	3,997,294	46.7	9,762,426	4,969,279	50.9	9,342,785	4,648,782	49.8
Industry	9,830,540	1,914,373	19.5	13,239,223	2,908,880	22.0	13,052,982	2,758,802	21.2
Trade and commerce	3,496,055	863,982	24.7	5,273,502	1,575,255	29.9	5,932,069	1,920,758	32.4
Civil service and professions	1,651,351	274,719	16.6	2,091,167	586,127	28.0	2,698,656	901,063	33.4
Domestic service	1,621,852	1,450,637	89.4	1,642,982	1,438,471	87.5	1,269,582	1,249,636	98.4
Total	25,156,017	8,501,005	33.8	32,009,300	11,478,012	35.9	32,296,074	11,479,041	35.5

Source: SdR, vol. 402, pp. 442, 446, 452; vol. 538, part 3, pp. 4–16.

Table 3.2 *Working women in the female population, 1907, 1925 and 1933*

Women	1907	1925	1933
Total	27,884,309	32,213,796	33,532,899
Of whom working	8,501,005	11,478,012	11,479,041
% working	30.5	35.6	34.2

Source: SdR, vol. 402, p. 424; vol. 458, p. 57.

Table 3.3 *The marital status of the female workforce, 1907, 1925 and 1933*

Status	1907		1925		1933	
	Number	%	Number	%	Number	%
Single	5,087,519	59.9	6,802,135	59.3	6,415,089	55.9
Married	2,494,178	29.3	3,645,326	31.7	4,177,404	36.4
Widowed	919,308	10.8	1,030,551	9.0	886,548	7.7
Total	8,501,005	100.0	11,478,012	100.0	11,479,041	100.0

Source: SdR, vol. 402, pp. 424, 439, 441; vol. 458, pp. 62, 76.

Table 3.4 *The marital status of the female population, 1907, 1925 and 1933*

Status	1907		1925		1933	
	Number	%	Number	%	Number	%
Single	15,949,747	57.1	16,516,715	51.3	15,878,191	47.3
Married	9,684,006	34.7	12,710,070	39.4	14,316,709	42.7
Widowed	2,250,556	8.2	2,987,011	9.3	3,337,999	10.0
Total	27,884,309	100.0	32,213,796	100.0	33,532,899	100.0

Source: SdR, vol. 401, p. 586; vol. 402, p. 442; StJhb 1935, p. 11.

During the Weimar Republic women dominated two occupational categories, those of family helper and domestic servant (see Table 3.6), and these two categories continued to be of significance for female employment before the Second World War.[30] In 1925 women dominated two sectors of employment, agriculture and domestic service (see Table 3.1.). As can be seen from Table 3.7, however, the share of the total female workforce employed in

Table 3.5 The number of working women according to their marital status and occupational category, 1925 and 1933

Occupation category	1925				1933			
	Total	Single	Married	Widowed/divorced	Total	Single	Married	Widowed/divorced
Family helper	4,132,956	1,538,480	2,501,335	93,141	4,149,035	1,234,664	2,834,933	79,438
Manual worker	3,503,826	2,468,069	708,061	327,696	3,488,698	2,260,541	931,306	296,851
White-collar worker or civil servant	1,437,655	1,301,955	82,537	53,163	1,694,621	1,512,830	115,379	66,412
Domestic servant	1,310,439	1,183,438	44,233	82,768	1,210,322	1,114,954	41,243	54,125
Independent worker[a]	1,093,136	310,193	309,160	473,783	936,365	292,100	254,543	389,722
Total	11,478,012	6,802,135	3,645,326	1,030,551	11,479,041	6,415,089	4,117,404	886,548

Note: [a] In the 1933 census homeworkers were no longer considered to be independent workers.

Source: SdR, vol. 402, pp. 452–3; vol. 458, p. 75.

Table 3.6 The number of working women according to occupational classifications, 1925 and 1933

Occupation category	1925			1933		
	Total	Women	% women	Total	Women	% women
Family helper	5,437,227	4,132,956	76.0	5,312,116	4,149,035	78.1
Manual	14,433,754	3,503,826	24.3	14,949,786	3,488,698	23.3
White-collar worker	5,274,232	1,437,655	27.1	4,032,345	1,566,754	
Civil servant				1,480,792	127,867	30.7
Domestic servant	1,325,587	1,310,439	98.9	1,218,119	1,210,322	99.4
Independent	5,538,500	1,093,136	19.7	5,302,916	936,365	17.7
Total	32,009,300	11,478,012	35.9	32,296,074	11,479,041	35.5

Source: SdR, vol. 402, p. 452; vol. 453, part 3, p. 16.

Table 3.7 The percentages of the male and female workforce in each area of employment, 1907, 1925 and 1933

Area of employment	1907		1925		1933	
	Men	Women	Men	Women	Men	Women
Agriculture	27.4	47.0	23.4	43.3	22.5	40.5
Industry	47.5	22.5	50.3	25.4	49.5	24.0
Trade and commerce	15.8	10.25	18.0	13.7	19.3	16.7
Civil Service and professions	8.3	3.25	7.3	5.1	8.6	7.8
Domestic service	1.0	17.0	1.0	12.5	0.1	10.0
Total	100.0	100.0	100.0	100.0	100.0	100.0

Source: SdR, vol. 402, pp. 442, 446, 452; vol. 453, part 3, pp. 4–16.

these two traditional areas of female employment, which not only involved physically hard labour and exploitation with little freedom but also frequently required women to live on the premises, had begun to dwindle. Women spurned them to take up manual work in industry and, increasingly, white-collar work in the rapidly expanding service and administration sectors, where working hours were fixed, working conditions regulated, the remuneration higher and, save for the period of the First World War, worker protection laws enforced. From the turn of the century, white-collar work was the fastest growing sector for female employment. These trends continued; by 1980 white-collar workers made up 51.9 per cent of West Germany's female workforce, while agriculture provided employment for only 7 per cent of employed women.[31]

Agriculture and domestic service

Domestic service had long been an area into which rural families had sent their daughters so that they could learn to run a household, earn a little for the family and not be a drain on its resources. With the growth of other employment opportunities in manual and white-collar work, domestic service became, in Helgard Kramer's words, 'a sluice through which women streamed from the countryside into the towns'.[32] A survey carried out in 1929 revealed that over one-third of those domestic servants interviewed wanted to change their job.[33] Domestic servants tended to be young and single, and they were to be found in the homes of property and business owners, civil servants and professional people in towns and cities.[34] On average they worked thirteen-and-a-half hours a day, though those who lived out worked fewer hours.[35] Although there were no regulated working conditions, many had one Sunday free and one afternoon off every two weeks. Between 1907 and 1925 the numbers of domestic servants who lived out increased by 15.6 per cent, and this trend continued to 1933. It was in particular domestic servants under twenty-five who preferred to live out, a sign of rebellion against domestic servants' working conditions.[36] The failure to introduce legislation regulating the employment of domestic servants meant that domestic service was the area of employment in which women had the least freedom and the fewest rights.[37] Women's organisations were concerned about the moral welfare of young domestic servants, who were thought to be in moral danger from the men of the household in which they worked and lived, both employers and fellow employees. Surveys carried out in the 1920s revealed their concern to be justified, as many prostitutes, unmarried mothers, venereally diseased women, and women under the care of the local welfare offices had been in domestic service.[38] Women were reluctant to enter domestic service if there were other jobs available, and the demand for domestics continued to exceed supply until 1924, when the impoverishment of middle-class families through the hyperinflation led to the dismissal of some. Thereafter, there was a surplus of female domestics, with 143,065 registered as unemployed in 1931, the largest group of women in that year (16.2 per cent).³⁹

In agriculture, the government moved swiftly to replace the *Gesindeordnung*, and the provisional agricultural labour decree of 24 January 1919 detailed working hours, wages and working conditions.⁴⁰ In an attempt to stem the flow of workers from agriculture into industry, the law of 16 March 1919 forbade non-agricultural employers from hiring anyone who had worked in agriculture before the war, but the demand for female agricultural labour exceeded supply until 1928, when there was an annual average of 101 applicants for every 100 available positions.⁴¹ Work in agriculture was divided into gender-specific tasks. Women's work consisted of dairying, looking after poultry, tending gardens, housework and, on smaller farms, helping in the fields at sowing and harvest time. Jones notes the Saxon farmers' adamant refusal in the early 1920s to employ men instead of *Mägde* (permanently employed female farm hands), which reflected the continuing belief in agricultural circles in the pre-war division of labour.⁴²

Agriculture tended to be a family business, and women were the mainstay of the agricultural labour force. In 1925, only 23 per cent of the total agricultural labour force were not members of farming families.⁴³ Women's work in agriculture was concentrated on smaller concerns, and the smaller the holding, the greater the dependence on female labour; as two-thirds of Germany's agricultural land was made up of farms of under 50 hectares, women's contribution was considerable.⁴⁴ It was especially strong in outlying rural areas near large industrial centres, where married women looked after the farms while their menfolk, and increasingly their daughters, went to work in the factories in the nearby towns.⁴⁵ Family helpers dominated the female agricultural workforce, with more peasants' wives working on the land than did peasants' daughters, and their numbers increased between 1925 and 1933 as daughters left and other helpers were let go.⁴⁶ The numbers of *Mägde*, the most respected of the paid female agricultural workforce, fell between 1925 and 1933, as the smaller farms on which they were employed could not afford to pay even their meagre wages during the Depression, though some may have left of their own volition to seek better-paid and better-regulated employment in industry.⁴⁷

Their tasks fell to female family members. The demand for female agricultural labourers also fell, as they were mostly to be found on larger farms which were mechanised in the 1920s.[48] While paid agricultural workers' hours were regulated and ranged between 2,725 and 2,900 annually, a peasant's wife had no such protection. One survey carried out in Württemberg revealed that a peasant worked on average 3,554 hours per year, and his wife 3,933.[49] 'A young peasant's wife with small children has the most miserable existence on earth; she is a genuine slave', concluded another survey. A peasant was often believed to think more highly of his cattle and fields than of his wife and children.[50] Young women were keen to escape this life of drudgery. Few women studied for a career in agriculture; in 1925 there were thirty-three women among 2,203 students at three forestry and four agricultural colleges.[51] Few were willing to marry young farmers, and in predominantly agricultural areas such as Brandenburg, Oldenburg, Mecklenburg and Pomerania men outnumbered women in the population up to the age of twenty-five.[52]

Industrial work

In the nineteenth century women had initially worked in industries related to the tasks they performed in the home, in textiles, clothing and food production, but the First World War opened other industries to women. Although there were mass dismissals of women workers during the demobilisation, Germany's inflation-fuelled economy soon required women workers, and by 1920 the numbers of women working in concerns overseen by the factory inspectorate exceeded the pre-war level. The numbers peaked in 1922, though even in the stabilisation of 1924 they were higher than before the war.[53] In 1925 nearly two-thirds (65.2 per cent) of all female manual workers in industry were still to be found in their traditional industries.[54] Female textile workers were atypical, being older, with higher skill levels, and having a greater share of married women than the average female manual workforce. More were able to reach supervisory positions, and their pay was closer to men's, though, as a whole, the pay in women's traditional industries was low; male weavers' earnings were consistently higher only than those of unskilled railway workers.[55] Women's domination of the textile industry declined slightly between 1925 and 1933 as rationalisation reduced the need for skilled women workers, whereas in other industries, rationalisation increased demand for cheaper, more dextrous machine-operators, and semi-skilled and unskilled women replaced skilled men.[56] Factory inspectors' returns for concerns with over fifty workers reveal an increase in women's share of the workforce between 1926 and 1930 in electrical engineering, the precision and optical instruments industry, the manufacture of metal goods and the toy industry among others.[57] By 1933 women had increased their share of the manual workforce in the chemical industry from 21.9 per cent in 1925 to 23.6 per cent, and increases were also recorded in the clothing, food, leather, rubber and toy industries.[58] Canning has noted that the rationalisation of German industry reinforced gendered notions of skill.[59] However, the continuing higher demand for unskilled female manual labour in rapidly mechanising male-dominated industries ensured not only that women were perceived as competitors in the job market but also that a return to pre-war notions of gendered industrial sectors was impossible.

During the Weimar Republic, the typical female manual worker was young, single and unskilled and had fewer opportunites for training and advancement and smaller remuneration than men, a situation which continued in West Germany at least into the 1980s.[60] Between 1925 and 1933, however, married women significantly increased their share of the industrial manual workforce.[61] Women were to be found predominantly in larger factories employing more than fifty people and undertaking mainly unskilled and semi-skilled work in their non-traditional industries.[62] Women remained entrenched in the lower rungs of the industrial workforce; they made up a mere 2.2 per cent of all supervisors in German industry in 1925, though in the textile industry the figure was 5 per cent.[63] Few women served apprenticeships; apprentices made up 6.3 per cent of the male manual workforce in the metal industry, but only 0.4 per cent of the female.[64] Women's lack of skill or training was one reason for the lower wages they received. Although women in some industries had been paid the same as men during the revolutionary upheaval, wage differentials soon became the norm.[65] In the metal industry women received on average 70 per cent of men's wages, while local authorities tended to pay their unskilled female workers 75 per cent of an unskilled man's wage.[66]

In addition, wage agreements were based on age differentials, with incremental pay scales up to the age of twenty or twenty-five, and the female manual industrial workforce was younger than the male one.[67] Poorer wages for women were also justified by the fact that women did not have a family to support – men continued to be perceived as the family breadwinner – and that employment was merely a stage between school and marriage. In addition, women, especially married women, constituted a reservoir of cheap labour and few of those women in work were members of trade unions. The highest number of women in the socialist Free Trade Unions during the Weimar Republic was 1,710,761 in 1920, constituting 21.7 per cent of the membership, and the numbers of women members fell steadily into the 1930s.[68] Many women were not convinced of the benefits of union membership, perhaps because they, too, saw work as only a temporary phase in their lives. They might have been unable to afford their union dues or have had little faith in the unions to improve women's working lives. Few women were union officials, though women were found in greater numbers in those unions of industries in which women played a major role; in 1920 321,532 women made up 65.4 per cent of the textile workers' union.[69]

The eight-hour day was introduced to German industry in a law of 23 November 1918 as part of the demobilisation decrees, and although working time was increased during the hyperinflation to ten hours for men and nine for women, the forty-eight-hour week became the norm by 1928, though women working in the textile industry were particularly affected by short time working during the Depression.[70] Several surveys of women's industrial working conditions revealed that many female manual workers were brought to the point of nervous exhaustion by having to do monotonous, repetitive work on increasingly fast assembly lines in badly lit and poorly ventilated factories with inadequate heating, noise protection and sanitary facilities, though some attempts were made during the Weimar Republic to improve the factory environment.[71] Insurance sickness funds' figures show that female manual workers were more often ill than their male counterparts, and for longer, with married women falling ill more frequently than single women, perhaps because pregnancy was classed as a case of sickness, though some employers believed that some married women reported sick when they had household chores to catch up on.[72] With large numbers of married women within the textile industry and an estimated 90,000 women pregnant at any one time, the German Textile Workers' Union conducted several surveys, which discovered that there was a higher proportion of stillbirths among working women than among those who did not go out to work, their babies were lighter, and that their babies' weights increased with the length of time for which the mother had given up work prior to the birth. The author of one survey, Dr Hirsch, a Berlin gynaecologist, reached the conclusion that pregnancy and industrial work were irreconcilable opposites.[73] The union led the campaign for improved worker protection for pregnant women, and on 16 July 1927 Germany became the first major industrialised nation to ratify the Washington Convention on the employment of women before and after childbirth in what was the only notable piece of female worker protection legislation during the Weimar Republic.[74] All women who paid into the sickness insurance funds, that is all manual and white-collar workers, were entitled to stop working six weeks before the expected date of confinement and were banned from working for six weeks after the birth. During these twelve weeks, and up to a maximum of eighteen weeks if the woman was not fully recovered, the woman could not be dismissed. Women could choose when they wanted to give up work, and though they were entitled to receive maternity benefit for four weeks before the expected date of confinement, many continued to work right up to the birth. In Baden, the Karlsruhe insurance funds of 1933 revealed that 67 per cent of pregnant women worked up to the day of the birth.[75] There were also reports of women being dismissed during the prohibited period, particularly unmarried women whose incapacity for work was seen as an act of negligence.[76] The 1927 law did not apply to women working in agriculture, in domestic service or as homeworkers. The latter had increased their number substantially between 1907 and 1925. They were usually aged over thirty and married, and were working at home on piece rates in the textile, tobacco and toy industries because they could not leave their children or other dependants. Figure 3.1 reveals an old homeworker, weighed down by the toys she is taking to the distributors. Homeworkers lost much of their wages to middlemen, and though the Homework Law of 27 June 1923 provided for the regulation of their pay by specially selected committees, many employers ignored it.[77]

Many girls did not relish combining industrial employment with

Women and work 149

Figure 3.1 Homework in the Weimar Republic: an old woman carries huge crates and baskets of toys over the mountains to the distributors (1925)

marriage and bringing up a family, as the personal reflections of textile workers make clear.[78] They saw their time at work as a transitory phase between leaving school and marrying, a time when they could enjoy their leisure, and believed that, once married, they would be permanently busy. Work also enabled them to contribute to the family's finances, and thus changed their status within the family. Initially, girls handed over their wages and received pocket money, but then, as they grew older, began to pay for their board. In a survey conducted in 1928–29, 97 per cent of female manual workers under the age of twenty-five still lived with their parents. Benninghaus believes that young women over the age of eighteen earned enough to be able to rent a room in lodgings or a hostel for young working women, but preferred to live at home. Young women who chose to live in lodgings were viewed with suspicion and were thought to be at risk of moral degeneracy.[79]

Within the home girls not only had to hand over more of their wages than their brothers did, but also had to help more with the household chores.[80] Some working-class girls would have liked to have apprenticeships, as tailors or hairdressers, but there were few vacancies.[81] Few actively aspired to do unskilled work in a factory, not merely because of the working conditions but also because factory girls suffered a tarnished reputation for coarseness and lack of refinement and respectability.[82] For many, the 'dream' job was as a sales assistant in a department store or in ladies' fashion; this white-collar work had higher social prestige, a cleaner working environment, neat attire, better pay and contact with customers of a higher social standing.[83]

White-collar employment

Although in 1925 white-collar workers and civil servants made up only 12.5 per cent of the female work force, the white-collar worker had become the 'typical gainfully employed woman of the masses' who was 'the dominant image of the city's streets'.[84] The female white-collar worker became the subject not only of newspaper attention but also of contemporary novels and films during the Weimar Republic. The typical 'new woman' of the 1920s, depicting her economic independence and her sexual emancipation in her bobbed hair and short skirt, was surely a white-collar worker based in Berlin or one of the other large cities. Thirty per cent of Berlin's female workforce was to be found in white-collar employment.[85] While the majority of white-collar workers were office workers or salesgirls, the occupational category also included telephonists, technicians, nurses and nuns (See Figures 3.2, 3.3 and 3.4).[86] With the rise of the department store and consumerism, the development of the social welfare state, the expansion of administrative bureaucracies and the rapid mechanisation of office equipment, there was a demand for young, attractive shop girls and cheap, semi-skilled female office personnel. While working-class girls sought shop work with its on-the-job training, lower-middle-class and middle-class girls were not thought to be demeaning themselves by taking office jobs, which were held in higher regard than sales work, and which usually required further educational qualifications.[87] The increase in office automation and the introduction of American office practices led to the continuing, gradual expansion of the

Women and work 151

Figure 3.2 The typing pool of a Berlin business (c. 1925)

Figure 3.3 Registrar: a young woman with a *Bubikopf* placing files in a cabinet (Berlin 1925)

Figure 3.4 Window dresser: a Berlin department store employee dresses the leg of a shop window mannequin (c. 1925)

female white-collar workforce between 1925 and 1930.[88] By 1933 women had increased their share of white-collar and civil service employment from 27.3 per cent in 1925 to 30.7 per cent, and this was the only category of employment in which the numbers of single, widowed and divorced women increased between 1925 and 1933; it also registered the largest percentage increase in married women.[89]

White-collar work and the civil service were the domain of the single woman; in 1925 90.6 per cent in this category were single, in 1933 89.2 per cent.[90] Youth and good looks were essential for female office staff and sales personnel. White-collar workers flocked to beauty parlours to remain smart and up to date. The manager of one Berlin department store reported that the main criterion in selecting female sales and office staff was a pleasant appearance. Women were expected to use their femininity to help sell goods or brighten up the office, and because many wanted this work the employers could pick the most attractive.[91] Because of the ready supply of young, good-looking white-collar workers, older ones had to do their best to remain smart and to keep up with the ever-increasing mechanisation of office equipment and the speedier, more efficient work methods. Young people were also cheaper to employ than older, more experienced hands.[92]

Age was one reason why female white-collar employees tended to be concentrated on the lower rungs of the employment ladder. A survey conducted in 1929 by the Trade Union of White-Collar Workers (Gewerkschaftsbund der Angestellten, GdA) revealed that 32.2 per cent of male white-collar workers were to be found in the lowest positions, 47.5 in the middle-ranking posts and 20.3 per cent in the most senior positions; for female white-collar workers the figures were 72, 25.5 and 2.5 per cent respectively.[93] The GdA survey also revealed that female white-collar workers had neither attended technical college nor served apprenticeships for as long as their male colleagues.[94] Their youth and lack of training were reasons for women's receiving lower pay than men, though they rarely did the same work, men being found in more responsible administrative positions. However, the difference between men's and women's wages was lower than was the case with manual workers; most wage agreements in the Weimar Republic envisaged a 10 per cent wage differential between men and women.[95] Many young women engaged in sales or office work received very poor wages, often below the subsistence minimum.[96] Most young female white-collar workers lived with their parents and, like young female manual workers, helped with household chores. A survey by the socialist Central Union of White-Collar Workers (Zentralvervand der Angestellten, ZdA) in 1929 revealed that 84 per cent of the female respondents lived with their parents or close relatives.[97] For most female office and sales personnel their employment did not enable them to be economically independent, but did enable them to purchase their own clothes and cosmetics and to indulge their leisure pursuits, as well as making a contribution to the family's finances. The GdA survey revealed that over a quarter (28.4 per cent) of the female respondents came from working-class families, and slightly fewer (23.2 per cent) had tradesmen or skilled craftsmen as fathers.[98] Surveys of the educational qualifications of female white-collar workers showed that these increased with age, an indication of the growth of working-class participation in white-collar employment, as educational achievements usually increased with social standing.[99] Male white-collar workers had long been anxious that the introduction of mechanical aids would lead to a proletarianisation of white-collar work, though women took on these more monotonous, repetitive functions, leaving more complex work to men. The ever-increasing tempo of the machines on which women worked led frequently to women office workers suffering from nervous exhaustion.[100]

Female white-collar workers appear to have been more convinced of the benefits of union membership than female manual workers were. Following a decrease in female membership after the demobilisation and during the hyperinflation, women's share of white-collar union membership increased from 1925, in contrast to the decrease in women's membership of the Free Trade Unions. The attacks on female employment during the Depression may have made women aware of their vulnerability, or it may have been that white-collar women were better able to afford their union dues than female manual workers. Women may also have wanted to take advantage of the services offered by their unions, which included legal aid, holiday homes, welfare benefits and, in the case of the Union of Female Commercial and Office Personnel, help from its job placement agency.[101]

Women in the professions

While office and sales work did not afford many women the chance to pursue a career, the professions and civil service did. A higher education qualification is normally a prerequisite for a professional career, and it was only in 1900 that Baden became the first German state to open its universities, in Heidelberg and Freiburg, to women. Mecklenburg was the final German state to follow Baden's example, in 1909. Prior to this, German women had attended university abroad, often to study medicine, usually in Switzerland, or had attended the training colleges for women teachers (*Lehrerinnenseminare*), which gave them the necessary qualifications to teach in elementary schools or the lower forms of girls' senior schools.[102] By 1914 women made up 6.7 per cent of the university student body, and in 1918 10 per cent, a share which fell slightly as young men began or resumed their studies at the war's end. Women's share of the university student body, which grew in the early post-war years, remained stable until 1923, when it began to rise, slowly at first in the early post-inflation years when student numbers experienced a substantial decrease, and then from 1928 more quickly, to reach 18.8 per cent in the winter of 1931, when student numbers were swollen with those opting to study rather than enter a depressed job market. The number of women studying at Germany's technical universities also increased steadily throughout the Weimar Republic, reaching 6.5 per cent in winter 1933–34.[103] The number of girls taking the *Abitur*, the school-leaving qualification which was the prerequisite for university entrance, quadrupled between 1926 and 1931, increasing women's share from 9.1 per cent of those taking it to 23.5 per cent at a time of diminishing career prospects in the professions.[104] Employment prospects played a large part in female students' choice of subject. The most popular subjects were the arts, medicine and pharmacy; in summer 1930 42.3 per cent of all female students were to be found in arts faculties, where they made up nearly one-third (31.8 per cent) of the student body. Few women studied theology, as they had little possibility of being ordained, and law remained male-dominated, though women were permitted to enter the legal profession in 1922.[105] Women preferred to attend universities in large cities or in areas known for their liberal outlook; thus, Berlin, Hamburg, Munich, Freiburg and Heidelberg universities were popular among women.[106] As there were few grants available to female students, a young woman's chance of going to university depended not only on her parents' financial standing but also on their liberal outlook, as the belief persisted that sons should be given the chance of a university education before daughters.[107] Most female students came from upper- or middle-class families. A mere 1.1 per cent of female university students in summer 1928 came from the working class, compared with 9 per cent of male students.[108]

Women's admittance to university had never been wholeheartedly accepted by some male academics, and their objections resurfaced during the Depression. Awareness among certain circles of the ever-increasing number of girls passing the *Abitur* and of women attending university, sharpened by dwindling professional employment prospects during the Depression, led to an open discussion of women's admittance to university within a general consideration of the overcrowding at universities. Although official committees suggested a range of solutions, including uniform cuts in the numbers of male and female students, one year's compulsory labour service, voluntary labour service or the channelling of large numbers of students with the *Abitur* into practical professions, male professional organisations were quick to demand a restriction on women's admittance to university.[109] In early 1932 Dr Hadrich, the general secretary of the Association of German Doctors, called for a two-year waiting period to be imposed immediately on all girls who had passed the *Abitur* in an attempt to combat university overcrowding. While the Association of Philologists at the University of Leipzig called for a complete ban on women studying chemistry, physics and history, other organisations promoted the notion of 'professional university study' for men, with examinations leading to professional qualifications, and 'educational study' for women, more suited to a woman's profession as mother and protector of the family.[110]

In 1927 Dr Käthe Gaebel, a senior civil servant in the Reich Office of Employment Exchanges, wrote that women had successfully established themselves in the teaching profession and had gained recognition in the medical profession, but that in all other professions in both the private and public sectors women were still in rather more or less pioneer positions.[111] Medical certification had been opened to women in 1899, and the number of female physicians increased gradually from fifty-five in 1908 to 196 in 1914. By 1925 2,572 women made up 5.4 per cent of Germany's physicians, and these figures increased to 4,367 and 8.6 per cent by 1933.[112] A survey conducted by the Federation of German Female Physicians (Bund Deutscher Ärztinnen, BdÄ) in 1924–25 revealed that of 1,395 female physicians in Germany over two-thirds (67.7 per cent) were to be found in cities with over 100,000 inhabitants, as many specialised in a single area of medicine and were bound to places with large populations. In addition, prejudice against female physicians was considerably less in cities than in the countryside. According to the BdÄ survey Berlin had 302 women physicians, over a third of whom were married.[113] About half of the female physicians were in general practice. Few female physicians were employed by the welfare or public services, and in some states women were barred from taking the necessary examinations to become district medical officers, while other states thought the job too demanding for a woman.[114] Few assistants' posts in university hospitals were offered to women; in 1926 women filled only sixteen (2.1 per cent) of 758 assistants' posts.[115] During the Depression, fears of competition in a shrinking labour market led the male physicians' professional organisations to demand that women be restricted to 5 per cent of those applying for certification.[116] During the Weimar Republic, women were also carving a niche for themselves in other areas of the medical sphere. By 1933 women had increased their share of dispensing chemists to 20.4 per cent and of dentists to 10.3 per cent, and between 1925 and 1933 more female dentists were founding their own practices, a clear indication that women were succeeding in establishing themselves in their chosen profession. Throughout the professions women tended to be younger than their male colleagues, because of the relatively short time for which universities and some professions had been open to them, and a higher percentage of women than men was to be found in salaried rather than independent positions.[117]

During the Weimar Republic several professions opened their doors to women, in keeping with the German Constitution of 11 August 1919, Article 128 of which proclaimed, 'All citizens without distinction are to be admitted to public office in accordance with the laws and according to their ability and qualifications.'[118] In the face of staunch opposition from the legal profession, a law of 11 July 1922 permitted women to become lawyers and judges. Prior to this some states had allowed women to take the first of the two state examinations necessary for certification, and had even allowed them to undertake the necessary period of preparatory service before taking the second examination, but had not allowed them to take that examination.[119] Between 1924 and 1931 145 women and 8,449 men passed the second examination in Prussia, 1.72 women for every 100 men.[120] Dr Marie Munk was the first solicitor in Prussia in 1924, and Fräulein Hilde Bott became the first female barrister to appear before Baden's state court on 9 July 1924; three years later the Prussian Justice Ministry appointed its first female judge, Dr Hagemeyer, to serve in district and regional courts.[121] By 1933 there were 251 female lawyers and 36 female judges in Germany, making up 1.3 per cent and 0.4 per cent respectively of the total numbers of lawyers and judges, and an increasing number of young women were choosing to study law at university.[122] However, a BdF survey of 1930 noted that although a career in the judiciary was open to women in theory, it was closed to them in practice.[123] Career opportunities were more promising for women lawyers, who could set up in practice, than for state prosecutors or judges, whose appointments were dependent on the goodwill and liberal outlook of the individual states. By 1930 no woman had been appointed as a public prosecutor in Prussia, and even in 1932 women were excluded from a career in the judiciary in Bavaria. In other places, such as Hamburg and Oldenburg, women were rejected as judges because it was believed their sensibilities made them unable to officiate in certain kinds of trials and because the workload was thought too demanding.[124]

Women also breached the male bastion of the Protestant Church. The state churches of Baden, Thuringia and Hamburg allowed women to take the two examinations and undertake the necessary preparatory service within the church to become parsons, and by early 1927 two female assistant parsons were employed in Baden, three in Thuringia and three in Hamburg. Their work included providing for the spiritual needs of women in prison or hospital as well as pastoral duties within the community.[125] Women were also being appointed to full professorships at German universities, after they were granted the right in 1918 to 'habilitate', to take the second doctorate necessary for appointment to university academic posts. In 1923 Dr Margarethe Wrangell became the first female full professor, taking up a post in botany at the agricultural University of Hohenheim, and Dr Mathilde Vaerting was appointed to a professorship in education at the University of Jena.[126] The number of female university lecturers increased steadily throughout the Weimar Republic, and in the winter semester of 1932 74 women made up 1.2 per cent of the lecturing staff at Germany's universities.[127] Women were also to be found in small numbers in other professions; in 1933 Germany had 175 female architects and 53 veterinary surgeons.[128]

The professional advances made by women can be seen in the number of professional women's associations founded during the Weimar Republic. The BdÄ was founded in 1924, and the Association of German Female University Lecturers in 1927, and on 11 May 1926 Dr Marie-Elisabeth Lüders had founded the German Federation of Female Academics (Deutsche Akademikerinnenbund, DAB) to ensure that professional women continued to have an influence on and a place in Germany's cultural life and to safeguard their economic and professional interests.[129] By June 1931 it was the second largest association of female professionals in the world, and a year later it had sixteen member organisations with 3,579 members, and twenty-seven local branches.[130] It was a member organisation of the International Federation of University Women, and supported student exchanges; it also provided residences for female students and supported financially the production of a bibliography on the women's movement. In the early 1930s it petitioned Reich ministers not to introduce legislation permitting the dismissal of married women civil servants, and sought the views of all political parties' leaders on professional women's employment. Lüders was instrumental in organising resistance within the women's movement to the suppression of women's professional opportunities, producing with the BdF the *Gelbe Blätter* material to publicise measures being taken against women's employment.[131]

Women in the civil service

In 1927 Käthe Gaebel noted that although women had registered significant achievements in the previous few years, the future for women in the professions was not altogether rosy. Only women who possessed tenacity and courage, as well as the necessary academic skills, should try in spite of all the forces ranged against them to have a professional career.[132] The revolution and the German Constitution had opened possibilities for women to enjoy a career in the professions, but the continuing economic problems which beset the Republic made it a challenging environment for women in which to grasp them. As early as 1921 Dr Elisabeth Altmann-Gottheiner was advising prospective female students to 'abandon hope, all ye who enter here'.[133] A year previously, young women had been warned by the Baden Education Ministry against taking up teaching as a career because of the large numbers of men returning from the war in search of teaching posts.[134] Teachers were civil servants employed by the individual states; their terms of employment were governed by a body of public law which ensured life tenure and a guaranteed level of work and remuneration. Teaching was the one profession in which single women had established themselves, albeit in positions with little or no responsibility. A career in teaching enabled women to become independent, and women teachers were, in general, older than other remunerated working women. In 1925 just under one-third (32.5 per cent) of teachers were under the age of thirty, one-third (33.8 per cent) were between the ages of thirty and forty, and 30.3 per cent were aged between forty and sixty. By 1933 these percentages had shifted to 26.6 per cent, 31.5 per cent and 39.6 per cent respectively, indicating the lack of employment opportunities for young female teachers.[135] In a 1927 survey conducted by the Association of Catholic Women Teachers, in which 9,392 women participated, nearly three-quarters (72 per cent) had their own household and a mere 11 per cent lived with their parents. However, 71.2 per cent of the respondents supported relatives, usually a mother or a sister, and so could not necessarily live an independent existence.[136]

During the Weimar Republic women's share of the teaching profession remained fairly stable, at just under one-third, in part because many states had established ratios for male and female teachers in certain kinds of school and in the allocation of teacher training places. Thus, women made up about one-quarter of elementary school teachers, and three-quarters of teachers in senior girls' schools. In Baden the ratio of male to female student teachers was 3:2, in Hesse and Thuringia 3:1 and in Saxony 4:1, and although it was decided in Prussia that the staff ratio in senior girls' schools should be one male to one female teacher, this never materialised.[137] Though teaching as a career for single women had gained acceptance, few women were to be found in the higher, more responsible and better-paid teaching positions; in 1933 women constituted 14.4 per cent of senior teachers (*Studienräte*).[138] A survey conducted by the General German Women Teachers' Association (Allgemeiner Deutscher Lehrerinnenverein, ADLV) on 1 May 1925 revealed that women made up 9.4 per cent of headteachers in Prussia's girls' senior schools, 6 per cent in girls' middle schools and 0.4 per cent in elementary schools. All elementary schools in Anhalt, Brunswick, Saxony, Thuringia and Württemberg were headed by men.[139] While women's lack of experience, ambition or self-belief or the authorities' reluctance to appoint women to headships might explain the small numbers of women in senior education posts, male teachers' professional jealousy and fear of competition and the attitudes of parents cannot be overlooked. When a woman was appointed to head a senior girls' school in Baden-Baden, after acting as the temporary head, the local male teachers' organisation publicly criticised the appointment and noted its expectation that the post should have gone to a family man with children, while in Moabit, Berlin, the Schools' Advisory Board's recommendation to give two of three vacant headships to women was refuted by the parents' associations and the teaching staff.[140] These events happened during the Depression, when, according to Gertrud Bäumer, the teaching profession was as good as closed to women.[141] Already in 1927 Prussia had 13,043 male and 7,853 female unemployed teachers, and by 1931 15,000 male and 7,500 female teachers were waiting for their first appointment.[142] In 1929 it limited the number of technical and physical education teacher training places for women, and by January 1933 it restricted to three the number of teacher training colleges that women could attend; here, too, women's numbers were cut as a temporary emergency measure.[143]

Women teachers made up half of Germany's female civil servants in 1933, and they appear to have fared better during the Weimar Republic than other female civil servants, whose numbers, along with those of female contractual employees in the public sector, fell more sharply between 1925 and 1933 than the numbers of their male colleagues. In 1933 one-quarter of Germany's female civil servants were to be found in the Reich Postal Service.[144] Women had first been employed in the postal service and on the railways in the 1860s and their numbers had gradually increased.[145] The number of female civil servants in the Reich Postal Service rose from 37,133 in 1918 to 66,552 in 1922, indicating the rapid expansion in public sector employment after the war.[146] Women had been given the right to life tenure on 1 January 1918, and in the early years of the Republic steps were taken to improve the position and standing of women civil servants within the communication and transport sectors, where they were to be found predominantly in middle-ranking posts. The personnel reform in the Reich Postal Service effective from 1 July 1922 placed women on an equal footing with men, granting them life tenure after five years, designated areas of the Postal Service primarily for women and provided women with a career structure, allowing them to sit examinations for promotion to more senior middle-ranking positions (*gehobener Dienst*) and higher-ranking positions (*höherer Dienst*) in the civil service. Between 1922 and 1933 eleven women were promoted to senior middle-ranking posts within the Reich Postal Service, but there was a reluctance to promote women to such posts, or to posts where they would be in charge of men.[147] Though a career structure was laid down for women civil servants on the Reich railways in December 1922, the Reich Transport Authority was adamant that no woman would ever be placed above men.[148] From 1922 the Reich Postal Service preferred to appoint women as contractual employees, with the possibility of transfer to the civil service if sufficient funding was provided in the annual budget, and within the Reich ministries, too, few women were taken on as candidates for the civil service. This led in 1927 to Dr Marie-Elisabeth Lüders spearheading a campaign for the transfer into the permanent civil service of female clerical workers with nine years' service in the Reich administration.[149] At local level, a survey conducted in 1928 in 190 towns and cities excluding Berlin discovered that of every 100 women working in local government, seventy-six were contractual employees and sixteen were civil servants.[150]

However, during the Weimar Republic women were appointed for the first time to so-called 'political' civil service posts, senior positions without tenure in Reich and state ministries from which women, along with socialists, liberals and Catholics, had been excluded in the Wilhelmine empire. At Reich level Dr Gertrud Bäumer was appointed under-secretary (*Ministerialrätin*) in the Reich Interior Ministry in 1920, with responsibility for schools and youth welfare, a post she held until 1933. A survey of 1928 revealed two other female under-secretaries: Dr Dünner in the Reich Labour Ministry and Frau Hirschfeld in the Reich Institute for Employment Exchanges and Unemployment Insurance, which also employed Dr Käthe Gaebel as a senior civil servant (*Oberregierungsrätin*). Dr Else Lüders held an equivalent post in the Reich Labour Ministry, but no women were to be found in senior civil servants' posts in the Reich Finance, Justice and Transport Ministries or the Reich Ministry for the Economy.[151] Margarete Kinsberger was appointed assistant consultant with responsibility for female personnel in the Reich Postal Ministry in 1919, rising to the post of ministerial adviser in 1930.[152] At state level, Helene Weber was an under-secretary in the Prussian Welfare Ministry from 1920 until 1933, and Dr Marie Baum was a consultant in Baden's Welfare Ministry from 1919 until her resignation in 1926.[153] The mid-1920s also saw the appointment of women to the police forces of Prussia, Baden and Saxony, with very gender-specific tasks relating to the care, interrogation and protection of women and children.[154]

The provision of a career structure for female civil servants within the Reich railways and the Reich Postal Service was, in part, an implementation of Article 128 of the Weimar Constitution, which stated, 'All discriminatory regulations against female civil servants are lifted.' Female civil servants could no longer be required to leave on marriage, and many states moved speedily to amend their regulations, though in Bavaria the Landtag refused to revoke its law dismissing female primary schoolteachers on marriage until it was forced to do so by the Supreme Court in 1921.[155] Although the Reich Interior Ministry issued guidelines on 3 September 1920 on the legal position of married female civil servants, upholding the Constitution and detailing the provisions for pregnant civil servants, his colleague the Reich Postal Minister favoured the introduction of severance payments to female civil servants who voluntarily left their posts on marriage, which had been proposed to him by the Association of German Female Reich Postal and Telegraph Civil Servants (Verband Deutscher Reichspost- und Telegraphenbeamtinnen, VRT).[156] The VRT's wish was to be granted when, with Germany's serious financial difficulties in 1922 causing ministers to plan reductions in public sector employment, the Reichstag approved the offer of a gratuity to married women civil servants willing to leave the transport and communications sectors, an offer implemented on 3 February 1923.[157] The Reich Postal Minister was happy to report the success of the scheme, with 83 per cent (3,429) of the eligible women taking advantage of it, a clear vindication of the VRT's campaign.[158] When Germany's extremely difficult financial situation led the Reichstag to pass an Enabling Act on 13 October 1923 to give the government powers to enact any financial, economic and social measures it deemed necessary, proposals to cut expenditure on public sector employment by 25 per cent could be implemented. Under Article 14 of the Personnel Reduction Decree (*Personalabbauverordnung*) of 27 October 1923, however, married women civil servants were singled out; unlike other dismissed civil servants, they were not entitled to receive a severance payment if their future seemed economically secure, and marriage was deemed to provide women with economic security.[159] By March 1924 the desired 25 per cent reduction had been achieved at Reich level, mainly at the expense of contractual employees and manual workers. The figures available make it clear that women, particularly married women, were harder hit than men. Of the 2,955 married female civil servants employed by the Reich on 1 October 1923 a mere 54 remained in post six months later (a cut of 98.2 per cent); of the 745 married female contractual employees, 139 remained and were to be found only in the Reich ministries (a cut of 81.3 per cent).[160] By 1 July 1928 the number of female civil servants in the Reich Postal Service had fallen from 60,884 on 1 October 1923 to 42,943, and the number of married female civil servants from 2,718 to 181.[161] The 1927 Salary Law, which substantially increased civil servants' pay, required every third civil service post that became vacant not to be filled, and as women tended to leave the civil service four times more frequently than did men, women were once again harder hit; this accounts in part for the larger fall in the number of women than of men civil servants between 1925 and 1933.[162] Between 1925 and 1933 the number of female civil servants in the Reich Postal Service fell by 30.1 per cent, and that of male civil servants by 6.6 per cent.[163]

When the Personnel Reduction Decree fell in August 1925, Article 14 continued until 31 March 1929, albeit in a less harsh form. No comprehensive statistics are available for its impact on married women teachers or other female civil servants employed by the states or local authorities, though the magazine of the Reich Association of Married Women Teachers gave frequent snapshots of the dismissals; in one area of Berlin in 1924, for example, twenty-seven out of thirty-one married women teachers were dismissed.[164] In Prussia, Elisabeth von Knobelsdorff, employed as a government architect in Prussia since summer 1921, was dismissed under Prussia's Personnel Reduction Decree in 1923.[165] Following the ending of Article 14, individual states introduced a range of measures to curb the number of married female civil servants, with Württemberg dismissing all its married female civil servants.[166] At Reich level, continuing discussions about the introduction of legislation governing the employment of married female civil servants were affected by the calls during the Depression for an end to double-earners (*Doppelverdiener*); this term originally referred to people with more than one job, but came to refer solely to married working women.

The effects of the Depression on female employment

With the exception of female civil servants, working women appear to have survived the Depression better than men, perhaps because those industries hardest hit, such as construction, were male-dominated.[167] Between September 1929 and December 1932 the number of employed men registered in the sickness insurance funds fell by 38 per cent, that of employed women by 29.1 per cent.[168] Women increased their share of the total insured workforce actually in work from 35.3 per cent in 1928 to 36 per cent in 1930 and to 37.3 per cent in 1931, though this fell slightly to 36.8 per cent in 1932.[169] In industry, it would seem that female employment was affected before male by the oncoming Depression. Between January and December 1929 the number of female applicants rose by 70.9 per cent, that of male applicants by 34.6 per cent.[170] From January 1930 the fluctuations in the labour market had the same effect on the employment of both sexes, though women's employment was slower to pick up than men's in 1933.[171]

As can be seen from Table 3.5, female manual workers appear to have been harder hit in the Depression than female white-collar workers, whose numbers increased between 1925 and 1933. The 1933 census data reveal that 17.3 per cent of female white-collar workers and civil servants and 19.5 per cent of female manual workers were unemployed, whereas for men these figures were 15.2 per cent and 36 per cent respectively. Hence women's share of the manual workforce actually in work increased, from 25.3 per cent in 1925 to 27.6 per cent in 1933.[172] Elizabeth Bright Jones believes that 'women's unskilled work and low wages may have insulated them more effectively from unemployment'.[173] Helgard Kramer, however, believes that working women were much more willing than men to be flexible and to adapt to employers' demands, reducing their expectations of the type of employment, pay and the permanency of a post.[174] This may have been because of the kind of work in which women were primarily engaged – unskilled or semi-skilled – or because women did not invest as heavily in their employment as men. They did not regard work as a lifetime career but merely as a stage in their lives between leaving school and getting married, a belief that continued to hold sway until at least the 1960s in West Germany.[175] Indeed, Ute Frevert has claimed that the acceptance by all social strata of women's employment as a natural stage before marriage was a sign of Weimar's modernity.[176] Young women between the ages of twenty and twenty-five seem to have been the group of women hardest hit by unemployment. Both boys and girls entering the job market at the age of fourteen benefited from the small birth cohorts from 1929 onwards, a result of the reduced birth rate during the First World War, and from the cheapness of their labour. Between the ages of fourteen and eighteen the unemployment rates of boys and girls were similar, but thereafter the difference between them widened, in part because more boys had apprenticeships and they were dismissed once these came to an end.[177] The authorities were more concerned about male than about female youth unemployment, as girls could be occupied in the home, doing housework.[178] A mere 5,000 of the 175,000 voluntary labour service places in January 1933 were filled by women.[179] One young woman on a voluntary labour service scheme run by the Lutheran Church in Hamburg in the winter of 1932–33 wrote, 'I am here because I got nothing from the welfare office and my mother cannot support me either, my brother is unemployed and doesn't get anything either, neither of us can live at home because my sister earns so little, and my mother only gets her pension.'[180]

In June 1931 young people under the age of twenty-one were excluded from unemployment benefit unless their families were unable to support them.[181] The same law introduced a means test for unemployed married women, and some claim that over one-third of unemployed married women lost their unemployment benefit.[182] Official statistics, however, show that women's share of those receiving unemployment benefit remained stable, and during the Depression married women constituted just over one-third of female recipients of unemployment benefit, indicating that unemployed married women needed financial support and had been working out of economic necessity.[183]

The demobilisation decrees at the war's end had linked the concept of 'economic need' with female employment, and this notion resurfaced at times of economic uncertainty. During the hyperinflation of 1923, when there were reports of mass dismissals of married female manual workers whose husbands were in employment, the Reich Labour Minister, Dr Brauns, wrote to the Union of German Employers' Associations, expressing his opinion that *Doppelverdiener* should, wherever possible, be replaced by the unemployed and should not be considered when new posts were being filled.[184] Dr Brauns's request was repeated in 1926 and by the new Labour Minister, Dr Stegerwald, in 1930, when he asked employers to prioritise the dismissal of *Doppelverdiener* and not to employ any if available unemployed persons were suitable.[185] With the onset of the Depression, calls were made for the dismissal of all employed married women, with claims that their removal from the workforce would eradicate male unemployment and allow women to return to their natural profession as wives and mothers.[186] Numerous petitions were laid before city councils, state parliaments and the Reichstag calling for the dismissal of *Doppelverdiener* from Reich and local government jobs, as it was far easier to regulate the employment of women by the state than by private concerns, though the political parties drawing up the petitions were also hoping to gain support by exploiting widely held views.[187] The staunchly anti-feminist DNHV demanded in November 1930 that Berlin's City Council should effect the dismissal of female sales personnel who were either married or had wealthy parents.[188] While feminists pointed out that at most 265,000 married women in wage-earning occupations could be replaced by men, their voices went unheeded in the general clamour for an end to married women's employment, which was also favoured by the churches.[189] In his encyclicals *Casti Connubii* of 31 December 1930 and *Quadragesimo Anno* of 15 May 1931 Pope Pius XI declared that a married woman's place was in the home, caring for her family, not in the labour market.[190] In March 1931 the government appointed a commission under Dr Brauns to examine the problem of unemployment; it concluded that married female civil servants whose future seemed economically secure should be dismissed, but could not agree on how to achieve the women's dismissal.[191] It was left to the Centre Party to secure support for a bill, passed in the Reichstag on 12 May 1932, which permitted married women civil servants in the Reich's employ to resign and Reich authorities to dismiss married women whose future seemed permanently secure, with all the women receiving severance payments.[192] The law affected some 1,200 women in the Reich Postal Service, of whom between 800 and 900 could be thought economically secure.[193] The Brauns Commission had also estimated that there were between 5,000 and 6,000 married women teachers, and some states lost no time in trying to pass similar laws, though it was not until 30 June 1933 that the law was formally extended to include the states and the local authorities. This law also permitted breaches of Article 128 of the Weimar Constitution, allowing women civil servants to be paid less than men, and set thirty-five as the minimum age at which a woman could be appointed to a civil service post on a permanent basis.[194] However, even during the Weimar Republic women civil servants had been placed on a lower salary scale than men doing the same work, and during the Depression several states, including Baden, Hesse and Thuringia, followed Prussia's example and cut the hours and salaries of their female teachers.[195] Although women teachers in Berlin and Baden successfully sued their education ministries, their victories were hollow. In its judgement the Baden Superior Court, while upholding Article 128 of the Constitution, stated that women teachers' physical weakness meant that they were not as equal as men to the demands of the teaching profession.[196]

The frequent attempts to curb married women's employment within the public sector reflect the dissatisfaction with the rights granted to women under Article 128 of the Weimar Constitution, rights which the courts sought to uphold but which were not universally wanted or welcomed. Karin Hausen has referred to the equal rights legislation as a 'provocation', and in the latter years of the Republic, single women in senior administrative positions were also dismissed, purportedly in order to curb expenditure.[197] These actions are indicative of wider concerns about women's role within the family and German society. One contemporary survey concluded that 'economic insecurity and unemployment tend to increase the number of women workers, whereas in prosperous times women, and especially married women, are much less likely to enter paid employment'.[198] Married women often went out to work because their husbands were unemployed, though most would have preferred to devote their whole time to their families rather than have the double burden of a job outside the home as well.[199] Even in working-class circles, where it had become accepted for married women to continue to work in the textile industry, often returning after having children, many did not believe in a married woman's right to work.[200] While a woman working in her husband's business was seen as strengthening the bond between the couple, a woman working outside the home was thought to rush her household chores and to have little time for her children, who were left in the care of others. Moreover, a woman working outside the home could hear opinions other than her husband's and gain self-confidence and, being no longer economically dependent on him, was more likely to leave him and break up the family. More often than not, however, working-class married women's paid work kept the family together, with the income saving the family from economic catastrophe.[201] Even professional women's organisations did not unanimously or unambiguously support married women's right to work. Both the Catholic and Protestant women teachers' associations believed that female civil servants should be single, while the ADLV remained reluctant to discriminate against married women. Its founder, Helene Lange, was adamant that women should not yield one inch of the rights they had been granted in the Constitution.[202] While the BdF campaigned against the continuation of Article 14 in 1925 and the introduction of the law of May 1932, it was aware that its position was tenuous, as its various member associations held differing views. One, the VRT, which could boast a membership of 85 per cent of female Reich postal civil servants in 1933, believed that a married female civil servant should be a rarity, and it welcomed the May 1932 law, regarding married women civil servants as competitors with single women and as a threat to single women's future in the civil service.[203] The VRT also believed that the married female civil servant was undermining the prestige and status of the civil service by combining two full-time careers, as wife and civil servant.[204] It sought severance payments in compensation for the women giving up their right to tenure and their careers. The small number of married female civil servants affected by the law of May 1932 highlights the fact that the campaign against the *Doppelverdiener*, which intensified during the Depression, was out of all proportion to the numbers of married working women who could be replaced by men. Indeed, the mayor of Hamburg recognised this when he noted that measures against *Doppelverdiener* aimed at a psychological impact, rather than relieving unemployment.[205]

Germany was not alone in acting against its married female civil servants in times of high unemployment. In 1924 the Dutch government decided to dismiss female civil servants on marriage, and in Great Britain, where, Meta Zimmeck believes, women civil servants were 'victims of both public policy and private prejudice', women continued to have to give up their teaching posts on marriage until 1944.[206] We have already noted the impact of the Nazis' law of 30 June 1933, but on coming to power, the Nazis had been quick to dismiss women in both senior civil servants' and 'political' civil servants' posts, most notably Dr Gertrud Bäumer, for reasons of political unreliability. Other women dismissed included Helene Weber, Else Lüders, and Käthe Gaebel in 'political' posts, Emmy Beckmann, a senior adviser on girls' schooling in Hamburg, and Else Ulich-Beil, the head of the Social Women's School in

Dresden.[207] The Nazis did, however, appoint women to 'political' posts, Paula Siber becoming an adviser on women's affairs in the Reich Interior Ministry and Hedwig Förster an adviser on girls' schooling in the Prussian Education Ministry, both with more gender-specific remits than their predecessors.[208] Although the anti-intellectual Nazi regime imposed a limit of 10 per cent on female participation in the student body, this was not strictly implemented, in part because of the dawning realisation that, in accordance with Nazi ideology, there had to be women doctors and teachers to care for female patients and pupils.[209] There was a general need for trained professionals, both male and female, because of the impact of the fall in social prestige of a university education as new elites such as the *Schutzstaffel* (protection squad, SS) rose in power, influence and standing, followed by the advent of the Second World War.[210] However, the tenuous footing which women had gained in the legal profession was taken away, at Hitler's wish, and after 1936 women were barred from becoming judges or setting up in legal practice, though there were career opportunities for women trained in law in the vast Nazi women's organisations.[211]

Conclusion

During the Weimar Republic structural changes in female employment which had begun at the turn of the century continued as women chose to leave their traditional areas of employment, agriculture and domestic service, to take up manual work in industry and, increasingly, white-collar work in the rapidly expanding service and administration sectors. The rationalisation of German industry during the 1920s facilitated women's entry into unskilled and semi-skilled work in newer industries such as optical engineering and chemicals, while during the Depression women were attractive to employers as cheap labour. Women could not have entered employment if the demand for their labour had not existed, but their entry into previously male-dominated domains led to them being seen as competitors in the job market.[212] As more women married, married women increased their share of the female workforce. However, attitudes in many sections of society towards female employment did not keep pace with the changing reality of it. Manual and white-collar work was hardly emancipatory for young women, the vast majority of whom lived with their parents, but it did give them the wherewithal to provide for their own needs and to furnish financial support to their families; this had long been customary within the working class, but was now becoming accepted practice among the impoverished middle class.

For determined young women with the necessary educational qualifications the Weimar Republic provided an opportunity to enter professional employment, to build a career of their choosing and to pursue an independent existence. Throughout the Weimar Republic an increasing number of girls were raising their educational standards, and many were going on to university, in order to train as teachers or for careers in a branch of medicine or one of the other professions now opening up for women, in line with the equality of the sexes laid down in the Weimar Constitution. During the Weimar Republic women were given a career structure within parts of the civil service and began to be appointed to permanent civil service positions under the same conditions as men. The advance of a woman was dependent to a large extent on the attitudes of her employer, the goodwill of her client base and the acceptance of other (male) professionals, with some, such as those in the legal profession, continuing to contest women's suitability.

While the Weimar Republic did not witness the economic liberation of the numbers of women indicated by Schoenbaum, there is little evidence to support Bridenthal's contention that women were 'pressed more and more into unskilled work with lessened responsibility or out of the economy altogether'. Indeed, Bridenthal's comments about the loss of a 'sense of competence and self-worth' could apply more readily to the millions of unemployed men during the Depression, unable to provide financially for their families and having to witness the women of the family assuming their role as family breadwinners.[213] As has been noted, the late Peukert argued that the Weimar Republic formed a critical phase in the era of classical modernity, which he understood to be the twentieth century's 'fully fledged industrialised society' with its 'highly rationalised industrial production' and 'a substantial degree of bureaucratised administrative and service activity'.[214] With the secular trends of the diminishing significance of traditional sectors and industries for the female workforce, the increase in women's employment in industry, administration and the service sector, as well as women's increasing educational achievements and entry into a range of professional posts, the Weimar Republic can be seen as the cradle for German women's position in employment to the present day.

Notes

1 D. Schoenbaum, *Hitler's Social Revolution: Class and Status in Nazi Germany 1933–1939* (London: Weidenfeld and Nicolson, 1967), p. 187.
2 R. Bridenthal, 'Beyond *Kinder, Küche, Kirche*: Weimar Women at Work', *Central European History*, 6:2 (1973), 149, 165.
3 BAK, Nachlass Lüders 157, Kriegsministerium, Kriegsamt. Anlagen 1 und 2 zu Nr. 40/11.18 A.Z.S.2.
4 BAB, R3901/567, 'Merkblatt für weibliche Angestellte'; 'Merkblatt für Arbeiterinnen'.
5 BAB, R3901/10399, E. Lüders, 'Die gewerbliche Frauenarbeit nach dem Krieg', pp. 2–3.
6 R. Bessel, 'Unemployment and Demobilisation in Germany after the First World War', in R. J. Evans and D. Geary (eds), *The German Unemployed: Experiences and Consequences of Mass Unemployment from the Weimar Republic to the Third Reich* (London: Croom Helm, 1987), pp. 23–39. Rouette notes that February 1919 was the worst month for unemployment in Berlin: S. Rouette, *Sozialpolitik als Geschlechterpolitik: Die Regulierung der Frauenarbeit nach dem Ersten Weltkrieg* (Frankfurt am Main: Campus Verlag, 1993), p. 60.
7 Rouette, '"Gleichberechtigung"', p. 171; Bessel claims that the demobilisation decrees 'were most consistently and effectively employed against women': Bessel, *Germany after the First World War*, p. 141.
8 Mai, 'Arbeitsmarktregulierung oder Sozialpolitik?', p. 219; ZStA, Reichstag, Nr. 127, Bl. 224, *Verhandlungen der verfassungsgebenden Deutschen Nationalversammlung*, vol. 329 (Berlin: Druck and Verlag der Nordeutschen Buckdruckerei und Verlags-Anstalt, 1920), pp. 2709–10.
9 Bessel, '"Eine nicht allzu grosse Beunruhigung des Arbeitsmarktes"', pp. 220–1; G. Schulz, 'Die weiblichen Angestellten vom 19. Jahrhundert bis 1945', in Pohl and Treue (eds), *Die Frau in der deutschen Wirtschaft*, p. 194.
10 Calculated from Mai, 'Arbeitsmarktregulierung oder Sozialpolitik?', p. 214.
11 Bessel, *Germany after the First World War*, p. 120; Bessel, '"Eine nicht allzugrosse Beunruhigung"', pp. 224–5.
12 'Vom Kampf gegen die Frauenarbeit', *Gewerkschaftliche Frauenzeitung*, 5:24 (1 December 1920), 177–8; Mai, 'Arbeitsmarktregulierung oder

Sozialpolitik?', p. 222; G. Hanna, 'Women in the German Trade Union Movement', *International Labour Review*, 8 (July 1923), 36–7.
13 'Interpellation. Nr. 746', *Verhandlungen der verfassungsgebenden Deutschen Nationalversammlung*, vol. 338 (Berlin: Julius Sittenfeld, 1920), pp. 530–1. A decree of February 1920 compelled demobilisation committees to include women as members: Rouette, *Sozialpolitik als Geschlechterpolitik*, p. 83.
14 'Verordnung über Erwerbslosenfürsorge. Vom 13. November 1918', *Reichsgesetzblatt 1918*, no. 153 (14 November 1918), 1305–9; S. Rouette, 'Mothers and Citizens: Gender and Social Policy in Germany after the First World War', *Central European History*, 30:1 (1997), 60.
15 ZStA, Reichsarbeitsministerium, Nr. 1170, Bl. 35, 'Verband Badischer Arbeitsnachweise ans Badische Arbeitsministerium. Karlsruhe 30 August 1920, Erwerbslosenfürsorge betr.'
16 For Baden see *ibid.*; LAB, BRep 235, HLA MF 2891, *Die Frau in schwerer Zeit* (10 April 1919) reports such courses being held in Bielefeld, Kassel, Karlsruhe, Breslau and Hamburg. In Karlsruhe the 200 participants each received a daily rate of 20 Pf and a self-prepared evening meal. In Britain, too, women who refused a domestic service post had their unemployment benefit withdrawn: see M. J. Boxer and J. H. Quataert (eds), *Connecting Spheres: Women in the Western World, 1500 to the Present* (Oxford: Oxford University Press, 1987), p. 207.
17 The numbers of insured domestic servants in Berlin rose from 72,714 in December 1918 to 96,628 a year later: Rouette, *Sozialpolitik als Geschlechterpolitik*, pp. 67–8; Rouette, '"Gleichberechtigung"', p. 177.
18 Bessel's figures show a higher percentage of female unemployment among trade union members until November 1920, and intermittently thereafter: Bessel, 'Unemployment and Demobilisation', p. 35. Between 1919 and 1923 the average annual unemployment among trade union members was higher for women than for men: *StJhb 1928*, p. 386.
19 The demand for women in agriculture continued to exceed supply throughout the 1920s: *StJhb 1920*, pp. 239, 241; *StJhb 1921/1922*, p. 424; *StJhb 1923*, p. 405; *StJhb 1924/1925*, p. 289; *StJhb 1926*, p. 297; *StJhb 1928*, p. 378.
20 The *Gesindeordnung* governed the terms and conditions of agricultural labourers and domestic servants: Bessel, *Germany after the First World War*, p. 201.
21 E. B. Jones, 'The Gendering of the Postwar Agricultural Labour Shortage in Saxony, 1918–1925', *Central European History*, 32:3

(1999), 324–5; Bessel, '"Eine nicht allzu grosse Beunruhigung"', pp. 222–3.
22 This trend continued into the Federal Republic of West Germany. In 1950 31.3 per cent of women worked, in 1961 33.4 per cent, in 1970 30.2 per cent and in 1980 32.6 per cent: Frevert, *Women in German History*, p. 333.
23 *SdR*, vol. 402, p. 424; vol. 458, pp. 57, 60.
24 Although there was an increase in married women working in all age-groups between 1907 and 1925, it was especially marked in those aged under thirty: *SdR*, vol. 402, p. 439; vol. 458, p. 77. In 1925 31 per cent of manual workers' wives were also classed as working: *SdR*, vol. 402, p. 440.
25 J. Stephenson, *Women in Nazi Germany* (Harlow: Longman, 2001), p. 54; Statistisches Bundesamt (ed.), *Statistisches Jahrbuch 1981 für die Bundesrepublik Deutschland* (Stuttgart: W. Kohlhammer GmbH, 1981), p. 101.
26 O. Opet and W. von Blume (eds), *Das Familienrecht des Bürgerlichen Gesetzbuches* (Berlin: Heymann, 1906), pp. 93–107. In 1925 33 per cent of women married to shopkeepers were classed as working: *SdR*, vol. 402, p. 440.
27 Bridenthal, 'Beyond *Kinder, Küche, Kirche*: Weimar Women at Work', p. 151.
28 Married women in the population:

Married women	1907		1925		1933	
	Number	%	Number	%	Number	%
Working	2,944,178	25.8	3,645,326	28.7	4,177,404	29.2
Without a profession	128,804	1.3	177,773	1.4	236,601	1.6
Housewives	7,061,024	72.9	8,886,971	69.9	9,902,704	69.2
Total	9,684,006	100.0	12,710,070	100.0	14,316,709	100.0

Source: *SdR*, vol. 402, pp. 439, 442; vol. 458, p. 76. In 1939 33 per cent of married women were working: Stephenson, *Women in Nazi Germany*, p. 54.

29 While the numbers of widowed and divorced women increased from 2,250,556 in 1907 to 3,337,999 in 1933, the numbers working fell from 919,308 to 886,548: *SdR*, vol. 402, pp. 442, 452; vol. 458, p. 76.
30 During the Third Reich, the downward trend stalled, with the share of family helpers within the female workforce rising from 36.1 per cent in 1933 to 36.4 per cent in 1939, but after the Second World War, this share fell to 22.1 per cent in West Germany in 1961 and 7.9 per cent

in 1980. Domestic servants constituted 10.5 per cent of the female workforce in 1939, falling to 3.4 per cent in West Germany in 1961, and they were no longer recognised as a category in 1980: Frevert, *Women in German History*, p. 334.
31 If civil servants are included the percentage rises to 55.9: Statistisches Bundesamt (ed.), *Statistisches Jahrbuch 1981*, p. 95.
32 H. Kramer, 'Frankfurt's Working Women: Scapegoats or Winners in the Great Depression?', in Evans and Geary (eds), *The German Unemployed*, p. 119.
33 J. Ernst, 'Jugendliche Hausangestellte', *Die Frau*, 37:2 (November 1929), 98–105.
34 In 1925 74.9 per cent of female domestic servants were under thirty, in 1933 72.9. In 1933 56.8 per cent of all resident domestic servants worked for property and business owners, and 26.1 per cent for civil servants or professionals: calculated from figures in *SdR*, vol. 402, p. 433; vol. 458, p. 64.
35 Results of a survey conducted by the Reich Labour Ministry in 1926: Allgemeiner Deutscher Gewerkschaftsbund, *Jahrbuch des Allgemeinen Deutschen Gewerkschaftsbundes 1928* (Berlin: Verlagsanstalt des Allgemeinen Deutschen Gewerkschaftsbundes, 1929), p. 141.
36 In 1925 77.5 per cent of female domestics resided under their employer's roof, in 1933 69.7: *SdR*, vol. 402, p. 433; vol. 458, p. 46. See also Kramer, 'Frankfurt's Working Women', p. 136.
37 For attempts to introduce legislation and the attitudes of the interested parties see R. Bridenthal, 'Class Struggle Around the Hearth: Women and Domestic Service in the Weimar Republic', in M. Dobkowski and I. Wallimann (eds), *Towards the Holocaust: The Social and Economic Collapse of the Weimar Republic* (Westport: Greenwood, 1983), pp. 243–64; I. Wittmann, '"Echte Weiblichkeit ist ein Dienen" – die Hausgehilfin in der Weimarer Republik und im Nationalsozialismus', in Frauengruppe Faschismusforschung (ed.), *Mutterkreuz und Arbeitsbuch*, pp. 21–4. Few domestic servants were organised in trade unions, some 10,845 women being members of the Central Federation of German Domestic Servants in 1922: Hanna, 'Women in the German Trade Union Movement', p. 27.
38 E. Hopmann, 'Die Gefährdung der Dienstboten', *Die christliche Frau*, 25:2 (February 1927), 38–45. According to one survey in the Rhineland 37.9 per cent of prostitutes were former domestic servants.
39 *StJhb 1924/1925*, p. 289; *StJhb 1932*, p. 291; *StJhb 1933*, p. 291. Domestic servants made up 19.5 per cent of unemployed women in 1932, which would refute Kramer's claim that unemployment in domestic service was lower than in other sectors: Kramer, 'Frankfurt's Working Women', p. 136.

40 In one third of the year agricultural workers were to work an average of eight hours daily, in another third ten hours and in the final third eleven hours: 'Verordnung betr. eine vorläufige Landarbeitsordnung. Vom 24. Januar 1919', *Reichsgesetzblatt 1919*, no. 21 (29 January 1919), 111–14.

41 'Verordnung zur Behebung des Arbeitermangels in der Landwirtschaft', *Reichsgesetzblatt 1919*, no. 60 (19 March 1919), 310–11; *StJhb 1929*, p. 273; *StJhb 1931*, p. 301.

42 Jones, 'The Gendering of the Postwar Agricultural Labour Shortage in Saxony', pp. 321, 325–7.

43 R. Kempf, *Die deutsche Frau nach der Volks-, Berufs- und Betriebszählung von 1925* (Mannheim: Bennsheimer Verlag, 1931), p. 73.

44 In 1925 90.1 per cent of all women working in agriculture were to be found on farms under 50 hectares: *StJhb 1930*, p. 58. See also R. Kempf, 'Die Stellung der Frau in der deutschen Landwirtschaft', in A. Schmidt-Beil (ed.), *Die Kultur der Frau* (Berlin: Verlag für Kultur und Wissenschaft, 1931), pp. 98–119.

45 In 1925 women made up 69.5 per cent of the agricultural workforce near the industrial centre of Pforzheim in Baden: calculated from figures in *SdR*, vol. 405, part 33, pp. 72–95. For Saxony see E. B. Jones, 'A New Stage of Life? Young Farm Women's Changing Expectations and Aspirations about Work in Weimar Saxony', *German History*, 19 (2001), 557–8.

46 In 1925 family helpers made up 72 per cent of the female agricultural workforce, and in 1933 74.6 per cent, with married women's share increasing from 59.1 per cent in 1925 to 67.2 per cent in 1933: calculated from figures in *SdR*, vol. 402, pp. 446, 452; vol. 453, pp. 4–16.

47 The numbers of *Mägde* fell from 540,426 in 1925 to 434,842 in 1933: E. Baldauf, 'Die Frauenarbeit in der Landwirtschaft' (PhD dissertation, University of Kiel, 1929), pp. 8, 11; *SdR*, vol. 458, p. 71. Women often earned less than half of a male agricultural worker's wage, which was considerably less than wages in industry. The *Mägde* tended to have yearly contracts and live in: M. Silberkühl-Schulte, 'Die Landfrauenfrage', *Die Frau*, 40:6 (March 1933), 363.

48 In 1933 agricultural labourers made up 45.5 per cent of female workers on farms of over 100 hectares, female seasonal workers 32.9 per cent and *Mägde* 10.7 per cent: M. B. von Brand, *Die Frau in der deutschen Landwirtschaft* (Berlin: F. Vahlen, 1939), p. xxiii; I. Strasser, *Frauenarbeit und Rationalisierung* (Berlin: Verlag der Roten Gewerkschafts-Internationale, 1927), p. 26.

49 Kempf, 'Die Stellung der Frau in der deutschen Landwirtschaft', p. 114. In the survey of nine concerns, the highest number of hours

worked by a woman was 4,396, and the lowest, in a concern without a male head of household, 3,151: M. Silberkühl-Schulte, 'Die Frau in der deutschen Landwirtschaft', *Die christliche Frau*, 31:4 (April 1933), 117.
50 Kempf, 'Die Stellung der Frau in der deutschen Landwirtschaft', p. 109; Silberkühl-Schulte, 'Die Landfrauenfrage', p. 364; Bridenthal, 'Beyond *Kinder, Kirche, Küche*: Weimar Women at Work', p. 152.
51 *StJhb* 1926, p. 404.
52 Brand, *Die Frau in der deutschen Landwirtschaft*, p. 48; *SdR*, vol. 410, p. 583.
53 E. Lüders, 'The Effects of German Labour Legislation on Employment Possibilities for Women', *International Labour Review*, 20 (1929), 394–5; Mai, 'Arbeitsmarktregulierung oder Sozialpolitik', p. 223; Deutscher Metallarbeiterverband, *Die Frauenarbeit in der Metallindustrie* (Stuttgart: Deutscher Metallarbeiterverband, 1930), p. vii.
54 *SdR*, vol. 408, p. 174. Women in the textile industry made up 28.4 per cent of the total female industrial manual workforce, in the clothing industry 25.4 per cent and in the food industry 11.4 per cent.
55 Allgemeiner Deutscher Gewerkschaftsbund, *Jahrbuch des Allgemeinen Deutschen Gewerkschaftsbundes 1927* (Berlin: Verlagsanstalt des Allgemeinen Deutschen Gewerkschaftsbundes, 1928), pp. 140–7. Women made up 60.5 per cent of the skilled workforce in the textile industry: E. Niewiera, 'Der Deutsche Textilarbeiterverband und die "Doppelverdiener"', *Die Genossin*, 8:6 (June 1931), 223. On average 28.6 per cent of the female workforce in textiles were married, but this figure varied with the type of job and area. In Berlin 68.4 per cent of female textile workers were married: *SdR*, vol. 402, p. 440; vol. 458, p. 71.
56 The female manual workforce in textiles decreased by 2.4 per cent, and the male increased by 7.6 per cent: calculated from figures in *SdR*, vol. 458, p. 53. In the cigar industry, for instance, four unskilled female machine-operators equalled the output of twelve skilled male cigar-makers: J. Grünfeld, 'Frauenarbeit im Lichte der Rationalisierung', *Die Arbeit*, 8 (1931), 921. Contrary to Grünfeld, Bridenthal believes that in most cases women did not replace men during the rationalisation of German industry: Bridenthal, 'Beyond *Kinder, Kirche, Küche*: Weimar Women at Work', p. 157.
57 Women made up 47.3 per cent of the workforce in the electrical engineering industry in 1926, 57.3 per cent in 1929 and 51.8 per cent in 1930. For the production of precision tools and optical instruments the figures are 36.1, 44.7 and 43.7 respectively; for metal goods 56.3, 61.4 and 60.8: Grünfeld, 'Frauenarbeit im Lichte der Rationalisierung', p. 922.

58 Calculated from figures in *SdR*, vol. 408, p. 74, and vol. 458, p. 43.
59 Canning, 'Women and the Politics of Gender', p. 160.
60 Frevert, *Women in German History*, pp. 276–7. In 1925 69.1 per cent of female manual workers in industry were under thirty, in 1933 60.4: calculated from figures in *SdR*, vol 401, p. 431, and vol. 458, p. 64.
61 The number of married female manual workers in industry increased by one-third between 1925 and 1933, from 420,299 to 560,376, taking their share of the female manual workforce from 21.4 per cent to 28.6 per cent: *SdR*, vol 401, p. 431, and vol. 458, p. 64.
62 Deutscher Metallarbeiterverband, *Die Frauenarbeit in der Metallindustrie*, pp. 19–20. In 1930 83.1 per cent of female manual workers in factories visited by the inspectorate were to be found in those with over fifty workers: Badisches Statistisches Landesamt, *Jahresbericht des Gewerbeaufsichts für das Jahr 1930* (Karlsruhe: Macklot'sche Druckerei, 1931), pp. 154–7. See also J. Grünfeld, 'Rationalisation and the Employment and Wages of Women in Germany', *International Labour Review*, 29 (1934), 617. In the metal industry 68 per cent of unskilled workers and 35 per cent of semi-skilled workers were women.
63 *SdR*, vol. 408, p. 158; A. Rühle-Gerstel, *Das Frauenproblem der Gegenwart: Eine psychologische Bilanz* (Leipzig: Verlag von S. Hirzel, 1932), p. 276.
64 Deutscher Metallarbeiterverband, *Die Frauenarbeit in der Metallindustrie*, p. 85. In 1928 girls made up 8.4 per cent of all craft apprentices: E. Harvey, *Youth and the Welfare State in Weimar Germany* (Oxford: Clarendon Press, 1993), p. 73.
65 Karbe, *Die Frauenlohnfrage*, p. 99; Bry, *Wages in Germany*, p. 96.
66 In the textile industry between 1924 and 1927 a skilled woman received 78 per cent of a skilled man's wage, an unskilled woman 74 per cent of an unskilled man's. In some areas, such as Aachen, Krefeld and Munich, male and female weavers earned the same, but the man received an extra 'social payment': *StJhb 1927*, p. 391; Allgemeiner Deutscher Gewerkschaftsbund, *Jahrbuch 1927*, pp. 140–7; J. Grünfeld, 'Das Lohnproblem der Arbeiterin', *Die Arbeit*, 6 (1929), 445–53.
67 In 1925 41.6 per cent of male and 55.9 per cent of female industrial workers were under twenty-five: *SdR*, vol. 402, p. 431; Bry, *Wages in Germany*, p. 89. In the Baden textile industry in 1927 a fourteen-year-old girl earned 96 per cent of a fourteen-year-old boy's wage, and the differential grew with age until the age of twenty: W. Jehle, 'Die Arbeiterlöhne in der Badischen Textilindustrie seit der Stabilisierung der Mark (1923–1933)' (PhD dissertation, University of Heidelberg, 1935), pp. 34–6.
68 Women's share of the membership peaked in 1918 with 25.4 per

cent (422,957 members): *StJhb 1922*, pp. 456–7. These are the yearly average figures. In 1931 570,836 women made up 13.8 per cent of the membership: *StJhb 1932*, p. 556. In times of unemployment women, especially married women, also showed a greater tendency to leave their unions: M. Thibert, 'The Economic Depression and the Employment of Women', *International Labour Review*, 27 (April 1933), 460.

69 Only two of the 282 officials at the 1927 General Congress of the General Federation of German Trade Unions were women: Allgemeiner Deutscher Gewerkschaftsbund, *Jahrbuch 1928*, p. 213; Hanna, 'Women in the German Trade Union Movement', p. 27. By 1929 women's share of the textile workers' union had fallen to 57.5 per cent, and by 1931 to 55.4 per cent: *StJhb 1930*, p. 576; *StJhb 1932*, p. 556.

70 'Anordnung über die Regelung der Arbeitszeit gewerblicher Arbeiter. Vom 23. November 1918', *Reichsgesetzblatt II 1918*, no. 162 (26 November 1918), 1, 333–6; 'Verordnung über die Arbeitszeit. Vom 21. Dezember 1923', *Reichsgesetzblatt 1923*, no. 134 (21 December 1923), 251. Over 80 per cent of women in the textile industry were working more than forty-eight hours per week in 1924, but by February 1930 31.9 per cent were on short-time working: L. Preller, *Sozialpolitik in der Weimarer Republik* (Düsseldorf: Athenäum-Droste, 1978), pp. 146–50.

71 G. Wellner, 'Industriearbeiterinnen in der Weimarer Republik: Arbeitsmarkt, Arbeit und Privatleben 1919–1933', *Geschichte und Gesellschaft*, 7 (1981), 545–6; Deutscher Textilarbeiterverband (ed.), *Mein Arbeitstag – mein Wochenende* (Berlin: Textilpraxis, 1928), *passim*; Bajohr, *Die Hälfte der Fabrik*, pp. 190–2; Hagemann, *Frauenalltag und Männerpolitik*, p. 409.

72 Between August 1923 and July 1924 there were 2.86 cases of illness for every 100 men registered in the insurance funds, and 3.47 for every 100 women: H. Adler, 'Die Gesunderhaltung der Industriearbeiterin in Beruf', *Die Frau*, 33:4 (January 1926), 204. A survey conducted by the Textile Industry's Employers' Organisation revealed that 46.05 per cent of the male and 61.91 per cent of the female workforce reported sick during 1925. On average each man was absent for ten days, each woman for eighteen: Arbeitgeberverband der deutschen Textilindustrie, *Die Frauenerwerbsarbeit in der Textilindustrie mit besonderer Berücksichtigung schwangerer Frauen* (Berlin: Elsner, 1926), pp. 12–13. Figures used by the German Metal Workers' Union, however, show that in 1925, 1926 and 1927 women were ill less often than men but absent from work for longer periods of time, a finding also of all sickness insurance funds reporting in 1930: Deutscher

Metallarbeiterverband, *Die Frauenarbeit in der Metallindustrie*, p. 185; *Berliner Tageblatt*, 278 (14 June 1932).

73 Deutscher Textilarbeiterverband, *Erwerbsarbeit, Schwangerschaft, Frauenleid* (Berlin: Verlag Deutscher Textilarbeiterverband, 1925), pp. 34–41. The union called *inter alia* for the prohibition of the employment of pregnant women for the last four months of pregnancy and a maximum of four hours' work per day in the fourth and fifth months of pregnancy.

74 'Gesetz über die Beschäftigung vor und nach der Niederkunft. Vom 16. Juli 1927', *Reichsgesetzblatt I 1927*, no. 31 (20 July 1927), 184–5; H. Goldschmidt, 'The Application in Germany of the Washington Convention concerning the Employment of Women before and after Childbirth', *International Labour Review*, 16 (1927), 637–47.

75 Badisches Statistisches Landesamt, *Berichte des Gewerbeaufsichtamtes für die Jahre 1933 und 1934* (Karlsruhe: Macklot, 1935) p. 24. Although the maternity benefit was supposed to be paid before the birth, surveys discovered that it was not generally paid until after it: Adler, 'Die Gesunderhaltung der Industriearbeiterin', p. 209; Usborne, *The Politics of the Body*, pp. 49–50. The Textile Industry's Employers' Organisation used the fact that one-quarter of pregnant textile workers worked up to the day of the birth and more than one-half up to within five days of their confinement to argue that the work was not too strenuous: Arbeitgeberverband der Deutschen Textilindustrie, *Die Frauenerwerbsarbeit in der Textilindustrie*, p. 26. The Metal Workers' Union noted that 60 per cent of women continued to work in the last four weeks of pregnancy and did not make use of the 1927 law: Deutscher Metallarbeiterverband, *Die Frauenarbeit in der Metallindustrie*, p. 175.

76 Allgemeiner Deutscher Gewerkschaftsbund, *Jahrbuch 1927*, pp. 204–9, and *Jahrbuch 1928*, p. 139.

77 By 1930 the number of committees had risen to fifty-eight, but they had little success in improving the abysmally low rates of pay: Kuczynski, *Studien zur Geschichte der Lage der Arbeiterin*, pp. 228–30; Allgemeiner Deutscher Gewerkschaftsbund, *Jahrbuch des Allgemeinen Deutschen Gewerkschaftsbundes 1930* (Berlin: Verlagsanstalt des Allgemeinen Deutschen Gewerkschaftsbundes, 1931), pp. 164–5. In 1925 there were 189,299 female homeworkers, 75.3 per cent of whom were over thirty and 57.9 per cent married: *SdR*, vol. 402, pp. 442, 446. Homeworkers were not included as a separate category in the census of 1933.

78 Deutscher Textilarbeiterverband (ed.), *Mein Arbeitstag – mein Wochenende*, pp. 12–13.

79 C. Benninghaus, 'Mothers' Toil and Daughters' Leisure: Working-

Class Girls and Time in 1920s' Germany', *History Workshop Journal*, 50 (2000), 54–6; C. Benninghaus, *Die anderen Jugendlichen: Arbeitermädchen in der Weimarer Republik* (Frankfurt: Campus, 1994), pp. 92, 198–9. In her belief that young women earned enough to enable them to leave the family home, Benninghaus revises previously accepted interpretations: cf. Hagemann, *Frauenalltag und Männerpolitik*, pp. 418, 769.

80 Wellner, 'Industriearbeiterinnen in der Weimarer Republik', p. 553; K. Hausen, 'Unemployment Also Hits Women: The New and the Old Woman on the Dark Side of the Golden Twenties in Germany', in P. Stachura (ed.), *Unemployment and the Great Depression in Weimar Germany* (Basingstoke: Macmillan, 1986), p. 102.

81 Of the 4,347 girls leaving elementary school in Cologne in 1924, just over a third (33.5 per cent) wanted to become tailors and 44 (1 per cent) wanted to become unskilled manual workers: Benninghaus, *Die anderen Jugendlichen*, p. 155. Hairdressing became a popular choice in the mid-1920s: GLA, 443/1054, *Nachrichtenblatt des Deutschen Roten Kreuzes*, 7 (1928), 153. Gaebel notes that girls had much slimmer chances of obtaining apprenticeships than boys: 15,000 girls were chasing 6,000 apprenticeships in tailoring in 1931, and 8,600 girls were applying for 1,700 hairdressing apprenticeships: K. Gaebel, *Die deutsche Wirtschaft und das Berufsschicksal der Frau* (Berlin: Bund Deutscher Frauenvereine, 1932), p. 12. Girls' apprenticeships lasted three years, boys' four.

82 'Aufzeichnungen einer Fabrikarbeiterin', *Die christliche Frau*, 22:5 (May 1924), 70–2; Benninghaus, *Die anderen Jugendlichen*, p. 175. There were reports during the demobilisation of housewives rejecting former factory workers as domestic servants: BAB, R3901/10400, newspaper report of 20 November 1919.

83 Benninghaus, *Die anderen Jugendlichen*, pp. 189, 243–5. Girls preferred not to work as salesgirls in food shops as these shops' hours were longer, the pay poorer and the temperature often kept lower in order to preserve the food.

84 S. Suhr, *Die weiblichen Angestellten* (Berlin: Zentralverband der Angestellten, 1930), pp. 3–4. The census of 1925 was more thorough than that of 1907, but the available statistics reveal an increase of 195.5 per cent in female and 43.7 per cent in male white-collar workers and civil servants: *SdR*, vol. 408, p. 141.

85 F. Glass and D. Kische, *Die wirtschaftlichen und sozialen Verhältnisse der berufstätigen Frauen* (Berlin: Heymann, 1930), p. 2. In 1925 56.5 per cent of all female white-collar workers and civil servants, 61.5 per cent of sales and office personnel and 41.3 per cent of technical and professional employees lived in cities: *SdR*, vol. 408, p. 173.

86 Three-quarters of the 1,437,655 women classified as white-collar workers and civil servants in 1925 were office workers and salesgirls. The remaining 24.4 per cent were classed as technical and professional employees and a mere 0.6 per cent as supervisors: *SdR*, vol. 408, pp. 147–50. Women made up 32.3 per cent of all office and sales staff, 22.5 per cent of technical and professional staff and 2.1 per cent of the staff in supervisory positions.

87 U. Frevert, 'Vom Klavier zur Schreibmaschine – weiblicher Arbeitsmarkt und Rollenzuweisungen am Beispiel der weiblichen Angestellten in der Weimarer Republik', in A. Kuhn and G. Schneider (eds), *Frauen in der Geschichte*, vol. 1 (Düsseldorf: Schwann, 1979), p. 94; Suhr, *Die weiblichen Angestellten*, p. 12; Benninghaus, *Die anderen Jugendlichen*, pp. 245–6.

88 Factory inspectors' returns for 1926 to 1930 reveal an increase of 29.4 per cent in female white-collar employment and a more modest 9.5 per cent increase in male white-collar employment: Grünfeld, 'Rationalisation', p. 613.

89 The increases were 16.2 per cent, 24.9 per cent and 39.8 per cent respectively: *SdR*, vol. 408, p. 141, and vol. 453, part 3, p. 16. Even with this increase, married women constituted a mere 6.8 per cent of female white-collar workers and civil servants in 1933.

90 Office workers and salesgirls tended to be younger than technical and professional employees: 8.2 per cent of the former were over the age of forty in 1925, and 29.3 per cent of the latter: *SdR*, vol. 408, pp. 143, 156, 170, and vol. 453, p. 65.

91 Rühle-Gerstel, *Das Frauenproblem der Gegenwart*, pp. 293–5; Bridenthal, 'Beyond *Kinder, Kirche, Küche*: Weimar Women at Work', pp. 162–3; S. Kracauer, *Die Angestellten* (Frankfurt am Main: Suhrkamp, 2nd edn, 1974), pp. 24–5.

92 For government and white-collar organisations' concerns about the problem of unemployment among older white-collar workers, particularly men, see GLA, 233/26078, Bund badischer Arbeitgeberverbände e.v., Mannheim, Nr. 28655, 1 November 1926. On the pressures on older office workers see the references to Elsa in the fictionalised account of a family in the Depression: Claire Bergmann, *What Will Become of the Children?*, trans. R. Bodek (Rochester: Camden House, 2010), p. 53.

93 Gewerkschaftsbund der Angestellten, *Die wirtschaftliche und soziale Lage der Angestellten* (Berlin: Sieben-Stäbe-Verlag, 1931), p. 12. The liberal GdA attracted mainly female office personnel, with only 20 per cent of its female members being shop assistants, and so its female membership tended to come from the middle class: U. Frevert, 'Traditionale Weiblichkeit und moderne Interessenorganisation:

Frauen im Angestelltenberuf 1918–1933', *Geschichte und Gesellschaft*, 7:3–4 (1981), 522–3.
94 GdA, *Die wirtschaftliche und soziale Lage der Angestellten*, pp. 48–50.
95 By 31 December 1931 816 of 1,037 wage agreements envisaged an average deduction of 10 per cent: BAK, Z.Sg.1 192/1 (14), *Zeitschrift des Gewerkschaftsbundes der Angestellten* (1 November 1932), 169.
96 A survey by the Central Union of White-Collar Workers in 1929 found that 81 per cent of its female respondents earned less than 200 RM monthly and a mere 3 per cent over 300 RM. These women were highly qualified and middle-aged, working in local government positions or insurance. BAK, Z.Sg.1 134/6, *Der freie Angestellte: Zeitschrift des Zentralverbandes der Angestellten*, 31:22 (16 November 1927), 338; GdA, *Die wirtschaftliche und soziale Lage der Angestellten*, p. 106; Suhr, *Die weiblichen Angestellten*, pp. 35–7.
97 Suhr, *Die weiblichen Angestellten*, p. 38; Frevert, 'Vom Klavier zur Schreibmaschine', pp. 95, 110. Another survey of 1928, answered by 24,676 women, revealed that 97.6 per cent of those under twenty, and 85 per cent of those aged between twenty and thirty, lived with their parents. Of those aged over forty, 25.2 per cent still lived in their parents' home: Glass and Kische, *Die wirtschaftlichen und sozialen Verhältnisse der berufstätigen Frauen*, pp. 33–6.
98 Just under a half (44.4 per cent) came from white-collar or civil servant families: GdA, *Die wirtschaftliche und soziale Lage der Angestellten*, p. 43.
99 88 per cent of those under twenty had attended only elementary school, 75 per cent of those aged between thirty and forty and 42 per cent of those over fifty. A mere 3 per cent of those under twenty had attended a grammar school, while for those over fifty this figure was 30 per cent: Suhr, *Die weiblichen Angestellten*, p. 13. The GdA survey revealed that of those female respondents whose fathers were manual workers 66.7 per cent were under the age of twenty-four and 0.6 per cent over fifty: GdA, *Die wirtschaftliche und soziale Lage der Angestellten*, p. 60.
100 Gaebel, *Die deutsche Wirtschaft und das Berufsschicksal der Frau*, p. 11.
101 In 1925 women made up 22.6 per cent of the GdA's membership, in 1931 31.5 per cent. For the ZdA the figures are 46.2 per cent and 50.1 per cent respectively. Schuckert notes that in 1927 71 per cent of male and 28.5 per cent of female white-collar workers and civil servants were organised in unions, but only 42 per cent of male and 24 per cent of female manual workers: M. Schuckert, 'Die Mitwirkung der Frau in Handel und Gewerbe', in Schmidt-Beil (ed.), *Die Kultur der Frau*, p. 137.

102 Before 1900 individual women had been allowed to attend university courses with the professor's permission. Prussia opened its universities to women in 1908: E. Boedeker, *25 Jahre Frauenstudium in Deutschland*, vol. 1 (Hanover: C. Trute, 1939), pp. 39–51. For the history of women's admittance to university see J. Albisetti, *Schooling German Girls and Women* (Princeton: Princeton University Press, 1988) and K. Rowold, *The Educated Woman: Minds, Bodies, and Women's Higher Education in Britain, Germany, and Spain, 1865–1914* (London: Routledge, 2010).

103 The actual number of women students peaked in summer 1931 with 19,394 out of a total of 103,912, the highest recorded in the Weimar Republic: *StJhb 1921/1922*, p. 320; *StJhb 1932*, p. 427; *StJhb 1934*, pp. 535, 537.

104 Calculated from figures in *StJhb 1929*, pp. 406–7, and *StJhb 1933*, p. 521. Bäumer puts the female share of pupils taking the examination at 10.9 per cent in 1925–26, 23.7 per cent in 1930–31 and 24.9 per cent in 1931–32: G. Bäumer, 'Krisis des Frauenstudiums', *Die Frau*, 39:6 (March 1932), 322–7, and 39:10 (July 1932), 611–19. Bäumer's figures are confirmed officially in GLA, 233/13046, 'Niederschrift über die am 23.1.1932 im Reichsministerium des Innern abgehaltene Sitzung, betr. Berufshilfemassnahmen für Abiturienten', III. 3381/23.1, p. 23.

105 Calculated from figures in *StJhb 1931*, pp. 430–1. Women made up 18 per cent of all medical students, 28.7 per cent of pharmacy students and 5.3 per cent of law students. See also M. Kater, 'Krisis des Frauenstudiums in der Weimarer Republik', *Vierteljahrschrift für Sozial- und Wirtschaftsgeschichte*, 59 (1972), 213–19, and K. von Soden and G. Zipfel, *Siebzig Jahre Frauenstudium: Frauen in der Wissenschaft* (Cologne: Pahl-Rugenstein, 1979), pp. 20–2.

106 Women's share of the student body in summer 1931 was as follows: Hamburg 24.7 per cent, Freiburg 23.4 per cent, Heidelberg 22 per cent, Berlin 21.3 per cent and Munich 18.4 per cent. The least popular universities for women were Erlangen, where women made up 8.4 per cent of the student body, and Giessen (8.6 per cent). Calculated from figures in *StJhb 1932*, pp. 426–7. Another factor in the popularity of city universities may have been cost; Benker notes that 50 per cent of Berlin's female students lived at home: G. Benker, *Studentinnen in der Weimarer Republik* (Pfaffenweiler: Centaurus-Verlag, 1990), p. 62. See also Kater, 'Krisis des Frauenstudiums', p. 210.

107 Some women also worked to support their studies. Benker notes that 12 per cent of Berlin's female students had jobs. Grants were available from a range of public and charitable sources and were dependent on a professor's recommendation, and the number of women from

working-class homes who received grants rose from zero in 1925 to 18 per cent of recipients in 1931. Students could also access loans from a students' union, with women making up some 6.5 per cent of recipients. Benker notes young women's reluctance to apply for such assistance: Benker, *Studentinnen in der Weimarer Republik*, pp. 56, 63–6.
108 GLA 235/4876, *Freiburger Zeitung*, 44 (14 February 1929). In the summer term of 1930 21.2 per cent of the female and 12.8 per cent of the male students had fathers in the more senior echelons of the civil service and 30 per cent of the women and 20 per cent of the men had fathers with academic degrees: *Deutsche Lehrerinnenzeitung*, 48:2 (10 January 1931), found in Archiv des ADLV, Berlin, collection 16. See also Kater, 'Krisis des Frauenstudiums', pp. 231–2.
109 J. Stephenson, 'Girls' Higher Education in Germany in the 1930s', *Journal of Contemporary History*, 10:1 (1975), 44–5, 48; GLA, 235/4876, *Denkschrift für das Reichsministerium des Innern auf Grund der Beratungen des Ausschusses für die Fragen der Überfüllung der Hochschulen und der Jungakademiker*, presented by Professor Tillman to the Reich Interior Minister on 24 October 1932; C. Führ, 'Schulpolitik im Spannungsfeld zwischen Reich und Ländern: Das Scheitern der Schulreform in der Weimarer Republik', *Aus Politik und Zeitgeschichte*, B 42 (1970), 29.
110 Bäumer, 'Krisis des Frauenstudiums', p. 615; G. Bäumer, 'Frauenschicksal in unserer Zeit', *Die badische Lehrerin*, 14:24 (15 December 1932), 173–5; *Die Bayerische Frau*, 1:10–11 (July–August 1932), 4.
111 K. Gaebel, 'Die Berufslage der Akademikerinnen', *Die Frau*, 34:4 (January 1927), 218–24, and 34:5 (February 1927), 278–82.
112 Kater notes that 'Germany was the last major European country to admit women to medical studies and to allow them to be certified as doctors': M. H. Kater, 'Professionalization and Socialization of Physicians in Wilhelmine and Weimar Germany', *Journal of Contemporary History*, 20 (1985), 686–7. The first two female physicians in Berlin were Franziska Tiburtius and Emilie Lehmus in 1877: Habeth, 'Die Freiberuflerin und Beamtin', pp. 156–7. Figures for 1925 and 1933 from *SdR*, vol. 402, p. 435, and vol. 458, pp. 49, 73. Statistical yearbook figures record smaller numbers of female physicians but do not include physicians working solely in institutions.
113 Gaebel, 'Die Berufslage der Akademikerinnen', pp. 220–1. By 1936 42 per cent of all female physicians were married, and of these 70 per cent had children: J. Stephenson, *Women in Nazi Society* (London: Croom Helm, 1975), p. 166. Huerkamp notes that in 1925 Prussia had 1,540 female physicians, of whom 21.4 per cent were Jewish;

for Berlin the figures were 532 and 40.4 per cent: C. Huerkamp, 'Jüdische Akademikerinnen in Deutschland 1900–1938', *Geschichte und Geseltschaft*, 19 (1993), 319.
114 Of 2,334 women physicians in 1929 1,233 (53.8 per cent) were in general practice: *Die Frau*, 37:1 (October 1929), 57. Kater claims that three-quarters of male physicians were in general practice: Kater, 'Professionalization and Socialization of Physicians', p. 687. Hesse, Mecklenburg-Strelitz, Schaumburg-Lippe and Waldeck refused to allow women to take the necessary examinations, while Prussia, Danzig and Brunswick thought the work too onerous for women: Gaebel, 'Die Berufslage der Akademikerinnen', p. 221.
115 L. Adelsberger, 'Die Frau als Ärztin', in Schmidt-Beil (ed.), *Die Kultur der Frau*, p. 199. On the hierarchical structure of medical education see Kater, 'Professionalization and Socialization of Physicians', p. 680.
116 Bäumer, 'Krisis des Frauenstudiums', p. 615.
117 In 1933 there were 3,716 female pharmacists, 93.5 per cent of them in salaried posts and 90.8 per cent of them under the age of forty. Of the male pharmacists, 59.8 per cent were in salaried posts, and 40.8 per cent were under forty. In 1925 there were 835 women dentists out of a total of 9,137, 49.9 per cent of them independent; in 1933 there were 1,250 women dentists out of 9,137, 55.4 per cent of them independent: *SdR*, vol. 402, p. 435; vol. 458, pp. 49, 73.
118 'Die Verfassung des Deutschen Reiches vom 11. August 1919', *Reichsgesetzblatt 1919*, no. 152 (14 August 1919), 1383–1418.
119 Bavaria had allowed women to take the first examination from 1903 but many states did not do so until after the war, among them Hamburg in 1919 and Baden in 1921: V. Lowitsch, 'Die Frau als Richter' (PhD dissertation, University of Freiburg im Breisgau, 1933), pp. 62–3.
120 Bäumer, 'Krisis des Frauenstudiums', p. 616. Between 1926 and 1931 158 women had taken the examination and 131 had passed: *Die Frau*, 40:8 (May 1933), 503.
121 *Freiburger Zeitung*, no. 184 (12 July 1924); *Karlsruher Zeitung*, no. 161 (12 July 1924); *Evangelische Frauenzeitung*, 30:1 (October 1928), 12. Marie Munk was made a District Court judge in Berlin-Charlottenburg in 1929.
122 There were fifty-four female lawyers in 1925, 0.4 per cent of the total: *SdR*, vol. 458, p. 49; Bäumer, 'Krisis des Frauenstudiums', p. 616. In the summer of 1923 736 women made up 3.3 per cent of those studying law and in summer 1930 1,175 women constituted 5.3 per cent of the law student body. Although by summer 1932 the number of female law students had fallen slightly to 1,137, they made up 6.2 per cent of law students: calculated from figures in *StJhb 1923*, p. 318, *StJhb 1931*, p. 430, and *StJhb 1933*, p. 522.

123 BAK, Nachlass Lüders 239, 'BdF betr. Minderbewertung der Frauenarbeit in Reichs-, Länder- und Kommunalverwaltungen', 20 June 1930; Gaebel, 'Die Berufslage der Akademikerinnen', p. 223. Kater notes that female law students had negligible chances of a legal career: Kater, 'Krisis des Frauenstudiums', p. 218.

124 M.-E. Lüders, 'Frauen als Richter', *Führer-Stimmen*, no. 10 (4 January 1930), 1–3, found in BAK, Nachlass Lüders 239; 'Frauen im Justizdienst', *Nachrichtenblatt des BdF*, 10:2 (February 1930), 15; S. Bajohr and K. Rödiger-Bajohr, 'Die Diskriminierung der Juristin in Deutschland bis 1945', *Kritische Justiz*, 13:1 (1980), 45–8; Stephenson, 'Women and the Professions in Germany', p. 277.

125 The women were not permitted to preach in a full church service, though some, for example Sophie Kunert, an assistant in Hamburg, did have the right in exceptional cases to administer the sacraments to women prisoners: Gaebel, 'Die Berufslage der Akadmikerinnen', pp. 280–2; A. von Zahn-Harnack, 'Die Mitarbeit der Frau in Kirche und Kirchengemeinde', in *Schriften und Reden* (Tübingen: Hopfer, 1964), p. 33; C. Jellinek, *Frauen unter deutschem Recht* (Mannheim: Bensheimer, 1928), p. 74. The Protestant Church in Prussia permitted women to train as vicars' helpers from 1927; they were regarded as assistants only, with no rights to administer the sacraments: Evangelisches Zentralarchiv Berlin, 51/GIII/2, letter of Female Protestant Theologians' Association to the General Synod of 1 December 1925 and the synod's decision of 6 May 1927.

126 Wrangell was appointed on 10 March 1923, Vaerting on 1 October: Soden and Gipfel, *Siebzig Jahre Frauenstudium*, pp. 22–4; Boedeker, *25 Jahre Frauenstudium*, vol. 1, p. 45. Seventy-one women habilitated before 1933. Habeth states that Prussia permitted women to habilitate only from 1920. Prior to this women had been appointed as 'honorary professors' to lecturing posts, for example, Dr Elisabeth Altmann-Gottheiner to Mannheim's University of Commerce in 1908: Habeth, 'Die Freiberuflerin und Beamtin', p. 168.

127 Fewer women were appointed to lecturing posts in technical universities; in 1932 the thirteen women in such posts constituted less than 1 per cent of such lecturing staff: *StJhb 1933*, pp. 524–5.

128 Women made up 0.5 per cent of architects and 0.8 per cent of veterinary surgeons: *SdR*, vol. 458, p. 49. For female chemists see J. A. Johnson, 'German Women in Chemistry, 1895–1925 (Part I)': *Zeitschrift für Geschichte der Wisssenschaften, Technik und Medizin*, NTM 6 (1998), 1–21, and 'German Women in Chemistry, 1925–1945 (Part II)', *ibid.*, pp. 65–90. Johnson claims that 'by 1925 women had won a foothold in the profession of chemistry'.

129 Zahn-Harnack, *Schriften und Reden*, pp. 1–6; *Die Frau im Staat*, 8:6/7

(June–July 1926), 15. The first chair, Dr Agnes von Zahn-Harnack, was succeeded in 1930 by Dr Lüders. In 1926 it had 3,787 members: LAB, BRep 235, HLA MF3634.

130 In 1928 the DAB had a total of 4,036 members, which fell to 3,559 in 1930. In 1932 the Association of Female Engineers had the smallest membership, with eleven, followed by the female theologians with fifteen, the female industrial chemists with seventeen and the female dentists with twenty. The largest member organisation was that of female philologists, with 2,400: LAB, BRep 235, HLA MF3633.

131 LAB, BRep 235, HLA MF3630, 'Bericht über die Tätigkeit des Deutschen Akademikerinnenbundes vom Juni 1929 bis Juni 1930'; BRep 235, HLA MF3631, letter to Reich ministers dated 26 April 1931; BRep 235, HLA MF 3632, letter to members dated June 1932; letter to party leaders dated 1 April 1932; BRep 235, HLA MF3633, 'Bericht über die Tätigkeit des Deutschen Akademikerinnenbundes vom Juni 1930 bis Oktober 1932'; 'Niederschrift über die Sitzung des Gesamtvorstandes des DAB am 30.9.32 im Harnackhaus zu Berlin-Dahlem'; *Gelbe Blätter*, found in LAB, BRep 235, HLA MF2906. The bibliography of the women's movement was H. Sveistrup and A. von Zahn-Harnack (eds), *Die Frauenfrage in Deutschland: Strömungen und Gegenströmungen, 1790–1930* (Magdeburg: Burg, 1934).

132 Gaebel, 'Die Berufslage der Akademikerinnen', p. 282.

133 Quoted in Benker, *Studentinnen in der Weimarer Republik*, p. 46.

134 *Freiburger Zeitung*, no. 129 (11 May 1928).

135 The 1933 census figures differentiate between different kinds of teacher, whereas the 1925 figures do not: SdR, vol. 402, p. 435, and vol. 458, p. 72.

136 Verein Katholischer Deutscher Lehrerinnen, *Statistische Erhebungen über die wirtschaftlichen Verhältnisse der Lehrerinnen* (Paderborn: Ferdinand Schöningh, 1928), pp. 2–3, 7.

137 *Nachrichtenblatt des BdF*, 5:10–11, (October–November 1925), 90; *Die Frau*, 38:10 (July 1931), 630; K. Gaebel, 'Frauenrecht = Mannesrecht? Der Weg bleibt uns versperrt', *Berliner Tageblatt* (23 June 1928), found in BAK, Nachlass Lüders 151. There were very few female teachers in boys' senior schools; in 1931–32 women made up 1.9 per cent of the staff, and girls 6.7 per cent of the pupils. With the impact of the fall in the war-time birth rate, some senior girls' schools had been closed and the girls sent to boys' senior schools. See also Kampmann, '"Zölibat – ohne uns!"'.

138 SdR, vol. 458, p. 78. Their relative youthfulness in comparison to their male colleagues – nearly half (48.4 per cent) were under the age of forty, but under one-third (29.6 per cent) of men – may have been due to women only recently having been considered for promotion or to

the fact that many women left on marriage. See Kampmann, '"Zölibat – ohne uns!"', pp. 80–1.
139 The most favourable position with regard to the headships of girls' senior schools was to be found in Hamburg, where four of seven schools had female headteachers. No woman was in charge of a girls' senior school in Baden, Anhalt or Saxony: Allgemeiner Deutscher Lehrerinnenverein, *Leitende Stellen im Mädchenschulwesen* (Hamburg: Blöß, 1926), pp. 11–15; *Die Frau*, 34:1 (October 1926), 53; Kampmann, '"Zölibat – ohne uns!"', pp. 96–8.
140 The parent–teacher committee in Baden-Baden apparently wanted a male headteacher: *Die Frau*, 38:10 (July 1931), 623–4; *Die Frau*, 38:7 (April 1931), 438. In Moabit in Berlin all schools were headed by men: LAB, BRep 235, HLA MF1954, 'Material zum Kampf der Frauen um Arbeit und Beruf', August 1932, p. 3, report entitled 'Gleichberechtigte Berufsausübung'.
141 Bäumer, 'Krisis des Frauenstudiums', p. 324.
142 Allgemeiner Deutscher Lehrerinnenverein, *Verhandlungen der XX. Generalversammlung des ADLV in Wien 19–22. Mai 1929* (Berlin,1929), pp. 104–5; *Die Bayerische Frau*, 1:5 (15 February 1932), 6; Führ, 'Schulpolitik im Spannungsfeld zwischen Reich und Ländern', p. 29. See also K. H. Jarausch, 'The Crisis of German Professions 1918–33', *Journal of Contemporary History*, 20 (1985), 377–98.
143 Stephenson, 'Girls' Higher Education in Germany', 44. The colleges were in Dortmund, Elbing and Beuthen: Archiv des BdF, Berlin, 10/3, letter of the Prussian Education Minister to the BdF of 30 January 1933.
144 Civil servants in Germany in 1933:

Sector	Total	Women	% women
Education	270,777	64,157	23.7
Postal service	225,110	33,843	15.0
Reich railway	276,142	3,564	1.3
Administration	436,307	10,432	2.4
Nursing	25,233	9,733	38.7
Welfare	13,548	3,556	26.2
Other	147,923	3,385	2.3
Total	1,395,040	128,670	9.2

Source: SdR, vol. 458, p. 37.

The 1925 census did not differentiate between civil servants and contractual employees.

145 On the history of women in the postal service see Doerner, 'Neun Jahrzehnte Frauenbeschäftigung'; Nienhaus, *Vater Staat und seine Gehilfinnen*. For the railways see B. Kerchner, *Beruf und Geschlecht* (Göttingen: Vandenhoeck & Ruprecht, 1992), pp. 168–9, and for women in the administration see E. Süersen, *Die Frau im deutschen Reichs- und Landesstaatsdienst* (Mannheim: Bensheimer, 1920), pp. 117–19.

146 For the public sector see J. P. Cullity, 'The Growth of Governmental Employment in Germany 1882–1950', *Zeitschrift für die gesamte Staatswissenschaft*, 123 (1967), 210–17; H. James, *The German Slump: Politics and Economics 1924–1936* (Oxford: Oxford University Press, 1986), pp. 39–41; Kunz, *Civil Servants and the Politics of Inflation in Germany*, pp. 54–7. Figures, excluding Bavaria and Württemberg (which until 1918 had run their own postal services), from E. Sommer, 'Aus der Werkstatt der Reichsadler', *Unter dem Reichsadler*, 21:1 (10 January 1929), 6–8.

147 *Unter dem Reichsadler*, 13:13 (14 July 1921), 200; *Unter dem Reichsadler*, 14:7 (13 April 1922), 101; C. Hahn, 'Der öffentliche Dienst und die Frauen – Beamtinnen in der Weimarer Republik', in Frauengruppe Faschismusforschung (ed.), *Mutterkreuz und Arbeitsbuch*, pp. 59–60. There were four ranking levels, from simple service to the higher civil service. Each required particular educational qualifications. See J. Caplan, 'The Imaginary Universality of Particular Interests: The "Tradition" of the Civil Service in German History', *Social History*, 4 (1979), 299–317. From 15 January 1923 male civil servants could be employed in those areas reserved for women as the Reich Postal Service attempted to address the surplus of male civil servants: 'Notstandsmassnahmen', *Unter dem Reichsadler*, 15:4 (22 February 1923), 37. For women in more senior middle-ranking posts see Doerner, 'Neun Jahrzehnte Frauenbeschäftigung', p. 387.

148 No areas of work were specially designated as suitable for women: H. Jende-Radomski, *Frauenberufe* (Dessau: Dünnhaupt, 1926), p. 69. For the Reich Transport Authority and the Reich Interior Minister's belief that women should be considered for senior civil service positions only if their presence seemed desirable in the areas concerned see BAK, R2/1291, pp. 97–8, letter of Reich Interior Minister to Prussian Finance Minister dated 22 January 1924.

149 Doerner, 'Neun Jahrzehnte Frauenbeschäftigung', p. 386; J. Caplan, *Government without Administration: State and Civil Service in Weimar and Nazi Germany* (Oxford: Oxford University Press, 1988), pp. 60–1; Kunz, *Civil Servants and the Politics of the Inflation in Germany*, p. 57; BAK, R2/1291, p. 140, Reichstag printed paper no. 3113, 15 March 1927; Nachlass Lüders 153, Reichstag printed paper

Women and work 191

no. 1887, 7 March 1928; Nachlass Lüders 135, Reichstag minutes of 18 March 1929 and *Denkschrift über die Überführung weiblicher Angestellter in das Beamtenverhältnis*, 14 January 1930.
150 In Anhalt women were appointed only as contractual employees, while several cities appointed women only to civil service posts without tenure: BAK, R36/93, p. 139; Nachlass Lüders 279, BdF, 'Minderbewertung der Frauenarbeit in Reichs-, Länder- und Kommnunalverwaltungen', 20 June 1930.
151 A total of fifteen women held senior civil service posts in Reich ministries on 1 April 1928: *Die Frau*, 35:8 (May 1928), 487. Most of these women had higher degrees and thus met the educational requirements for senior civil servants.
152 *Unter dem Reichsadler*, 11:17 (11 September 1919), 180; *Unter dem Reichsadler*, 14:7 (13 Apri 1922), 101; *Unter dem Reichsadler*, 22:11 (12 June 1930), 174.
153 In 1928 there were twenty-three women in senior civil service posts in the states: Rühle-Gerstel, *Das Frauenproblem der Gegenwart*, p. 307. F. von Magnus-Hausen, '10 Jahre deutsche Staatsbürgerin', *Die Frau*, 37:5 (February 1930), 273–81, and 37:6 (March 1930), 351–7; M. Baum, *Rückblick auf mein Leben* (Heidelberg: Kerle, 1950), p. 229.
154 Henriette Arendt had been appointed a police assistant in Stuttgart in 1903, and by 1912 nineteen cities had appointed women welfare officers in police departments. Following an experiment with British policewomen in Cologne in 1923, Prussia appointed its first female police officer on 11 June 1926, Saxony on 15 April 1927, Hamburg on 15 August 1927 and Baden on 1 October 1927. By 1932 Prussia had 109 female police officers: G. Langheld, 'German Women Police Work', found in LAB, BRep 235, HLA MF1283 with accompanying letter to the BdF of 8 November 1932; L. Barck, *Ziele und Aufgaben der weiblichen Polizei in Deutschland* (Berlin: Deutscher Polizei-Verlag, 1928), p. 33.
155 In Prussia the discriminatory clauses were lifted on 22 October 1919: D. Lande, 'Die Frauenbewegung', *Sozialistische Monatshefte*, 26 (1920), 198. The Bavarian law had been passed before the Constitution but came into effect after it: 'Die Rechtsstellung der weiblichen Beamten', *Nachrichtenblatt des BdF*, 12:1 (January 1932), 3; 'Entscheidung des Reichsgerichts auf Grund des Artikel 13 Absatz 2 der Verfassung des Deutschen Reiches. Vom 10. Mai 1921', *Reichsgesetzblatt 1921*, no. 61 (17 June 1921), 315. For more detail on the following see H. Boak, 'The State as an Employer of Women in the Weimar Republic', in W. R. Lee and E. Rosenhaft (eds), *The State and Social Change in Germany, 1880–1980* (London: Berg, 1990), pp. 61–98.
156 ZStA, Reichsministerium des Innern, nr. 2233, Bl. 189ff; BAK,

R2/1291, pp. 61–2; 'Richtlinien über die rechtliche Stellung der verheirateten Beamtinnen', *Die Frau*, 28:1 (October 1920), 25. The guidelines were reaffirmed at cabinet meetings on 24 July 1923 and 2 August 1923: BAK, R2/1291, pp. 49–51, letter of Reich Interior Minister to the Reich Chancellery, ref. V5360A of 10 July 1923; R36/93, Reich Interior Minister to all Reich authorities, ref. V6001A of 13 August 1923; ZStA, Reichstag 3328, 292; *Unter dem Reichsadler*, 12:14 (22 July 1920), 165. The VRT submitted the proposal on 9 July 1919.
157 For details of the 1923 scheme see Boak, 'The State as an Employer of Women', pp. 74–5.
158 BAK, R2/1291, pp. 37–8 and 65–6, letters of the Reich Postal Minister to the Reich Finance Minister of 21 June and 20 September 1923. Women constituted 67 per cent of all married female civil servants within the Reich Postal Service; of the 1,701 remaining in post on 1 April 1923 over 1,000 were not eligible for compensation under the scheme. See also 'Die Kernfragen des weiblichen Beamtentums bei der Deutschen Reichspost', *Unter dem Reichsadler*, 23:18 (24 September 1931), 273–4.
159 'Verordnung zur Herabminderung der Personalausgaben des Reiches. (Personalabbauverordnung.) Vom 27. Oktober 1923', *Reichsgesetzblatt I 1923*, no. 108 (30 October 1923), 999–1011. The law came into effect on 31 October 1923 and was adopted by all the states. See also A. Kunz, 'Stand versus Klasse: Beamtenschaft und Gewerkschaften im Konflikt um den Personalabbau 1923/24', *Geschichte und Gesellschaft*, 8 (1982), 55–86, and Caplan, *Government without Administration*, pp. 51–7.
160 The numbers of Reich contractual employees fell by 49.7 per cent, of Reich manual workers by 32.9 per cent and of Reich civil servants by 16.3 per cent: BAK, R43I/2613, 289, 'Denkschrift des Reichsfinanzministeriums über den Personalabbau', 15 May 1924. See also Kunz, 'Stand versus Klasse', p. 63, and Caplan, *Government without Administration*, p. 56. For detailed figures of the cuts see Boak, 'The State as an Employer of Women', pp. 78–9.
161 BAK, Nachlass Lüders 153, Reich Finance Minister, Reichstag printed paper no. 2895, 7 January 1927, ref. IB19146, 'Übersicht über den Personalstand', p. 26; ZSg.I.90/25, *SPD Parteikorrespondenz 1929*, p. 20. Fuller figures for the period in Boak, 'The State as an Employer of Women', pp. 78–80.
162 'Reichsbesoldungsgesetz. Vom 17. Dezember 1927', *Reichsgesetzblatt I 1927*, no. 52 (19 December 1927), p. 349; Caplan, *Government without Administration*, p. 92; BAK, Nachlass Lüders 154, *Vossische Zeitung*, 20 January 1928.
163 Boak, 'The State as an Employer of Women', p. 73. See also Hahn, 'Der öffentliche Dienst und die Frauen', p. 77.

164 *Die verheiratete Lehrerin*, 1:3 (August 1925). See also Boak, 'The State as an Employer of Women', pp. 79–81.
165 She had married in 1922: Stratigakos, 'The Professional Spoils of War', pp. 470–3.
166 The Württemberg law came into effect on 1 April 1929 and contravened a Supreme Court ruling of July 1927 that the states had no right to make Article 14 more discriminatory: M.-E. Lüders, 'Grundsatz oder Vorteil', *Die Frau*, 36:4 (January 1929), 198–201.
167 On 15 March 1931 17.8 per cent of all men receiving unemployment benefit were building workers: BAK, R2/18809, 'Statistische Beilage zum Reichsarbeitsblatt 1932', no. 4, p. 11. In 1925 building workers made up 12.1 per cent of the male manual workforce: *StJhb 1932*, p. 20. Hausen, 'Unemployment Also Hits Women', p. 109. Hausen does, however, draw attention to the 'invisible unemployed' missing from the statistics.
168 *StJhb 1932*, p. 290; *StJhb 1933*, p. 290. In September 1929 12,214,000 men in work made up 86.8 per cent of the total male insured workforce, and in December 1932 7,578,000 made up 65.5 per cent. For women the figures were 6,213,000 and 78.1 per cent and 4,405,000 and 63.5 per cent respectively.
169 Figures given for the December of each year. On average in 1933 women made up 35.3 per cent of the insured workforce: *StJhb 1932*, p. 290; *StJhb 1934*, p. 296. Grünfeld has slightly different figures but the same findings: Grünfeld, 'Rationalisation', p. 609.
170 Between February and December 1929 women's share of those receiving unemployment benefit rose from 13.7 per cent to 18.4 per cent, though the actual number of people receiving benefit fell. Calculated from figures in BAK, R2/18809, 'Statistische Beilage zum Reichsarbeitsblatt 1930', no. 4, p. 8. The number of women seeking employment may well have been swollen by those made recently unemployed and by women entering the workforce because their husbands or other relatives had lost their jobs.
171 Between January and May 1933 the number of insured male workers in employment rose by 18 per cent, and that of insured female workers by 9.2 per cent: calculated from figures in BAK, R2/18809, 'Statistische Beilage zum Reichsarbeitsblatt 1933', no. 19, p. 3. On the swifter decline in male than in female unemployment, see BAK, R2/16809, Der Reichsarbeitsminister, IVa, 20201/33, end of October 1933, 'Der Stand der deutschen Arbeitsschlacht', p. 5.
172 Calculated from figures in *StJhb 1935*, p. 19. The 1933 census referred to working persons, dividing them into the economically active and the unemployed: 10,336,455 women were economically active, and 1,142,586 unemployed. The 1925 census data were then adjusted to

the 1933 methodology, so that 158,924 of the 11,478,012 working women were classed as unemployed. Women's share of the economically active white-collar and civil servant workforce increased from 27.1 per cent in 1925 to 30.2 per cent in 1933. In Hamburg, women's share of the manual workforce increased from 20 per cent in 1929 to 25 per cent in 1932, while their share of white-collar work remained stable at 37 per cent: Hagemann, *Frauenalltag und Männerpolitik*, p. 448.

173 Jones, 'A New Stage of Life?', p. 560; see also Harvey, *Youth and the Welfare State*, p. 110.
174 Kramer, 'Frankfurt's Working Women', pp. 130–2, 135–7; see also Hagemann, *Frauenalltag und Männerpolitik*, pp. 376, 448.
175 Frevert, *Women in German History*, pp. 276–7.
176 *Ibid.*, p. 185.
177 This also affected girls who had served apprenticeships in tailoring or hairdressing and who now sought manual work in industry or a domestic service post: Harvey, *Youth and the Welfare State*, pp. 108–9.
178 *Ibid.*, pp. 119–20.
179 Stephenson, *Women in Nazi Society*, p. 84. Kleiber claims that women made up 5 per cent of those doing labour service at the end of the Weimar Republic: L. Kleiber, 'Wo ihr seid, da soll die Sonne scheinen!' – der Frauenarbeitsdienst am Ende der Weimarer Republik und im Nationalsozialismus', in Frauengruppe Faschismusforschung (ed.), *Mutterkreuz und Arbeitsbuch*, p. 196. On obligatory and voluntary work schemes see Harvey, *Youth and the Welfare State*, pp. 131–47.
180 Quoted in Harvey, *Youth and Welfare State*, p. 146.
181 The age limit had been raised to seventeen, except for orphans, in July 1930, when provision was also made to cut the benefit paid to an unemployed married person, depending on their partner's income and family size: 'Verordnung des Reichspräsidenten zur Behebung finanzieller, wirtschaftlicher und sozialer Notstände: Vierter Abschnitt. Arbeitslosenversicherung, Krankenversicherung und Reichsversorgung. Vom 26. Juli 1930', *Reichsgesetzblatt I 1930*, no. 31 (27 July 1930), 318–27; 'Zweite Verordnung des Reichspräsidenten zur Sicherung von Wirtschaft und Finanzen: Dritter Teil. Arbeitslosenhilfe. Vom 5. Juli 1931', *Reichsgesetzblatt I 1931*, no. 22 (6 June 1931), 293–301.
182 M. Ehlert, 'Zur Arbeitslosigkeit der Arbeitnehmerin in den Jahren 1929 and 1930', *Die christliche* Frau, 29:4 (April 1931), 110. For details of the history of unemployment benefit during the Republic and its impact on women see Hausen, 'Unemployment Also Hits Women', pp. 87–97. Arendt claims that 34.9 per cent of unemployed

married women lost their benefit: H.-J. Arendt, 'Das Schutzprogramm der KPD für die arbeitende Frau vom 15. Oktober 1931', *Beiträge zur Geschichte der Arbeiterbewegung*, 11:2 (1969), 293.

183 In June 1930, according to Reich Labour Ministry figures, women made up 20.9 per cent of the unemployed, 20.2 per cent of those receiving unemployment benefit and 18.5 per cent of those receiving emergency relief. A year later the figures were 19.7, 22.1 and 13.6 respectively, and in June 1932 20.4, 29.6 and 15.3: BAK, R2/18809, 'Statistische Beilage zum Arbeitsblatt 1931', no. 4, pp. 8–10; 'Statistische Beilage zum Arbeitsblatt 1932', no. 4, pp. 8–10; 'Statistische Beilage zum Arbeitsblatt 1933', no. 4, pp. 1–2. Stephenson has different figures but the same findings: Stephenson, *Women in Nazi Society*, p. 83. Married women made up 15.6 per cent of the paid female workforce in 1925 and 18.3 per cent in 1933. In February 1931 married women constituted 34.8 per cent of female recipients of unemployment benefit, and in February 1933 37.2 per cent: calculated from figures in *StJhb 1931*, p. 307, and *StJhb 1933*, p. 303.

184 Kuczynski, *Studien zur Geschichte der Lage der Arbeiterin*, p. 218; BAK, R43I/612, p. 193, Reichsarbeitsministerium X 7607/23, 19 November 1923; Sozialdemokratische Partei Deutschlands, *Reichstag und Frauenrechte* (Weimar: Verlag SPD Bezirksverband Grossthüringen, 1924), pp. 19–21.

185 BAK, R36/1598, RAM IV nr. 11905.26, 24 September 1926; R43I/2042, p. 323; R36/2198, letter from the *Deutscher Städtetag* to its affiliates, no. 1641/30 dated 31 December 1930 referring to Dr Stegerwald's letter of 22 December 1930.

186 BAK, R43I/2039, pp. 231–58; M. Corssen, 'Frauenbewegung', *Sozialistische Monatshefte*, 37:2 (1931), 678; Hausen, 'Unemployment Also Hits Women', p. 81.

187 For example, the petitions to the Reichstag of the Economics Party, the DNVP and the NSDAP of 11 December 1930 and of the Centre Party of 3 March 1931, and the DVP petition of 4 December 1930 to Berlin's City Council, among many: BAK, R36/2198, 'Vorbericht für die Vorstandssitzung des Deutschen Städtetages am 20. März 1931 zu Berlin'; M. Juchacz, 'Der Kampf der verheirateten Lehrerin', *Die Genossin*, 8:6 (June 1931), 236–8.

188 BAK, Nachlass Lüders 135, letter of DNHV Gau Brandenburg-Pommern of 21 November 1931; see also G. Hanna, 'Vom Kampf gegen die verheirateten erwerbstätigen Frauen', *Die Arbeit*, 8 (1931), 253–60.

189 'Nimmt die berufstätige Frau dem Mann den Arbeitsplatz weg?', *Nachrichtenblatt des BdF*, 12:7 (July 1932), 53; M. Hellersberg, 'Die Berufsarbeit der Frau', *Die Bayerische Frau*, 1:5 (15 February 1932),

2; F. Schmidt, 'Die Doppelverdiener', *Die Genossin*, 8:6 (June 1931), 216–18. See also Stephenson, *Women in Nazi Society*, p. 83.
190 'Die christliche Ehe: Enzyklika des Papstes Pius XI vom 31. Dezember 1930', printed in *Archiv für Bevölkerungspolitik, Sexualethik und Familienkunde*, 1:1 (1931), 24–55; Pius XI (Papa), *Rundschreiben über die gesellschaftliche Ordnung* (Freiburg im Breisgau: Herder, 1931); G. Stoffel, 'Die Arbeitslosigkeit und die Frauenarbeit', *Die Frau im Staat*, 13:8–9 (August–September 1931), 5–7; BAK, Nachlass Katharina von Kardorff 34a, 'Papst contra Frau?', pp. 79–98.
191 The majority favoured persuasion, with the women being offered severance payments for voluntarily leaving their posts, while the minority favoured coercion: BAK, R43I/2039, pp. 387–9, 'Gutachten zur Arbeitslosenfrage', 27 March 1931. One of the ten members of the commission was a woman, Antonie Hopmann, the general secretary of the Catholic Women's Association.
192 'Gesetz über die Rechtstellung der weiblichen Beamten. Vom 30. Mai 1932', *Reichsgesetzblatt I 1932*, no. 31 (3 June 1932), 245–6. The SPD supported the bill only if it did not apply to the states or local authorities: Boak, 'The State as an Employer of Women', pp. 85–9.
193 Figures given by Dr Völter (SPD) in his Reichstag speech, printed in 'Die Rechtsstellung der verheirateten Beamtin', *Die Genossin*, 9:5–6 (May–June 1932), 125–8; J. McIntyre, 'Women and the Professions in Germany, 1930–1940', in A. J. Nicholls and E. Matthias (eds), *German Democracy and the Triumph of Hitler* (London: Allen and Unwin, 1971), pp. 186–7.
194 Centre Party draft bill of 24 May 1932 to the Prussian Landtag, found in BAK, R36/93, pp. 217, 407; law of 20 December 1932 in Anhalt, found in Staatsarchiv Hamburg (StAH), 131-10[I] 1931Ja23, *Der Beamtenbund*, 10 February 1933; 'Gesetz zur Änderung von Vorschriften auf dem Gebiete des allgemeinen Beamten-, des Besoldungs- und Versorgungsrechts. Vom 30. Juni 1933. Kapitell III. Rechtstellung der weiblichen Beamten', *Reichsgesetzblatt I 1933*, no. 74 (1 July 1933), 435; Stephenson, *Women in Nazi Society*, pp. 157–8. Women civil servants tended to marry men in well-paid, secure jobs. The Reich Postal Service reported that of its 7,092 female civil servants who had married between July 1926 and March 1929 a third (33.7 per cent) had married civil servants, another third (34.6 per cent) white-collar workers, one-fifth (19.7 per cent) self-employed men and one-tenth (11.7 per cent) contractual employees or manual workers in the Reich's employ: BAK, R2/1291, p. 237, *Übersicht über die Berufe der Ehemänner der weiblichen Beamten der deutschen Reichspost*, July 1929. A 1930 survey of 430 married women teachers revealed that 41.6 per cent had married civil servants, 17.2 per cent white-collar

workers, 11.9 per cent professional men and 21.9 per cent men of independent means: *Die verheiratete Lehrerin,* 7:3 (June 1931), 34.
195 M.-E. Lüders, 'Besoldungsreform', *Die Frau,* 27:8 (May 1920), 229–32; E. Kolshorn, 'Die Lage der weiblichen Post- und Telegraphenbeamten', *Jahrbuch für Frauenarbeit,* 1 (1924), 79–85; M. Ortmann-Sarnecki, 'Die Reichsbahnbeamtin', *Jahrbuch für Frauenarbeit,* 4 (1928), 110–13; Hahn, 'Der öffentliche Dienst und die Frauen', p. 64. Married female civil servants received smaller supplementary allowances than their male colleagues. The Prussian Salary Law of 1927 had allowed the hours and salaries of women teachers whose contracts did not stipulate the number of working hours to be cut by 10 per cent: 'Preussisches Gesetz über die Dienstbezüge der unmittelbaren Staatsbeamten (Preusiches Besoldungsgesetz). Vom 17. Dezember 1927', *Das gesamte deutsche und preussische Gesetzgebungsmaterial* (Berlin: Verlag des Gesetzsammlungsamts, 1927), pp. 826ff.; *Nachrichtenblatt des BdF,* 12:7 (July 1932), 54.
196 Archiv des ADLV, Berlin, collection 16, cases of Clara Paschke and Susanne Stork against the city of Berlin in March 1932 and of Paula Rheiner, Hedwig Bodenheimer and P. Prochaska against the Baden Education Ministry, decided on 20 December 1932; letter of Martha Schmidt to Emmy Beckmann of 23 January 1932.
197 Hausen, 'Unemployment Also Hits Women', p. 81. Following the removal of the Social Democrat-led Prussian government by Chancellor von Papen in July 1932, five of the nine senior female administrators in Prussian ministries were dismissed. The women's section in the Prussian Agricultural Ministry was closed and two women in senior positions in the Prussian Culture Ministry were dismissed, as was one of three senior administrators in the Education Ministry: *Nachrichtenblatt des BdF,* 12:12 (December 1932), 111–12, and 13:1 (January 1933), 4.
198 Thibert, 'The Economic Depression and the Employment of Women', pp. 450–1.
199 *Ibid.,* p. 451. A small survey in 1928 found that 60.4 per cent of married working women were the only or main providers for their families: Blos (ed.), *Die Frauenfrage im Lichte des Sozialismus,* p. 189.
200 Only 29 per cent of respondents in a survey conducted in 1929 believed it was right for a married woman to have a job: E. Fromm, *The Working Class in Weimar Germany. A Psychological and Sociological Study* (London: Berg, 1984), pp. 162–6.
201 A. Geyer, 'Die Bedeutung der Erwerbsarbeit verheirateter Frauen für die wirtschaftliche Lage und den Zusammenhalt der Familie', *Arbeiterwohlfahrt,* 5:20 (15 October 1930), 609–13, found in BAK, Z.Sg.1/5; H. Heberiz, 'Gedanken zur Berufsarbeit der verheirateten

Frau', *Die christliche Frau*, 26:5 (May 1928), 155–7; see also Hausen, 'Unemployment Also Hits Women', p. 83.
202 *Die christliche Frau*, 19:12 (December 1921); ZStA, Reichsministerium des Innern, Nr. 2232, Bl. 163, letter of the Catholic Women Teachers' Association of 9 November 1920 condemning the equality of married female civil servants; Nr. 2233, Bl. 420, ADLV's general meeting in Karlsruhe in May 1923, central committee's decision not to recommend any restrictions on the rights of married women teachers; letter of Helene Lange to Emmy Beckmann of 22 January 1923, found in BAK, Kl.Erw. 268-4, p. 8. See also Kampmann, '"Zölibat – ohne uns!"', pp. 84–5.
203 See *Nachrichtenblatt des BdF*, 5:2 (February 1925), 12 for petitions calling for the end of Article 14; *Die Frau im Staat*, 14:8 (August 1932), 10; *Die Bayerische Frau*, 1:6 (15 March 1932), 5; BAK, Nachlass Lüders 154, BdF declaration of 2 October 1931; StAH, 131-10¹, 1931Ja23, VRT petition of 21 May 1932; *Nachrichtenblatt des BdF*, 9:12 (December 1929), 93. The Reich Postal Minister lifted the embargo on appointing women to tenured civil service posts on 8 June 1932: Boak, 'The State as an Employer of Women', p. 88.
204 The VRT fought hard to uphold the standing of the civil service, and its rebuttal of attempts to prevent the dismissal of unmarried mothers from the civil service should be seen in this light. It resolved by 229 votes to one at its 1920 congress in Hamburg that unmarried motherhood in the civil service was a disgrace and that unmarried mothers should be summarily dismissed: *Sozialistische Monatshefte*, 27 (1921), 619; *Die Frau im Staat*, 2:7–8 (July–August 1920), 25. The ADLV thought that every case should be judged on its merits but believed in principle that unmarried motherhood constituted grounds for disciplinary action: H. Lange, 'Die uneheliche Mutterschaft als Disziplinverfahren', *Die Frau*, 28:9 (June 1921), 270–2.
205 StAH, 131-10¹, memorandum from Lohse (Employment Office) to Senator Kaven dated 29 December 1930, referring to a meeting of 10 December 1930 where a decision was taken to try to avoid employing man and wife in the public sector, and of women whose husbands were employed elsewhere. See also Hausen, 'Unemployment Also Hits Women', p. 112.
206 In Sweden, Canada and some of the United States women civil servants whose husbands were employed were also dismissed: H. Fuss, 'Unemployment and Employment among women', *International Labour Review*, 31 (1935), 465. British female civil servants did not enjoy the same pay as their male colleagues, nor were they admitted to the highest ranks of the civil service until 1925: V. Douie, *The Professional Position of Women* (London: British Federation of

Business and Professional Women, 1947), pp. 10–12; M. Zimmeck, 'Strategies and Stratagems for the Employment of Women in the British Civil Service, 1919–1931', *Historical Journal*, 27 (1984), 901–24, reveals that in spite of the Sex Disqualification (Removal) Act of 1919 the retention of married women remained exceptional.

207 Bäumer was granted indefinite leave of absence on 27 February 1933 and dismissed on 21 April 1933. She took some consolation from the fact that two men had to be appointed to replace her, as no one person had the necessary knowledge or the ability to master it: G. Bäumer, *Des Lebens wie der Liebe Band: Briefe*, ed. E. Beckmann (Tübingen: Wunderlich, 1956), p. 50; Stephenson, *Women in Nazi Society*, p. 155; A. Schaser, *Helene Lange und Gertrud Bäumer: Eine politische Lebensgemeinschaft* (Cologne: Böhlau Verlag, 2000), p. 286.

208 *Die Frau*, 40:10 (July 1933), 635. Even after the Second World War, however, women experienced difficulty in advancing into the senior civil service, with only 0.4 per cent of such posts being held by women in West Germany in 1960: Lüders, *Fürchte dich nicht*, p. 98.

209 For detailed studies of female students under Nazism see Stephenson, 'Girls' Higher Education in Germany'; Stephenson, *Women in Nazi Society*, pp. 116–46; J. R. Pauwels, *Women, Nazis, and Universities: Female University Students in the Third Reich* (Westport: Greenwood Press, 1984).

210 The SS began as Hitler's bodyguard and expanded under Himmler's leadership to become a multi-faceted organisation which was in the vanguard of implementing the Nazis' new racial order and which had policing, security and military duties.

211 Stephenson, *Women in Nazi Society*, pp. 169–72. For an account of discrimination against women in the legal profession in the Third Reich see A.-G. Meier-Scherling, 'Die Benachteiligung der Juristin zwischen 1933 und 1945', *Deutsche Richterzeitung*, 53 (1975), 10–13. According to Frevert women made up only 3 per cent of West Germany's lawyers in 1977: Frevert, *Women in German History*, p. 276.

212 J. Stephenson, 'Modernization, Emancipation, Mobilization: Nazi Society Reconsidered', in Jones and Retallack (eds), *Elections, Mass Politics and Social Change*, pp. 228–9.

213 Silke Neunsinger has referred to a crisis in masculinity caused by men's unemployment during the Depression: S. Neunsinger, 'Die Arbeit der Frauen – die Krise der Männer: Die Erwerbstätigkeit verheirateter Frauen in Deutschland und Schweden 1919–1939' (PhD dissertation, University of Uppsala, 2001), pp. 250–1, 260–1.

214 Peukert, *The Weimar Republic*, pp. 81–2.

4
Women, the family and sexuality

Reproductive rights have been one area in which historians have seen great improvements in women's lives during the Weimar Republic. Easier access to birth control, the relaxation in the abortion laws, the decriminalisation of prostitution, the openness about sexual matters, sex reformers' desire to improve the nation's knowledge about sexual pleasure and techniques and a thriving lesbian sub-culture all contributed. However, the dark side of modernity has also been seen in welfare and population policy. Peukert saw in the implementation of youth welfare policies attempts to impose social discipline and to normalise the behaviour of the working class. Others have also noted the increasing espousal of negative eugenics in the late 1920s, drawing allegations of continuity with the Nazi regime.[1] Michelle Mouton, however, sees a distinct difference between the Weimar Republic, which had no agreed official family policy, and the Third Reich, which had, even if it was not uniformly implemented throughout Germany.[2] This chapter seeks to explore woman's role within the family, primarily as wife and mother, the impact of the changes in family and population policy and attitudes towards female sexuality, both heterosexual and homosexual.

The surplus of women (*Frauenüberschuss*)

The 'new woman', sexually emancipated and childless, symbolised both the liberating changes in sexual mores and the nightmare of nationalists concerned that the German nation was in danger of dying out. Population experts believed that each woman needed to have three children in order to maintain the nation.[3] Nationalists' concern had been heightened by the fall in both the marriage rates and birth rates during the war, by the increase in divorce at the war's end and by women's reduced marriage prospects caused by servicemen's deaths in the war. Some 1,935,712 German servicemen died during the First World War, substantially reducing the marriage opportunities of German women.[4] The 1925 census revealed 1,067 women for every 1,000 men in Germany. There had in fact been a surplus of women (*Frauenüberschuss*) in Germany before the First World War, but this had declined steadily from 1,043 women to 1,000 men in 1885 to 1,026 women to 1,000 men in 1910.[5] The surplus was not uniform across Germany; in general, it increased with the size of the community. Indeed, an estimated 900,000 of the 2,016,973 surplus women in 1925 were to be found in cities, perhaps swelling the ranks of the 'new women', though even here there were differences; Wiesbaden recorded the largest surplus, with 1,296 women to every 1,000 men.[6] In predominantly agricultural areas such as Oldenburg and Schleswig-Holstein, and in heavy industrial regions such as Westphalia, the *Frauenüberschuss* was below average. It varied between the different age groups: in 1925 it was largest (1,480 women to 1,000 men) in the age group over eighty, owing to women's longer life expectancy, and second largest in the age group between thirty and thirty-five with 1,259 women to 1,000 men, a direct consequence of the slaughter of the First World War. However, with the predominance of births of boys over girls, there was in fact a surplus of males up to the age of nineteen throughout Germany, though this lasted only until the ages of thirteen to fourteen in the cities because of the numbers of girls aged between fifteen and twenty who went to the cities to find work.[7] Jay Winter has claimed that 'it is one of the myths of the war that it produced a generation of spinsters. Nothing of the kind happened', and he notes the impact of the fall in emigration and women's willingness to marry men who were younger than themselves or from a lower social class, trends noticed in Germany, too.[8] It is true that more couples were marrying (see Table 4.1), so that in 1925 39.4 per cent of all women in Germany were married, compared with 35.6 per cent in 1910, though this increase was due in part to the shifting age of the population. However, married women's share of the female population over the age of fifteen fell slightly from 53.4 per cent in 1910 to 52.3 per cent in 1925; every female age group up to the age of forty-five recorded a smaller percentage of married women in 1925 than in 1910, whereas men recorded an increase in

Table 4.1 The marital status of the population, 1910, 1925 and 1933

Status	Total	%	Men	%	Women	%
1910						
Single	33,746,242	58.4	17,266,176	60.6	16,480,066	56.2
Married	20,841,088	36.1	10,401,035	36.5	10,440,053	35.6
Widowed	3,082,519	5.3	776,856	2.7	2,305,663	7.9
Divorced	128,578	0.2	45,779	0.2	82,799	0.3
Total	57,798,427	100.0	28,489,846	100.0	29,308,581	100.0
1925						
Single	33,009,152	52.9	16,492,437	54.6	16,516,715	51.3
Married	25,437,499	40.8	12,727,429	42.2	12,710,070	39.4
Widowed	3,680,829	5.9	876,354	2.9	2,804,475	8.7
Divorced	283,139	0.4	100,603	0.3	182,536	0.6
Total	62,410,619	100.0	30,196,823	100.0	32,213,796	100.0
1933						
Single	32,091,072	49.2	16,212,881	51.2	15,878,191	47.4
Married	28,627,849	43.9	14,311,140	45.1	14,316,709	42.7
Widowed	4,005,018	6.1	978,541	3.1	3,026,477	9.0
Divorced	494,522	0.8	183,000	0.6	311,522	0.9
Total	65,218,461	100.0	31,685,562	100.0	33,532,899	100.0

Source: SdR, vol. 401, p. 586; StJhb 1935, p. 11.

every age group.⁹ Usborne has noted that these unmarried women were perceived as a social problem, as they provided competition with men in the job market and a temptation for husbands to be unfaithful.¹⁰ They swelled the ranks of the 'new women' in the cities, threatening the social and moral order in the eyes of those seeking a return to pre-war gender norms and an increase in the birth rate.

Among the *Frauenüberschuss* in 1918 were some 600,000 war widows, who differed from traditional widows through their youth, the age of their children and the higher pensions they received.¹¹ Under the 1920 National Pension Law they could apply for a pension equivalent to 30 per cent of the pension of a severely disabled serviceman, but this brought them to the notice of the welfare office, and the pension's value was decimated in the hyperinflation of the early 1920s.¹² As one widow wrote in 1930, 'the great inflation was the most terrible time for the dependents of the war dead. The state can never redress what we and our children had to suffer through the total devaluation of our pensions.'¹³ An estimated one-third of war widows remarried soon after the war, helped by match-making schemes such as the one in Magdeburg which introduced war widows to disabled soldiers.¹⁴ In 1919 105,749 widows remarried, making up 12.5 per cent of women marrying that year.¹⁵

In 1924 364,950 war widows were in receipt of a pension, the vast majority being between the ages of thirty and fifty and 78.5 per cent of them having children.¹⁶ In Hamburg in 1925 widows made up 42.2 per cent of social welfare recipients.¹⁷ Single women were dependent on their own labour, pensions, inherited wealth or families for their livelihood, with social welfare the safety net. During the Republic, before the onset of the Depression, women outnumbered men as recipients of welfare.¹⁸ Their numbers were swollen in the early 1920s by small rentiers, middle-class widows and unmarried women who had lived on their savings and investments or inherited wealth until their value had been wiped out during the hyperinflation.¹⁹ Figure 4.1 shows the facility set up by the Berlin Housewives' Associations for the sale of private property to protect pensioners and the impoverished middle class from being swindled. The impoverished middle class joined working-class female social pensioners who were unable to survive on their pensions or receive support from their families and were

Figure 4.1 Inflation: Germany is being liquidated. The Berlin Housewives' Associations' facility for the sale of private property (1923)

dependent on welfare. In Hamburg in July 1927 77.5 per cent of small rentiers and 59.4 per cent of social pensioners in receipt of social welfare were women.[20] During the Depression women with no means of financial support and no family to provide for them were forced to enter homeless shelters (see Figure 4.2). Some of those with no hope chose suicide, and the number of female suicides in 1932 was almost 50 per cent higher than that in 1924.[21] According to one contemporary, Germany had the highest rate of female suicides in Europe; Goeschel attributes the increasing number of female suicides to rising unemployment, while Nazi and Communist contemporaries were keen to blame the Weimar government's failure to deal with Germany's political and economic problems.[22] Other reasons for women committing suicide may have included lovesickness, unplanned pregnancy or mental illness. Suicide tended to be an urban, especially big-city phenomenon, and women's preferred methods were gassing, hanging and drowning.[23] For women, marriage provided security and protection from the vicissitudes of life.

Figure 4.2 Women's dormitory in a Berlin homeless shelter (December 1930)

Marriage

Article 119 of the Weimar Constitution of 11 August 1919 proclaimed that marriage, as the foundation of the family and of the preservation and reproduction of the nation, was based on the equality of the sexes.[24] This contradicted the German Civil Code of 18 August 1896, which had come into force on 1 January 1900 and which, in its determination of the legal aspects of marriage, granted the husband the right to make the decisions in all matters relating to married life.[25] Article 119 also proclaimed that it was the duty of the state and of local communities to keep the family pure and healthy, and to support it publicly.

Marriage was seen as the bedrock of a stable society by those with, in Heineman's words, 'uniquely bourgeois notions of the significance of marriage'.[26] There were, however, some radical feminists who challenged these notions. Helene Stöcker, leader of the BfM, espoused free love, the right of a man and a woman to have an open relationship outside marriage, and a woman's right to choose whether to become a mother.[27] In the working class, cohabitation and unmarried motherhood were common, though Hagemann notes a change in attitude during the Weimar Republic, with pressure being placed on working-class couples to marry. In Hamburg over one-quarter of illegitimate births were subsequently legitimised through marriage during the Republic.[28] In many rural areas it was traditional for couples to wait until the woman became pregnant, as proof of her fertility, before they married.[29] Economic factors also played their part in changing attitudes towards marriage. Gertrud Bäumer believed that in many cases marriage was possible only if both partners were employed, and Heineman notes that the Depression meant that marriage no longer 'brought a woman access to a male income'.[30] The use of reliable forms of contraception meant that couples were able to plan their families, and some enjoyed 'companionate marriages', consciously deciding not to have children. In 1933 35 per cent of marriages were childless in Berlin, 30.4 per cent in Hamburg.[31]

At the war's end, couples took the opportunity of marrying, the marriage rate peaking in 1920 at 14.5 per 1,000 of the population (see Table 4.2). As marriage was seen by the state as the basis for reproduction, and there were concerns about the 'fitness' to reproduce of some in society, specifically the mentally ill and those suffering from hereditary diseases, there were calls for couples to obtain compulsory health certificates before marriage, a demand made by the BfM in 1907.[32] The government could not agree on this, though the Interior Minister decreed on 30 May 1921 that all couples about to marry should be given a leaflet, drawn up by the Reich Health Council in August 1920, which detailed the dangers of a variety of diseases, including mental illness and venereal disease, for any potential offspring.[33] To facilitate the issue of health certificates and to 'promote healthy and high-quality offspring', the Prussian Welfare Minister passed a decree on 19 February 1926 encouraging local authorities to set up medically led marriage guidance clinics offering advice to prospective couples on health and eugenics. The first municipal marriage guidance clinic in Berlin was opened in Prenzlauer Berg on 1 June 1926, and by 1928 Prussia had 224 such centres.[34] Grossmann believes that the authorities wished to offer an alternative to the birth control clinics being set up by a range of organisations, and there was some debate about whether the municipal marriage guidance clinics should also offer contraceptive advice, especially as it was clear that it was this kind of advice that

Table 4.2 *Marriages and live births in selected years, 1885–1933*

Year	Marriages	Per 1,000 of the population	Live births	Per 1,000 of the population
1885	368,619	7.9	1,729,927	37.0
1900	476,491	8.5	1,996,139	35.6
1910	496,396	7.7	1,924,778	29.8
1916	279,076	4.1	1,029,484	13.9
1918	352,453	5.4	926,813	14.3
1919	844,339	13.4	1,260,500	20.0
1920	894,978	14.5	1,599,287	25.9
1921	731,157	11.8	1,560,447	25.3
1922	681,891	11.1	1,404,215	23.0
1923	581,277	9.4	1,297,449	21.1
1924	440,039	7.1	1,270,820	20.5
1925	482,792	7.7	1,292,499	20.7
1926	483,198	7.7	1,227,900	19.5
1927	538,463	8.5	1,161,719	18.4
1928	589,611	9.2	1,182,815	18.6
1929	589,611	9.2	1,147,458	17.9
1930	562,648	8.8	1,127,450	17.5
1931	515,403	8.0	1,031,770	16.0
1932	509,597	7.9	978,210	15.1
1933	630,826	9.7	956,915	14.7

Source: StJhb 1934, p. 27.

most people wanted.[35] Usborne claims that 'the marriage clinics in Prussia attracted a derisively small number of clients', but Paul Weindling regards them as precursors to the Nazis' racial health clinics and points out the crucial role they played in transforming eugenics 'from being the concern of an educated elite to providing the rationale of expert planners supporting a state-imposed population policy' under the Nazis.[36]

Contraception

During the Weimar Republic sex reformers challenged existing attitudes towards sexuality; they promoted sex education and improved knowledge of sexual techniques. According to Weitz, 'sex reformers played a central role in making Germany in the Weimar period a more modern, open and humane society'.[37] Believing in an individual's right to control his or her own body and hence in a woman's right to choose to have as many or as few children as she wanted, they promoted the use of birth control. Everyone, male and female, had the right to an enjoyable sex life, free from the worry of an unplanned pregnancy. Grossmann, however, emphasises that sex reformers were less concerned with women's individual rights over their bodies than with the inequalities caused by class and about the welfare of the population.[38] The fear of an unplanned pregnancy meant, according to Usborne, that many working-class women 'dreaded rather than enjoyed sex'.[39] Women's sexual pleasure was also marred by drunken and brutal husbands.[40] Pamela Swett writes of women's fear of Friday evenings when men came home drunk after having been paid, and contemporaries expressed concern that the experience of violence and brutality during the war had made some men addicted to violence in their sex lives.[41] Sex reformers sought to end 'sexual misery' and to inform Germans how to improve their sex lives. *The Ideal Marriage* (1926), by a Dutch gynaecologist, Theodor van de Velde, was one of several popular sex and marriage manuals, explicitly detailing sexual techniques and encouraging men to educate their wives in sexual matters and to learn how to give them sexual pleasure.[42]

The Weimar Republic witnessed the gradual acceptance of contraception as a means of limiting family size and the growth of a range of organisations, some with links to the SPD and KPD, offering contraceptive advice and contraception at affordable prices. The first sexual advice clinic was opened by Magnus Hirschfeld, a noted sexologist, in Berlin in July 1919, and during its first year it had 3,000 visitors, the vast majority of whom sought advice about birth control. Usborne believes that the Prussian government's willingness to take over the funding and management of the clinic after the hyperinflation in February 1924 was a significant step in the acceptance of contraception.[43] By the end of the Republic Berlin alone had forty of the 400 such clinics across Germany, and there were some 100 travelling clinics in addition to these.[44] The clinics were set up by sex reform organisations such as the BfM and the Society for Sexual Reform (*Gesellschaft für Sexualreform*, Gesex, founded in 1913) and by working-class lay organisations, originally for commercial gain, although Usborne believes that their commercial nature has been overstated.[45] Grossmann claims that the lay organisations had 150,000 members in 1932, and as membership organisations they were able to circumvent Article 184 of the Criminal Code of 1871 prohibiting the public display of contraceptives, which were deemed articles for obscene use.[46] Contraception was also available from 1928 to members of Berlin's sickness insurance funds, though the most popular methods of birth control for many couples remained *coitus interruptus*, douching and pessaries, cheap methods that did not require medical intervention.[47] The 1927 Law for Combating Venereal Diseases permitted the display of contraceptives that could be used as prophylactics, and by 1932 1,300 condom-dispensing machines had been installed in public lavatories. Roos has noted that 'for women, improved access to certain contraceptives after 1927 marked an important gain in reproductive rights'.[48]

In spite of the fact that the Constitution proclaimed marriage to be the foundation for the family, more and more couples were consciously limiting their family size. Contraception enabled women to control their fertility. They were no longer condemned to a thirty-year circle of pregnancy and child-rearing. Burgdörfer noted in 1929 that the fall in the national birth rate (see Table 4.2) was primarily attributable to the working class copying the reproductive behaviour of the upper and middle classes: according to Hagemann, working-class couples having families in the 1920s and 1930s became the first generation to realise 'the ideal of the modern, small family'.[49] In Hamburg in 1900 the birth rate in the working-class district of Uhlenhorst was 36.3 per 1,000 of population, and in the up-market residential district of Harvestehude it was 17.5; by 1933 the figures had fallen to 10 and 7.2 respectively.[50] During the Weimar Republic the birth rate was the lowest in the cities, with Germany's fifty cities of over 100,000 inhabitants recording a birth rate of 10.8 in 1932, and it increased to 17.9 in smaller communities of under 15,000. Berlin had the lowest birth rate in the world, at 8.1 births per 1,000 of the population in 1932.[51] Couples in the countryside had always had more children than those living in the cities, and this trend continued; in 1925 there were 252 births per 1,000 married men under the age of fifty among Prussia's agricultural population, and 132 in the non-agricultural population. However, the 1920s witnessed an accelerated decrease in the birth rate among the rural population so that by 1930 the birth rate in both rural and urban areas of Prussia was just under half of what it had been at the turn of the century.[52] Figures from Baden reveal no difference between the birth rates of Catholic and Protestant areas, and Usborne believes that the Protestant Church came to accept birth control because it was so widely practised, while in the Catholic Church lack of agreement led at the end of 1930 to Pope Pius XI's encyclical *Casti Connubii*, which condemned the use of artificial contraception and abortion.[53] The national birth rate reached a nadir of 14.7 in 1933, before rising to 20.4 in 1939 as the Nazis closed down the birth control clinics and sex reform organisations and attempted to restrict access to contraception for racially valuable women while also offering financial inducements for Aryan families to have children; improving economic prospects also encouraged couples to start or increase their families.[54] John Knodel believes that the early 1930s witnessed the 'end of Germany's fertility transition', with birth rates higher in the mid-to-late 1930s and in the early years of the Federal Republic than during the Depression.[55]

Abortion

One reason for the growing acceptance of contraception was the belief that it was preferable to abortion, which, according to Usborne, was the most prevalent form of birth control for many working-class and lower middle-class women.[56] During the Republic the estimated annual number of abortions grew to one million during the Depression, and estimations of the numbers of women dying as the result of botched abortions varied from 4,000 to 40,000, with cases of morbidity estimated at between 50,000 and 100,000.[57] Cases of abortion were thought to increase during periods of economic hardship, and during the Depression there were claims that the number of abortions exceeded the number of births.[58] The majority of women having abortions were married with children, though Hagemann believes that throughout the Republic the share of young, married childless women and of single women having abortions increased.[59] Usborne has clearly shown women's agency in determining to limit their family size and their belief in their right to do so. In many cases, they were dependent in their choice of contraceptive method on the co-operation of their male partner, and Usborne has shown the supportiveness of some husbands to women wishing to seek an abortion, in finding a reputable lay practitioner or in attending the termination. Abortion was popularly accepted as a means for ending an unwanted pregnancy, and could be self-administered; if women sought help it was from a lay practitioner, wise woman or midwife, known locally by word of mouth, whose services were cheaper and less judgemental than a physician's. Contrary to the portrayals of lay abortionists as greedy, unhygienic practitioners endangering desperate women's lives, found in contemporary films, plays and literary texts which brought the issue of abortion to the masses, Usborne claims that 'the majority of lay abortionists acted conscientiously and safely because of their skill and the precautions they took', and contrasts their wealth of knowledge and practical experience with that of physicians, some of whom botched terminations.[60] Usborne found little difference in attitudes towards abortion between town and country or between Protestant and Catholic. It was perceived as neither criminal nor immoral, and at a time when there was no reliable test for pregnancy, women could believe they were acting to bring on a late period.[61]

However, Article 218 of the 1871 Criminal Code threatened a pregnant woman who aborted her child, or anyone who did so with her permission, with a minimum sentence of six months or a maximum sentence of five years' penal servitude; Article 219 prescribed up to ten years' penal servitude for someone who aborted or gave the woman the means to abort a child for monetary gain, and Article 220 prescribed a sentence of not less than two years' penal servitude for someone carrying out an abortion without the mother's consent; if the mother died as a result of the abortion, the sentence increased to not less than ten years or life.[62] Cases came to the attention of the authorities when something went wrong, when abortionists were denounced, or when a lay abortionist confessed, as was the case with a Berlin chemist, Paul Heiser, who confessed in 1924 to having performed 11,000 abortions in order to bring about a change in the law.[63] Heiser had invented a paste that brought on a miscarriage which, according to Usborne, was 'the only really significant new development in abortion technology during the inter-war period', and it came to be used throughout Germany and in Britain and the United States.[64] In 1921, of 5,169 people prosecuted under Article 218, 921 were acquitted and 3,216 (75.7 per cent) of those found guilty were women. Of those convicted 69 (1.6 per cent) were sentenced to penal servitude and 285 (6.7 per cent) to a prison sentence longer than one year. By 1925, the highpoint of convictions, of the 6,707 people found guilty, 113 (1.7 per cent) were sentenced to penal servitude and 233 (3.5 per cent) to a prison term of longer than one year.[65] The abortion laws were considered class-discriminatory as only wealthy middle- and upper-class women could afford to obtain a discreet medical termination or to pay for reliable artificial forms of contraception.[66]

In the early years of the Republic the parties of the left, in response to grass-roots protests against Article 218 and often at the instigation of female parliamentarians, initiated motions to reform the abortion laws. In the National Assembly the SPD called in March 1920 for abortion to be permitted on social and eugenic grounds, and four months later in the first Reichstag it responded to the USPD's motion to repeal Articles 218-20 by calling for abortion to be permitted within the first three months of pregnancy if carried out by the woman herself or by a physician. From 1924 the KPD, believing that abortion was a necessary evil until the state could ensure the material well-being of all children, called for the repeal of Articles 218 and 219; it later integrated this demand into a comprehensive maternity and child welfare programme, which was discussed in the Reichstag's population policy committee.[67] The liberal parties, the DVP and the DDP, said little on abortion but were willing to support moderate reform, while the Centre Party and the DNVP were totally opposed to any relaxation in the abortion laws, reflecting the attitude of the Catholic and Protestant Churches.[68] The German Doctors' Association, meeting in Leipzig in 1925, opposed any change to the abortion laws, though it believed that a termination on medical grounds, under strictly controlled procedures, should be lawful.[69] In the face of this opposition the amendment proposed by the SPD and approved by the Reichstag in May 1926 was, in Usborne's words, 'a significant improvement' and gave Germany the most lenient abortion laws in Western Europe.[70] Under the new Article 218, which replaced Articles 218-20, abortion became a misdemeanour, not a crime; for a woman who aborted her child or someone who performed an abortion with the woman's consent, and in extenuating circumstances, the punishment could be a small fine or one day in prison, a reduction from the previous law's six months. Performing an abortion without the woman's consent or for financial gain remained a crime, punishable by penal servitude, and the maximum sentence was increased to fifteen years. The amendment bore a remarkable similarity to the BdF's standpoint on abortion, approved in 1908, which, while upholding Article 218, had called for the removal of penal servitude and a reduction in the sentence for a woman found guilty of having an abortion, and for legal terminations when pregnancy threatened the life or health of the mother, when the child could be expected to be born mentally or physically disabled, or in cases of rape. The BdF re-affirmed this position in 1925, adding that social conditions should also be taken into consideration when determining the threat to the mother's health.[71] A Supreme Court ruling in March 1927 permitted abortion on medical grounds, fulfilling another part of the BdF's demand.[72] Its call for abortion on eugenic grounds was supported by several different groups, including some women doctors who shared the widespread belief that eugenics was a progressive and humanitarian science. Some, like Agnes Bluhm, were motivated by considerations of what was best for the future of the German race.[73] While the BdF favoured custodial care for the mentally handicapped and those thought 'unfit' to reproduce, some of its members, such as Dr Anne-Marie Durand-Wever, joined sex reformers, socialist feminists and others in advocating sterilisation, including compulsory sterilisation, as a cost-effective and safe method of preventing those deemed 'unfit' from reproducing.[74] Usborne claims that some 50,000–100,000 sterilisations were being performed annually by the early 1930s, many for eugenic reasons, but many, also, as a method of long-term birth control.[75] In some cases physicians sterilised women by stealth, believing that their fecklessness in the use of contraception showed them to be lacking in intelligence, but in others doctors were implored by women to prevent them suffering future pregnancies. In a much-publicised case tried in Offenburg in 1931, Dr Merk and a male and a female colleague who were accused of having performed forty-one sterilisations were found guilty of causing bodily harm.[76] In their Law to Prevent Hereditarily Diseased Offspring of July 1933 the Nazis ensured that those deemed 'unfit' to reproduce faced compulsory sterilisation, whereas voluntary sterilisation as a means of birth control for those deemed racially valuable became illegal.[77]

Following the 1926 amendment, the numbers of prosecutions under Article 218 fell, with 5,313 convictions in 1927, 3,892 in 1928 and 3,597 in 1929, before they began to rise again, with 4,233 convictions in 1932.[78] The KPD continued to petition the Reichstag for the repeal of the abortion law within a comprehensive welfare programme, and in 1929 the SPD added its voice to the call for repeal in discussions on the redrafting of the Criminal Code.[79] Opinions within the SPD were, however, divided on the issue of abortion, as they were within the medical profession. On 25 May 1930 the majority of Berlin's female physicians within the BdÄ, 356 of 476, petitioned the Reichstag for abortion to be illegal only when it was not performed by a registered physician or without the woman's consent, and within weeks 400 women doctors from across Germany counter-petitioned, calling for abortion to be legal only on strictly controlled medical grounds.[80]

During the early years of the Republic demonstrations against Article 218 and against the trials of doctors accused of performing abortions were a common occurrence across Germany, usually orchestrated by the left or by sex-reform organisations.[81] In spring 1931 public discussion of the new draft Criminal Code and a campaign by a coalition of Communist women's organisations, the BfM and the IFFF against the papal encyclical *Casti Connubii* coalesced with a groundswell of protest, much of it orchestrated by the KPD, against the arrest on 19 February 1931 of two Stuttgart doctors, Dr Friedrich Wolf and Dr Else Kienle, for having performed abortions. Wolf, a KPD member, was well known for having written an anti-Article 218 play, *Cyankali*, which had been performed throughout Germany.[82] The campaign against Article 218, which included a committee for self-denunciation which encouraged women to speak and write about their abortion experiences, saw over 1,500 demonstrations across Germany on 8 March 1931, International Women's Day, and culminated with Wolf and Kienle speaking in Berlin's Sportpalast to 15,000 on 15 April 1931. The campaign fizzled out, perhaps because of the decree of 28 March 1931 which severely limited demonstrations and increased press censorship, because of the rapidly deteriorating economic and political situation, or because of the KPD's failure to maintain leadership of the campaign.[83] Within months of coming to power the Nazis, who on 12 March 1930 petitioned the Reichstag for anyone who tried artificially to impede the natural fertility of the German race to be punished with penal servitude for 'racial treason', amended Article 218, adding two new paragraphs which forbade the advertising of abortifacients and abortion.[84] The Nazis' attitude towards abortion was governed by their theories of race. Abortion was, therefore, permitted for those deemed less racially valuable than hereditarily healthy Aryan women; in 1935 it was permitted on eugenic grounds for pregnant women slated for sterilisation, and in 1943 for pregnant foreign workers from the East, at a time when capital punishment was introduced for serial abortionists of foetuses deemed racially valuable.[85]

Prostitution and the fight against venereal disease

The 1926 amendment enshrined in law a significant shift in attitudes towards an aborting mother. A more radical change in attitudes towards women was to be found in the Law for Combating Venereal Diseases of February 1927. Roos, while acknowledging the potentially repressive aspects of this law, claims that it 'represented important advances in women's rights' because it decriminalised prostitution, and that its success can be seen in the force of the backlash against it in the early 1930s, which 'ultimately helped destroy Weimar democracy'.[86] Victoria Harris, however, sees the law 'as part of the continued and intensified policy of the internment and exclusion of both prostitutes and a growing section of the non-prostitute female population', and as social exclusion 'by different means'.[87] Although prostitution was illegal before 1927, authorities across Germany had adopted systems of regulation whereby prostitutes had to register with the morals police (*Sittenpolizei*), undergo regular examinations and abide by restrictions on their movements, place of residence and behaviour in public. In some areas prostitutes were restricted to living and working in brothels or designated streets. Many more women than were registered worked clandestinely as prostitutes, and their numbers swelled in times of economic uncertainty.[88] Prostitutes were thought to be major carriers of venereal disease, and abolitionists, seeing in the regulation of prostitution a misogynist double standard as male clients were not prosecuted nor were they placed under police or medical supervision, sought to decriminalise prostitution. At the war's end, when the authorities believed there that was no greater danger to the future of the German people than 'extensive moral degeneracy' and the 'contamination of the population' through venereal disease, laws were passed in December 1918 permitting local health authorities to order the compulsory treatment of all infected men and women and imprisonment for up to three years for those who had sexual intercourse knowing they were infected with venereal disease.[89] In 1921 653 people, of whom 542 were women, were prosecuted under this law, highlighting the continuing prejudice against women, whose sexual behaviour was now perceived to be as promiscuous as men's.[90] The major women's organisations, the BdF, the DEF and the KFB, were all against regulation, and on 22 October 1919 women from all the political parties petitioned the National Assembly to end regulation and to replace the supervision of registered prostitutes by the *Sittenpolizei* with health care and welfare.[91] In 1921, at the instigation of female city councillors, it was agreed to close the brothels in Hamburg and Leipzig, though some prostitutes campaigned against this, fearing not only the loss of secure accommodation but also competition from unlicensed prostitution.[92] The formal end to regulation was to come after five years of debate in the Reichstag, in the Law for Combating Venereal Diseases, which came into effect on 1 October 1927.[93] Regulation was thought to be incompatible with the equality of the sexes and the individual human rights enshrined in the Constitution and was perceived to have failed to halt the spread of venereal disease, much to the concern of those interested in population policy. Accurate figures for the numbers of people infected with venereal disease were difficult to obtain, because of the difficulties in diagnosing syphilis in its early stages, the desire of those infected for confidentiality and the lack of compulsory registration for all those infected. A survey conducted for one month between November and December 1918 revealed 136,328 people receiving treatment, from which the authorities extrapolated that there were 528,288 new cases each year. However, only 55 per cent of physicians answered the survey, and claims of an epidemic of venereal disease, fuelled by the rapid demobilisation, were common in the early years of the Republic.[94] Paula Mueller-Otfried, speaking in Mannheim in January 1921, claimed that the number of sufferers from venereal disease had risen from two million in 1914 to six million and that in 1919 one child in twenty-five had been born with syphilis.[95] Population policy experts were concerned about the impact on the birth rate, with some claiming that venereal disease caused between 40,000 and 100,000 fewer births annually, while of 36,000 cases of babies born blind in 1925, 30,000 were attributed to gonorrhoea.[96] Although it remained illegal under the 1927 law to solicit in communities with under 15,000 inhabitants or in the vicinity of churches, schools or areas popular with young people, prostitutes were no longer subject to restrictions on their movements, their domicile, their code of dress or their right to keep a pet, and they could choose private physicians to carry out medical examinations.[97] The primary focus of the law was on curbing the spread of venereal disease, and it was incumbent upon any individual infected with venereal disease, male or female, to seek medical treatment from a registered physician of their choosing; if the individual was impecunious, the public purse would fund the treatment, though in some areas infected women once treated were forced to work in a workhouse to cover the cost.[98] Local health offices were given the responsibility of ensuring the implementation of the law, and if they suspected that an individual had venereal disease, they could demand medical certification or that the individual undergo a medical examination and, if infected, treatment, using force if necessary. Anyone knowingly infected with venereal disease who had sexual intercourse could face imprisonment for up to three years. Harris believes that the law widened the circle of women who could be made to undergo medical examination and treatment and who were subject to the supervision of the local health and welfare offices.[99] Freund-Widder notes that the number under supervision in Cologne and Berlin doubled, while in Münster eight women were under supervision before the law was passed, but over 100 afterwards.[100] However, this law was, in essence, a consolidation of the December 1918 emergency decrees which had permitted the compulsory treatment of men and women suspected of having venereal disease. The increase in the number of women under the supervision of the local health offices may be attributable to the transfer of the supervision of prostitutes from the *Sittenpolizei*. Indeed, after 1927 the numbers of women prosecuted under the law for having sexual intercourse knowing they were infected with venereal disease fell, from 458 in 1926 to 119 in 1932, though higher numbers of women than men continued to be prosecuted.[101]

Harris notes that in some areas the police ignored the 1927 law, causing prostitutes to protest about police repression and excessive surveillance which prevented them from carrying out their lawful business, and their protests were, according to Roos, 'a crucial factor in the backlash against prostitution reforms during the early 1930s'.[102] Other factors included the perceived increase in prostitution caused by mass unemployment, resulting in a visible deterioration in the 'streetscape' where prostitutes solicited; the concern about the increased number of advertisements for prostitutes' services in newspapers; complaints about the fall in property values when prostitutes moved into an area; and the concern about public decency and the danger to metropolitan youth. In 1932 one Catholic organisation called for an emergency decree to end the plague of prostitution.[103] The deposition of the SPD-led government in Prussia by Chancellor Franz von Papen in July 1932 led to the appointment of several right-wing police chiefs, some of whom forbade street soliciting, and this ban was extended across Germany by the Nazis in May 1933. Many prostitutes were arrested during 1933 in the regime's fight against immorality, and in autumn 1933 several cities re-introduced state-regulated prostitution.[104]

The 1927 law fulfilled a long-standing demand of the abolitionists, the BdF and the DEF, and significantly improved the rights of a very small number of women, the registered prostitutes, though not all prostitutes welcomed the law, with some bemoaning the loss of the warmth and security of the brothel and the constant fear of arrest.[105] It also legalised not only the inoffensive public display of prophylactics but also the dissemination of information about venereal disease, though leaflets, lectures, travelling exhibitions and films warning about the dangers of venereal disease had proliferated since the end of the war. Annette Timm writes that 'educational and propaganda campaigns about VD in the Weimar years displayed an incredible degree of publicity'.[106] Socialist attempts to include in the law the provision of compulsory sex education for schoolchildren over the age of fourteen were unsuccessful, though Prussian school leavers were lectured on the dangers of venereal disease from 1919.[107] The authorities could not agree on the introduction of sex education in schools, believing that parents were responsible for the sex education of their children, and where sex education for girls did take place, the emphasis was on chastity until marriage.[108] However, in many working-class and middle-class families discussions of sexuality were taboo, perhaps out of embarrassment or ignorance. Although the well-known Jewish doctor Rahel Strauss wrote a pamphlet advising mothers on how to explain sex to their daughters, she failed to provide her own children with sex education.[109] In Fromm's survey of 1929 fewer than one-quarter of respondents favoured early sex education for children, but nearly one-half (46 per cent) failed to answer.[110] Although many working-class children, forced to share bedrooms with parents, witnessed sexual activity, they gleaned their sex education from socialist youth organisations.[111]

Sexual behaviour

During the Weimar Republic young working-class women's sexual behaviour became the focus of several studies by middle-class women, some of whom were shocked by the young women's openness about their promiscuity, while others accepted that pre-marital sex was the norm, even for girls between the ages of fourteen and eighteen.[112] It is probable that this had been accepted practice in working-class circles before the war. The war had, however, challenged bourgeois standards of sexual behaviour, and the hyperinflation further eroded the belief in a woman's chastity before a marriage which would provide for her economically and in which the paternity of any inheriting offspring had to be beyond doubt. As one woman commented, 'when the money became worthless, it destroyed the whole system for getting married, and so it destroyed the whole idea of remaining chaste until marriage'.[113] Middle-class girls no longer remained virgins before marriage. While some impoverished young middle-class women entered sexual relationships with nouveau-riche businessmen for financial security, others believed that even though they might not have the opportunity to marry they were entitled to be sexually active.[114] Grossmann writes of women physicians' distress at young middle-class women's ability to divorce sex from procreation and from love, and Hans Ostwald, writing about the moral impact of the hyperinflation, noted that women 'asserted their demands, particularly their sexual demands, much more clearly'.[115] This may, however, have been a big-city phenomenon, while in rural and Catholic areas traditional patterns of behaviour continued. The perceived transformation in single women's sexual mores, at a time when higher standards of behaviour were expected of women than of men, reinforced traditional beliefs that single women who were sexually active damaged their reputation and raised concerns about the spread of venereal disease and an increase in illegitimate births.[116] Unmarried motherhood brought shame and scandal, as well as accusations of stupidity, because of the belief that knowledge about contraception was widespread, though this was not always the case.[117] There were reports of girls committing infanticide and abandoning their babies, though Patricia Stokes claims that during the Weimar Republic fewer families than before rejected their pregnant single daughters.[118]

Illegitimacy

Under the Civil Code of 1900 an illegitimate child was not related to its father; its mother had custody, but no legal parental authority, and could claim from the father the costs of her confinement and subsistence for the first six weeks following the birth and maintenance for the child in accordance with her financial circumstances, though if it was proved that she had had sexual intercourse with others during the probable period of conception, paternity could not be proved.[119] Official attitudes towards illegitimate children were to change during the war, as their importance in maintaining 'the health of the next generation' came to be realised. Illegitimate children were eligible to receive Family War Benefit, and on 20 February 1918 the Reichstag agreed that a father had to pay maintenance, dependent on his income, until the child reached the age of eighteen.[120] Article 121 of the Weimar Constitution proclaimed that illegitimate children were to be assured, through legislation, of the same conditions for their bodily, spiritual and social development as legitimate children. However, attempts to introduce legislation amending the Civil Code were unsuccessful, being blocked by the Centre Party and DNVP, which believed that such legislation undermined the family.[121] The proportion of illegitimate births rose from 9.1 per cent of all births in 1910 to 13.1 per cent in 1918, and then fell to 10.4 per cent in 1923 before averaging around 12 per cent until 1932.[122] Unmarried mothers tended to be younger than married ones, and illegitimate children were more likely than legitimate ones to die during their first year, though infant mortality improved during the Weimar Republic. In 1919 26 per cent of illegitimate and 13 per cent of legitimate children died before their first birthday, and in 1931 12.3 per cent and 7.8 per cent respectively.[123] Mouton credits the Reich Youth Welfare Law of 9 July 1922, which Lilienthal claims 'was a milestone in the care of illegitimacy', with this fall.[124] Under this law, child welfare offices oversaw the wellbeing of illegitimate children and acted as guardians for them. Part of their remit was ensuring that the father paid maintenance, which they collected and then passed on to the mother, having set aside funds for the child's education. Figures revealed that paternity was acknowledged in 60 per cent of cases without going to court, and in 25 per cent of cases after going to court, while in the 6 per cent of cases in which multiple intercourse was proven, the child received public welfare.[125] Of those fathers acknowledging paternity in Hamburg between 1929 and 1933 67.9 per cent were manual workers, 10.5 per cent white-collar workers and 2.2 per cent civil servants, and 10.5 per cent had other occupations.[126] Mouton claims that the increasing number of men paying maintenance helped to improve single mothers' lives, and while wealthy men were the least likely to acknowledge paternity, they might come to a private arrangement with the mother.[127] The law placed the mother and child under the surveillance of the youth welfare office and its appointed guardian until the child reached maturity, though youth welfare offices differed in their zealousness in implementing the law. David Crew believes that many youth welfare offices preferred to put illegitimate children into foster care while forcing the father, mother or other relatives to pay for the care, though a child could not be put up for adoption without the mother's consent.[128] Hagemann notes that working-class families saw fostering as a way to supplement their income, though the hyperinflation forced some to give up fostering. Increased rates of pay for fostering after July 1925 meant that the numbers of families willing to foster children increased, though they were now subject to stringent checks from the local youth welfare offices.[129] While the youth welfare offices during the Weimar Republic tried to place children in emotionally stable homes, the Nazis placed more emphasis on the racial heritage of the foster parents.[130] In the Third Reich the proportion of illegitimate births fell, from 10.7 per cent of all births in 1933 to 7.8 per cent in 1939, perhaps because working-class couples were encouraged to marry by the provision of marriage loans or because unmarried mothers of several children were deemed promiscuous asocials and were sterilised, while the mothers of illegitimate, racially valuable children were deemed worthy of support.[131] Traditional attitudes, however, continued to stigmatise unmarried mothers.

Divorce

The churches, DNVP and Centre Party had fought to prevent any improvement in the legal status of illegitimate children, and the

Catholic Church and its political representatives, the Centre Party and the Bavarian People's Party, were intransigent in their opposition to divorce reform. The increase in divorce during the Republic was regarded by some as a symptom of the Republic's moral decline.[132] Divorce was governed by the Civil Code of 1900, which had replaced a variety of state laws. It introduced absolute and relative grounds for divorce and normally required guilt to be attributed to one party. Absolute grounds for divorce included adultery, bigamy, wilful desertion, death threats and unnatural sexual acts, while relative grounds, which permitted judges some discretion in their judgement, included immoral or dishonourable behaviour which made it impossible for one party to stay in the marriage, and mental illness.[133] In Prussia before the war, religiously mixed couples were the most likely to divorce, Catholic couples the least; adultery was the major cause, and for every 100 women found guilty in a divorce, there were 174 men.[134] From 1915 the number of men instigating divorce proceedings grew, usually because of a wife's adultery, and during the war and in the immediate post-war years the ratio of women to men pronounced guilty fell to 100:115; Mouton claims that in 1917 women were found guilty in 55.6 per cent of Prussian divorce cases.[135] In 1920 the divorce rate was 2.5 times its pre-war average (see Table 4.3), perhaps because the war had fundamentally altered the relationship between the couple, those who had rushed to marry in 1914 realised their mistake, or those who had been intending to divorce had been forced by the war to delay, and the divorce rate continued at what was perceived to be a high level throughout the Republic. Divorce was regarded as a big-city phenomenon, as was confirmed by pre-war and post-war figures. In Prussia between 1919 and 1922 the divorce rate per 100,000 head of population was 1.79 in rural areas, 9.85 in towns and 14.26 in cities.[136] During the Republic Berlin vied with Hamburg for the title of divorce capital of Germany, followed more distantly by Bremen and Lübeck.[137] On average nearly one-third of marriages had lasted for less than five years, and over 60 per cent fewer than ten.[138] Mouton notes that 'judges increasingly assigned guilt to women when men were clearly the guilty parties', though figures from Prussia show a fall in women's share of those pronounced individually guilty.[139] However, expectations placed on women's behaviour were higher than those placed on men's. A court in Karlsruhe determined that a man who had a mistress did

Table 4.3 *The divorce rate, 1910–33*

Year	Divorces	Per 100,000 of the population
1910	15,016	23.3
1911	15,780	24.1
1912	16,911	25.6
1913	17,835	26.6
1914	17,740	26.2
1915	10,791	a
1916	10,494	a
1917	11,603	17.7
1918	13,344	20.6
1919	22,022	35.0
1920	36,542	59.1
1921	39,211	62.9
1922	36,587	59.7
1923	33,939	55.0
1924	35,936	57.8
1925	35,451	56.8
1926	34,105	54.3
1927	36,449	57.6
1928	36,928	58.0
1929	39,424	61.6
1930	40,722	63.3
1931	39,971	61.8
1932	42,202	65.0
1933	42,485	65.1

Note: [a] Not available, or not recorded.

Source: Relevant years of *StJhb*.

not have to put up with a wife with a lover, while in another case a judge granted a divorce to a man who had discovered that his wife had had several affairs before their marriage, noting that 'a wife's love affairs before marriage are different from a husband's. According to contemporary views, a bachelor's fast-living and dissolute lifestyle is not held against him but when a woman has several lovers, it is regarded as a serious moral failing and a lack of control in relationships with the opposite sex.'[140]

During the Republic two trends became discernible: the number of cases in which both parties were found guilty increased, and immoral or dishonourable behaviour supplanted adultery as the major cause of divorce.¹⁴¹ Mouton sees in these trends judges being swayed by considerations of 'irreconcilable differences', though Blasius notes that the concept of guilt remained, as did the public opprobrium and financial penalties that went with it, which were particularly harsh on women, as being found guilty meant penury, and even if the woman was the innocent party she was entitled to maintenance from her ex-husband only if she had no private means or if it had not been customary for her to work.¹⁴² Divorced men were more likely to remarry than were divorced women, though under Article 1312 of the Civil Code they could not marry the person cited as co-respondent in their divorce case without special dispensation from the court.¹⁴³ Feminists wished to repeal this paragraph, and the BdF called for divorce on the grounds of irretrievable breakdown, without allocation of guilt, on the grounds of mutual consent and on the grounds of one partner's insuperable dislike of the other.¹⁴⁴ In the early years of the Republic Marie-Elisabeth Lüders led the fight for divorce reform, first raising the issue in the Reichstag on 26 January 1921, when she called for divorce to be made easier, for the introduction of the principle of irretrievable breakdown in place of the principle of guilt, for divorce on the grounds of mutual consent and even for divorce on the application of only one party.¹⁴⁵ Thereafter she and her party submitted petitions and drafts introducing divorce on the grounds of irretrievable breakdown and calling for an end to the principle of guilt.¹⁴⁶ In 1928 the DDP, SPD and Economics Party and Dr Kahl of the DVP also called for divorce to be possible after five years' separation.¹⁴⁷ By 1928 the DVP supported divorce on the grounds of irretrievable breakdown. The KPD wanted marriage to be regarded as a private contract between the two persons concerned, a contract that could be terminated if both parties so agreed or one partner so desired.¹⁴⁸ The DNVP and DEF, while thinking that divorce reform was needed, believed firmly in the principle of guilt and that the proposal to allow for just one party to demand a divorce would be detrimental to older women.¹⁴⁹ The Catholic Church, the Centre Party and the BVB held fast to the belief in the indissolubility of marriage; when the Democratic Justice Minister drew up a draft law for the reform of divorce in early 1929, introducing irretrievable breakdown as an additional grounds for divorce, the Centre Party, having failed to secure the Chancellor's agreement to delay discussions, withdrew its members from the Reichstag's legal committee, effectively ending any discussions of reform.[150] It was left to the Nazis to reform the divorce laws, and on 6 July 1938 they introduced divorce for couples who had been separated for three years and whose marriage appeared to have broken down irretrievably.[151] Their reasons for doing so had little to do with liberal ideals, but stemmed from a desire to increase the number of reproductive marriages.

Motherhood

Under Article 119 of the Weimar Constitution motherhood had a right to the protection and care of the state, but Crew notes that 'the child, not the mother, was the primary focus of the welfare state's commitment to the protection of motherhood'.[152] Before the war a small number of ante-natal advice centres had been set up by organisations such as the BfM, and Leipzig was the first city to fund an ante-natal advice centre in 1915.[153] Berlin followed in 1917, having implemented a system of social worker visits to all unmarried pregnant women the previous year, and on 20 August 1920 the Prussian Welfare Minister directed all communities to create ante-natal advice centres.[154] By 1928 Prussia had 898 publicly funded ante-natal advice centres, with thirty-eight in Berlin alongside eighteen clinics funded by the sickness insurance funds, which had first opened in 1925, and several privately run centres.[155] A government survey found 1,426 publicly funded and 1,883 privately funded ante-natal advice centres in Germany in 1928.[156] The centres offered an external medical examination and medical, legal and economic advice; very few offered medical treatment, the Berlin sickness insurance funds' centres being an exception.[157] Stokes claims that by 1929 42 per cent of all pregnant women in Berlin visited an ante-natal advice centre.[158] In other towns and cities, however, far fewer pregnant women visited the centres unless they were induced by material benefits such as groceries, bed linen or baby clothes, as authorities were reluctant to give impoverished women money, fearing that it would be squandered, perhaps by alcoholic husbands.[159] There were few ante-natal advice centres in rural areas, with women relying on relatives and informal networks for support. While middle- and upper-class women could afford to consult a physician during their pregnancy, it was the norm for working-class and rural women to consult a midwife only during the later stages of pregnancy.[160] However, many women had the right of access to a physician in cases of complications under the three schemes pertinent to pregnant women that were developed during the early years of the Republic. Insured working women were eligible for Maternity Benefit, a continuation of the First World War scheme; female relatives of insured working men were entitled to the Family Maternity Benefit; and impoverished women could receive Maternity Welfare, which was paid for by the community. Pregnant women were entitled to receive a weekly cash sum (*Wochengeld*) for four weeks before the due date, which they had to have certified by a physician, and for six weeks after the birth, which could be extended at the discretion of the insurance fund to ten weeks. Nursing mothers received a supplementary sum for twelve weeks, with a possible extension to twenty-six weeks, but had to have their nursing verified by a social worker. In 1929 26.5 per cent of all women who had a baby received Maternity Benefit, 44.8 per cent Family Maternity Benefit and 9 per cent Maternity Welfare.[161] As *Wochengeld* was initially paid following the birth, many women, out of economic necessity, continued to work until the birth, while following the introduction of the Law on the Employment of Women before and after Childbirth in 1927 some women received both their wages and maternity benefit.[162] During the hyperinflation maternity benefit rapidly lost value, and during the Depression the additional discretionary payments were scrapped.[163]

During the Republic the majority of women gave birth at home with the assistance of a midwife, who was legally required to call out a physician in cases of complications and who could not administer pain relief. From the mid-1920s, hospital births became common in major cities as married women, in their search for pain relief, overcame the stigma associated with hospital birth, which had been the domain of the unmarried mother. In 1931 across Germany 16.3 per cent of births took place in a hospital or maternity home; in Hamburg the figure was 61.3 per cent, in Berlin 64.3 per cent and in Frankfurt am Main 73.5 per cent.[164] The numbers then fell because the Fourth Emergency Decree of December 1931 permitted the insurance funds to cover only the costs of a home birth.[165] The risks inherent in childbirth and women's contribution to the survival of the German race through having children were often equated with the dangers and contribution to the nation of men's military service.

Between 1900 and 1930 maternal mortality increased. In 1913 15.9 women per 10,000 head of population died of childbed fever, and a further 17.8 of other illnesses such as eclampsia or haemorrhage; in 1930 the figures were 26.6 and 25.4 respectively.[166] An estimated 30,000–40,000 women annually suffered long-term complications following childbirth, such as prolapse or incontinence.[167] The share of stillbirths remained relatively stable at around 3 per cent. The high maternal mortality rate was due to a lack of obstetric care, poor obstetric practice and the insanitary conditions in which some urban working-class and rural women were forced to give birth.[168] Not only could poor working-class women not afford clean linen, but many also lacked privacy in their confinement and lying-in.[169] Poverty, poor housing and lack of hygiene were also reasons given for the high rate of infant mortality, which improved significantly during the life of the Republic. In Berlin infant mortality fell from 140 per 1,000 live births in 1920 to 67 in 1932.[170] The infant mortality rate was considerably higher in working-class districts than in middle-class ones.[171] Although rent controls meant that the share of a family's income spent on accommodation fell significantly in the early inflationary years after the war, working-class families struggled to meet the rising cost of food, even though price controls and rationing of various foodstuffs continued until 1922.[172] In 1921 28.7 per cent of German babies under six months and 41.1 per cent of infants between six months and one year suffered from rickets.[173] Many were dependent on the food kitchens opened by the Quakers; Ostwald claims that 60,000 children were being fed daily.[174] As poverty and poor housing continued throughout the Republic, with many Germans being dependent on welfare during the hyperinflation and the Depression, the fall in infant mortality can be attributed to the measures taken to improve infant care among the working class.[175] Figures from Hamburg reveal that the primary cause of infant mortality changed between 1900 and 1931 from food disorders to premature birth or complications at birth.[176] Crew has claimed that 'the protection of motherhood frequently translated in practice into an intrusive policing of mothers', and he writes of the welfare agencies' 'invasive practices of "normalization and surveillance"' as middle-class female social workers tried to inculcate their ideals of a healthy, orderly and efficient lifestyle on their working-class clients.[177] Hagemann has also noted that the granting of public welfare was combined with considerable social control and discipline.[178] Larry Frohman, however, in his exploration of measures to combat tuberculosis and infant mortality, argues for the popularity of these programmes among grateful working-class recipients, and states that 'they gave the Weimar welfare system a genuinely liberal, emancipatory dimension'.[179]

In her study of Hamburg Hagemann has noted 'that infant mortality fell first, and most sharply, in those working-class quarters reached earliest by infant welfare programmes'.[180] Following Empress Auguste Victoria's expression of concern about baby and child welfare in 1904, infant welfare clinics began to appear in 1905. They offered sterilised milk and advice on hygiene and household management. Breastfeeding was encouraged as a means to restrict infant mortality, and this campaign continued into the Weimar Republic.[181] During the war breastfeeding increased, primarily because of the shortage of cow's milk. In Hamburg 75 per cent of mothers nursed their babies before the war, 96 per cent after it.[182] There were regional variations in the infant welfare services offered and in the range of providers, which included publicly funded, church and women's organisations. In Münster the infant welfare centre was run by the Catholic and Protestant Churches.[183] In 1928 Prussia had 2,656 publicly funded infant welfare centres and 342 clinics run by voluntary organisations.[184] In Hamburg, where the regional office of the German Infant Protection Association worked with health and welfare offices and was funded during the Republic by the city, a system began before the war in which the registry office notified the infant welfare centre of every birth and a social worker would visit mothers to identify those in need of support; the social worker would encourage mothers to visit the infant welfare centre and have their babies examined by a physician. The number of social workers working with babies and infants in Hamburg rose from twenty in 1917 to 108 in 1927, and during the 1920s they were able to increase their house visits to an average of eleven in the child's first year. However, by 1933, with the rising caseloads occasioned by the Depression and mass unemployment, the number of visits halved to an average of five per year.[185] One of the social workers' tasks was to certify that a mother was breastfeeding and hence entitled to claim the nursing supplements; another was to encourage mothers to visit infant welfare centres, where, in addition to medical checks for the child, they could receive baby clothes, bed linen, additional groceries and access to holidays in the countryside for their children. In 1919 55 per cent of mothers under the supervision of social workers attended an infant welfare centre, in 1925 67 per cent and in 1933 89 per cent, each woman attending an average five or six times per year. Frohman claims that by the mid-1920s in many cities, two-thirds of babies were coming under the attention of the infant welfare centres, a clear indication that working-class women believed these visits to be beneficial for their children.[186] Hagemann believes that it was primarily first-time mothers married to skilled workers who were willing to take advantage of the facilities of the infant welfare centres and to embrace their advice not only on hygiene, infant care and nutrition, but also on the efficient management of a rationalised household.[187]

While the state concentrated its efforts on the child, charitable organisations also tried to help exhausted mothers of several children by funding a stay in a mothers' recuperation home. The largest Protestant women's organisation, the Protestant Women's Aid (Evangelische Frauenhilfe), initially rented homes but by 1923 had ten of its own; by 1933 this number had risen to thirty-five, and it leased an additional seven. In 1932 it provided 16,000 mothers with respite totalling 400,000 days, which means that the average stay was twenty-five days.[188] In Westphalia, the Catholic organisation Caritas also provided recuperative care from 1931.[189] The Protestant Women's Aid also ran courses for mothers in both towns and countryside. By 1932 it had forty-eight schools for mothers, and 40,000 women attended a course; in the winter of 1932 alone it ran 260 courses in the countryside.[190] The Protestant Women's Aid was not alone in believing that women needed training for motherhood. Some firms provided courses for their employees' wives, while in Hamburg the demand for a course offered in 1919 by the city's largest maternity hospital led to the development of courses by other providers.[191] In Hamburg, too, childcare became part of the curriculum in vocational training colleges, along with home economics, as motherhood came to be regarded as a profession for which training was required.[192]

Between 1930 and 1933 the Protestant Women's Aid collected money for its recuperation homes on Mother's Day.[193] It was affiliated to the Working Group for the Recovery of the Volk (Arbeitsgemeinschaft für Volksgesundung), an organisation which from 1925 included the German Florists' League, which had been campaigning for a Mother's Day since 1922. The first Mother's Day, on 13 May 1922, was to be a private, domestic occasion 'to honour the mother', but once the Working Group took over its organisation it became a public occasion on which local communities could pay tribute to 'child-rich' mothers.[194] In Münster women with several children each received a cup and a cake plate, in Brunswick a brooch and 'honorary gift', in Kiel a savings book worth 20 RM. From 1927 in Prussia mothers of impeccable reputation and good education and in financial need who had twelve or more children could apply to be honoured, and if successful they could receive a porcelain cup or 100 RM.[195] In addition to uniting the nation in honour of its mothers, the organising committee hoped to convince young women of the joys of motherhood. Weyrather sees in the campaign for a Mother's Day a reaction to the 'new woman' and to the campaign for the reform of Article 218.[196] In 1933 Mother's Day became a national holiday.[197]

Housework and housing

Hagemann believes that working-class women's household chores changed little until the 1950s, and von Saldern has noted that the working class experienced few improvements in their living conditions during the Republic.[198] Many urban working-class families lived in badly lit, cramped apartments in multi-storey tenements, built around a series of courtyards. They shared toilet facilities with other families, and only the wealthier working-class families could afford an apartment with a parlour, which was used only on special occasions.[199] A housewife's standing in her local community was judged by her ability to maintain a clean and tidy home and dress her family in clean and tidy clothing, or by the pristine whiteness of her apron when she bought from traders in the courtyard. Her housewifery skills were monitored in the twice-yearly 'big cleaning' or the cleaning of communal stairwells.[200] Without modern appliances for washing, ironing, cleaning the floors, cooking and sewing, it is not surprising that contemporary accounts revealed working-class housewives spending eighty-seven hours a week caring for their families.[201] Although Article 155 of the Weimar Constitution assured every German of a healthy dwelling, it was not until 1924 that the state began to subsidise housing projects to try and address the Republic's housing crisis. Figures in 1927 revealed an estimated shortage of over 900,000 dwellings and a further 300,000 deemed unfit for habitation.[202] In Berlin, which had the worst housing of any European city until the mid-1920s, such was the shortage that 100,000 people were living in makeshift homes on garden allotments in 1925, while over 30,000 of Berlin's poorest families were to be found living in the eighty tented cities which mushroomed during the Depression.[203] In Hanover the very poorest families were condemned to living in emergency shelters such as railway carriages.[204] The shortage was, in part, caused by the lack of housing construction during the war, the influx of refugees and the increased incidence of marriage, as well as the demand for smaller dwellings as family sizes fell.[205] The average household size fell between 1910 and 1933: in 1910 54.6 per cent of households contained up to four people or fewer, in 1925 64.2 per cent and in 1933 71.8 per cent.[206] In general, the smaller the community, the larger the average household size. In 1933 the average household size was 3.61, though it was 2.92 in Berlin.[207] The fall in family size must have eased overcrowding, and in 1927 over half of Munich's population lived in apartments with three rooms or fewer, whether because of family size or cost.[208] By 1932 17.5 per cent of the housing stock, some 2.88 million dwellings, were new.[209] Only the more affluent, skilled working class, white-collar workers and lower-ranking civil servants could afford the rents of apartments in the newly built housing estates, with their own bathroom, hot and cold running water and electricity, and few of them could afford the range of household appliances, such as washing machines, electric irons, refrigerators and vacuum cleaners, that some middle-class housewives needed to enable them to run their household when they could no longer employ domestic servants.[210] In 1918 under 7 per cent of Berlin's households had electricity. By 1928 the figure had risen to 45 per cent; only 56 per cent of these households had an electric iron, 27.5 per cent a vacuum cleaner, 0.5 per cent a washing machine and 0.2 per cent a refrigerator, and these were probably to be found in the homes of the upper and middle classes.[211] The loss of domestic servants and the change in middle-class women's experience may have been one reason behind the housewives' organisations' attempts to professionalise the work of housewives and raise their status by portraying them as 'scientific household managers'.[212] No one challenged the belief that housework was women's work, but attempts were made to persuade women to become more efficient in carrying out their household duties, by introducing either technology or rationalisation into their homes and thus reducing the labour-intensive, often physically demanding aspects of housework.[213] Working-class women, however, resisted attempts to rationalise housework which aimed to save time, money, energy and resources and give them more time for their children or for self-improvement.[214] Rationalisation also meant decluttering the home, ridding it of oversized furniture, heavy curtains or knick-knacks that needed dusting.[215] Housing officers on the new estates in Frankfurt noted that 'the most unbelievable junk can often be found in the apartments, furniture that is inappropriate and unnecessary'.[216] Not only could working-class families not afford to buy new furniture, but they also attached status to what they regarded as bourgeois furnishings.[217]

Some of the new housing projects incorporated modernist designs proposed by architects who attempted to influence the lifestyle of residents, applying rational notions of scientific management to housework and designing kitchens as functional work spaces physically separated from the family's living and socialising spaces.[218] Such was the Frankfurt kitchen designed by Grete Schütte-Lihotzky in 1926, which housewives disliked because they were unable to converse with family while working in it and because of the lack of storage space for potatoes in the in-built drawers.[219] They preferred the more traditional layout of combined kitchen and living room. Von Saldern notes that it was young married couples who were more open to adopting 'rationally organized living'.[220] The new housing estates of the late 1920s were built for modern small families, although Article 155 of the Constitution promised housing and financial benefits to 'child-rich' families, deemed to be those with four children under working age and those consisting of a widow with three children. At the war's end some industrial concerns began to pay supplementary allowances to workers with children, but these allowances, with the exception of the pharmacists' scheme, did not survive the hyperinflation. The state, however, introduced a supplementary allowance for children in the Civil Service Remuneration Law of April 1920, and in 1926 the allowance was being paid for 103,242 children.[221] It was left to the Nazis to introduce family allowances in 1935.[222]

Female homosexuality

The newly open and relaxed atmosphere of the Weimar Republic permitted a vibrant lesbian sub-culture in many cities, with Berlin becoming 'the lesbian Eldorado of the 1920s'.[223] Some fifty clubs for homosexual women were a popular destination for sex tourists; fourteen of them were the subject of a 1928 guide, and scenes from them featured heavily in the work of the artist Jeanne Mammen.[224] The clubs catered for a broad, socially diverse clientele and hosted dances, fashion shows, excursions and events put on by homosexual organisations. Some of the clubs had close links to the League for Human Rights (until 1925 the German Friendship Association), an organisation for homosexuals which in 1929 claimed a membership of 48,000, of whom 1,500 were women.[225] One of the league's major demands was the abolition of Article 175 of the Criminal Code, which criminalised homosexual acts between men. During discussions on the reform of the Criminal Code in the late 1920s there were demands for this law to be extended to women, an indication of the large prejudice against homosexual women.[226] Some of the Berlin clubs had their preferred magazines, with the Violetta's 400 members backing *Die Freundin*, while the Monbijou club preferred the *Garçonne*. These were the foremost among the several magazines aimed at a lesbian readership. *Die Freundin*, the most popular, appeared between 1924 and 1933, with a year's interruption from June 1928 when it was banned under the Law to Protect Young People from Trashy and Smutty Literature. The *Garçonne*, (1930–October 1932), a continuation of *Frauenliebe* (1926–30), had a print run of 10,000 and from June 1931 could be sold only under the counter.[227] Sub-cultural magazines engaged with the complexity of the application of current sexological theories to homosexual women, whom the popular press often caricatured and portrayed as perverse and failing in their reproductive duties. The magazines included short stories, poems, educational pieces and serialised novels, and their notices and small personal advertising sections not only helped some rural homosexual women overcome their physical and psychological isolation but also facilitated the coming together of like-minded women, not just in their imagination but also physically with the impetus to create groups.[228]

In society at large, however, female homosexuality remained a taboo, with lesbians compelled to hide their sexuality from their colleagues and families.[229] Hilde Radusch, a councillor in Berlin between 1929 and 1932, was barred from the KPD because she was a lesbian.[230] During the Republic, disciplinary proceedings were brought against female homosexual civil servants; in a case that featured prominently in the newspapers, Josephine Erkens, the head of the female police force in Hamburg, was dismissed following the suicide in July 1931 of two of her subordinates who were lesbians. Her superiors, insinuating that Erkens's behaviour had led to the suicides and that women's emotional instability made them unsuitable for leadership positions, used the case to close down the women's section.[231] In 1933 the Nazis closed down homosexual organisations, clubs and magazines, and homosexual women lost their communication networks; some felt compelled to adopt a more feminine appearance or to marry to avoid attention.[232]

Conclusion

The Weimar Republic witnessed considerable change in men's and women's personal lives as the small, modern family became the norm. Marriage became popular, but not necessarily for the purpose of procreation, as the widespread use of contraception ensured that sexual intercourse could be divorced from reproduction, and some couples consciously enjoyed companionate marriages. Contraception had become an accepted means to limit family size in both town and country and in both Protestant and Catholic regions. This led to a consideration among those concerned about the future of the German nation of not just the quantity but also the quality of progeny. Some population policy experts regarded 'child-rich' families as at best irresponsible, at worst degenerate.[233] The use of contraception and the ensuing fall in the birth rate have been seen as part of the rationalisation of reproduction, on a par with the rationalisation of German industry or the attempted rationalisation of the household. Rationalisation of sexuality was espoused by sex reformers, who, according to Grossmann, 'wanted to teach men techniques and to teach women birth control ... as a means of stabilizing and harmonizing the nuclear family'.[234] It was the skilled working class who could afford to move into the new housing estates and who were more open to a rationalised lifestyle, and it was this section of the working class who were the first to welcome attempts to improve ante-natal care and reduce infant mortality. The promotion of new rationalised lifestyles by the developers of the new housing estates has been seen as an example of attempts to discipline or normalise the residents, and we have noted Crew's reference to the 'invasive practices of "normalization and surveillance" of the Republic's welfare provision. He has suggested that the welfare practices relating to illegitimate children 'baffled, puzzled, and perhaps enraged many unmarried mothers', but this criticism does not pay due regard to the improved financial situation of some unmarried mothers or to the manner in which some practices, such as moves to reduce infant mortality, were welcomed by the recipients.[235] Social welfare provided a safety net for many old, impoverished women who had been left on their own through divorce, widowhood or spinsterhood.

The significant fall in infant mortality was not matched by any improvement in maternal mortality, perhaps because of a lack of obstetric knowledge or care, or a lack of priority in health care. Throughout the Republic aspects of reproduction were heavily contested, not just by population policy experts, but also by those in the medical profession who sought to remove the influence and participation of lay practitioners in the areas of contraception, abortion and venereal disease. Changes in the law, which turned abortion from a crime into a misdemeanour, decriminalised prostitution, protected pregnant working women and gave financial support to new mothers, brought significant improvements to women's rights and an openness about sexual matters, while readily available manuals and advice columns in magazines meant that ignorance could be overcome. However, traditional attitudes remained; unmarried motherhood was still stigmatised in some sections of society, housework remained the domain of the woman, female homosexuality was still a taboo, and the double standard with regard to the sexual behaviour of men and women continued. The churches continued to uphold traditional values, and the Catholic Church did its utmost to ensure that reform of the divorce laws was not added to the Republic's achievements. Ironically, while many of these achievements were reversed during the Third Reich, the Nazis introduced divorce reform in 1938.

In some ways elements of population and family policy during the Weimar Republic paved the way for more repressive measures during the Third Reich. During the Weimar Republic there was a range of views on eugenics, abortion reform, sex education, divorce reform, prostitution and combating the spread of venereal disease, and many of these views were based on notions of progressive welfare reform and the belief that circumstances, rather than any failings on the part of the individual, were responsible for the vicissitudes which befell him or her. The provision of welfare by a multiplicity of organisations, the local authorities, churches, women's organisations, and the Social Democratic *Arbeiterwohlfahrt*, ensured that family and population policy were matters of public debate, while the implementation of welfare granted social workers access to individuals' homes and private lives and an opportunity to monitor their behaviour and to inculcate their own beliefs and values. In the Third Reich, however, the state sought to implement the Nazis' population and family policy, which was based on racism, with scant regard to individual need; support was granted to those deemed valuable for the race, while those deemed not valuable and a danger to the racial purity of the state were marginalised, and some ultimately faced elimination.

Notes

1 Usborne, *The Politics of the Body*, pp. 204–5; Dickinson, 'Biopolitics, Fascism, Democracy', pp. 15–18.
2 M. Mouton, *From Nurturing the Nation to Purifying the Volk: Weimar and Nazi Family Policy, 1918–1945* (Cambridge: Cambridge University Press, 2007). Grossmann likewise believes that '1933 represented a radical break': Grossmann, *Reforming Sex*, p. vii.
3 F. Burgdörfer, *Zurück zum Agrar-Staat? Stadt und Land in volksbiologischer Betrachtung* (Berlin: Kurt Vowinckel, 1933), p. 12. Burgdörfer calculated that if only married women were considered the necessary number of children was 3.4, but if unmarried women were included it was 3.1.
4 Bessel, *Germany after the First World War*, p. 6. Jay Winter puts the figure at 2,037,000: J. Winter, 'Demography', in J. Horne (ed.), *A Companion to World War 1* (Oxford: Wiley-Blackwell, 2010), p. 249.
5 For the nineteenth-century women's movement's exploitation of the *Frauenüberschuss* to gain educational and professional opportunities for women see C. Dollard, 'Marital Status and the Rhetoric of the Women's Movement in World War 1 Germany', *Women in German Yearbook: Feminist Studies in German Literature and Culture*, 22 (2006), 218–19, and I. Sharp, 'The Disappearing Surplus: The Spinster in the Post-War Debate in Weimar Germany, 1918–1920', in Sharp

and Stibbe (eds), *Aftermaths of War*, p. 153. Every country in Europe had a surplus of women after the war, with France's being the highest in 1921 with 1,103 women to 1,000 men, though in the United States of America there was a surplus of men: *SdR*, vol. 401, pp. 580–1.
6 *SdR*, vol. 401, p. 582. Six of Germany's forty-five cities actually recorded a surplus of men: C. Lorenz, 'Der Frauenüberschuss im Deutschen Reich', *Die Frau*, 34:8 (May 1927), 493. Berlin had a surplus of 1,117 women to 1,000 men, and in 1933 it was estimated that one-sixth of the surplus was to be found there: A. Niemeyer, 'Zahlen sprechen', *Die Frau*, 41:1 (October 1933), 25.
7 Westphalia recorded a surplus of men in 1925: *SdR*, vol. 401, pp. 580–4. In 1910 there had been 1,438 women over the age of eighty, and 1,007 women aged between thirty and thirty-five, to 1,000 men.
8 Winter, 'Demography', p. 259; E. Meissner, 'Der Frauenüberschuss nach dem Kriege im Lichte der Statistik', *Die Frau*, 43:9 (June 1936), 540.
9 *SdR*, vol. 401, p. 590. While the population increased by 8 per cent between 1910 and 1925, the numbers under the age of fifteen fell by 17.9 per cent: *StJhb 1932*, p. 12
10 Usborne, 'The New Woman and Generational Conflict', p. 155.
11 Hausen, 'The German Nation's Obligation', p. 129.
12 The pension increased to 50 per cent of a severely disabled serviceman's if the woman was unable to work, had children to look after or was over fifty years of age: Y.-S. Hong, *Welfare, Modernity and the Weimar State, 1919–1933* (Princeton: Princeton University Press, 1998), p. 95.
13 Quoted in Hausen, 'The German Nation's Obligation', p. 128.
14 E. Kuhlman, *Reconstructing Patriarchy after the Great War: Women, Gender, and Postwar Reconciliation between Nations* (Basingstoke: Palgrave Macmillan, 2008), p. 152.
15 In 1918 36,891 remarried, in 1920 94,114 and in 1921 68,516, making up 10.5 per cent of women marrying in 1918 and 1920 and 9.4 per cent in 1921. By 1930 widows made up 3 per cent of women marrying: *StJhb 1921/22*, p. 40; *StJhb 1923*, p. 30; *StJhb 1932*, p. 30.
16 Hausen, 'The German Nation's Obligation', p. 128. In 1925 the number of widows aged thirty to forty (224,566) was more than double the number in 1910 (107,959): *SdR*, vol. 401, p. 586.
17 Women made up 65.6 per cent: Hagemann, '"… wir werden alt vom Arbeiten": Die soziale Situation alternder Arbeiterfrauen in der Weimarer Republik am Beispiel Hamburgs,' *Archiv für Sozialgeschichte*, 30 (1990), 273.
18 D. F. Crew, *Germans on Welfare: From Weimar to Hitler* (Oxford: Oxford University Press, 1998), p. 206. On 31 July 1927 social

pensioners made up 36.7 per cent and small rentiers 21.1 per cent of people in receipt of welfare, with 37.5 per cent receiving supplementary unemployment relief. On 31 March 1932 the unemployed made up 55.5 per cent of welfare recipients, with an additional 5.6 per cent receiving supplementary relief; social pensioners made up 14.9 per cent and small rentiers 7.4 per cent: Hong, *Welfare, Modernity and the Weimar State*, p. 137.
19 At least two-thirds of small rentiers were women. For DNVP and DVP female politicians' campaigns on their behalf see Scheck, *Mothers of the Nation*, pp. 107–13.
20 Hagemann, '"... wir werden alt vom Arbeiten"', p. 275.
21 1924 was the low point, with 3,926 female suicides; they then rose to 5,818 in 1932, an increase of 48.2 per cent: *StJhb 1926*, p. 37; *StJhb 1934*, pp. 43–4.
22 Dr Roesle cited in A. Grossmann, 'Abortion and Economic Crisis: The 1931 Campaign against §218 in Germany', *New German Critique*, 14 (1978), 125. Peukert notes that in 1932 Germany had 260 suicides per million inhabitants, France 155 and Great Britain 85: Peukert, *The Weimar Republic*, p. 280; C. Goeschel, *Suicide in Nazi Germany* (Oxford: Oxford University Press, 2009), pp. 15, 21–9.
23 In 1930 28.5 per cent of female suicides were by gassing, 28.4 per cent by hanging and 18.4 per cent by drowning. In 1933 the figures were 27.2 per cent, 30 per cent and 15.9 per cent respectively. Men's preferred methods were hanging and shooting: in 1930 46.7 per cent of male suicides were by hanging, 16.9 per cent by shooting, and in 1933 the figures were 50.1 per cent and 17.8 per cent respectively: *StJhb 1932*, pp. 42–3; *StJhb 1933*, p. 45; *StJhb 1935*, pp. 54–5.
24 *Reichsgesetzblatt II 1919*, no. 152 (14 August 1919), 1406.
25 Opet and Blume (eds), *Das Familienrecht*, p. 93 ff. Attempts to revise the Civil Code in the light of the Constitution came to nought.
26 E. D. Heineman, *What Difference does a Husband Make? Women and Marital Status in Nazi and Postwar Germany* (Berkeley: University of California Press, 1999), p. 7.
27 Allen, *Feminism and Motherhood*, pp. 58, 101, 108. Stöcker practised what she preached, living with Bruno Springer.
28 Heineman, *What Difference does a Husband Make?*, p. 7; Hagemann, *Frauenalltag und Männerpolitik*, pp. 176, 182. In 1929 32 per cent of Hamburg's illegitimate children were legitimised.
29 M. Meusel, *Lebensverhältnisse lediger Mütter auf dem Lande* (Berlin: Müller, 1933), p. 51.
30 Baümer, *Die Frau im neuen Lebensraum*, p. 212; Heineman, *What Difference does a Husband Make?*, p. 7.
31 Weitz, *Weimar Germany*, p. 305; Hagemann, *Frauenalltag und*

Männerpolitik, p. 203. In 1939 19 per cent of all marriages contracted between 1925 and 1929 remained childless, and for those in rural areas the figure was 10.2 per cent: M. Niehuss, 'Lebensweise und Familie in der Inflationszeit', in Feldman et al. (eds), *Die Anpassung an die Inflation*, p. 240.

32 Wickert, Hamburger and Lienau, 'Helene Stöcker', p. 614. The Nazis introduced pre-marital health certificates in 1935.

33 Usborne, *The Politics of the Body*, pp. 142–3; K. von Soden, *Die Sexualberatungsstellen der Weimarer Republik, 1919–1933* (Berlin: Druckhaus Hentrich Verlag, 1988), p. 25.

34 Soden, *Die Sexualberatungsstellen*, pp. 68–70; Weindling, *Health, Race and German Politics*, pp. 424–6 details marriage guidance clinics elsewhere.

35 Grossmann, *Reforming Sex*, p. 10. The clinics in Berlin did give contraceptive advice if medical or eugenic reasons called for it, and Usborne notes that by the early 1930s Berlin's city council had decided to set up marriage and sex-counselling clinics across the capital: Usborne, *The Politics of the Body*, p. 145.

36 C. Usborne, 'Rhetoric and Resistance: Rationalisation of Reproduction in Weimar Germany', *Social Politics*, 4:1 (1997), 72; Weindling, *Health, Race and German Politics*, pp. 429–30.

37 Weitz, *Weimar Germany*, p. 302. The key text is Grossmann, *Reforming Sex*.

38 Weitz, *Weimar Germany*, pp. 297–305; A. Grossmann, '"Satisfaction is domestic happiness": Mass Working-Class Sex Reform Organisations in the Weimar Republic', in Dobkowski and Wallmann (eds), *Towards the Holocaust*, p. 284.

39 C. Usborne, 'Rebellious Girls and Pitiable Women: Abortion Narratives in Weimar Popular Culture', *German History*, 23 (2005), 330.

40 Grossmann, '"Satisfaction is domestic happiness"', p. 284.

41 The phenomenon was known as *Prügelfreitag* (beating Friday): Swett, *Neighbors and Enemies*, p. 76. Little is known about domestic violence in the Weimar Republic, though Dickinson writes of police concern at men's sexual abuse of women, with rates for crimes of rape, sexual assault and abuse of family dependents being significantly higher than before the war: E. R. Dickinson, 'Policing Sex in Germany, 1882–1982: A Preliminary Statistical Analysis', *Journal of the History of Sexuality*, 16:2 (2007), 220; see also B. Ziemann, 'Germany after the First World War – a Violent Society? Results and Implications of Recent Research on Weimar Germany', *Journal of Modern European History*, 1 (2003), 594.

42 Weitz, *Weimar Germany*, pp. 299–302; Grossmann, 'The New Woman and the Rationalization of Sexuality', p. 197.

43 Soden, *Die Sexualberatungsstellen*, p. 99; Usborne, *The Politics of the Body*, pp. 119–20.
44 Soden, *Die Sexualberatungsstellen*, p. 9.
45 Usborne, *The Politics of the Body*, p. 124. Usborne also points out the commercial nature of the medical profession's involvement in providing contraception: Usborne, 'Rhetoric and Resistance', pp. 73–4. For the commercial nature of the organisations see Grossmann, '"Satisfaction is domestic happiness"', p. 265, and H. Lehfeldt, 'Die Laienorganisationen für Geburtenregelung', *Archiv für Bevölkerungspolitik*, 2 (1932), 64.
46 Grossmann, *Reforming Sex*, p. 32. Article 184 banned the advertising of contraceptives but not their manufacture or sale.
47 Usborne, *The Politics of the Body*, pp. 129–30.
48 Roos, *Weimar through the Lens of Gender*, p. 113; L. D. H. Sauerteig, '"The Fatherland is in danger, save the Fatherland": Venereal Disease, Sexuality and Gender in Imperial and Weimar Germany', in R. Davidson and L. A. Hall (eds), *Sex, Sin and Suffering: Venereal Disease and European Society since 1870* (London: Routledge, 2001), p. 83.
49 F. Burgdörfer, *Der Geburtenrückgang und seine Bekämpfung: Die Lebensfrage des deutschen Volkes* (Berlin: Schoetz, 1929), p. 89; Hagemann, *Frauenalltag und Männerpolitik*, p. 204.
50 Hagemann, *Frauenalltag and Männerpolitik*, pp. 200–1.
51 Burgdörfer, *Zurück zum Agrar-Staat?*, pp. 17, 114.
52 In Bavaria the figures were 212 and 142 respectively: *ibid.*, pp. 15, 113.
53 M. Hecht, 'Der Geburtenrythmus Badens in den letzten 100 Jahren', *Archiv für Bevölkerungswissenschaft (Volkskunde) und Bevölkerungspolitik*, 5:5 (1935), 353–5; C. Usborne, 'The Christian Churches and the Regulation of Sexuality in Weimar Germany', in J. Obelkevich, L. Roper and R. Samuel (eds), *Disciplines of Faith: Studies in Religion, Politics and Patriarchy* (London: Routledge and Kegan Paul, 1987), pp. 107–8.
54 Stephenson, *Women in Nazi Germany*, pp. 24, 37–8.
55 J. E. Knodel, *The Decline of Fertility in Germany, 1871–1939* (Princeton: Princeton University Press, 1974), p. 247. The post-war birth rate peaked at 18.3 in 1963, and fell below the 1933 level in 1970: Statistisches Bundesamt (ed.), *Statistisches Jahrbuch für die Bundesrepublik Deutschland 1972* (Stuttgart: W. Kohlhammer GmbH, 1973), p. 43.
56 Usborne, 'Rhetoric and Resistance', p. 79.
57 Usborne estimates the number of abortions in 1919 at 300,000, in 1925 at 500,000, reaching 1 million in 1929, a figure Grossmann uses for 1931: C. Usborne, 'The Christian Churches', p. 101; Grossmann,

'Abortion and Economic Crisis', p. 121. The figure of 4,000 was an estimate by the socialist doctor Julius Moses: *Die Genossin*, 6:9 (September 1929), 376, whereas the Protestant Women's Aid put the figure at 30,000: Evangelisches Zentralarchiv Berlin, 7/3989, pp. 164–5, 'Helft den Müttern!'; the figures of 40,000 deaths and 50,000 cases of morbidity come from Soden, *Die Sexualberatungsstellen*, p. 144. Usborne puts the morbidity figure at 100,000: C. Usborne, 'Abortion for Sale! The Competition between Quacks and Doctors in Weimar Germany', in M. Gijswijt-Hofstra, H. Marland and H. De Wardt (eds), *Illness and Healing Alternatives in Western Europe* (London: Routledge, 1997), p. 185.
58 C. Usborne, 'Abortion in Weimar Germany – the Debate amongst the Medical Profession', *Continuity and Change*, 5:2 (1990), 203.
59 Hagemann, *Frauenalltag und Männerpolitik*, p. 257.
60 Usborne, 'Rhetoric and Resistance', pp. 80–4. The key text which gives a voice to some of those who had abortions during the Weimar Republic is Usborne, *Cultures of Abortion*. For the portrayal of abortion in popular culture see Usborne, 'Rebellious Girls and Pitiable Women', p. 327.
61 Usborne, 'Rhetoric and Resistance', p. 80. Two doctors in Berlin, Aschheim and Zondek, were experiencing some success in devising a test by 1930: Stokes, 'Contested Conceptions', pp. 489–90.
62 D. V. Glass, *Population Policies and Movements in Europe* (London: Frank Cass & Co. Ltd, 1967), p. 281.
63 Woycke, *Birth Control in Germany*, pp. 145–6. Historians differ over the details of his trial: Woycke places it in May 1924, Usborne in January 1925 and Grossmann in May 1927. Heiser was found guilty and sentenced to two years imprisonment but released on probation: Grossmann, *Reforming Sex*, pp. 102, 247; Usborne, *Cultures of Abortion*, p. 120.
64 Usborne, *Cultures of Abortion*, p. 120.
65 C. Usborne, 'Abtreibung: Mord, Therapie oder weibliches Selbstbestimmungsrecht? Der §218 im medizinischen Diskurs der Weimarer Republik', in J. Geyer-Kordesch and A. Kuhn (eds), *Frauenkörper, Medizin, Sexualität* (Düsseldorf: Patmos, 1986), p. 222. Grossmann and König both give the number of convictions in 1925 as 7,193, which may include those persecuted under the other two abortion paragraphs: Grossmann, *Reforming Sex*, p. 247; J. K. König, *Seid fruchtbar und mehret Euch!* (Berlin: Verlagsanstalt der Proletarischen Freidenker, 1931), p. 18.
66 Usborne, *Cultures of Abortion*, p. 213.
67 For details of motions see Usborne, *The Politics of the Body*, pp. 217–19.

68 For the churches' attitude see Usborne, 'The Christian Churches'.
69 *Die Frau*, 33:1 (October 1925), 57; Usborne, *The Politics of the Body*, p. 183.
70 Usborne, *The Politics of the Body*, pp. 169–74. The amendment was based on a draft revision of the Civil Code drawn up by Justice Minister Radbruch in 1922.
71 BAK, Nachlass Lüders 169, BdF General Assembly decision on 9 October 1908 in Breslau and BdF decision at its fourteenth General Assembly meeting in Dresden in 1925. See also K. Hagemann (ed.), *Eine Frauensache: Alltagsleben und Geburtenpolitik 1919–1933* (Pfaffenweiler: Centaurus, 1991), pp. 128–9.
72 Usborne, *The Politics of the Body*, p. 177.
73 *Ibid.*, p. 197; Usborne, 'The Christian Churches', p. 108.
74 A. Grossmann, 'German Women Doctors from Berlin to New York: Maternity and Modernity in Weimar and in Exile', *Feminist Studies*, 19:1 (1993), 75–6; Allen, 'Feminism and Eugenics', pp. 492–3. Usborne claims there was widespread support for voluntary sterilisation on eugenic grounds by the early 1930s: Usborne, 'Rhetoric and resistance', p. 73.
75 Usborne, 'Rhetoric and Resistance', pp. 72–3; Usborne, *The Politics of the Body*, p. 148.
76 Usborne, *The Politics of the Body*, pp. 154–5; P. R. Stokes, 'Pathology, Danger and Power: Women's and Physicians' Views of Pregnancy and Childbirth in Weimar Germany', *Social History of Medicine*, 13:3 (2000), 364.
77 For discussions on the implementation of sterilisation laws in various states during the Republic see Weindling, *Health, Race and German Politics*, pp. 390–3, 453–7, 523–5.
78 *Die Genossin*, 9:11–12 (November–December 1932), 259. Dickinson's claim that the criminality rate for abortion fell by 50 per cent after the law's introduction holds good for a comparison of the number of convictions in 1925 and in 1929, when the lowest number of convictions was recorded: Dickinson, 'Policing Sex in Germany', pp. 226–9. In 1926 there had been 6,268 convictions: *StJhb 1927*, p. 491; *StJhb 1928*, p. 573; *StJhb 1929*, p. 478; *StJhb 1930*, p. 554; *StJhb 1931*, p. 540; *StJhb 1932*, p. 535; *StJhb 1933*, p. 533.
79 Usborne, *The Politics of the Body*, p. 175.
80 BAK, Nachlass Lüders 133, petition to the Reichstag and its Legal Committee of 25 May 1930, and petition to the Legal Committee on 18 June 1930. A group of women including doctors from Württemberg had written to the DDP's *Reichsfrauenausschüsse* on 15 June 1929 to uphold Article 218: BAK, Nachlass Lüders 133, letter to Martha

Women, the family and sexuality 243

Dönhoff of 15 June 1929. For the variety of views see Usborne, *The Politics of the Body*, pp. 183–201.

81 C. Usborne, 'Body Biological to Body Politic', in G. Eley and J. Palmowski (eds), *Citizenship and National Identity in Twentieth-Century Germany* (Stanford: Stanford University Press, 2008), pp. 139–41.

82 *Cyankali* opened in Berlin on 6 September 1929: Hagemann, *Eine Frauensache*, p. 155; Grossmann, 'Abortion and Economic Crisis', pp. 127–9.

83 Grossmann, *Reforming Sex*, pp. 83–6.

84 W. Frick, *Die Nationalsozialisten im Reichstag 1924–1931* (Munich: Eher, 1932), p. 63, petition no. 1741, 'Gesetz zum Schutz der deutschen Nation'; K. Kern, *Frauen, entscheidet Euch!* (Berlin: J. H. W. Dietz, 1931), p. 7.

85 G. Czarnowski, 'Women's Crimes, State Crimes: Abortion in Nazi Germany', in M. L. Arnot and C. Usborne (eds), *Gender and Crime in Modern Europe* (London: Routledge, 1999), pp. 241–4, 250–2.

86 Roos, *Weimar through the Lens of Gender*, pp. 212–13.

87 V. Harris, 'In the Absence of Empire: Feminism, Abolitionism and Social Work in Hamburg (c. 1900–1933)', *Women's History Review*, 17:2 (2008), 287.

88 For details of the regulation of prostitution see Roos, *Weimar through the Lens of Gender*, pp. 16–22. Roos estimates that there were between five and ten times as many unregistered prostitutes as registered ones, while Dickinson claims that unregistered women made up between 80 and 90 per cent of prostitutes: Dickinson, 'Policing Sex in Germany', p. 217.

89 BAB, R3201/21, K. M. Kriegsamt und das Reichsamt für die wirtschaftliche Demobilmachung, 14 November 1918, Bl. 8-10; Weindling, *Health, Race and German Politics*, p. 357.

90 LAB, BRep 235 HLA MF 1248, Reichsministerium des Innern II 5079 A Nr. 975, 'Entwurf eines Gesetzes zur Bekämpfung der Geschlechtskrankheiten', 6 June 1925, 'Begründung', p. 7; 251 women were acquitted. Sauerteig claims that the majority of sentences amounted to less than three months: Sauerteig, '"The Fatherland is in danger"', p. 85.

91 For the women's organisations' attitudes see Roos, *Weimar through the Lens of Gender*, pp. 187–90; LAB, HLA BRep 235, MF 1248, printed paper no. 1324 (Dr M Baum and colleagues).

92 'Der Abbau der Bordelle in Leipzig', *Evangelische Frauenzeitung*, 27:3 (March 1926), 8–10; Harris, *Selling Sex*, pp. 155–6, 161. Other cities closing their brothels included Dresden and Frankfurt am Main. For prostitutes' protests see Roos, *Weimar through the Lens of Gender*, pp. 84–90.

93 'Gesetz zur Bekämpfung der Geschlechtskrankheiten', *Reichsgesetzblatt* 1927, no. 9 (22 February 1927), pp. 61–3. (The law was passed on 18 February)
94 The highest rates were recorded in Hamburg and Bremen: LAB, HLA BRep 235 MF 1248, Reichsministerium des Innern II 5079 A Nr. 975, 'Entwurf eines Gesetzes zur Bekämpfung der Geschlechtskrankheiten', 6 June 1925, 'Begründung', p. 4; Roos, *Weimar through the Lens of Gender*, pp. 43–4, 243.
95 *General-Anzeiger*, 48 (29 January 1921).
96 The figure of 40,000 comes from A. F. Timm, *The Politics of Fertility in Twentieth-Century Berlin* (Cambridge: Cambridge University Press, 2010), pp. 60–1; 100,000 is from Roos, *Weimar through the Lens of Gender*, p. 43; *Evangelische Frauenzeitung*, 28:10 (October 1926), 5.
97 Prostitutes were forbidden to live in housing where children aged between three and eighteen resided. Frau Neuhaus (Z) was the key figure behind the insertion of the so-called 'church tower paragraph': BAK, Z.Sg.1 108/6, *Nationale Arbeit* (1929), pp. 247–8.
98 Harris, *Selling Sex*, pp. 172–3. In Hamburg women were expected to work in the hospital while undergoing treatment.
99 *Ibid.*, p. 165; Crew, *Germans on Welfare*, p. 122.
100 M. Freund-Widder, *Frauen unter Kontrolle: Prostitution und ihre staatliche Bekämpfung in Hamburg vom Ende des Kaiserreichs bis zu den Anfängen der Bundesrepublik* (Münster: Lit Verlag, 2003), pp. 85–6.
101 In 1926 women made up 74.7 per cent of those found guilty, and in 1932 69.2 per cent, while in 1933 111 women made up 68.1 per cent of those convicted. The numbers of women convicted almost halved between 1927 and 1928, from 309 to 155: *StJhb 1928*, p. 574; *StJhb 1929*, p. 479; *StJhb 1930*, p. 553; *StJhb 1934*, p. 545.
102 Harris, *Selling Sex*, p. 163; Roos, 'Weimar's Crisis', pp. 135–40. Roos also believes that the law's removal of police authority over prostitutes increased the hostility of police officers to the Republic.
103 BAB, R1501/126315, Bl. 16, Arbeitsgemeinschaft der Kölner Katholiken, 19 April 1932; Bl. 11, letter of Reichstag delegate Dr Cremer to the Interior Ministry of 15 April 1932; BAK, R36/1323, P. Suewen, 'Ist das Gesetz zur Bekämpfung der Geschlechtskrankheiten reformbedürftig?'
104 Roos, *Weimar through the Lens of Gender*, pp. 203–4. For the Nazis' policies on prostitution see J. Roos, 'Backlash against Prostitutes' Rights: Origins and Dynamics of Nazi Prostitution Policies', in D. Herzog (ed.), *Sexuality and German Fascism* (Oxford: Berghahn, 2005), pp. 67–94.
105 Roos, *Weimar through the Lens of Gender*, p. 94.

106 Timm, *The Politics of Fertility*, p. 70.
107 Usborne, 'The Christian Churches', p. 105; L. Sach, '"Gedenke, daß du eine deutsche Frau bist!" Die Ärtzin und Bevölkerungspolitikerin Ilse Szagunn (1887–1971) in der Weimarer Republik und im Nationalsozialismus' (PhD dissertation, University of Berlin, 2006), pp. 99–101.
108 Sach, '"Gedenke, daß du eine deutsche Frau bist!"', pp. 100–1, 196; Timm, *The Politics of Fertility*, p. 67. Although the authorities in Hamburg envisaged some form of sex education in schools, it was not compulsory and none of Hagemann's interviewees received it: Hagemann, *Frauenalltag und Männerpolitik*, p. 241.
109 C. Prestel, 'The "New Jewish Woman" in Weimar Germany', in W. Benz, A. Paucker and P. Pulzer (eds), *Jüdisches Leben in der Weimarer Republik / Jews in the Weimar Republic* (Tübingen: Mohr Siebech, 1998), pp. 140–1.
110 Fromm, *The Working Class*, pp. 174–6.
111 S. Bajohr, 'Sexualaufklärung im proletarischen Milieu, Geschlechtskrankheiten und staatliche Eheberatung 1900 bis 1933', in P. Pasteur, N. Niederacher and M. Mesner (eds), *Sexualität, Unterschichtenmilieus und ArbeiterInnenbewegung* (Leipzig: Akademische Verlagsanstalt, 2003), pp. 60–5; Hagemann, *Frauenalltag und Männerpolitik*, pp. 234–6. Estimates claimed that 20 per cent of young people shared a bed: K. Philipp, 'Die Wohnungsnot und ihre Bekämpfung', *Die christliche Frau*, 26:3 (March 1928), 68.
112 There were estimates of 90 per cent of young women in this age group having sexual relations: Usborne, 'The New Woman and Generational Conflict', pp. 150–3.
113 O. Friedrich, *Beyond the Deluge: A Portrait of Berlin in the 1920s* (New York: Harper and Row, 1972), p. 127.
114 Widdig portrays the mistresses of Raffkes (black market profiteers) as symbols of luxury who were seen more generally as symbols of amorality and decadence: B. Widdig, *Culture and Inflation in Weimar Germany* (Berkeley: University of California Press, 2001), pp. 208–9; Usborne, 'The New Woman and Generational Conflict', pp. 141, 157; Soden, *Die Sexualberatungsstellen*, p. 48.
115 Grossmann, 'German Women Doctors', p. 72. Ostwald quoted in Widdig, *Culture and Inflation*, p. 201.
116 Hagemann, *Frauenalltag und Männerpolitik*, p. 240; Stokes, 'Contested Conceptions', p. 592.
117 Mouton, *From Nurturing the Nation*, p. 233.
118 Stokes, 'Contested Conceptions', p. 592. For infanticide cases see BAK, Nachlass Lüders 233, Reichstag minutes of the 39th and 40th sittings, 4 February 1929, pp. 1021–2; Zentrale der KPD, *Referentenmaterial:*

Mutter und Kind in Deutschland und Russland (Berlin: Zentrale der KPD, 1926), p. 20.
119 G. Lilienthal, 'The Illegitimacy Question in Germany, 1900–1945: Areas of Tension in Social and Population Policy', *Continuity and Change*, 5:2 (1990), 250–1.
120 *Ibid.*, p. 258.
121 See *ibid.*, 262–3 for the proposals; BAK, Nachlass Lüders 233, Reichstag minutes of the 39th and 40th sittings, 4 February 1929, pp. 1015–23.
122 In 1926 11.9 per cent of all births were illegitimate, in 1926 12.5 percent, in 1930 12 per cent and in 1932 11.6 per cent: *StJhb 1935*, p. 36.
123 *StJhb 1933*, p. 46. In 1925 68.1 per cent of unmarried mothers and 26.3 per cent of married mothers in Hamburg were under the age of twenty-five: Hagemann, *Frauenalltag und Männerpolitik*, p. 181.
124 Mouton, *From Nurturing the Nation*, p. 202; Lilienthal, 'The Illegitimacy Question', p. 265.
125 BAK, Nachlass Lüders 233, Reichstag minutes of the 39th and 40th sittings, 4 February 1929, p. 1019. In 9 per cent of cases the father could not be traced.
126 Hagemann, *Frauenalltag und Männerpolitik*, p. 185.
127 Mouton, *From Nurturing the Nation*, pp. 210, 233.
128 *Ibid.*, pp. 210–11; Crew, *Germans on Welfare*, pp. 123–5. For fostering in the Republic see M. Mouton, 'Rescuing Children and Policing Families: Adoption Policy in Weimar and Nazi Germany', *Central European History*, 38:4 (2005), 545–71.
129 In Hamburg the number of children in foster families rose from 1,731 in 1925 to 2,805 in 1930, even though the proportion of rejected applicants rose from 3 per cent of the total to 53 per cent: Hagemann, *Frauenalltag und Männerpolitik*, pp. 194–5.
130 Mouton, *From Nurturing the Nation*, pp. 268–70.
131 *Ibid.*, pp. 212–20; *StJhb 1943*, p. 66; Stephenson, *Women in Nazi Germany*, pp. 41–3.
132 'Zur Reform des Ehescheidungsrechts', *Evangelische Frauenzeitung*, 28:6 (June 1927), 131.
133 Munk, *Recht und Rechtsverfolgung*, pp. 59–65. Prior to 1900 in Prussia, for example, a childless couple could divorce on grounds of mutual agreement or insuperable dislike on the part of one partner.
134 Calculated using figures from 1905 to 1913: D. Blasius, *Ehescheidung in Deutschland 1794–1945* (Göttingen: Vandenhoeck & Ruprecht, 1987), pp. 159–60.
135 *Ibid.*; Mouton, *From Nurturing the Nation*, p. 79. In Kiel before the war, women were the plaintiffs in 60 per cent of divorce cases, but in

1919 men made up 66 per cent of the plaintiffs, and in that year the number of women found guilty of adultery was double that of men: Heinemann, *Familie zwischen Tradition und Emanzipation*, p. 154. In Prussia, the number of divorce cases where women's adultery was the cause exceeded those caused by men's adultery until 1921.
136 Blasius, *Ehescheidung*, p. 158.
137 Hamburg had a higher divorce rate in 1919, 1920, 1927–30 and 1933. In 1920 Hamburg had 223.6 divorces per 100,000 inhabitants, Berlin 219.7, Bremen 149.2 and Lübeck 126.1. Waldeck had the lowest divorce rate in 1920, with 5.9 per 100,000 inhabitants: *StJhb 1923*, p. 37. In two-thirds of German states the divorce rate was below the national average: K. Goetz, 'Die Ehescheidungen im Deutschen Reich', *Die Frau*, 35:2 (November 1927), 96.
138 Goetz, 'Die Ehescheidungen in Deutschen Reich', p. 97. Figures for divorces in 1933 show similar findings: *StJhb 1935*, p. 59.
139 Mouton, *From Nurturing the Nation*, pp. 79–81; Blasius, *Ehescheidung*, p. 160.
140 'Ehekämpfe vor Gericht', *Der Montagmorgen* (10 March 1930), found in BAK, Nachlass Katharina von Kardorff 44; Blasius, *Ehescheidung*, pp. 161–2.
141 In Prussia in 1925, men were pronounced guilty in 55.4 per cent of cases, women in 20.4 per cent and both parties in 24.2 per cent; in 1929 the figures were 52.6, 19.4 and 28 respectively: calculated from figures in Blasius, *Ehescheidung*, p. 160.
142 Working-class women, therefore, did not normally receive maintenance: *ibid.*, p. 161; Hagemann, *Frauenalltag und Männerpolitik*, p. 326.
143 Blasius, *Ehescheidung*, p. 156. For examples of couples seeking dispensation see Mouton, *From Nurturing the Nation*, pp. 83–6.
144 M. Munk, *Vorschläge zur Umgestaltung des Rechts der Ehescheidung und der elterlichen Gewalt nebst Gesetzentwurf* (Berlin: Herbig, 1923), p. 7.
145 BAK, Nachlass Lüders 148, 57th sitting of the Reichstag, Wednesday, 26 January 1921, p. 2135.
146 BAK, Nachlass Lüders 232, DDP draft of 30 June 1922, Reichstag printed paper no. 4649 of 30 June 1922, Reichstag printed paper no. 74 of 6 January 1925, no. 462 of 1925 and no. 113 of 1926.
147 BAK, Nachlass Lüders 232, Reichstag printed paper no. 472 of 14 February 1928.
148 BAK, Nachlass Lüders 232, Reichstag printed paper no. 94 of 26 June 1928 and proceedings of the 22nd sitting of the Reichstag, 30 November 1928, pp. 574–8; Munk, *Recht und Rechtsverfolgung*, p. 64.

149 ADEF, BB4, letter of DEF to Reichstagsfraktion of the DNVP, DVP and Economics Party of 1 May 1929; Max Weiss (ed.), *Politisches Handwörterbuch (Führer ABC)* (Berlin: Deutschnationale Schriftenvertriebsstelle, 1928), p. 218.
150 This was regarded as a great victory: R. Morsey, *Die Protokolle der Reichstagsfraktion und des Fraktionsvorstandes der deutschen Zentrumspartei, 1926–1933* (Mainz: Matthias-Grünewald-Verlag, 1969), pp. 333–40; H. Weber, 'Die Ehescheidungs-"Reform" im Reichstag', *Die christliche Frau*, 28:1 (January 1930), 6–7. For details of the change in the Justice Minister and the impact of the differences over divorce on the SPD/Centre Party coalition, see Blasius, *Ehescheidung*, pp. 183–6.
151 Divorce could also be granted if one partner, without good reason, refused to have children or if one used illegal means to prevent a birth: Stephenson, *Women in Nazi Germany*, p. 29.
152 Crew, *Germans on Welfare*, p. 121.
153 The BfM, which Stokes claims was 'the primary force' in the pre-war ante-natal advice movement, opened its first ante-natal advice centre in Mannheim in 1906: Stokes, 'Contested Conceptions', p. 301.
154 *Ibid.*, p. 302; Mouton, *From Nurturing the Volk*, p. 156.
155 P. Weindling, 'Eugenics and the Welfare State during the Weimar Republic', in W. R. Lee and E. Rosenhaft (eds), *State, Social Policy and Social Change in Germany 1880–1994* (Oxford: Berg, 2nd edn, 1997), p. 147.
156 Stokes, 'Contested Conceptions', pp. 303–4. These figures were contested. Württemberg had no publicly funded centre. Hong says there were 2,144 ante-natal advice centres in 1924: Y.-S. Hong, 'The Weimar Welfare System', in McElligott (ed.), *Weimar Germany*, p. 197.
157 Stokes, 'Contested Conceptions', p. 327.
158 *Ibid.*, p. 355.
159 *Ibid.*, pp. 196, 319–20.
160 *Ibid.*, p. 299; Stokes, 'Pathology, Danger and Power', pp. 370, 379.
161 Stokes, 'Contested Conceptions', pp. 179, 181. The system evolved over time, settling down by 1926.
162 This amounted to 150 per cent of their wages. In Saxony, 56.3 per cent of women continued working: Stokes, 'Contested Conceptions', pp. 190, 221.
163 *Ibid.*, p. 188.
164 In East Prussia it was 3.95 per cent: *ibid.*, pp. 530, 593, 610, 715.
165 *Ibid.*, p. 814.
166 *StJhb 1928*, p. 48; *StJhb 1933*, p. 40.
167 Stokes, 'Contested Conceptions', p. 389.

168 Stokes, 'Pathology, Danger and Power', 361–2; Usborne, *The Politics of the Body*, p. 52.
169 Stokes notes that 49 per cent of apartments in Berlin comprised just one room in 1918: Stokes, 'Contested Conceptions', pp. 557–8.
170 S. Stöckel, 'Infant Mortality and Concepts of Hygiene: Strategies and Consequences in the Kaiserreich and the Weimar Republic. The Example of Berlin', *History of the Family*, 7 (2002), 611.
171 *Ibid.*, 608; K. Hagemann, 'Rationalizing Family Work: Municipal Family Welfare and Urban Working-Class Mothers in Germany', *Social Politics*, 4:1 (1997), 26.
172 For the impact on rent controls on housing see Bessel, *Germany after the First World War*, pp. 177, 181, 192; H. Ostwald, *Sittengeschichte der Inflation* (Berlin: Neufeld & Henius, 1931), p. 94; for the expenditure of a middle-income family see Widdig, *Culture and Inflation*, pp. 46–7, which shows that at the height of the hyperinflation 91.6 per cent of the family's spending went on food.
173 Niehuss, 'Lebensweise und Familie in der Inflationszeit', p. 256. Cases of tuberculosis among young children also rose.
174 Ostwald, *Sittengeschichte der Inflation*, p. 193. Stibbe says the Quakers fed over one million children: Stibbe, *Germany 1914–1933*, p. 106.
175 For Germans on welfare see Crew, *Germans on Welfare*, pp. 11–12.
176 Hagemann, *Frauenalltag und Männerpolitik*, p. 214.
177 Crew, *Germans on Welfare*, pp. 121, 208.
178 Hagemann, '"… wir werden alt vom Arbeiten"', p. 270.
179 L. Frohman, 'Prevention, Welfare, and Citizenship: The War on Tuberculosis and Infant Mortality in Germany, 1900–1930', *Central European History*, 39:3 (2006), 437, 480.
180 Hagemann, 'Rationalizing Family Work', p. 26.
181 Bottle-fed babies were five times more likely to die than breastfed ones: Frohman, 'Prevention, Welfare, and Citizenship', pp. 454, 449–50; Hong, *Welfare, Modernity and the Weimar State*, p. 27; Hagemann, 'Rationalizing Family Work', pp. 26–8. Stokes says that it was not typical for women in Berlin and Bavaria to breastfeed: for different regional attitudes towards breastfeeding see Stokes, 'Contested Conceptions', p. 573.
182 Hagemann, 'Rationalizing Family Work', p. 29.
183 Across Westphalia the infant welfare centres were run by church and women's organisations as well as by municipal welfare offices: Mouton, *From Nurturing the Nation*, pp. 157–9.
184 There were an additional 1,517 publicly funded centres for small children, and a further 150 run by voluntary organisations: Weindling, 'Eugenics and the Welfare State', p. 146. Crew claims that there were

6,159 municipal and 3,617 private maternal, infant and child welfare clinics throughout Germany: Crew, *Germans on Welfare*, p. 118.
185 Hagemann, *Frauenalltag und Männerpolitik*, p. 217; Hagemann, 'Rationalizing Family Work', pp. 29–31.
186 Frohman, 'Prevention, Welfare, and Citizenship', pp. 464–5. For the provision in Düsseldorf see D. F. Crew, 'German Socialism, the State and Family Policy 1918–1933', *Continuity and Change*, 1 (1986), 243–8.
187 Hagemann, 'Rationalizing Family Work', pp. 35, 39–40.
188 In 1931 women had benefited from 300,000 days of holiday: Evangelisches Zentralarchiv Berlin 7/3989, pp. 165–7. Mouton says the length of stay ranged between ten and forty days: Mouton, *From Nurturing the Nation*, p. 167.
189 Mouton, *From Nurturing the Nation*, p. 167.
190 By 1933 it had fifty-four schools for mothers: Evangelisches Zentralarchiv Berlin, 7/3989, pp. 166–7.
191 Mouton, *From Nurturing the Nation*, p. 163; Hagemann, 'Rationalizing Family Work', p. 33.
192 Hagemann, 'Rationalizing Family Work', p. 32.
193 I. Weyrather, *Mutterkreuz und Muttertag: Der Kult um die 'deutsche Mutter' im Nationalsozialismus* (Frankfurt am Main: Fischer Taschenbuch Verlag, 1993), p. 49.
194 The Working Group amalgamated with the German Society for Population Policy in 1926: K. Hausen, 'Mothers, Sons, and the Sale of Symbols and Goods: The "German Mother's Day" 1923–33', in H. Medick and D. W. Sabean (eds), *Interest and Emotion: Essays on the Study of Family and Kinship* (Cambridge: Cambridge University Press, 1984), pp. 374–8. Caritas joined the committee preparing for Mother's Day in 1930.
195 Weyrather, *Mutterkreuz*, p. 24. For celebrations in Westphalia see Mouton, *From Nurturing the Nation*, pp. 112–13.
196 Weyrather, *Mutterkreuz*, p. 24; Hausen, 'Mothers, Sons, and the Sale of Symbols and Goods', pp. 386–7; Mouton, *From Nurturing the Nation*, pp. 110–11.
197 For Mother's Day in the Third Reich see Mouton, *From Nurturing the Nation*, pp. 116–22 and Weyrather, *Mutterkreuz*, pp. 49–54.
198 K. Hagemann, 'Of "Old" and "New" Housewives: Everyday Housework and the Limits of Household Rationalisation in the Urban Working-Class Milieu of the Weimar Republic', *International Review of Social History*, 41:3 (1996), 317; A. von Saldern, 'Social Rationalization of Living and Housework in Germany and the United States in the 1920s', *History of the Family*, 2:1 (1997), 90.
199 For working-class housing see W. L. Guttsman, *Workers' Culture in*

Weimar Germany: Between Tradition and Commitment (Oxford: Berg, 1990), pp. 121–4; Weitz, Weimar Germany, pp. 70–3.
200 Hagemann, 'Of "Old" and "New" Housewives', pp. 317–24.
201 Hausen, 'Mothers, Sons, and the Sale of Symbols and Goods', p. 397.
202 The housing census conducted on 16 May 1927 recorded figures for 8,052 communities with over 5,000 inhabitants and 6,876 with under 5,000, and discovered 791,094 families with no home of their own in the former and 111,442 in the latter, making a total of 902,536 families who shared other families' accommodation. This survey also revealed 490,000 overcrowded dwellings: 'Das Wohnungselend in Deutschland', *Evangelische Frauenzeitung*, 30:9 (September 1929), 230. Preller refers to 791,000 dwellings: Preller, *Sozialpolitik*, p. 483; Hausen, 'Mothers, Sons, and the Sale of Symbols and Goods', p. 393.
203 Swett, *Neighbors and Enemies*, pp. 40, 72–3.
204 A. von Saldern, *The Challenge of Modernity: German Social and Cultural Studies, 1890–1960* (Ann Arbor: University of Michigan Press, 2002), pp. 175–8.
205 G. Stahl, 'Von der Hauswirtschaft zum Haushalt oder wie man vom Haus zur Wohnung kommt', in Neue Gesellschaft für Bildende Kunst (ed.), *Wem gehört die Welt: Kunst und Gesellschaft in der Weimarer Republik* (Berlin: Neue Gesellschaft für Bildende Kunst, 1977), pp. 95–6.
206 These households contained 35.9 per cent, 46.4 per cent and 55.2 per cent of the population respectively: *StJhb 1936*, p. 34.
207 *StJhb 1935*, pp. 28, 35.
208 L. Jerram, 'Kitchen Sink Dramas: Women, Modernity and Space in Weimar Germany', *Cultural Geographies*, 13 (2006), 547.
209 Preller, *Sozialpolitik*, p. 485. Guttsman notes the increase in the number of dwellings per 1,000 of population from 222 in 1919 to 249 in 1932: Guttsman, *Workers' Culture in Weimar Germany*, p. 115.
210 Von Saldern, 'Social Rationalization of Living', pp. 77, 84; M. Peach, '"Der Architekt denkt, die Hausfrau lenkt": German Modern Architecture and the Modern Woman', *German Studies Review*, 18:3 (1995), 449. For a rare experiment bringing fifty electric stoves to a Bavarian village for four months in 1927 see E. Duffy, 'Oskar von Miller and the Art of the Electrical Exhibition: Staffing Modernity in Weimar Germany', *German History*, 25:4 (2007), 517.
211 Reagin, *Sweeping the German Nation*, p. 87. Across Germany about 10 per cent of households had electricity in 1914, 56 per cent in 1925, 69 per cent in 1928 and 72 per cent in 1936: M. Hessler, '"Do companies know what women want?" The Introduction of Electrical Domestic Appliances during the Weimar Republic', *Technology/Technologies*, 13 (1998–99), http://hdl.handle.net/2027/spo.ark5583.0013.002

(accessed 19 November 2011). Duffy has figures from two 1928 surveys in Berlin: Duffy, 'Oskar von Miller', p. 532.
212 Von Saldern, 'Social Rationalization of Living', p. 83; Reagin, *Sweeping the German Nation*, pp. 72–3; 102. Hagemann, 'Of "Old" and "New" Housewives', p. 306.
213 Peach, '"Der Architekt denkt, die Hausfrau lenkt"', p. 449; M. Nolan, '"Housework made easy": The Taylorized Housewife in Weimar Germany's Rationalised Economy', *Feminist Studies*, 16:3 (1990), 563.
214 Hagemann, 'Of "Old" and "New" Housewives', pp. 305–8. Some saw in this an attempt to masculinise women by giving them time to leave the private sphere and enter the public sphere: F. Fritzen, '"Neuzeitlich Leben": Reformhausbewegung und Moderne, 1925–1933', in Föllmer and Graf (eds), *Die 'Krise' der Weimarer Republik*, p. 182. Duffy believes that technology merely reinforced traditional gender roles in the home: Duffy, 'Oskar von Miller', p. 532. In the countryside, less time spent on household tasks meant more time available for work on the farm: Jones, *Gender and Rural Modernity*, p. 130.
215 Nolan, '"Housework made easy"', p. 563.
216 Quoted in von Saldern, *The Challenge of Modernity*, p. 125.
217 Jerram, 'Kitchen Sink Dramas', p. 548; von Saldern, 'Social Rationalization of Living', p. 90.
218 Jerram points out that most design was not modernist in the 1920s: Jerram, 'Kitchen Sink Dramas', p. 540.
219 *Ibid.*, p. 549.
220 A. von Saldern, '"Neues Wohnen": Housing and Reform', in McElligott (ed.), *Weimar Germany*, p. 222.
221 Burgdörfer, *Der Geburtenrückgang*, p. 84. At the time there were 90,248 middle-ranking Reich civil servants, of whom 81,114 were married. For industry schemes see Glass, *Population Policies*, p. 293. For 'child-rich' families see 'Der Reichsbund der Kinderreichen Deutschlands', *Archiv für Bevölkerungspolitik*, 2 (1932), 108–9.
222 Stephenson, *Women in Nazi Germany*, p. 30.
223 Claudia Schoppmann, *Days of Masquerade: Life Stories of Lesbians during the Third Reich*, trans. A. Brown (New York: Columbia University Press, 1996), p. 24.
224 The guide *Berlins lesbische Frauen* was written by Ruth Roellig: K. Sutton, *The Masculine New Woman in Weimar Germany* (Oxford: Berghahn, 2011), p. 7. For Mammen see L. Lampela, 'Portrait of a Lesbian Couple', *Journal of Gay and Lesbian Issues in Education*, 3:4 (2006), 7–10. For details of some of the clubs see F. Tamagne, *A History of Homosexuality in Europe: Berlin, London, Paris 1919–1939*, vol. 1 (New York: Algora Publishing, 2004), pp. 53–7.

225 Kokula notes two major centres, one in the west for wealthier patrons and one in the east around Alexanderplatz for the working class: I. Kokula, 'Freundinnen: Lesbische Frauen in der Weimarer Zeit', in K. von Soden, M. Schmidt, A. Delille and B. Becker (eds), *Hart und Zart: Frauenleben 1920–1970* (Berlin: Elefantenpress, 1990), pp. 128–31. Internal disagreements within the league led to the reformation of the German Friendship Association in the mid-1920s. The league is not to be confused with the German League for Human Rights, the successor organisation to the pacifist Bund Neues Vaterland.
226 Schoppmann, *Days of Masquerade*, p. 6.
227 *Ibid.*, p. 6; Kokula, 'Freundinnen', pp. 130–1. *Die Freundin* was close to the League for Human Rights, whose chairman, Friedrich Radszuweit, was its publisher, while the *Garçonne* had links to the German Friendship Association: Sutton, *The Masculine Woman*, p. 91.
228 Sulton, *The Masculine Woman*, pp. 154–5; A. Espinaco-Virseda, '"I feel that I belong to you": Subculture, *Die Freundin* and Lesbian Identities in Weimar Germany', *Spaces of Identity*, 4:1 (2004), 88. Tamagne notes the disappearance of the classified advertisements from *Die Freundin* in 1932, when suicides began to be notified: Tamagne, *A History of Homosexuality in Europe*, vol 1, pp. 107–10.
229 Schoppmann, *Days of Masquerade*, p. 80.
230 R. Dyer, 'Less and More than Women and Men: Lesbian and Gay Cinema in Weimar Germany', *New German Critique*, 50 (1990), 44.
231 M. M. Lybeck, 'Gender, Sexuality and Belonging: Female Homosexuality in Germany, 1890–1933', *Bulletin of the German Historical Institute*, 44 (2009), 37–8. For Erkens see Nienhaus, *Nicht für eine Führungsposition geeignet*.
232 For Nazi attitudes towards and treatment of lesbians see Schoppmann, *Days of Masquerade*, pp. 11, 15–23.
233 Grossmann, 'Crisis, Reaction, and Resistance', p. 65.
234 *Ibid.*, p. 71.
235 Von Saldern, '"Neues Wohnen"', p. 222; Crew, *Germans on Welfare*, pp. 124, 208.

5

Women in the public realm

Photographs of the 'new woman', sitting astride a motorcycle smoking a cigarette or alone in the Romanisches Cafe in Berlin (see Figure 5.1), reveal the visibility of women in Weimar Germany, the opportunities open to them in their employment and leisure time and the challenges to accepted patterns of behaviour that these opportunities represented. During the Weimar Republic women's

Figure 5.1 Young woman alone in the Romanisches Cafe, Berlin (1924)

visibility became omnipresent, both physically and in images used in advertising, the media and party-political propaganda on hoardings in the cities' streets. Before the war, the presence of working-class women in the streets had been deemed suitable only within very restricted circumstances, when they were going to work or shopping, though the rise of the department store in the late 1890s had provided a safe destination for respectable middle-class women, who would not otherwise have been seen without chaperones. Otherwise, the only women on the streets were regarded as prostitutes. In Weimar Germany the reasons for women's presence on the streets multiplied as they took part in mushrooming political, organisational, leisure or sporting activities, while the increase in glass-fronted department stores encouraged window shopping even at night.[1] However, Katharina von Ankum notes the continuation of male prejudices about single women appearing alone in a public space, and Swett has alluded to working-class women's fear of being accosted even in the communal areas of their tenement buildings.[2] The public realm remained one in which single women did not linger, but in which women could now move more freely with friends, both male and female. As Stefan Zweig noted, 'in no other area of public life has there been such total transformation within one generation as in relations between the sexes'.[3] This chapter will explore the interactions and depictions of women outside the home, particularly as consumers of leisure and mass culture, which, as Corey Ross has noted, 'remained closely tied to class, region and milieu', with variable socially levelling effects.[4] The Weimar Republic also witnessed the beginnings of a mass urban consumer society in which women featured strongly as producers, commodified objects, targeted recipients, critical observers and discerning purchasers.

Women's leisure time

Leisure activities from Wilhelmine Germany continued, including reading and needlework in the home and, for the working class, going to dances and the cinema while the middle classes enjoyed visits to restaurants and the more intellectual entertainment provided by the theatre and the opera.[5] During the Weimar Republic the cinema became more accepted among the middle class, while in the countryside fairs and events linked to associational activities and religious festivals continued to be the mainstays of leisure pursuits. Throughout the Republic the most popular leisure activity among women was probably reading, though there were concerns among publishers about the decline in book reading as new leisure activities such as sports, dancing and going to the cinema became popular, as did the reading of illustrated newspapers and magazines.[6] Middle-class women and girls found more time to read than the working class, who might do so only at the end of the day or on a Sunday.[7] There was a distinct female reading culture, which was often viewed pejoratively by critics as 'low-brow'. Information gleaned from Leipzig's public libraries between 1922 and 1926 reveals a clear distinction between the books read by men and women on any given topic. Women also read more fiction than men and were more willing to read books by female authors.[8] Several surveys conducted during the Republic found that girls' reading began to diverge from boys' at the age of ten, when girls began to read the so-called *Backfischbücher*, teenage coming-of-age stories, until the age of about sixteen, when they began to read adult women's literature, primarily romantic fiction. The best-selling author throughout the Weimar Republic was a romantic novelist, Hedwig Courths-Mahler, who produced 122 novels during the Republic with an average print run of 145,000.[9] A writing competition for girls aged between fifteen and twenty, linked to the 1931 'Day of the Book', an event which was devoted to women, revealed young women's preference for characters they could identify with, indicating the view that many women were uncritical, emotionally engaged readers who read for entertainment rather than self-improvement.[10]

Reading and needlework were leisure activities which earned parental approval. Many parents were protective of their daughters, not allowing them to go out alone in the evenings or to join youth groups, and some families enjoyed outdoor leisure activities together, going cycling, hiking or swimming.[11] In 1926 about one-third of Germany's young people were to be found in youth organisations, and young women made up one-third of these members.[12] Although the largest number of male members was to be found in sports groups, it was the Catholic youth movement that attracted the most young women. Indeed, nearly half of the young women organised in youth groups were to be found in church organisations, indicating not only the important role the churches played within German society but also, perhaps, what activities parents considered suitable for their daughters.[13] Peukert claims that there were some 368,000 in the workers' youth organisations, but young working-class women were believed to prefer enjoying popular culture outside the socialist milieu or going out with their boyfriends to joining the Social Democratic women's movement, while young Communist women preferred to join co-educational organisations.[14]

Dancing was a popular activity among working-class girls who could go to local dance halls, or, if they had more money, to afternoon tea dances or dance coffee-houses.[15] The gramophone popularised dance music, and by 1930 Berlin had 899 dance locales. Dancing classes were taken by some 7 million Germans between 1924 and 1929, though many girls learned from friends or their brothers.[16] New dances such as the Charleston, with women dancing independently, not requiring a male partner, and moving their arms as well as their feet in syncopated movements, seemed to some to symbolise the independence of the 'new woman'.[17] The change in fashions enabled women to be more agile in their dancing, and this contributed, too, to the growing interest in body culture and sport.

Of 1,400 girls at further education colleges who wrote essays about their free time, half stated that they went dancing while 70 per cent said they went to the cinema.[18] The cinema was accessible to all classes, though it was perhaps only in the newly built cinema complexes in major city centres that all classes could watch the same film together.[19] Elsewhere, cinemas catered for a price-segregated audience, often showing different silent films. American films, especially westerns, and German comedies were popular in cinemas in working-class districts, where they were accompanied by much audience participation, whereas the love scenes and emancipated women in Hollywood films were reputed to offend small-town Catholic audiences.[20] In 1925 there were 3,878 cinemas in Germany, most concentrated in cities with several screenings daily, while those in small towns would open only at weekends with one or two screenings.[21] Cinema audiences peaked at 352.4 million per year in 1928–29, falling to 238.4 million in 1931–32.[22] A normal two-hour programme consisted of two silent films, a newsreel and perhaps a couple of short films, and women and young people were reputedly the most avid cinema-goers. The cinema industry believed that up to 75 per cent of its audience was female.[23] Lynn Abrams believes that working-class women may have gone to the cinema with their children during the day, but given the time-consuming nature of housework and the expense involved in a cinema visit, it is unlikely that the less affluent working-class mother had much opportunity to go.[24] Female unskilled manual workers, however, had an estimated 3 RM per week to spend on leisure, and with local cinema seats costing 40 or 50 Pf, they could afford to attend.[25] Siegfried Kracauer, perhaps sharing the socialist belief that workers going to the cinema were uncritical recipients of bourgeois propaganda, and that their leisure time should be spent on more educational or political pursuits, wrote disparagingly of 'little shop girls, typists and cleaning girls' going to the cinema to be enthralled by the escapist entertainment they saw on screen. As one contemporary wrote, 'the young proletarian woman learns through the cinema to venerate those Olympian heights where the stars show her how to attract love and gain money, drive in motorcars, dance and wear beautiful clothes forever'.[26] A young woman would go to the cinema with friends or with a boyfriend, as an entertaining diversion from her humdrum working life, perhaps to escape overcrowded living conditions and to have some independence from her family. There were, however, few cinemas in smaller towns. Only 2 per cent of Germany's towns with fewer than 10,000 inhabitants had a cinema in 1925.[27] Here, visiting funfairs, dances and religious festivals provided entertainment opportunities.

The cinema, therefore, was not accessible to all and cannot be termed a universal mass culture. That role was fulfilled during the Weimar Republic by the press which remained 'the most important mass media of the age', with 7,303 newspapers and magazines in 1931 and over 20 million newspapers sold daily, though two-thirds of newspapers had a circulation of under 5,000, testimony to the fragmentation of the press along sectarian, political and regional lines.[28] Women were believed to decide which newspaper the family subscribed to, and, in an attempt to win women readers, papers introduced women's supplements and more diverse, entertaining articles.[29] To boost sales, magazines and newspapers published serialised novels, the middle-class women's magazine *Die Dame* serialising Anita Loos' *Gentlemen Prefer Blondes* in 1925 and the *Vossische Zeitung* Erich Remarque's *All Quiet on the Western Front* in 1928.[30] The *Berliner Illustrirte Zeitung*'s serialisation of Vicki Baum's *Stud. Chem. Helene Willfüer* in 1928 reportedly increased its circulation by 200,000.[31] In 1921 Gertrud Bäumer and Marie-Elisabeth Lüders expressed concern at the *Berliner Tageblatt*'s serialisation of Fritz Reck-Malleczewen's *Die Dame aus New York*, the story of an upper-class woman's descent into degradation in the company of blacks and criminals, and asked for more care to be given in the choice of entertainment literature.[32] Although some observers believed that women read newspapers to keep abreast of political developments, others claimed that they were more interested in reading the advertisements.[33] In the late 1920s advertising made up on average half of newspapers' income, and was worth an estimated 1 billion RM to newspapers and 2 billion RM to magazines.[34] As readers, women were thought to prefer images to prose, and as technological advances in both photography and printing reduced the cost and complexity of including images in the press, newspapers and illustrated magazines began to include photographs (often depicting women) and photojournalism.[35] In 1931 readers could choose from 227 non-political illustrated magazines and 175 women's and fashion magazines, several of which offered accident and life assurance with subscriptions to attract female readers.[36] Reuveni notes that the number of insurance newspapers grew from 69 in 1913 to 118 in 1928 and that much of this increase came from women's and fashion magazines such as Ullstein's *Blatt der Hausfrau* ('Housewife's Magazine'), which had a circulation of half a million in the late 1920s.[37] The most popular illustrated magazine was the weekly *Berliner Illustrirte Zeitung*, with a circulation of over 1.9 million in 1931.[38] Women's magazines included the renowned quality fortnightly *Die Dame*, aimed at wealthier middle-class women, with a circulation of 53,500 in 1928 and containing a mixture of fashion and lifestyle articles and short stories, and *Elegante Welt*, likewise appearing fortnightly with a circulation of 50,000.[39]

While women could read newspapers and magazines at home, on public transport, in cafes and in waiting rooms, listening to the radio tended to take place in a domestic setting, often with family and friends listening together (see Figure 5.2), though there was some provision for collective listening.[40] Following the first broadcast on 29 October 1923, daytime programmes for women began to appear on the nine regional stations in spring 1924, addressing women as wives, mothers and consumers; the housewives' associations and

Figure 5.2 The radio provides the entertainment on a Berlin roof-top in summer (1926)

advertisers played influential roles in programming. The Beyer sewing pattern company, for example, funded an hour-long weekly broadcast for women on Leipzig radio from July 1924. When in 1931 a washing powder manufacturer offered free samples, 400,000 people applied, revealing not only the size of the audience but also the significant role that women's radio programmes could play in advertising.[41] Lacey has noted that the working class and women were 'disenfranchised by Weimar radio', and that 'most programmes managed to bypass the interests of ordinary working women'.[42] In 1929 a mere 2.3 per cent of broadcasting time on Bavaria's *Deutsche Stunde* was devoted to women's programmes.[43] In 1932 there were 4.3 million registered radio sets, encompassing an estimated 11 million listeners, but the high cost of a radio set, the 2 RM monthly licence fee, the restricted reception range and the 'stodgy and highbrow' programming meant that radio was primarily an urban middle-class medium. Across Germany only 7.9 per cent of households in the countryside had a licensed radio set.[44] Radio was not a significant element in Weimar's mass culture, nor did it engage significantly with constructions and representations of women. Before the First World War, corsets and long skirts had impeded women's mobility and participation in sport, and few sports such as tennis and segregated swimming were open to women. Gymnastics was introduced into girls' education in the late nineteenth century but concerns about women's decorum and the impact of sport on their reproductive health and their physique remained.[45] In 1914 an estimated 27,000 women were members of sports associations and 88,000 were to be found in the two major gymnastics organisations.[46] At the war's end, however, with many men left disabled, women and children malnourished and physically weak and the removal of military service to ensure the fitness of young men, the government encouraged participation in sporting activities to ensure the physical and psychological health of the German people.[47] Some employers believed that physical exercise could improve the health and productivity of its female employees; Leiser, a chain selling shoes in Berlin, encouraged its shop assistants to do gymnastics in their breaks.[48] While gymnastics was perceived as a suitable physical activity for women, women's participation in competitive sports was controversial and some sports, such as football and ski-jumping, were deemed totally unsuitable. The formation of a female football club in Frankfurt in 1930 was met with such ridicule that it folded in 1931.[49] However, the number of women taking part in sports increased dramatically. Marsha Meskimmon believes that 'women's sport ... was a genuine part of a newly-emergent women's culture among a generation of women reaching maturity in 1930', and the English writer Cicely Hamilton was struck by young German women's interest in sport and physical education, which she regarded as indicative of their 'new aims and ambitions'.[50] In 1930 there were 200,946 women in gymnastics associations and 761,387 in sports associations, making up 25.3 per cent and 5.8 per cent of the members respectively, though many women may have taken part in recreational sports without being club members.[51] The largest number of women was to be found in the German Sport Authority for Athletics, which in 1919 had asked its member organisations to create sections for women, followed by the swimming and tennis associations. The smallest number of women was to be found in the National Association for Jiu-Jitsu, though with the increase in political violence on the streets, the

Figure 5.3 A lone female driver defends herself against a would-be attacker (July 1931)

Communist women's magazine *Der Weg der Frau* encouraged women to take up this form of self-defence in 1932.[52] Figure 5.3 shows a demonstration of how a single female car driver could use jiu-jitsu to defend herself. Between 1921 and 1924 women even competed in boxing matches in Berlin, though some of these had the definite air of the burlesque about them. These female boxers came from the working class, but during the 1920s boxing training became a popular workout for upper-class women and personalities, such as the writer Vicki Baum and the actresses Marlene Dietrich and Carola Neher.[53] Class played its part in sport, too. In 1931 over 1,800,000 women took part in 150,000 classes run by the Workers' Gymnastics and Sports Association, which, according to Dagmar Reese, had a membership of 400,000 including 130,000 were women.[54]

Many women engaged in sporting activity not merely for leisure but also to keep healthy and to hone their bodies into the slender, svelte form that became the ideal in the 1920s. Some were dedicated sportswomen, and successful sportsmen and women were feted in newspapers and magazines, becoming household names.

In 1931 Cilly Aussem became the first German woman to win the Wimbledon tennis championship, following her success in the Paris Open, and she defeated her fellow German Hilde Krahwinkel in the final. Germany's female athletes were particularly successful: in 1928 Lina Radke-Batschauer won Germany's only gold medal at the Amsterdam Olympic Games, running the 800 metres in a world record time, but attention focused on two Canadian women who collapsed at the end of the race, raising concerns that some sporting events were physically too demanding for women.[55] The fear that too much sporting activity was detrimental to women's reproductive organs was proven unfounded by a study of 10,000 women in 1932, and those in socialist sports organisations believed that sport made girls' bodies strong and healthy, giving 'the race the mothers it needs'.[56] Concerns remained, however, about the increasing masculinisation of women's physique through sporting activity, to be frequently defused in the press through caricature and humorous cartoons.[57] Such was women's success in sport that the times between men's and women's performances narrowed, challenging accepted views about the gender order and the biological differences between the sexes.[58]

Although the image of a short-haired, healthy, physically honed and svelte young female athlete, dressed in singlet and shorts, became an accepted norm for women engaged in sporting competitions by the end of the Republic, the radical change in women's attire for sporting activities was not universally approved, particularly not by the Catholic Church.[59] In Munich in 1925 women were banned from wearing ski pants within the city limits, and there were reports that the Catholic Church in Bavaria had forbidden female tourists from climbing mountains in trousers.[60] In Prussia, there were claims of some 3 million nudists in 1930, and out of concern about the perceived increasing popularity of naturism the Interior Ministry introduced the so-called 'gusset law' of 28 September 1932, specifying that both male and female swimming costumes had to have legs and a gusset; a woman's swimming costume could not be lower at the back than the bottom of the shoulder blades, and at the front her bosom and upper body had to be completely covered.[61] Whereas before the war it had been customary for men and women to swim separately, the Republic saw the building of publicly funded mixed-sex swimming pools, reflecting not just financial pressures but also the

Figure 5.4 Eight young people on an excursion into the Berlin countryside (1928)

changing relationships between the sexes in public.[62] Figure 5.4 shows a group of four couples on an excursion to the countryside outside Berlin and reveals the more relaxed relationships between the sexes. Other popular outdoor activities included walking and hiking in the countryside at weekends. By 1929 the sale of Sunday day-return railway tickets had increased six-fold since before the war, and the 4 million overnight stays in youth hostels in that year reveal the growing interest in getting to know Germany.[63] Hiking and rambling had been an important feature of the Wandervogel youth movement since the turn of the century and were popular with both boys and girls.[64] Steffi Orfali writes of her time with the Kameraden, a Jewish youth group, which would meet at Nuremberg railway station at 7 a.m. on a Sunday to travel to the foothills of Franconian Switzerland to hike, and of an Easter vacation spent hiking with four girlfriends and a chaperone in northern Bavaria and the Thuringian forest, staying overnight in youth hostels.[65] The co-educational socialist youth movement likewise enjoyed rambling and camping holidays, promoting comradeship and also inculcating an appreciation of culture and art with visits to concerts and museums.[66] Motorised transport was the ultimate symbol of personal freedom, and young women were keen to master modern forms, if they could afford them. Hanni Köhler became a well-known motorcyclist, racing against men and winning her class in the 1924 night race between Leipzig and Frankfurt; she went on to set record times for twelve-hour and a twenty-four-hour periods on a 119 c.c. machine in 1927 and undertook a 2,000 km trip to India in 1931.[67] Clärenore Stinnes, the daughter of the industrialist Hugo Stinnes, became the most successful female rally driver in Europe, winning seventeen races, and on 27 May 1927 she set off on a 760-day drive around the world, becoming the toast of Berlin on her return.[68] Erika Mann, daughter of the novelist Thomas Mann, also raced cars, winning a 10,000 km rally in southern Europe in 1931, while Elly Beinhorn achieved celebrity as a long-distance aviatrix.[69] All were featured in the illustrated press and some appeared in cinema newsreels.[70]

Elly Beinhorn continued to be a media personality in the Third Reich, becoming even more of a celebrity after she married the motor racing driver Bernd Rosemeyer in 1936.[71] However, the most high-profile aviatrix was perhaps Hanna Reitsch, a world-record-setting glider pilot who became a test pilot for the Luftwaffe, the German air force, and was given her Iron Cross, First Class, by Hitler personally.[72] Although the Nazis had originally opposed competitive sport for women, Hitler appreciated its propaganda value, and the regime supported its female athletes in the 1936 Olympic Games in Berlin, where, according to the *New York Times*, 'This masculine Third Reich owes much of its success to its women athletes.'[73] Female gold medal winners included Gisela Mauermayer in the shot put and Tilly Fleischer in the javelin.[74] The Nazis, however, refused to acknowledge the achievements of Jewish athletes, and so Gretel Bergmann was not selected for the high jump, though the Nazis did allow a half-Jew, Helene Mayer, to compete in the fencing competition, as lip service to their claim that athletes were chosen on merit.[75] According to Erik Jensen, the Nazis 'continued and accelerated most of the athletic trends that had begun under the Weimar Republic', though Lisa Pine points out that 'sport was not an end in itself, but a means of training German youth in accordance with National Socialist ideals'.[76] This involved primarily creating physically fit girls who would become healthy mothers of healthy babies. German women were able to participate in sporting activities run by the Nazi organisation Strength through Joy (Kraft durch Freude, KdF), though Baranowski notes that 'they were concentrated in the putatively less physically taxing activities'.[77] Strength through Joy attempted to meet the demands of consumers and to provide leisure activities for the masses, sometimes as a reward for work performance or to incentivise workers. It offered not only visits to cultural events such as concerts and the theatre, whose programmes had faced Nazification, but also cruises and holidays and the possibility of saving to buy the KdF car, the Volkswagen, the fulfilment of Hitler's promise to 'motorize the masses'.[78] As part of the Nazis' attempt to create a people's racial community, KdF tried to break down distinctions of class and regional differences, particularly in its holiday provision. Baranowski notes the high participation of women, especially single women, on KdF holidays, where some earned criticism for the ostentatious display of their middle-class status through their choice of jewellery or clothes or for their inappropriate behaviour with men of inferior race.[79]

Women as consumers

The importance of household consumption to the national economy had been acknowledged during the war, and after the hyperinflation advertisers targeted women as consumers. From 1924 advertising boomed in Germany, with American advertising agencies founding branches there, and advertisements, which included imagery as well as text, focused less on the qualities of the product than on the perceived needs, desires and aspirations of the consumer, who was gendered female.[80] Women were believed to be responsible for 75 per cent of all purchases and were thought to be gullible, emotional and conservative consumers.[81] Buerkle has noted that the women featured in advertisements were either housewives or 'new women', but glamorous female models also provided a cachet of luxury and indulgence to advertisements for up-market products such as cars.[82] Advertisements played on women's anxieties and desires. The 'new woman' provided the aspirational model in advertisements for fashion and beauty products, urging young working women to stay young and beautiful in order to keep their jobs or to attract a husband.[83] The desired look was of healthy, well-groomed 'naturalness', and advertisements featured soaps, creams and hair products; the use of face powder and lipstick was not regarded by many as a sign of the emancipation of the 'new woman', but of immorality, as make-up continued to be associated with prostitution.[84] In Fromm's survey, 84 per cent of respondents claimed not to like the use of powder, lipstick or perfume by a woman.[85] Advertisements encouraged women to have cosmetic surgery to maintain their youthful appearance, to use sun lamps and depilatories to improve their looks, or to diet, take diet pills or use exercise equipment to stay slim.[86] Women's magazines detailed ideal body measurements and weights, and striving to acquire and then maintain the ideal svelte figure came at a price. Janet Ward has noted that the 1920s saw an increase in cases of anorexia and bulimia.[87] The 1920s also saw the first beauty contests and their coverage in the media. In December 1925 the first German fashion queen, Sonja Jovanowitsch, was crowned in Berlin, and just over a year later, in March 1927, the first Miss Germany contest was won by Hildegard Quandt.[88] The BdF, KFB and DEF all wanted beauty contests to be banned, believing that they devalued women.[89]

Women's physical and external appearance changed fundamentally during the Weimar Republic. Some have seen in the new fashions 'female political liberation's direct visual translation', while others have linked them to the increase in women's interest and participation in sports.[90] Berlin was the centre of Germany's fashion trade, with a highly successful ready-to-wear industry whose exports to other European countries amounted in value to 15 per cent of all German exports in 1913. Its designers would transform the latest Parisian fashions into mass-produced, affordable clothes that could be bought from department stores and clothes shops. During the First World War designers could no longer visit Paris, and emphasis was placed on producing good-quality, functional and chaste clothing, which, from August 1918, was exhibited twice yearly in Berlin fashion week. The ready-to-wear industry improved its mass production techniques in the rush to produce military uniforms, while women discarded their corsets and shortened their skirts to improve their mobility at work and on public transport.[91] The German fashion industry boomed during the Weimar Republic, with so many shows and contests in Berlin in the late 1920s that the fashion press could not cover them all.[92] In 1925 some 500 ready-to-wear firms employed over 200,000 people in Berlin, with an additional 80,000–100,000 homeworkers on piece rates.[93] The introduction of synthetic materials, in particular rayon, which was known as artificial silk in Germany, obscured the visual differences between the appearances of working-class and middle-class women's clothing. Sewing patterns enabled working-class and lower middle-class women to enjoy the latest fashions and were even included in some women's magazines. In the 1920s the publishing company Ullstein sold over 6 million paper patterns a year.[94] The latest fashion trends became accessible to all, and the young working woman, who needed neat, tidy and comfortable clothing suitable for the work environment and her daily commute, could appear stylish. A survey in the late 1920s revealed that a female white-collar worker could spend over 25 per cent of her income on maintaining her wardrobe.[95] Women learned about the latest fashion trends from newspapers, from illustrated and women's magazines and also from the cinema. On the screen they would see the latest fashions worn by popular film stars who also featured in fashion magazines, and fashion shows were also covered in newsreels.[96] While a working-class women's wardrobe might consist of work, day and Sunday clothes, middle-class and upper-class women enjoyed different styles of morning, afternoon and evening wear. Women were not, however, slaves to fashion; they could not afford to be. When fashion houses tried to introduce new trends such as long jackets in 1920 or more feminine styles in 1925, they were unsuccessful.[97] After the war, several fashion trends were discernible, with an emphasis on unobtrusiveness, muted colours and thrift, thanks in part to the shortage of textile material. While designs emphasised women's natural curves at the bust, waist and hips, short-skirted sports clothing presaged later fashions. Skirts varied from calf to ankle length.[98] Following on from trends during the war, corsets were no longer *de rigueur*, and increasingly day-wear clothes became straighter and simpler, which, in the economically straitened times of the early 1920s, enabled existing clothes to be altered. The resulting slender silhouette led to discussions about male and female categories of clothing. In 1923 the smoking costume, as it was known in German, featured a good-quality straight skirt, usually in a dark-coloured wool, with a tuxedo jacket and stressed simplicity, functionality and seriousness, while the *Bubikopf* extended the slender silhouette, as did the cloche hat.[99] The page-boy haircut had first appeared in the United States during the war; in 1920 personalities such as Isadora Duncan and Coco Chanel sported it, and by the early 1920s several German film stars had a *Bubikopf*. Some women went further, adopting the Eton crop, even shorter hair with a side parting.[100] The *Bubikopf* was seen as another trend from the United States that was taking over Germany and also as one of the visible signs of the masculinisation of women in general. In 1928 the *Berliner Illustrirte Zeitung* ran a competition inviting readers to guess the gender of young people in six photographs; this was one of a wealth of media articles in which the ability to distinguish between the sexes was challenged and which point to the increasing androgyny in visual portrayals of women.[101] A further example can be seen in the *Berliner Illustrirte Zeitung*'s RM 3,000 competition in November 1927 for the wittiest reply to the question 'What do you say about Fräulein Mia?', featuring a young woman sporting an Eton crop, smoking costume with tie, and a monocle, carrying a cigarette holder and walking across a room with a man of similar features (see Figure 5.5).

The winter season 1923–24 saw the disappearance of the waist from garments, and in spring 1924 the short skirt, finishing just below the knee, appeared. It was to dominate German fashion for the next few years, becoming the iconic apparel of the 'new woman': the knee-length, low-waisted dress teamed with higher heeled shoes with a strap, worn by a young woman with a *Bubikopf*. As Mila Ganeva notes, this was the first time in the history of women's fashion in the West that skirts had risen to knee level.[102] As can be seen from Figure 5.6, the *Berliner Illustrirte Zeitung*'s front cover of 6 September 1925 highlighted the change in fashion. The new fashion proved popular with women of all ages and classes, as it was very practical, allowing freedom of movement.[103] In Fromm's study, 78 per cent of respondents claimed to like present-day fashions, though one did note, 'summer comfortable; winter flu'.[104] With shorter skirts came the need for flesh-coloured silk stockings, another item for advertisers to merchandise. The lack of emphasis on women's natural curves, the simplicity and uniformity of the designs and the use of lapels, taken from men's tailoring, led to claims of a masculinisation of women's fashion and of its wearers.[105] As one article in the popular *Berliner Illustrirte Zeitung* claimed in 1925: 'it would scarcely be noticed this spring if a woman absent-mindedly put on her husband's coat', and it condemned the current trends as 'odious fashions' which had 'been transplanted

Figure 5.5 'What do you say about Fräulein Mia?', *Berliner Illustrirte Zeitung* (13 November 1927)

Figure 5.6 'The change in women's fashions: the fashionable woman of today and from our grandfathers' time', *Berliner Illustrirte Zeitung* (6 September 1925)

from America'.[106] These odious fashions included the tuxedo and the silk pyjama suit, popular with upper-class women as leisure wear. The wearing of trousers, other than by women riding a horse or bicycle or for ski-ing, was not widely accepted and was regarded as a contravention of gender norms.[107] Kessemeier claims that by 1927 the straight and slender female silhouette was no longer regarded as masculine, but as youthful and sporty.[108] At the end of the 1920s skirts became slightly longer and fuller, while accessories such as fur collars and cuffs detracted from the straight line. Bows and frills made clothes appear more feminine and hair styles became softer.[109] As curves became fashionable, sales of girdles soared.[110]

Mass-produced fashion gave women the freedom to dress as they wished, to suit their lifestyle. Changes in fashion trends throughout the Republic masked the fundamental change in the ideal of the young female body to one that was slender, supple and made fit by physical exercise, an ideal that continued into the Third Reich. Mila Ganeva has claimed that fashion was 'central to women's experience of modernity in Weimar Germany'.[111] It has become, in its imagery of the 'new woman', a marker for Weimar modernity itself, and in its commodification an example of a nascent mass consumer culture, rendered accessible through the illustrated press, cinema and department stores, where not only mannequins but also live models displayed the latest wares.[112] It also became during the Republic a focus for the discussion about accepted gender attributes, be they physical or behavioural. Helene Weber noted that although complaints about the masculinisation of women, with women deemed to be going against their intrinsic nature and striving to adopt and conform to masculine values, were rife, no one could state explicitly what was meant by 'masculinisation'; people could only refer to instances such as women entering professions that were not directly linked to the maternal or feminine sphere, the fall in the birth rate or the masculine cut in women's fashions and appearance.[113] No such concerns were supposed to be heard in the Third Reich, where images of healthy Aryan mothers abounded. The Nazis attempted, unsuccessfully, to encourage women to purchase German fashions and to wear the traditional dirndl.[114] Emphasis was placed on women's natural beauty, free of cosmetic artifice, and smoking was deemed a threat to their reproductive organs. In some towns women were requested not to smoke in public; Ilse Guenther tells of one visitor to Berlin in March 1933 who had her cigarette snatched from her lips by a stormtrooper 'who informed her that "the *Führer* disapproved of women smoking"'.[115] German women, however, including those such as Magda Goebbels who were married to prominent members of the regime, continued to smoke and wear cosmetics.

Women in culture

Cultural historians have examined depictions of women in film, literature and art to explore contemporary male anxieties about women's rapidly changing role in the German economy, society and politics. Stephen Brockmann, drawing on the work of Klaus Theweleit which examined the writings of seven members of irregular troops in the *Freikorps*, notes that 'hatred towards women was widespread in the culture of the Weimar Republic' he cites seven reasons for this hatred, all primarily relating to women's behaviour during the First World War: women had suffocated men before the war; they had allowed men to go to war; they did not understand them nor support them sufficiently; they had betrayed them, either sexually or emotionally; they did not fight in the war; they had played a part in Germany's losing the war; and they had feminised German society.[116] Maria Tatar has seen in the *Lustmord* (sexual murder) paintings of Georg Grosz and Otto Dix the displacement of the trauma inflicted on soldiers' bodies during the war to the female body and, in their dismembering of women's reproductive organs, an attempt to regain their own creative powers.[117] Beth Irwin Lewis, examining the sexual murder works of seven artists, believes that they reveal 'an overpowering fascination with sexuality combined with an obsessive dread of woman' and 'a reactionary response that had its roots deep in contemporary cultural and social misogyny.'[118] Dorothy Rowe, too, sees in the 'dismemberment of a woman's body ... a major and disturbing hallmark of male modernist culture' and notes that many portrayals of sexual murder have a cityscape as their backdrop, thus depicting for her 'the punitive consequences for women who step out of the rigidly defined bourgeois spheres of the private and into the public realm of the masculinized spaces of urban modernity'.[119] 'Cut, mutilated, fragmented, dismembered and maimed, the female body is put on display as an icon of cultural crisis', claims Tatar.[120] The same could, perhaps, be said of the maimed, mutilated bodies of crippled war veterans that populate artistic works of the early 1920s. These artistic works are social products, creations that may reveal more about the obsessions of the artist and the interests of the critic than about social reality. The numbers of murdered females did rise substantially in 1919 to 615 from 373 in 1918, but details of how many of these could be classed as sexual murders are not available.[121]

Stephen Brockmann claims that the prostitute became 'a symbol for Weimar woman in general'.[122] The prostitute features in works of art, literature and film. Bernd Widdig has noted how the prostitute was one of four female figures used to symbolise the cultural impact of the hyperinflation, signifying 'sexual permissiveness coupled with economic and social misery.'[123] Many of Grosz's portrayals of women are as prostitutes, often depicting aggressive female sexuality, disease and decadence, and they contrast sharply with paintings of prostitutes by female artists such as Elsa Haensgen-Dingkuhn, or with Gerta Overbeck's representation of a prostitute as a working woman buying a contraceptive douche.[124] In Karl Grune's 1923 film *The Street (Die Straße)* the dangerous world of the street, represented by the prostitute threatening to use her sexuality and criminal connections to destroy the naive bourgeois man, is juxtaposed with the safety of the home and his virtuous, caring wife, 'the patriarchal female ideal'.[125] In another street film, *Asphalt* (1929), the portrayal of a female jewel thief who uses her overt sexuality to avoid arrest reflects the views of Erich Wulffen, a criminologist and author of *Woman as Sexual Criminal (Das Weib als Sexualverbrecherin*, 1923) who believed that there was a direct link between excessive sexuality, latent in every woman, and criminal behaviour. Women were by nature instinctive, emotional and amoral, but normally their sexuality was more passive than men's and would remain so within the confines of their role as wife and mother.[126] Gabriele Tergit, a journalist who covered criminal trials in Berlin, likewise believed that 'female criminals were driven by their emotions'.[127] According to Barbara Hales, 'the lustful and lascivious woman criminal was a media obsession' and she sees in this obsession 'a signifier for the fear of women's liberation'.[128] In committing crimes, women were perceived to be acting in a masculine way. During the Weimar Republic the initial post-war increase in crime fell after 1923, in which year 134,943 women had formed 16.4 per cent of those convicted. By 1933 the figures had fallen to 58,173 and 11.2 per cent respectively, so fears of an increase in crime were unfounded.[129] Theft was the most common crime; in 1923 42.6 per cent of convicted women were guilty of theft, in 1933 23.3 per cent.[130] The female proportion of convicted murderers and manslaughterers peaked at 17.8 per cent in 1924, falling to 8.1 per cent in 1932, and during the Republic seven women had the death penalty imposed on them.[131] In his *Die beiden Freundinnen und ihr Giftmord* (*Two Women Friends and How they Murdered with Poison*, 1924) Alfred Döblin fictionalised the case of Ella Klein and Margarete Nebbe, two young wives living in Berlin who fell in love, began a lesbian relationship and were subsequently found guilty of murdering Klein's husband in April 1922 and attempting to murder Nebbe's by poison. In their trial, which attracted widespread publicity, experts testified that their actions were rooted in their homosexuality and that 'they suffered from a sexual pathology'.[132]

A lesbian's coming-of-age was the topic of Anna Weirauch's popular trilogy *Der Skorpion* (1919, 1921, 1931), of which Hilde Radusch wrote, 'For me the book was a revelation, I recognized myself there', and lesbians featured as minor characters in several popular novels such as Kästner's *Fabian* (1931).[133] The best-known work about lesbianism is the 1931 film *Mädchen in Uniform* (*Girls in Uniform*), written and directed by women with an all-female cast, which was perceived by many at the time as anti-authoritarian and critical of Prussian militarism. Set in a girls' boarding school, it tells the tale of a schoolgirl's crush on one of her teachers and has subsequently been reclaimed as a lesbian film, though Richard Dyer notes that '*Mädchen*'s lesbianism is so obvious that it is difficult to believe that anyone could downplay it.'[134] Rich notes that all the 'most fundamentally lesbian scenes' were cut by the New York censors before they approved the film in August 1932.[135] McCormick, however, believes that *Der blaue Engel* (*The Blue Angel*, 1930) was more popular with Berlin's lesbian community than *Mädchen in Uniform* because of its star, Marlene Dietrich. Dietrich played the role of Lola-Lola, a cabaret singer who possesses many characteristics deemed masculine: she is sexually aware, unemotional and controlled and openly pursues her desires. Her sexuality enthrals Professor Unrat, whose love for her leads to his downfall from respectable schoolmaster to cabaret clown and to his eventual suicide.[136]

Mädchen in Uniform is the one film seen by Irmgard Keun's protagonist Doris in her 1932 novel *Das kunstseidene Mädchen* (*The Artificial Silk Girl*). This is one of several popular novels by female authors, written towards the end of the Republic, which explore topical issues of interest to women such as sexuality, motherhood, abortion, sexual harassment in the workplace and the impact of the Depression on the family. Irmgard Keun's first novel, *Gilgi, eine von uns* (*Gilgi, One of Us*, 1931), tells the story of an unemotional young female secretary, who has a strict daily regime of exercise and beauty care, and is keen to improve herself and her employment chances by taking language classes in an evening; she is aware of all the latest trends and has a belief in the naturalness of her sexuality. Independently minded, she resigns when her boss makes inappropriate advances towards her. She falls in love with a bohemian poet, becomes pregnant and, having considered an abortion, moves to Berlin to have her child and raise it alone. Keun's novel sold 30,000 copies in its first year and was subsequently serialised in *Vorwärts* in autumn 1932 when the SPD newspaper attempted to win women readers and women's votes.[137] *Das kunstseidene Mädchen*, Keun's second novel, tells the tale of Doris, another secretary, who dreams of becoming a film star and steals a fur coat; she moves to Berlin where she has a number of liaisons, faces homelessness and narrowly avoids a descent into prostitution. Another popular author, Vicki Baum, told the story in *Stud. Chem. Helene Willfüer* of a single mother, Helene, who obtains her doctorate, works in a laboratory on a successful rejuvenation technique and marries her former professor. A member of the Federation of Catholic Women Students' Associations repudiated Baum's depiction of female students, claiming that women did not go to university to indulge in free love, and that Helene, in conceiving a child with another student, attempting to get an abortion and contemplating suicide, was far removed from the feminine ideal to which they aspired.[138] Baum's other major work, *Menschen im Hotel* (1929, translated as *Grand Hotel*), includes the character of Fräulein Flamm, a temporary secretary who also poses nude for advertising photographs and occasionally turns to prostitution, which she matter-of-factly acknowledges is more lucrative than secretarial work.[139] For her, there is no stigma attached to prostitution. The women in all these novels could be seen to be 'new women'. However, both Gilgi and Helene choose to become unmarried mothers, which, while challenging conventional bourgeois morality, calls into question popular concerns about the 'new woman's' attitude towards motherhood.[140]

Meskimmon has noted the existence of a distinct women's culture during the Republic: 'women wrote books and articles, edited journals, produced art, mass media imagery and fashion'.[141] This distinctiveness can be clearly seen in the visual representations of women created by women artists and photographers, which tended not to commodify women as sexual objects. Innovative female photographers would focus on the item being advertised rather than on the woman modelling it.[142] Clear distinctions can also be seen in visual representations of working-class women by socialist print media and artists. Perhaps the best-known female artist during the Weimar Republic, Käthe Kollwitz, became the first female member of the Prussian Academy of Arts in 1919.[143] Her lithographs, drawings and posters of homeworkers, pregnant women, hungry children and dead infants depict the unromanticised reality of working-class life.[144] The depictions of young women in the *Arbeiter Illustrierte Zeitung* (*Workers' Illustrated Newspaper*) were, according to Jennifer Lynn, not as eroticised as those in the middle-class illustrated magazines, and the women's self-assuredness and confidence come from their strength, health and athleticism, not clothing and cosmetics.[145] Meskimmon notes women's tendency to seek out the work of other women.[146] In this they were encouraged by the radio. In Hamburg, for example, the success of a series of discussions with women artists led to the first women's college on the radio, with a thirty-minute programme featuring women's art, literature and science every Thursday, and to exhibitions such as that dedicated to 'Women's Creativity in the Twentieth Century' held in Hamburg in October 1927.[147] Prejudices about women's creative abilities remained, however. At the Bauhaus female students faced discrimination in admissions policies and areas of work, with weaving, pottery and book-binding deemed suitable, but not architecture.[148]

Women's participation in popular artistic productions was not universally welcomed. In the countryside and among the staunchly religious, some of the entertainments available to pleasure-seekers in the cities were viewed as both decadent and depraved. In 1923 there were 360 variety and political-literary cabaret theatres in 119 cities throughout Germany, though Berlin was the centre, the city where 'anything goes'.[149] Its three revue and three variety theatres offered audiences a choice between Klein's nude reviews and Haller's lavishly orchestrated entertainments, in which the Tiller girls, a troupe of scantily clad dancing girls performing high, synchronised kicks in a line, were the main attraction.[150] Here women were seen to represent the decadence and depravity of modern urban culture. In late 1928 some 10,000 citizens joined a demonstration in Düsseldorf organised by Catholic and Protestant associations to protest about the immorality of city life and to call for an end to shameless revues and morally offensive theatre and cinema performances.[151] In June 1932 the Centre Party's Women's Advisory Committee wrote to the Reich Interior Minister calling for an end to nude matinees given by the Adolf Koch Nude Culture School in Berlin's Großes Schauspielhaus, which it believed offended the sensibilities of Christian circles and which were not a worthy expression of German culture or art.[152] Although the Council of People's Delegates' programme of 12 November 1918 ended censorship, and freedom of expression was guaranteed under Article 118 of the Weimar Constitution, the mass of obscene, pornographic and 'educational' films dealing with venereal disease, prostitution and homosexuality led to the re-introduction of film censorship on 12 May 1920, and throughout the Republic various works of art and plays attracted the courts' attention for violating public morality, though this censorship tended to target anti-militaristic and socialist works.[153]

During the Third Reich women continued to be active in cultural production, provided that they, and what they created, conformed to Nazi ideals. Leni Riefenstahl was entrusted with producing documentary films of the 1934 party rally (*Triumph of the Will*) and the 1936 Olympic Games (*Olympia*). Föllmer notes a newspaper report that she was also asked to make a film about the German army in 1935 'because her intuition made her superior to her male colleagues'.[154] Intuition was deemed by the Nazis to be a feminine characteristic. Some women, such as Liselotte Purpur, worked as photojournalists for the regime during the war, at home and abroad.[155] However, many of those working in the cultural industries left Germany, as they faced persecution for their political beliefs, race or sexuality. Marlene Dietrich had already left Germany in 1930 to pursue her film career in Hollywood, and she refused Nazi requests for her to return.[156] Vicki Baum had moved to California in 1932, and, as a Jew, found that her books were banned in Germany. Irmgard Keun's work was also banned, as was Anna Weirauch's *Der Skorpion*, deemed to be 'damaging and undesirable literature'.[157] The Jewish painters Lotte Laserstein and Lea Grundig emigrated, while those who had been politically active, like Alice Lex-Nerlinger, faced arrest and imprisonment. Of those who stayed in Germany some, like Grete Jürgens, were not allowed to exhibit, while Käthe Kollwitz was forced to renounce her membership of the Prussian Academy of Arts.[158]

Conclusion

One young woman, in her essay for the 'Day of the Book' competition in 1931, wrote: 'Now we are struggling to shape our personalities as women. We are forced to struggle because today, there is no ideal woman. The old ideal no longer exists, and the new one has not yet been discovered.'[159] A journalist writing in 1927 had, however, claimed that there were now three types of women living in Germany: the 'Gretchen', naive, conservative and hidebound by tradition; the 'Girl', the American girl-next-door, self-reliant and calculating; and the 'Garçonne', sexually and intellectually potent and combining 'comradely male entrepreneurial sense with heroic, feminine devotion'. Lynne Frame claims that these types had become so entrenched in the German mindset by their depiction in the mass media that the slightest allusion to a woman's appearance or character could instantly trigger an association with one of them.[160] This claim reveals not only the obsession with taxonomies during the Republic but also the preponderance of images and depictions of women within the mass media, as producers sought to encourage women, be they housewives or young women with financial resources of their own, however limited, to purchase their wares, whether films, newspapers, magazines, consumer goods or membership of political parties.

The Weimar Republic witnessed significant changes in women's lives outside the home as they accessed the public realm to pursue a variety of interests. Young women working with the public in offices and shops were expected to maintain their looks, and advertisers provided them with a range of products, displayed by a series of celebrity role models drawn from the world of film or sport, to help them. The introduction of the eight-hour day in 1918 enabled more men and women to indulge in leisure pursuits and sporting activities: the Republic witnessed an upsurge of interest in health and physical fitness which gave rise to expectations of adherence to a new body shape and physical appearance, with recommended body weights and calorie intakes. Women had the opportunity to take part in a range of sporting activities, some more contested than others, and the improvements in their performance challenged notions of male athletic and physical supremacy. Writing in 1928, the sports commentator Willy Meisl noted that 'it was sports that cleared the way for the emancipation of women', and sport also caused traditional attitudes towards the differences between male and female attributes to be reassessed.[161] Women were also prominent as producers and consumers of German culture, though the distinctive female culture, in literature and elsewhere, was viewed pejoratively by contemporary critics such as Kracauer. The iconic androgynous appearance of the 'new woman' with her *Bubikopf* and short skirt first came to light in 1924 at the end of the period of hyperinflation, coinciding with the so-called 'Golden Years' between 1924 and 1928, which witnessed apparent political and economic stability and the expansion of advertising. The high visibility of women, in the city streets and in the media, not only challenged notions of the traditional spheres of the sexes, but also bore testimony to women's changed status in German society.

Notes

1 In 1926–27 70 per cent of window displays in forty-six German cities had electric lighting installed. By 1929 there were around 700 department stores across Germany, with sixty-five in Berlin: J. W. Langstrum, 'The Display Window: Designs and Desires of Weimar Consumerism', *New German Critique*, 76 (1999), 136, 140.
2 K. von Ankum, 'Gendered Urban Spaces in Irmgard Keun's *Das kunstseidene Mädchen*', in von Ankum (ed.), *Women in the Metropolis*, p. 165; Swett, *Neighbors and Enemies*, p. 87.
3 Quoted in Frevert, *Women in German History*, p. 201.
4 C. Ross, *Media and the Making of Modern Germany* (Oxford: Oxford University Press, 2008), pp. 185–6.
5 L. Abrams, 'From Control to Commercialisation: The Triumph of Mass Entertainment in Germany, 1900–25?', *German History*, 8:3 (1990), 281.
6 For the bourgeois concern that the decline in book reading was synonymous with the decline in high culture and the rise of mass culture see G. Reuveni, 'Reading, Advertising and Consumer Culture in the Weimar Period', in K. Führer and C. Ross (eds), *Mass Media, Culture*

and *Society in Twentieth-Century Germany* (Basingstoke: Palgrave Macmillan, 2006), pp. 207, 214.

7 G. Reuveni, *Reading Germany: Literature and Consumer Culture in Germany before 1933* (Oxford: Berghahn, 2006), p. 224; Guttsman, *Workers' Culture in Weimar Germany*, p. 119; E. Harvey, 'Private Fantasy and Public Intervention: Girls' Reading in Weimar Germany', in J. Birkett and E. Harvey (eds), *Determined Women: Studies in the Construction of the Female Subject, 1900–1990* (London: Macmillan, 1991), p. 41.

8 Reuveni, *Reading Germany*, pp. 225–8; K. Barndt, 'Mothers, Citizens, and Consumers: Female Readers in Weimar Germany', in Canning, Barndt and McGuire (eds), *Weimar Publics*, p. 102.

9 R. Wittmann, *Geschichte des deutschen Buchhandels* (Munich: Verlag C. H. Beck, 1999), p. 355.

10 Barndt, 'Mothers, Citizens, and Consumers', pp. 96, 99, 104–5; Reuveni, *Reading Germany*, pp. 241–2.

11 Reese, *Growing Up Female*, p. 125; Benninghaus, 'Mothers' Toil', p. 53.

12 Some 1,440,000 women made up 33.8 per cent of the 4,353,450 members of youth organisations: A. Schmidt, 'Die Mädchen in den Jugendverbänden und ihre Stellung zur Frauenbewegung', *Die Frau*, 36:9 (June 1929), 544.

13 Some 441,700 young women were in Catholic youth groups, constituting 52 per cent of the membership, while 260,100 girls made up 15.9 per cent of sports groups' membership: 'Die Mädchen in den Jugendverbänden', in E. Wolff (ed.), *Jahrbuch des Bundes Deutscher Frauenvereine 1927–28* (Mannheim: J. Bensheimer, 1929), p. 81. There were 224,800 young women in Protestant youth groups, making up 48.9 per cent of the membership. In total church organisations accounted for 46.3 per cent of young women in youth groups.

14 Peukert, *Weimar Republic*, p. 90; von Saldern, 'Modernization', pp. 120–1; *Sozialdemokratischer Parteitag 1927*, p. 306; Grossmann, 'German Communism', p. 150. Peukert's figures contrast with contemporary ones which give a figure of 57,450, of whom 20,750 were female: 'Die Mädchen in den Jugendverbänden', p. 81.

15 Reese, *Growing Up Female*, pp. 209–10. The war-time ban on dance halls was lifted on 31 December 1918, though some authorities only permitted them to open on only two or three days a week: Ross, *Media and the Making of Modern Germany*, pp. 74–6.

16 Ross, *Media and the Making of Modern Germany*, p. 184; Reese, *Growing Up Female*, p. 209.

17 S. L. Funkenstein, 'A Man's Place in a Woman's World: Otto Dix, Social Dancing, and Constructions of Masculinity in Weimar

Germany', *Women in German Yearbook: Feminist Studies in German Literature*, 21 (2005), 165–6.
18 Benninghaus, 'Mothers' Toil', p. 54.
19 The largest cinema in Europe, a 2,667-seater in Hamburg, opened in 1929: K. C. Führer, 'Auf dem Weg zur "Massenkultur"? Kino und Rundfunk in der Weimarer Republik', *Historische Zeitschrift*, 262:3 (1996), 742–3.
20 Ross notes that cinema audiences were 'still visibly divided among lines of region, milieu, and class': Ross, *Media and the Making of Modern Germany*, pp. 159–62.
21 Führer, 'Auf dem Weg zur "Massenkultur"?', p. 743.
22 Ross, *Media and the Making of Modern Germany*, p. 173.
23 Führer, 'Auf dem Weg zur "Massenkultur"?', p. 750.
24 Abrams, 'From Control to Commercialisation', p. 283; Petro, *Joyless Streets*, pp. 19–20. On the popularity of the cinema among young people see Swett, *Neighbors and Enemies*, pp. 75–6. Children under the age of six were banned from cinemas under the 1920 law on film censorship. This age was raised to ten in 1929: Büttner, *Weimar*, p. 261.
25 Reese, *Growing Up Female*, pp. 205–9. Ross believes that young working women could not afford to go to the cinema often, but a survey of 10,000 young Berliners revealed that two-thirds went once a week: C. Ross, 'Cinema, Radio, and "Mass Culture" in the Weimar Republic: Between Shared Experience and Social Division', in J. A. Williams (ed.), *Weimar Culture Revisited* (Basingstoke: Palgrave Macmillan, 2011), p. 26; Petersen, *Women and Modernity in Weimar Germany*, p. 66.
26 Quoted in Guttsman, *Workers' Culture in Weimar Germany*, p. 264.
27 Ross, 'Cinema, Radio, and "Mass Culture" in the Weimar Republic', p. 25.
28 Reuveni, 'Reading, Advertising and Consumer Culture', pp. 207, 214; Ross, *Media and the Making of Modern Germany*, p. 179; B. Fulda, 'Industries of Sensationalism: German Tabloids in Weimar Berlin', in Führer and Ross (eds), *Mass Media*, p. 183.
29 Reuveni, 'Reading, Advertising and Consumer Culture', p. 212. The liberal *Berliner Tageblatt* introduced a four-to-eight-page women's weekly supplement, the *Moden-Spiegel*, in July 1921, initially restricting itself to fashion and beauty before adding cultural items from the mid-1920s: G. Kessemeier, *Sportlich, sachlich, männlich: Das Bild der 'Neuen Frau' in den zwanziger Jahren* (Dortmund: Edition Ebersbach, 2000), p. 210.
30 Von Ankum, 'Gendered Urban Spaces', p. 169.
31 Petro, *Joyless Streets*, pp. 90–1.

32 LAB, BRep 235 HLA MF 1262, G. Bäumer and M.-E. Lüders, letter of 5 August to Th. Wolff, the editor.
33 Reuveni, *Reading Germany*, pp. 137–8.
34 Reuveni, 'Reading, Advertising and Consumer Culture', p. 207. Advertising generated up to two-thirds of some newspapers' income.
35 M. Ganeva, 'Fashion Photography and Women's Modernity in Weimar Germany: The Case of Yva', *NWSA Journal*, 15:3 (2003), 2.
36 There were also 301 sports and 58 broadcasting magazines: Reuveni, *Reading Germany*, p. 128.
37 *Ibid.*, p. 118; M. Ganeva, *Women in Weimar Fashion: Discourses and Displays in German Culture, 1918–1933* (Rochester: Camden House, 2008), p. 54.
38 16 per cent were sold in Berlin: H. Hardt, 'Pictures for the Masses: Photography and the Rise of Popular Magazines in the Weimar Republic', *Journal of Communication Inquiry*, 13:1 (1989), 14–16.
39 Kessemeier, *Sportlich, sachlich, männlich*, pp. 275–7, 280–1.
40 There were a reported 749 listening communities across Germany in 1932, including workers' radio clubs: Ross, *Media and the Making of Modern Germany*, pp. 182–3.
41 The key text is K. Lacey, *Feminine Frequencies: Gender, German Radio, and the Public Sphere, 1923–1939* (Ann Arbor: University of Michigan Press, 1996), pp. 57–62, 64.
42 *Ibid.*, pp. 61, 66.
43 K. C. Führer, 'A Medium of Modernity? Broadcasting in Weimar Germany, 1923–32', *Journal of Modern History*, 69:4 (1997), 743.
44 *Ibid.*, pp. 722, 731, 737, 751; Ross, *Media and the Making of Modern Germany*, p. 186.
45 G. Pfister, 'Sport for Women', in R. Naul and K. Hardman (eds), *Sport and Physical Education in Germany* (London: Routledge, 2002), p. 167.
46 Estimated by C. Eisenberg, 'Massensport in der Weimarer Republik', *Archiv für Sozialgeschichte*, 33 (1993), 159. Eisenberg believes that an additional 12,000 women were members of non-affiliated gymnastics organisations.
47 M. Hau, 'Sports in the Human Economy: "Leibesübungen", Medicine, Psychology, and Performance Enhancement during the Weimar Republic', *Central European History*, 41:3 (2008), 382–7.
48 *Ibid.*, p. 400.
49 A. C. Stanley, *Modernising Tradition: Gender and Consumerism in Interwar France and Germany* (Baton Rouge: Louisiana State University Press, 2008), p. 149.
50 Meskimmon, *We Weren't Modern Enough*, p. 166; M. C. Storer, 'Weimar Germany as Seen by an Englishwoman: British Women

Writers and the Weimar Republic', *German Studies Review*, 32:1 (2009), 140.

51 Eisenberg, 'Massensport', p. 160.

52 There were 62,060 women in the athletics association, 44,825 in the swimming organisation, 39,100 in tennis associations and 95 in the jiu-jitsu association: *ibid.*, 160; E. N. Jensen, *Body by Weimar: Athletes, Gender, and German Modernity* (Oxford: Oxford University Press, 2010), p. 83.

53 Adolf Hitler is reported to have attended a women's boxing match at Lunapark: *ibid.*, pp. 51, 57, 71, 92–5.

54 Over a million women attended an additional 100,000 mixed classes. Berghaus claims that the association had 90,000 female members: G. Berghaus, 'Girlkultur – Feminism, Americanism, and Popular Entertainment in Weimar Germany', *Journal of Design History*, 1:3–4 (1988), 211; Reese, *Growing Up Female*, p. 67. The workers also had their own Olympics, the first being held in Frankfurt am Main in 1925.

55 Jensen, *Body by Weimar*, pp. 124–7. The event was not reinstated until 1960.

56 K. Sutton, 'The Masculinized Female Athlete in Weimar Germany', *German Politics and Society*, 27:3 (2009), 40; G. Pfister, 'Demands, Realities and Ambivalences – Women in the Proletarian Sports Movement in Germany (1893–1933)', *Women in Sport and Physical Activity Journal*, 3:2 (1994), 49.

57 M. Hau, *The Cult of Health and Beauty in Germany: A Social History, 1890–1930* (Chicago: University of Chicago Press, 2003), p. 182; Sutton, *The Masculine Woman*, pp. 33, 68, 72–3.

58 Sutton, 'The Masculinized Female Athlete', p. 31.

59 *Ibid.*, pp. 34, 38–40.

60 I. Guenther, *Nazi Chic? Fashioning Women in the Third Reich* (Oxford: Berg, 2004), pp. 57–8; Kessemeier, *Sportlich, sachlich, männlich*, p. 210.

61 M. Jefferies, '"For a genuine and noble nakedness"? German Naturism in the Third Reich', *German History*, 24:1 (2006), 66. The law also introduced a 150 RM fine for swimming nude.

62 D. Imhoof, 'The Game of Political Change: Sports in Göttingen during the Weimar and Nazi Eras', *German History*, 27:3 (2009), 381–2.

63 P. Fritzsche, 'The Economy of Experience in Weimar Germany', in Canning, Barndt and McGuire (eds), *Weimar Subjects*, p. 361. Frevert has slightly different figures but believes that one-third of the 3.6 million youth hostel visitors in 1929 were female: Frevert, *Women in German History*, p. 202. Baranowski writes of the Friends of Nature group, with its socialist and Communist group-

ings, which had 100,000 members and '230 hiking and vacation hostels': S. Baranowski, *Strength through Joy: Consumerism and Mass Tourism in the Third Reich* (Cambridge: Cambridge University Press, 2004), p. 53.
64 On women's involvement in the Wandervogel movement and its successors in the Weimar Republic see M. E. P. de Ras, *Body, Femininity and Nationalism: Girls in the German Youth Movement, 1900–1934* (London: Routledge, 2008).
65 S. Orfali, *A Jewish Girl in the Weimar Republic* (Berkeley: Ronin Publishing, 1987), pp. 126–7, 139–41.
66 Guttsman, *Workers' Culture in Weimar Germany*, pp. 298–302.
67 S. Disko, 'Men, Motorcycles and Modernity: Motorisation during the Weimar Republic' (PhD dissertation, New York University, 2008), pp. 227–31.
68 'Vor 80 Jahren um die Welt', *Welt Online* (3 March 2007), www.welt.de/welt_print/article743782/Vor_80_Jahren_um_die_Welt.html (accessed 18 February 2012).
69 A. Hertling, 'Representing Gender: Automobility in Discourse of Femininity in the Weimar Republic' (2004), 4–6, www.carstudies.de/gender/repr_gender/representinggender.pdf (accessed 26 March 2012).
70 Female athletes and celebrities like Stinnes appeared in newsreels. Swett claims that women featured in fourteen stories in forty-eight newsreels between 1929 and 1933: Swett, *Neighbors and Enemies*, p. 74.
71 'Vor 80 Jahren um die Welt'. Rosemeyer died when attempting to break a world speed record in 1938.
72 I. Kershaw, *Hitler. 1936–45: Nemesis* (London: Allen Lane, 2000), pp. 621, 820. Reitsch was an ardent supporter of Hitler and reputedly flew the last plane out of Berlin on 28 April 1945.
73 Quoted in Jensen, *Body by Weimar*, p. 132; Pfister, 'Sport for Women', p. 171.
74 Jensen, *Body by Weimar*, pp. 132, 138.
75 Mayer won the silver medal and gave the Hitler salute on the podium. For Bergmann see *ibid.*, p. 132. For Mayer see M. Mogulof, *Foiled, Hitler's Jewish Olympian: The Helene Mayer Story* (Oakland: RDR Books, 2002).
76 Jensen, *Body by Weimar*, pp. 137–8; L. Pine, *Education in Nazi Germany* (Oxford: Berg, 2010), p. 123. For the physical education curriculum for girls see *ibid.*, pp. 64–5. For the popularity of sport within the Nazi Girls' League see Reese, *Growing Up Female*, pp. 60–2.
77 Baranowski, *Strength through Joy*, p. 97.

78 *Ibid.*, pp. 6, 35, 56–9.
79 *Ibid.*, pp. 68, 150, 174, 180–2.
80 In 1928 there were a reported 2,000 advertising agencies in Germany: Reuveni, *Reading Germany*, p. 129; Stanley, *Modernising Tradition*, pp. 20–1.
81 One advertising journal in 1932 claimed this figure to be 85 per cent: M. Lavin, *Clean New World: Culture, Politics and Graphic Design* (London: MIT Press, 2001), p. 50. The figure of 75 per cent comes from H. Kropff, 'Women as Shoppers', in A. Kaes, M. Jay and E. Dimendberg (eds), *The Weimar Republic Sourcebook* (Berkeley: University of California Press, 1994), p. 660.
82 D. Buerkle, 'Gendered Spectatorship, Jewish Women and Psychological Advertising in Weimar Germany', *Women's History Review*, 15:4 (2006), 630. Buerkle argues that while in the 1920s the 'new woman' in advertisements could be thought to be Jewish, by the early 1930s any trace of Jewishness had disappeared. For housewives in advertisements see Stanley, *Modernising Tradition*, pp. 31–55. See also J. Sneeringer, 'The Shopper as Voter: Women, Advertising, and Politics in Post-Inflation Germany', *German Studies Review*, 27:3 (2004), 475–501.
83 I. Sharp, 'Riding the Tiger: Ambivalent Images of the New Woman in the Popular Press of the Weimar Republic', in A. Heilmann and M. Beetham (eds), *New Woman Hybridities: Femininity, Feminism and International Consumer Culture, 1880–1930* (London: Routledge, 2004), pp. 130–2.
84 C. Ross, 'Visions of Prosperity: The Americanisation of Advertising in Interwar Germany', in P. E. Swett, S. J. Wiesen and J. R. Zatlin (eds), *Selling Modernity: Advertising in Twentieth-Century Germany* (London: Duke University Press, 2007), p. 64; Kessemeier, *Sportlich, sachlich, männlich*, pp. 132–3.
85 Fromm points out that the use of perfume was perceived differently from the use of make-up and was widely accepted: Fromm, *The Working Class*, pp. 158–61, 164–5.
86 Hau, *The Cult of Health*, p. 180; Prestel, 'The "New Jewish Woman"', p. 151.
87 J. Ward, *Weimar Surfaces: Urban Visual Culture in 1920s Germany* (Berkeley: University of California Press, 2001), p. 89. One magazine, *Die Dame*, reported that a woman 1.5 m. tall had an ideal weight of 100 pounds, and that every centimetre in height above that equated to two pounds: Kessemeier, *Sportlich, sachlich, männlich*, pp. 141–3; G. Berghaus, 'Girlkultur', p. 205.
88 Ganeva, *Women in Weimar Fashion*, p. 135.
89 ADEF, G2d, report of negotiations about a possible joint request to

the Reich Interior Minister to ban beauty contests. The Nazis banned the contest after 1933.
90 Guenther, *Nazi Chic?*, p. 55.
91 M. Makela, 'The Rise and Fall of the Flapper Dress: Nationalism and Anti-Semitism in Early-Twentieth-Century Discourse in German Fashion', *Journal of Popular Culture*, 34:3 (2000), 188, 191, 197; Guenther, *Nazi Chic?*, pp. 56–7.
92 Ganeva, *Women in Weimar Fashion*, pp. 136–7.
93 There were some 600 firms across Germany in the mid-1920s, rising to over 800 in 1927: Guenther, *Nazi Chic?*, pp. 80–1.
94 *Ibid.*, p. 56. Ullstein believed that about ten million dresses were sewn at home in the mid-1920s: *ibid.*, p. 56; Kessemeier, *Sportlich, sachlich, männlich*, p. 8.
95 Kessemeier, *Sportlich, sachlich, männlich*, p. 179; Ganeva, *Women in Weimar Fashion*, p. 4.
96 In one film, *Die Geliebte Roswolskys (Roswolsky's Mistress)*, its star, Asta Nielsen, was seen in thirty-six outfits: Ganeva, *Women in Weimar Fashion*, p. 114.
97 Kessemeier, *Sportlich, sachlich, männlich*, pp. 85, 104.
98 *Ibid.*, pp. 86–9, 92.
99 *Ibid.*, pp. 92–5.
100 S. Hake, 'In the Mirror of Fashion', in von Ankum (ed.), *Women in the Metropolis*, p. 187; Ward, *Weimar Surfaces*, p. 58.
101 M. Lavin, 'Androgyny, Spectatorship, and the Weimar Photomontages of Hanna Höch', *New German Critique*, 51 (1990), 75.
102 Ganeva, *Women in Weimar Fashion*, p. 3.
103 Kessemeier, *Sportlich, sachlich, männlich*, p. 105.
104 Fromm, *The Working Class*, pp. 152–7.
105 Kessemeier, *Sportlich, sachlich, männlich*, pp. 98–106.
106 'Enough is Enough! Against the Masculinisation of Women', in Kaes, Jay and Dimendberg (eds), *The Weimar Republic Sourcebook*, p. 659.
107 Kessemeier, *Sportlich, sachlich, männlich*, pp. 253–4.
108 *Ibid.*, p. 114.
109 *Ibid.*, pp. 109–13.
110 Guenther, *Nazi Chic?*, p. 86.
111 Ganeva, *Women in Weimar Fashion*, pp. 1, 193.
112 On live models appearing in window displays see *ibid.*, pp. 156–8; Ward, *Urban Surfaces*, p. 221.
113 H. Weber, 'Die "Vermännlichung" der Frau', *Die christliche Frau*, 24:4 (April 1926), 91.
114 Guenther, *Nazi Chic?*, pp. 109–19.
115 *Ibid.*, pp. 107–8.
116 S. Brockmann, 'Weimar Sexual Cynicism', in T. W. Kniesche and

S. Brockmann (eds), *Dancing on the Volcano: Essays on the Culture of the Weimar Republic* (Columbia: Camden House, 1994), pp. 170–1.
117 M. Tatar, *Lustmord: Sexual Murder in Weimar Germany* (Princeton: Princeton University Press, 1995), pp. 68, 80.
118 B. I. Lewis, '*Lustmord*: Inside the Windows of the Metropolis', in von Ankum (ed.), *Women in the Metropolis*, p. 226.
119 D. Rowe, *Representing Berlin: Sexuality and the City in Imperial and Weimar Germany* (Aldershot: Ashgate, 2003), pp. 155–9.
120 Tatar, *Lustmord*, p. 173.
121 While the number of murders of females increased by 64.9 per cent between 1918 and 1919, that of murders of males not in the military rose 118.3 per cent: calculated from figures in *StJhb 1924*, pp. 45–9. In the early 1930s about one-third of female murder victims were under the age of five: *StJhb 1932*, p. 37; *StJhb 1933*, pp. 43–5. The female share of murder victims was 30.9 per cent in 1919 and reached a highpoint of 42.4 per cent in 1928, falling to 35.1 per cent in 1932 with 485 murders. This fall may have been due to the fact that fewer women than men were killed in political violence.
122 He believes that the Weimar woman was 'now thrown from the protection of the patriarchal family unit and forced to sell herself on the open market': Brockmann, 'Weimar Sexual Cynicism', p. 174.
123 Widdig, *Culture and Inflation*, pp. 196–220. The other three figures were the witch, the starving mother and the mistress.
124 Meskimmon, *We Weren't Modern Enough*, pp. 23–38. See also Hans Baluschek's 1923 painting of a suburban prostitute: Rowe, *Representing Berlin*, pp. 146–7.
125 B. Murray, 'The Role of the Vamp in Weimar Cinema: An Analysis of Karl Grune's *The Street (Die Straße)*', in S. Frieden, R. W. McCormick, V. P. Petersen and L. M. Vogelsang (eds), *Gender and German Cinema: Feminist Interventions*, vol. 2: *German Film History: German History on Film* (Oxford: Berg, 1993), p. 39.
126 Sharp, 'Riding the Tiger', p. 121; B. Hales, 'Woman as Sexual Criminal: Weimar Constructions of the Criminal Femme Fatale', *Women in German Yearbook: Feminist Studies in German Literature and Culture*, 12 (1996), 104.
127 D. Siemens, 'Explaining Crime: Berlin Newspapers and the Construction of the Criminal in Weimar Germany', *Journal of European Studies*, 39:3 (2009), 339.
128 Hales, 'Woman as Sexual Criminal', pp. 107, 116.
129 *StJhb 1937*, p. 591.
130 *StJhb 1926*, pp. 439–40; *StJhb 1935*, pp. 530–1.
131 In 1924 107 women were convicted of murder and manslaughter, in 1932 53: *StJhb 1927*, p. 491; *StJhb 1934*, p. 544. One woman was

executed in 1920, one in 1921, two in 1925 and three in 1933: *StJhb 1924*, pp. 45–9; *StJhb 1929*, p. 45; *StJhb 1935*, pp. 48–9. Figures for 1928–30 are missing, but Evans claims that no executions were carried out in 1928 and 1929 as the use of the death penalty was being publicly debated and that the three women, executed for political crimes in 1933, were the first since before the war: R. J. Evans, *Rituals of Retribution: Capital Punishment in Germany 1600–1987* (Oxford: Oxford University Press, 1996), pp. 564, 646.

132 T. Herzog, *Crime Stories: Criminalistic Fantasy and the Culture of Crisis in Weimar Germany* (Oxford: Berghahn, 2009), pp. 57–63. Klein was sentenced to four years in prison, Nebbe to eighteen months of hard labour.

133 Radusch quoted in Tamagne, *A History of Homosexuality in Europe*, p. 266; Sutton, *The Masculine Woman*, pp. 151–80.

134 Dyer, 'Less and more than women and men', p. 34. For the film's reception see Sutton, *The Masculine Woman*, pp. 142–3. Petro claims that Countess Geschwitz in *Pandora's Box* (1928) is the first screen lesbian: Petro, *Joyless Streets*, p. 80.

135 B. R. Rich, 'From Repressive Tolerance to Erotic Liberation: *Girls in Uniform* (*Mädchen in Uniform*)', in Frieden et al. (eds), *Gender and German Cinema*, vol. 2, p. 93.

136 McCormick, *Gender and Sexuality in Weimar Modernity*, p. 34. On *The Blue Angel* see J. T. Zagula, 'Saints, Sinners and Society: Images of Woman in Film and Drama, from Weimar to Hitler', *Women's Studies*, 19 (1991), 63–9.

137 The book, however, met with a mixed reaction from readers: Barndt, 'Mothers, Citizens, and Consumers', pp. 107–10; Usborne, *Cultures of Abortion*, pp. 40–2.

138 'Our German people needs pure women who will lead it again to a higher moral and spiritual standard': M. T. Bewerunge, 'Stud. Chem. Helene Willfüer, Roman eines jungen Mädchens von heute', *Die christliche Frau*, 27:1 (January 1928), 32.

139 J. S. Smith, 'Working Girls: White-Collar Workers and Prostitutes in late Weimar fiction', *German Quarterly*, 81:4 (2008), 457.

140 K. Barndt, 'Aesthetics of Crisis: Motherhood, Abortion, and Melodrama in Irmgard Keun and Friedrich Wolf', *Women in German Yearbook: Feminist Studies in German Literature and Culture*, 24 (2008), 76.

141 Meskimmon, *We Weren't Modern Enough*, p. 3. For an introduction to twenty female artists see Meskimmon and West, *Visions of the Neue Frau*. Many of the editors and journalists on women's magazines were women: Kessemeier, *Sportlich, sachlich, männlich*, p. 9.

142 There were over 100 photographic 'studios in Berlin owned and

managed by women': Ganeva, 'Fashion Photography', pp. 2, 13–15. See also Lavin, *Clean New World*, pp. 50–67, on the work of two female photographers, Ellen Auerbach and Grete Stern.
143 Büttner, *Weimar*, p. 301.
144 See also Martha Schrag's work and Lea Grundig's: Meskimmon, *We Weren't Modern Enough*, pp. 90–9.
145 J. M. Lynn, 'Contesting Images: Representations of the Modern Woman in the German Illustrated Press, 1924–1933' (MA dissertation, University of North Carolina, 2008), p. 90.
146 Meskimmon, *We Weren't Modern Enough*, p. 4.
147 Lacey, *Feminine Frequencies*, pp. 75–8. The radio station later organised a conference in Gandersheim, which was broadcast nationwide.
148 K. R. Ray, 'Bauhaus Hausfraus: Gender Formation in Design Education', *Journal of Architectural Education*, 55:2 (2001), 78.
149 Berghaus, '*Girlkultur*', p. 199.
150 *Ibid*., pp. 99–201. The Tiller girls were only one of a number of well-known dancing troupes.
151 The theatre had sued the Düsseldorf Association of Catholic Organisations for loss of earnings after it urged residents to boycott it for six months because of its immoral revues: 'Eine Kundgebung in Düsseldorf gegen die Entsittlichung des Großstadtlebens', *Die christliche Frau*, 27:1 (January 1929), 31–2.
152 ADKFB, Collection 1-47-10, letter from the Women's Advisory Committee to the Reich Interior Minister, 19 June 1932.
153 Stibbe, *Germany 1914–1933*, pp. 135–6; Büttner, *Weimar*, p. 302. The Law to Protect Young People from Trashy and Smutty Literature of 18 December 1926, under which some 143 works had been banned by 1932, and an attempt to extend it to popular amusements in 1927 highlight the concern of some sections of society about the perceived immoral impact of elements of culture on young people: Ross, *Media and the Making of Modern Germany*, p. 77.
154 Föllmer, 'Was Nazism Collectivistic?' p. 77.
155 E. Harvey, '"Ich war überall": Die NS-Propagandaphotographin Liselotte Purpur', in Steinbacher (ed.), *Volksgenossinnen*, pp. 138–53. Harvey notes that a war-time article discussed six female photojournalists.
156 Guenther, *Nazi Chic?*, p. 114.
157 C. Schoppmann, 'Anna Elisabet Weirach (1887–1970)', www.lesbengeschichte.de/bio_weirauch_d.html (accessed 25 July 2012). Schoppmann notes that this was the only one of Weirauch's works to be banned. She had joined the Reich Chamber of Literature and was allowed to continue writing. She produced no fewer than twenty-one novels during the Third Reich.

158 Meskimmon, *We Weren't Modern Enough*, pp. 243–5; D. Welch, *The Third Reich: Politics and Propaganda* (London: Routledge, 2nd edn, 2002), p. 32.
159 Quoted in Barndt, 'Mothers, Citizens, and Consumers', p. 105.
160 L. Frame, 'Gretchen, Girl, Garçonne? Weimar Science and Popular Culture in Search of the Ideal New Woman', in Ankum (ed.), *Women in the Metropolis*, pp. 12, 25.
161 Quoted in Jensen, *Body by Weimar*, p. 134.

Conclusion

Weitz has claimed that during the Weimar Republic, 'women had greater choices in their lives than ever before'.[1] However, not all these choices were available to all women in equal measure. The revolution granted all women over the age of twenty the same political and citizenship rights as men, and women all over Germany could exercise them.[2] The Weimar Constitution in principle enshrined the equality of the sexes, but not all women could benefit from the range of opportunities, benefits and life choices which became available through its implementation and through the improvements in some welfare provision. Women living in rural communities in Pomerania or in the Alps in Bavaria who continued to rely heavily on local support networks were little affected by the increasing range of employment opportunities, the improved antenatal care or the opportunity to give birth in a hospital, and their experience of and attitudes towards the Republic may have been determined by the impact of its economic difficulties on their lives. These did not affect the lives of middle- and upper-class women of independent means, who were able to adopt the latest trends in fashion, leisure and lifestyle. Young, urban women were, however, able to take advantage of the 'multiple development opportunities' opening up for women, particularly in employment.

Else Hermann, writing about the 'new woman' in 1929, claimed that 'the woman of today is oriented exclusively toward the present'. She contrasted her with the woman of yesterday, who had 'lived exclusively for and geared her actions towards the future' – the future of her husband and children. Hermann's women of today were going out to work to become economically independent, which, according to Hermann, was 'the necessary pre-condition for a self-reliant personality'.[3] While only older, professional women were able to lead economically independent lives during the Weimar Republic, a greater range of professional employment opportunities was becoming available for women, and increasing numbers of young women were staying at school to take the *Abitur*, go to university and pursue professional careers, usually in salaried positions in the cities, or, as with university study, in areas known for their liberal outlook before the First World War. Less academic young women also had a greater range of employment opportunities. Article 145 of the Constitution introduced compulsory education until the age of eighteen, improving women's vocational training. They could reject work in domestic service and agriculture, the two most exploitative, least regulated areas of employment, and enter paid employment as manual workers in industry or white-collar workers in the expanding retail and administrative sectors. Although manual and white-collar work may have been physically and nervously exhausting, and women were confined, through their youth and their lack of training and skill, to the lower echelons of the workforce, women had better pay relative to men's, regulated working conditions and better trade union organisational structures to represent their interests. Women were not paid the same as men during the Weimar Republic but wage differentials were narrowing slowly, with the smallest obtaining in white-collar work, which became a much-sought-after area of employment among working-class girls.[4] It was also an acceptable form of employment for young middle-class women whose parents could no longer afford to support them after the hyperinflation. Young women were no longer confined to manual work in the textile, clothing and food industries, but could seek employment in industries that women had breached during the war and in newer industries such as the electro-technical industry, since the rationalisation of German industry in the mid-1920s was increasing the demand for unskilled and semi-skilled workers. The erosion of gender-segregated industries and the entry of women into professional employment, particularly the legal profession, challenged the pre-war gender order, which owed much to the belief in 'separate spheres', with the public sphere of employment, politics and public life being deemed a masculine sphere, and the home, the private sphere, a feminine one. Professional women faced staunch opposition from some male colleagues who sought to undermine their capabilities and capacities, particularly during the Depression, when professional employment opportunities were limited. In manual and white-collar work, however, women had a better chance of retaining their employment than men during the Depression, in part because of the sectors in which they worked, in part because of the cheapness of their labour. Men regarded women as competitors in the job market, being aided in this mistaken view, according to Hilde Walter, by the mass publicity that women's work and 'moderate professional successes' had attracted in the media.[5] While it became accepted during the Republic that young women should find employment between leaving school and getting married, there was very limited acceptance of married women's right to work.

Although the Constitution proclaimed that marriage was based on the equality of the sexes, the Civil Code of 1900 was not amended, and it was to be 1975 before the Federal Republic enacted a law granting men and women equality in marriage.[6] Any attempt to improve women's status within marriage, to improve the status of illegitimate children or to amend the divorce laws was fiercely opposed by the Catholic Church, and the Protestant and Catholic women's organisations continued to act as the guardians of the nation's moral standards and the traditional family. While traditional notions of 'separate spheres' were being challenged outside the home, within it they held sway. The BdF proclaimed that 'the main focus of a woman's life remains the family', which reflected the experience of the majority of married women.[7] Although the BdF regarded marriage as a full-time occupation, it believed that if a married woman wished to pursue a career she should be free to do so. Other confessional and professional women's organisations such as the VRT did not share this liberal view. Marriage was a profession in its own right, though in contravening the Constitution and dismissing married women civil servants from October 1923 until 1929 and from May 1932 the state was also acting from the belief that marriage provided a woman with economic security. Within middle-class marriage the traditional gender order obtained: the husband was the breadwinner and head of household, with the legal right to make all the decisions, and the wife remained responsible for the smooth running of the household and the upbringing of the children. Even in working-class households where the wife had to go out to work to ensure the family's finances, she still had these responsibilities, which is why so many young women admired their mothers but did not want to share their fate.[8] A young working woman's ability to aid the family's finances enhanced her standing within the family, and she was able to benefit from the more relaxed social mores of the Republic, taking part in a range of leisure activities with female friends or even enjoying platonic friendships with members of the opposite sex within the co-educational youth organisations. Hermann noted the 'fundamental change in the orientation of women toward men which acquires its basic tone from concerns of equality and comradeship'.[9] Young women no longer saw the necessity for a separate women's movement.

Women were able to take advantage of the employment and professional opportunities that the Weimar Republic was making accessible because they were able to control their fertility. Contraceptive advice became more widespread, and the use of contraception to limit family size became accepted as couples sought to ensure a better future for their children. Even in the countryside, where traditionally gendered work practices continued within agriculture and exposure to the emerging mass culture of the Republic was extremely limited, women were able to benefit from what was perhaps the most significant improvement in women's lives during the Republic – their ability to control their fertility. However, the ensuing fall in the birth rate fuelled nationalists' concerns that the nation was in danger of dying out, and women, in particular the 'new woman', were blamed. The 'new woman' was representative of women who were able to break free of the traditional expectations of them. The young woman with her *Bubikopf* and short skirt, working in new white-collar positions or in industries that had mechanised and rationalised to gain some economic independence, embracing the latest ideas from the United States and enjoying the latest offerings of mass culture, represented for some the positive impact of modernity, while for others women's participation not just in nude reviews but in leisure activities alongside men, their perceived openness about their sexuality and their failure to have children represented the decadent and degenerate excesses of urban life.

The revolution granted women equal suffrage rights, and women could participate actively in politics, at all levels, in keeping with their ideological beliefs. In France women were not given the vote until 1944, and it was only in 1928 that all women over the age of twenty-one were given equal suffrage with men in Great Britain. In December 1918 one woman, one of seventeen female candidates out of 1,623, was elected to serve in the British parliament.[10]

However, the German electoral system ensured that women were dependent on the goodwill of their parties to be elected, and many village councils and even some state assemblies had no elected female representatives. While the growing influence of interest groups harmed women's chances of being chosen to stand for election, the increasing masculinisation of politics and street violence from 1930 circumscribed women's full participation in the political process. The Constitution granted women equal citizenship rights with men, at a time when one of the pillars on which male citizenship was based, their ability to bear arms in defence of their country, was being eroded by the Treaty of Versailles. McCormick has noted that modernity in Weimar Germany 'was often experienced as a crisis of traditional male authority, agency, and identity', while Petro, among others, has claimed that 'modernity, in turn, was almost always represented as a woman'.[11]

As Stibbe has astutely pointed out, historians' concerns about the crisis of modernity mask the battles between the adherents of conservative and liberal values during the Republic.[12] The improvements in women's lives and in the opportunities open to them, equal political and citizenship rights, the removal of restrictions within professional employment, the best protection laws for pregnant workers and the most lenient abortion laws in Western Europe, the decriminalisation of prostitution, the decrease in infant mortality, the financial support for new mothers and for unmarried mothers, and the more relaxed relationships between the sexes were considerable achievements. But, as Weitz notes, 'It was Weimar's many *achievements* that the Nazis could not abide.'[13] Many of the rights and opportunities granted to women in the early years of the Republic were not universally welcomed, by either men or women. The octogenarian Helene Lange noted in 1928 that 'The fact that we are now not making any progress is much more the fault of women than of men; on average they cannot make the most of the favourable situation which the revolution created for them.'[14] In her book exploring Danish women's experiences in the 1920s, Brigitte Søland has written that 'In the course of little more than a decade, the existence of "modern" young women – women who wore short dresses and bobbed hair, who worked during the day and enjoyed themselves at night, and who expected romance and egalitarianism within marriage – had been largely accepted.'[15] This was not the case in Germany, a country coming to terms with a lost war, occupied territory, a new political system and turbulent economic conditions. Felix Gilbert has pointed out that the difference between 'actual behaviour and publicly accepted values' may be 'considered characteristic of contrasting attitudes that had developed in Germany in the twenties. Revolution and inflation in Germany, which had encouraged radical convictions and notions more quickly and strongly than in other countries, also strengthened a belief in the need to maintain traditional customs and values.'[16] Young women were caught between the possibilities opening up for them to exercise freedom of choice, be it which career they might pursue, how they spent their earnings and leisure time, or how many children they had, and the expectations placed on them by the continuation of long-held beliefs that they were predestined to fulfil women's primary role as wife and mother.

The opportunities that grew out of the First World War and out of the rights granted to women in the revolution and by the Constitution blurred the pre-war gender order; they signified to all those who hated the Republic all that was wrong with it. German women were not immune to the perceived shame of the lost war and Germany's loss of standing in the international community, nor to the Republic's economic woes, which the democratic government seemed unable to master. Some wanted to play a full role in revitalising the German nation, and saw in the appointment of a strong leader a man who could lead Germany back to national greatness and self-respect and the unemployed back to work. The man whom many Germans entrusted with this task, Adolf Hitler, led a party that stressed the differences between the sexes; for him a woman's world was 'her husband, her family, her children, and her home'.[17] The blurring of the 'traditionally gendered roles and behaviour' which McCormick found so emancipatory during the Republic was to be reversed to some extent, though it returned during the Second World War. Although the demands of an economy geared towards rearmament and the needs of individuals to earn their living ensured that not all women could return to the home, the Nazi regime did reverse some of the rights which the Weimar Republic had granted women, particularly with regard to the public sphere, such as passive suffrage and women's employment within the judiciary. The Nazis' accession to power was to prove a distinct rupture in the lives of Social Democrat and Communist women who were ideologically opposed to Nazism, or women deemed politically unreliable who were fired from their jobs. It was, however, to be the Nazis' racist ideology which was to have the most impact on women's lives, with those deemed racially inferior or of little value to the Aryan race, including those with hereditary illnesses, asocials, the Jews, and the gypsies, facing discrimination and exclusion from the national, racial community.

Notes

1. E. Weitz, 'Weimar Germany and the Dilemmas of Liberty', in J. C. Friedman (ed.), *The Routledge History of the Holocaust* (London: Routledge, 2010), p. 59.
2. An exception was to be women who lost their German citizenship on marrying a foreigner under a law of 22 July 1913. Lüders campaigned unsuccessfully to change this law: BAK, Nachlass Lüders 245, Reichstag printed papers nos. 3210 of 15 December 1921, 5324 of 5 December 1922, 3056 of 26 February 1927 and 3629 of 15 September 1927.
3. E. Hermann, 'This is the New Woman', in Kaes, Jay and Dimendberg (eds), *The Weimar Republic Sourcebook*, pp. 206–7.
4. In April 2011 the SPD fraction in the German parliament, the Bundestag, noted that German women received 23 per cent less pay than men doing the same work or work of equal value: 'Gleicher Lohn für gleiche Arbeit: Eckpunkte für gesetzliche Regelung', *Fraktion Intern*, 3 (11 April 2011), 11, www.spdfraktion.de/cnt/rs/rs_datei/0,,14434,00.pdf (accessed 21 April 2012).
5. H. Walter, 'Twilight for women', in Kaes, Jay and Dimendberg, *The Weimar Republic Sourcebook*, p. 210.
6. Frevert, *Women in German History*, p. 323.
7. Wolff (ed.) *Jahrbuch des Bundes Deutscher Frauenvereine 1932*, p. 73.
8. Deutscher Textilarbeiterverband (ed.), *Mein Arbeitstag – mein Wochenende, passim*.
9. Hermann, 'This is the New Woman', in Kaes, Jay and Dimendberg p. 207.
10. Countess Markievicz represented Sinn Fein and never took her seat. In subsequent by-elections two women were elected: W. S. G. Kohn, *Women in National Legislatures* (New York: Praeger, 1980), p. 72.
11. McCormick, *Gender and Sexuality in Weimar Modernity*, p. 3; Petro, *Joyless Streets*, p. 40.
12. Stibbe, *Germany 1914–1933*, p. 151.
13. Weitz, 'Weimar Germany and the Dilemmas of Liberty', p. 59.

14 Helene Lange letter to Emmy Beckmann of 15 June 1928, in *Was ich hier geliebt*, ed. Beckmann p. 319.
15 B. Søland, *Becoming Modern: Young Women and the Reconstruction of Womanhood in the 1920s* (Princeton: Princeton University Press, 2000), p. 173.
16 F. Gilbert, *A European Past: Memoirs, 1905–1945* (New York: W. W. Norton Company, 1988), p. 68.
17 Hitler speaking to the NSF at the Nuremberg party rally on 8 September 1934, quoted in Stephenson, *Women in Nazi Germany*, p. 142.

Bibliography

Primary sources
Archival sources
Archiv des Allgemeinen Deutschen Lehrerinnenvereins (ADLV), Berlin
Collections 7, 10, 11, 12, 15, 16

Archiv des Bundes Deutscher Frauenvereine (BdF), Berlin
Collections 1, 3, 7, 8, 10, 11, 12, 14, 15

Archiv des Deutsch-Evangelischen Frauenbundes, Archiv der deutschen Frauenbewegung, Kassel (ADEF)
Collections (Mappen) A, B, E, F, G, K, N, O, P, Q

Archiv des Katholischen Deutschen Frauenbundes, Cologne (AKDFB)
Collections (Mappen) 1-15, 1-16, 1-17, 1-22, 1-43, 1-44, 1-47, 1-108

Bayerisches Hauptstaatsarchiv, Munich
MInn Bavarian Interior Ministry

Bundesarchiv Berlin (BAB)
60 Vo 1 Deutsche Volkspartei
60 Vo 2 Deutschnationale Volkspartei
61 Re Reichslandbund
62 DAF Deutsche Arbeitsfront
R1501 Reichministerium des Innern
R1507 Reichskommissar für die Überwachung der öffentlichen Ordnung
R3201 Reichsministerium für wirtschaftliche Demobilmuchung
R3901 Reichsarbeitsministerium

R703 Reichstag
R8005 Deutschnationale Volkspartei
R8034II Reichslandbund
R8083 Reichsgemeinschaft Deutscher Hausfrauen
R901 Auswärtiges Amt

Bundesarchiv Koblenz (BAK)
Kleine Erwerbungen (Kl.Erw.)
Nachlass Gertrud Bäumer
Nachlass Hermann Dietrich
Nachlass Camilla Jellinek
Nachlass Katharina von Kardorff
Nachlass Marie-Elisabeth Lüders
Nachlass Adele Schreiber
R2 Finanzministerium
R36 Deutscher Gemeindetag
R43I Reichskanzlei
R45II Deutsche Volkspartei
R45III Deutsche Demokratische Partei
R45IV Kommunistiche Partei Deutschlands
R134 Reichskommissar für die Überwachung der öffentlichen Ordnung und Nachrichtensammelstelle im Reichsministerium des Innern
Zeitgeschichtliche Sammlung (Z.Sg.)

Evangelisches Zentralarchiv Berlin
7 Evangelischer Oberkirchenrat
51 Ökumenisches Archiv

Generallandesarchiv, Karlsruhe (GLA)
231 Landtag
233 Staatsministerium
235 Kultusministerium
443 Badischer Frauenverin vom Roten Kreuz

Landesarchiv Berlin (LAB)
BRep 235 Helene-Lange-Archiv (HLA)
FRep 240 Zeitgeschichtliche Sammlung
FRep 260 Plakatsammlung

Staatsarchiv Freiburg im Breisgau
317 Landeskommissär Konstanz
1257 Die politische Lage

Staatsarchiv Hamburg (StAH)
Senat
131-10[1] Personalabteilung

Stadtarchiv Konstanz
SII Stadt Konstanz

Stadtarchiv Mannheim
S2 Ortsgeschichte

Zentrales Staatsarchiv Potsdam (ZStA)
Auswärtiges Amt
Deutschnationale Volkspartei (60 Vo 2)
Reichsarbeitsministerium
Reichskommissar für die Überwachung der öffentlichen Ordnung (St. 12)
Reichsministerium des Innern
Reichstag

Published sources

Official publications

Badisches Statistisches Landesamt, *Über die deutschen Nationalversammlungswahlen in Baden, die badischen Gemeinde-, Bezirksrats- und Kreisabgeordnetenwahl und das Frauenwahlrecht* (Karlsruhe: C. F. Müller, 1921)
Badisches Statistisches Landesamt, *Statistisches Jahrbuch für das Land Baden 1925* (Karlsruhe: Macklot, 1925)
Badisches Statistisches Landesamt, *Jahresbericht des Gewerbeaufsichts für das Jahr 1930* (Karlsruhe: Macklot'sche Druckerei, 1931)
Badisches Statistisches Landesamt, *Berichte des Gewerbeaufsichtamtes für die Jahre 1933 und 1934* (Karlsruhe: Macklot, 1935)
Das gesamte deutsche und preussische Gesetzgebungsmaterial (Berlin: Verlag des Gesetzsammlungsamts, 1927)
Handbuch der verfassungsgebenden deutschen Nationalversammlung (Berlin: Carl Heymanns Verlag, 1919)
Reichsgesetzblatt
Reichstags-Handbuch. I.–VIII. Wahlperiode (Berlin: Karl Heymanns Verlag, 1919; J. Sitten Feld, 1920; Verlag der Reichsdruckerei, 1924–33)
Statistisches Reichsamt, *Statistik des Deutschen Reiches* (Berlin)
Statistisches Reichsamt, *Statistisches Jahrbuch für das Deutsche Reich* (Berlin)
Stenographische Berichte über die Verhandlungen des Reichstages (Berlin)

Newspapers, magazines and periodicals
Archiv für Bevölkerungspolitik
Die Bayerische Frau
Die christliche Frau
Evangelische Frauenzeitung
Die Frau
Die Frauenfrage
Die Frau im Staat
Die Genossin
Die Gleichheit
Freiburger Zeitung
General-Anzeiger (Mannheim)
Gewerkschaftliche Frauenzeitung
Heidelberger Tagblatt
Jahrbuch für Frauenarbeit
Jus suffragii
Karlsruher Zeitung
Nachrichtenblatt des Bundes deutscher Frauenvereine
Sozialistische Monatshefte
Unter dem Reichsadler
Zeitschrift des bayerischen statistischen Landesamtes

Secondary sources

Contemporary published sources

Adler, H., 'Die Gesunderhaltung der Industriearbeiterin in Beruf', *Die Frau*, 33:4 (January 1926), 203–12

Allgemeiner Deutscher Gewerkschaftbund, *Jahrbuch des Allgemeinen Deutschen Gewerkschaftsbundes 1927* (Berlin: Verlagsanstalt des Allgemeinen Deutschen Gewerkschaftsbundes, 1928)

Allgemeiner Deutscher Gewerkschaftbund, *Jahrbuch des Allgemeinen Deutschen Gewerkschaftsbundes 1928* (Berlin: Verlagsanstalt des Allgemeinen Deutschen Gewerkschaftsbundes, 1929)

Allgemeiner Deutscher Gewerkschaftbund, *Jahrbuch des Allgemeinen Deutschen Gewerkschaftsbundes 1930* (Berlin: Verlagsanstalt des Allgemeinen Deutschen Gewerkschaftsbundes, 1931)

Allgemeiner Deutscher Lehrerinnenverein, *Leitende Stellen im Mädchenschulwesen* (Hamburg: Blöß, 1926)

Allgemeiner Deutscher Lehrerinnenverein, *Verhandlungen der XX. Generalversammlung des ADLV in Wien 19.–22. Mai 1929* (Berlin, 1929)

Altmann-Gottheiner, E. (ed.), *Kriegsjahrbuch des Bundes Deutscher Frauenvereine 1915* (Leipzig and Berlin: Teubner, 1915)

Altmann-Gottheimer, E. (ed.), *Jahrbuch des Bundes Deutscher Frauenvereine 1920* (Berlin: Teubner, 1920)
Arbeitgeberverband der Deutschen Textilindustrie, *Die Frauenerwerbsarbeit in der Textilindustrie mit besonderer Berücksichtigung schwangerer Frauen* (Berlin: Elsner, 1926)
Bäumer, G., 'Heimatchronik', *Die Frau*, 21:12 (September 1914), 748–53
Bäumer, G., *Die Frau im neuen Lebensraum* (Berlin: Herbig, 1931)
Bäumer, G., *Die Frau im deutschen Staat* (Berlin: Junker und Dünnhaupt, 1932)
Bäumer, G., 'Krisis des Frauenstudiums', *Die Frau*, 39:6 (March 1932), 322–7, and 39:10 (July 1932), 611–19
Bäumer, G., *Lebensweg durch eine Zeitwende* (Tübingen: Rainer Wunderlich Verlag, 1933)
Bäumer, G., *Des Lebens wie der Liebe Band: Briefe*, ed. E. Beckmann (Tübingen: Wunderlich, 1956)
Barck, L., *Ziele und Aufgaben der weiblichen Polizei in Deutschland* (Berlin: Deutscher Polizei-Verlag, 1928)
Beyer, H., *Die Frau in der politischen Entscheidung* (Stuttgart: Enke, 1933)
Blos, A. (ed.), *Die Frauenfrage im Lichte des Sozialismus* (Dresden: Kadan, 1930)
Blücher, Evelyn, Princess, *An English Wife in Berlin* (New York: E. P. Dutton & Company, 1920)
Burgdörfer, F., *Der Geburtenrückgang und seine Bekämpfung: Die Lebensfrage des deutschen Volkes* (Berlin: Schoetz, 1929)
Burgdörfer, F., *Zurück zum Agrar-Staat? Stadt und Land in volksbiologischer Betrachtung* (Berlin: Kurt Vowinckel, 1933)
Cooper, C. E., *Behind the Lines: One Woman's War 1914–18*, ed. D. Denholm (Sydney: Collins, 1982)
Deutsch, R., *Die politische Tat der Frau* (Gotha: Perthes, 1920)
Deutsch, R., *Zwei Jahre parlamentarischer Frauenarbeit* (Gotha: Perthes, 1923)
Deutsch, R., *Parlamentarische Frauenarbeit II: Aus den Reichstagen von 1924–1928* (Berlin: Herbig, 1928)
Deutscher Metallarbeiterverband, *Die Frauenarbeit in der Metallindustrie* (Stuttgart: Deutscher Metallarbeiterverband, 1930)
Deutscher Textilarbeiterverband, *Umfang der Frauenarbeit in der deutschen Textilindustrie* (Berlin: Verlag Deutscher Textilarbeiterverband, 1923)
Deutscher Textilarbeiterverband, *Erwerbsarbeit, Schwangerschaft, Frauenleid* (Berlin: Verlag Deutscher Textilarbeiterverband, 1925)
Deutscher Textilarbeiterverband (ed.), *Mein Arbeitstag – mein Wochenende* (Berlin: Textilpraxis, 1928)
Diehl, G., *Was wir wollen: Frage und Antwort über den Neulandbund* (Eisenach: Neulandverlag, 1918)

Frauenliga für Frieden und Freiheit (Deutsches Zweig), *Völkerversöhnende Frauenarbeit* (Munich: Heller, 1920)
Frick, W., *Die Nationalsozialisten im Reichstag 1924–1931* (Munich: Eher, 1932)
Fuss, H., 'Unemployment and Employment among Women', *International Labour Review*, 31 (1935), 463–97
Gaebel, K., 'Die Berufslage der Akademikerinnen', *Die Frau*, 34:4 (January 1927), 218–24, and 34:5 (February 1927), 238–82
Gaebel, K., *Die deutsche Wirtschaft und das Berufsschicksal der Frau* (Berlin: Bund Deutscher Frauenvereine, 1932)
Gerard, J. W., *My Four Years in Germany* (London: Hodder and Stoughton, 1917)
Gewerkschaftsbund der Angestellten, *Die wirtschaftliche und soziale Lage der Angestellten* (Berlin: Sieben-Stäbe-Verlag, 1931)
Glass, F., and D. Kische, *Die wirtschaftlichen und sozialen Verhältnisse der berufstätigen Frauen* (Berlin: Heymann, 1930)
Goetz, K., 'Die Ehescheidungen im Deutschen Reich', *Die Frau*, 35:2 (November 1927), 94–7
Goldschmidt, H., 'The Application in Germany of the Washington Convention concerning the Employment of Women before and after Childbirth', *International Labour Review*, 16 (1927), 637–47
Grünfeld, J., 'Das Lohnproblem der Arbeiterin', *Die Arbeit*, 6 (1929), 445–53
Grünfeld, J., 'Frauenarbeit im Lichte der Rationalisierung', *Die Arbeit*, 8 (1931), 911–24
Grünfeld, J., 'Rationalisation and the Employment and Wages of Women in Germany', *International Labour Review*, 29 (1934), 605–32
Hanna, G., 'Women in the German Trade Union Movement', *International Labour Review*, 8 (1923), 21–37
Hartwig, Dr, 'Wie die Frauen im Deutschen Reich von ihrem politischen Wahlrecht Gebrauch machen', *Allgemeines statistisches Archiv*, 17 (1928), 497–512
Hartwig, Dr, 'Das Frauenwahlrecht in der Statistik', *Allgemeines statistisches Archiv*, 21 (1931), 167–82
Hellersberg, M., *Die soziale Not der weiblichen Angestellten* (Berlin: Sieben-Stäbe-Verlag, 1928)
Hermann, E., 'This is the New Woman', in A. Kaes, M. Jay and E. Dimendberg (eds), *The Weimar Republic Sourcebook* (Berkeley: University of California Press, 1994), pp. 206–7
Hoffmann, E., *Die Gemeindewahlen in Mannheim 1911–1930* (Mannheim: Gengenbach & Hahn, 1932)
Jahrbuch der deutschen Sozialdemokratie (Berlin: J. H. W. Dietz, 1930)
Jellinek, C., *Frauen unter deutschem Recht* (Mannheim: Bensheimer, 1928)

Jende-Radomski, H., *Frauenberufe* (Dessau: Dünnhaupt, 1926)
Karbe, A., *Die Frauenlohnfrage und ihre Entwicklung in der Kriegs- und Nachkriegszeit* (Rostock: C. Hinstorffs, 1928)
Kempf, R., *Die deutsche Frau nach der Volks-, Berufs- und Betriebszählung von 1925* (Mannheim: Bennsheimer Verlag, 1931)
Kempf, R., 'Die Stellung der Frau in der deutschen Landwirtschaft', in A. Schmidt-Beil (ed.), *Die Kultur der Frau* (Berlin: Verlag für Kultur und Wissenschaft, 1931), pp. 98–11
Kern, K., *Frauen, entscheidet Euch!* (Berlin: J. H. W. Dietz, 1931)
König, J. K., *Seid fruchtbar und mehret Euch!* (Berlin: Verlagsanstalt der Proletarischen Freidenker, 1931)
Kropff, H., 'Women as Shoppers', in A. Kaes, M. Jay and E. Dimendberg (eds), *The Weimar Republic Sourcebook* (Berkeley: University of California Press, 1994), pp. 660–2
Kuhr, P., *There We'll Meet Again: The First World War Diary of a Young German Girl*, trans. W. Wright (Gloucester: Walter Wright, 1998)
Kuntze, L., 'The Extension of German Women's Work in War Time', *Jus suffragii*, 11:4 (1 February 1917), 66–7
Lange, H., *Die Frauenbewegung in ihren gegenwärtigen Problemen* (Leipzig: Quelle & Meyer, 3rd edn, 1924)
Lange, H., *Was ich hier geliebt: Briefe von Helene Lange*, ed. E. Beckmann (Tübingen: Wunderlich, 1957)
Lorenz, C., 'Die gewerbliche Frauenarbeit während des Krieges', in J. T. Shotwell (ed.), *Der Krieg und die Arbeitsverhältnisse* (Stuttgart: Deutsche Verlagsanstalt, 1928), pp. 311–91
Lüders, E., 'The Effects of German Labour Legislation on Employment Possibilities for Women', *International Labour Review*, 20 (1929), 385–96
Lüders, M.-E., 'Die Entwicklung der gewerblichen Frauenarbeit im Kriege', *Schmollers Jahrbuch für Gesetzgebung, Verwaltung und Volkswirtschaft im Deutschen Reiche*, 44 (1920), 241–75 and 569–93
Magnus-Hausen, F., *Zehn Jahre deutsche Staatsbürgerin* (Berlin: Herbig, 1930)
Meerwarth, R., A., Günther and W. Zimmermann, *Die Einwirkung des Krieges auf Bevölkerungsbewegung, Einkommen und Lebenshaltung in Deutschland* (Stuttgart: Deutsche Verlagsanstalt, 1932)
Meusel, M., *Lebensverhältnisse lediger Mütter auf dem Lande* (Berlin: Müller, 1933)
Munk, M., *Vorschläge zur Umgestaltung des Rechts der Ehescheidung und der elterlichen Gewalt nebst Gesetzentwurf* (Berlin: Herbig, 1923)
Munk, M., *Recht und Rechtsverfolgung im Familienrecht* (Berlin: Liebmann, 1929)
Nationaler Frauendienst, *Der Nationale Frauendienst in Berlin, 1914–17* (Berlin: Vaterländische Verlags- und Kunstanstalt, 1917)

Opet, O., and W. von Blume (eds), *Das Familienrecht des Bürgerlichen Gesetzbuches* (Berlin: Heymann, 1906)

Ostwald, H., *Sittengeschichte der Inflation* (Berlin: Neufeld & Henius, 1931)

Pius XI (Papa), *Rundschreiben über die gesellschaftliche Ordnung* (Freiburg im Breisgau: Herder, 1931)

Protokoll über die Verhandlungen des Parteitages der Sozialdemokratischen Partei Deutschlands abgehalten in Weimar vom 10. bis 15. Juni 1919 (Berlin: Buchhaltung Vorwärts Paul Singer, 1919)

Rabe, S., *Die Frau im nationalsozialistischen Staate* (Munich: Münchener Druck- und Verlagshaus, 1932)

Reichsorganisationsleiter der NSDAP (ed.), *NSDAP Partei-Statistik* (Munich: Zentralverlag der NSDAP, 1935)

Rühle-Gerstel, A., *Das Frauenproblem der Gegenwart: Eine psychologische Bilanz* (Leipzig: Verlag von S. Hirzel, 1932)

Salomon, A., 'Women's Hopes for the New Order', *Jus suffragii*, 13:5 (February 1919), 62

Schmidt-Beil, A. (ed.), *Die Kultur der Frau* (Berlin: Verlag für Kultur und Wissenschaft, 1931)

Silberkühl-Schulte, M., 'Die Landfrauenfrage', *Die Frau*, 40:6 (March 1933), 361–5

Sozialdemokratische Partei Deutschlands, *Reichstag und Frauenrechte* (Weimar: Verlag SPD Bezirksverband Grossthüringen, 1924)

Sozialdemokratischer Parteitag 1924 (Berlin: J. H. W. Dietz, 1924)

Sozialdemokratischer Parteitag 1925 in Heidelberg (Berlin: J. H. W. Dietz, 1925)

Sozialdemokratischer Parteitag 1927 in Kiel (Berlin: J. H. W. Dietz, 1927)

Strasser, I., *Frauenarbeit und Rationalisierung* (Berlin: Verlag der Roten Gewerkschafts-Internationale, 1927)

Stritt, M., 'German Women have Got the Vote', *Jus suffragii*, 13:4 (January 1919), 44–6

Stritt, M., 'Germany', *Jus suffragii*, 13:6 (March 1919), 76

Süersen, E., *Die Frau im Deutschen Reichs- und Landesstaatsdienst* (Mannheim: Bensheimer, 1920)

Suhr, S., *Die weiblichen Angestellten* (Berlin: Zentralverband der Angestellten, 1930)

Sveistrup, H., and A. von Zahn-Harnack (eds), *Die Frauenfrage in Deutschland: Strömungen und Gegenströmungen, 1790–1930* (Magdeburg: Burg, 1934)

Thibert, M., 'The Economic Depression and the Employment of Women', *International Labour Review*, 27 (April 1933), 443–70, and 27 (May 1933), 620–30

Verein Katholischer Deutscher Lehrerinnen, *Statistische Erhebungen über*

die wirtschaftlichen Verhältnisse der Lehrerinnen (Paderborn: Ferdinand Schöningh, 1928)
Verhandlungen der verfassungsgebenden Deutschen Nationalversammlung, vol. 329 (Berlin: Druck und Verlag der Nordeutschen Buchdruckerei und Verlags-Anstalt, 1920)
Verhandlungen der verfassungsgebenden Deutschen Nationalversammlung, vol. 338 (Berlin: Julius Sittenfeld, 1920)
Weiss, M. (ed.), *Politisches Handwörterbuch (Führer ABC)* (Berlin: Deutschnationale Schriftenvertriebsstelle, 1928)
Wex, E., *Staatsbürgerliche Arbeit deutscher Frauen 1865 bis 1928* (Berlin: Herbig, 1929)
Wolff, E. (ed.), *Jahrbuch des Bundes Deutscher Frauenvereine 1927–28* (Mannheim: J. Bensheimer, 1929)
Wolff, E. (ed.), *Jahrbuch des Bundes Deutscher Frauenvereine 1932* (Berlin and Leipzig: Bensheimer, 1932)
Wurm, M., *Die Frauenerwerbsarbeit: Rede auf der Leipziger Frauenkonferenz am 29. November 1919* (Berlin: 'Freiheit', 1920)
Zentrale der KPD, *Referentenmaterial: Mutter und Kind in Deutschland und Russland* (Berlin: Zentrale der KPD, 1926)

Books and articles

Abrams, L., 'From Control to Commercialisation: The Triumph of Mass Entertainment in Germany, 1900-25?', *German History*, 8:3 (1990), 278–93
Albisetti, J., *Schooling German Girls and Women* (Princeton: Princeton University Press, 1988)
Allen, A. T., *Feminism and Motherhood in Germany 1800–1914* (New Brunswick: Rutgers University Press, 1991)
Allen, A. T., 'Feminism, Venereal Diseases, and the State in Germany', *Journal of the History of Sexuality*, 4:1 (1993), 27–50
Allen, A. T., 'Feminism and Eugenics in Germany and Britain, 1900–1940: A Comparative Perspective', *German Studies Review*, 23:3 (2000), 477–505
Allen, A. T., *Feminism and Motherhood in Western Europe, 1890–1970* (Basingstoke: Palgrave Macmillan, 2005)
Allen, K., 'Sharing Scarcity: Bread Rationing and the First World War in Berlin, 1914–1923', *Journal of Social History*, 32:2 (1998), 371–93
Allen, K., 'Food and the German Home Front: Evidence from Berlin', in G. Braybon (ed.), *Evidence, History, and the Great War: Historians and the Impact of 1914–18* (Oxford: Berghahn, 2003), pp. 172–97
Altenhoner, F., 'Das "Heimatheer deutscher Frauen": Propaganda durch bürgerliche Frauen in Berlin 1918 zwischen Aufklärung und Denunziation', *Ariadne*, 47 (May 2005), 38–43

Ankum, K. von, 'Gendered Urban Spaces in Irmgard Keun's *Das kunstseidene Mädchen*', in K. von Ankum (ed.), *Women in the Metropolis: Gender and Modernity in Weimar Culture* (Berkeley: University of California Press, 1997), pp. 162–84

Ankum, K. von (ed.), *Women in the Metropolis: Gender and Modernity in Weimar Culture* (Berkeley: University of California Press, 1997)

Arendt, H.-J., 'Das Schutzprogramm der KPD für die arbeitende Frau vom 15. Oktober 1931', *Beiträge zur Geschichte der Arbeiterbewegung*, 11:2 (1969), 291–311

Arendt, H.-J., 'Weibliche Mitglieder der KPD in der Weimarer Republik – zahlenmässige Stärke und soziale Stellung', *Beiträge zur Geschichte der Arbeiterbewegung*, 19 (1977), 652–60

Arendt, H.-J., 'Die "Gleichschaltung" der bürgerlichen Frauenorganisationen in Deutschland 1933/34', *Zeitschrift für Geschichtswissenschaft*, 27 (1979), 615–27

Arendt, H.-J., 'Weibliche Opfer militäristischen Terrors in Deutschland (1918–1920)', *Beiträge zur Geschichte der Arbeiterbewegung*, 26:2 (1984), 228–37

Arendt, H.-J., and W. Freigang, 'Der Rote Frauen- und Mädchenbund – die revolutionäre deutsche Frauenorganisation in der Weimarer Republik', *Beiträge zur Geschichte der Arbeiterbewegung*, 21 (1979), 249–58

Arendt, H.-J., S. Hering and L. Wagner (eds), *Nationalsozialistische Frauenpolitik vor 1933* (Frankfurt am Main: Dipa Verlag, 1995)

Arendt, H.-J., J. Kirchner, J. Müller, E. Schotte and F. Staude (eds), *Dokumente der revolutionären deutschen Frauenbewegung zur Frauenfrage, 1848–1974* (Leipzig: Verlag für die Frau, 1975)

Bajohr, S., *Die Hälfte der Fabrik: Geschichte der Frauenarbeit in Deutschland 1914 bis 1945* (Marburg: Verlag Arbeiterbewegung und Gesellschaftswissenschaft, 1979)

Bajohr, S., 'Sexualaufklärung im proletarischen Milieu, Geschlechtskrankheiten und staatliche Eheberatung 1900 bis 1933', in P. Pasteur, N. Niederacher and M. Mesner (eds), *Sexualität, Unterschichtenmilieus und ArbeiterInnenbewegung* (Leipzig: Akademische Verlagsanstalt, 2003), pp. 59–69

Bajohr, S., and K. Rödiger-Bajohr, 'Die Diskriminierung der Juristin in Deutschland bis 1945', *Kritische Justiz*, 13:1 (1980), 39–51

Baranowski, S., *Strength through Joy: Consumerism and Mass Tourism in the Third Reich* (Cambridge: Cambridge University Press, 2004)

Barndt, K., 'Aesthetics of Crisis: Motherhood, Abortion, and Melodrama in Irmgard Keun and Friedrich Wolf', *Women in German Yearbook: Feminist Studies in German Literature and Culture*, 24 (2008), 71–95

Barndt, K., 'Mothers, Citizens, and Consumers: Female Readers in Weimar Germany', in K. Canning, K. Barndt and K. McGuire (eds), *Weimar*

Publics / Weimar Subjects: Rethinking the Political Culture of Germany in the 1920s (Oxford: Berghahn, 2010), pp. 95–115

Baum, M., *Rückblick auf mein Leben* (Heidelberg: Kerle, 1950)

Baumann, U., 'Religion, Emancipation, and Politics in the Confessional Women's Movement in Germany, 1900–1933', in B. Melman (ed.), *Borderlines: Genders and Identities in War and Peace, 1870–1930* (London: Routledge, 1998), pp. 285–306

Benker, G., *Studentinnen in der Weimarer Republik* (Pfaffenweiler: Centaurus-Verlag, 1990)

Benninghaus, C., *Die anderen Jugendlichen: Arbeitermädchen in der Weimarer Republik* (Frankfurt: Campus, 1994)

Benninghaus, C., 'Mothers' Toil and Daughters' Leisure: Working-Class Girls and Time in 1920s' Germany', *History Workshop Journal*, 50 (2000), 45–72

Berghaus, G., 'Girlkultur – Feminism, Americanism, and Popular Entertainment in Weimar Germany', *Journal of Design History*, 1:3–4 (1988), 193–219

Bergmann, C., *What Will Become of the Children?*, trans. R. Bodek (Rochester: Camden House, 2010)

Berliner Geschichtswerkstatt e.V. (ed.), *August 1914: Ein Volk zieht in den Krieg* (Berlin: Nishen, 1989)

Berntson, M. A., and B. Ault, 'Gender and Nazism: Women Joiners of the Pre-1933 Nazi Party', *American Behavioral Scientist*, 41 (1998), 1193–1218

Bessel, R., '"Eine nicht allzu grosse Beunruhigung des Arbeitsmarktes": Frauenarbeit und Demobilmachung in Deutschland nach dem Ersten Weltkrieg', *Geschichte und Gesellschaft*, 9 (1983), 211–29

Bessel, R., *Germany after the First World War* (Oxford: Clarendon Press, 1993)

Bessel, R., 'Mobilizing German Society for War', in R. Chickering and S. Förster (eds), *Great War, Total War: Combat and Mobilization on the Western Front, 1914–1918* (Cambridge: Cambridge University Press, 2000), pp. 437–51

Bessel, R., 'Unemployment and Demobilisation in Germany after the First World War', in R. J. Evans and D. Geary (eds), *The German Unemployed: Experiences and Consequences of Mass Unemployment from the Weimar Republic to the Third Reich* (London: Croom Helm, 1987), pp. 23–43

Birkett, J., and E. Harvey (eds), *Determined Women: Studies in the Construction of the Female Subject, 1900–1990* (London: Macmillan, 1991)

Blackbourn, D., and G. Eley, *The Peculiarities of German History: Bourgeois Society and Politics in Nineteenth-Century Germany* (Oxford: Oxford University Press, 1984)

Blasius, D., *Ehescheidung in Deutschland 1794–1945* (Göttingen: Vandenhoeck & Ruprecht, 1987)
Blom, I., K. Hagemann and C. Hall (eds), *Gendered Nations: Nationalisms and Gender Order in the Long Nineteenth Century* (Oxford: Berg, 2000)
Boak, H. L., '"Our last hope": Women's Votes for Hitler – A Reappraisal', *German Studies Review*, 12:2 (May 1989), 289–310
Boak, H., 'The State as an Employer of Women in the Weimar Republic', in W. R. Lee and E. Rosenhaft (eds), *The State and Social Change in Germany, 1880–1980* (London: Berg, 1990), pp. 61–98
Boak, H., 'Women in Weimar Politics', *European History Quarterly*, 20:3 (1990), 369–99
Boak, H., 'National Socialism and Working-Class Women before 1933', in C. Fischer (ed.), *The Rise of National Socialism and the Working Classes in Weimar Germany* (Oxford: Berghahn, 1996), pp. 163–88
Boak, H., 'Mobilising Women for Hitler: The Female Nazi Voter', in A. McElligott and T. Kirk (eds), *Working towards the Führer* (Manchester: Manchester University Press, 2003), pp. 68–92
Boedeker, E., *25 Jahre Frauenstudium in Deutschland*, vol. 1 (Hanover: C. Trute, 1939)
Bölke, C., *Die Wandlung der Frauenemanzipationsbewegung von Marx bis zur Rätebewegung* (Hamburg: Verlag Association, 1975)
Bonzon, T., and B. Davis, 'Feeding the Cities', in J. Winter and J.-L. Robert (eds), *Capital Cities at War: Paris, London, Berlin 1914–1919* (Cambridge: Cambridge University Press, 1997), pp. 305–41
Boxer, M. J., and J. H. Quataert (eds), *Connecting Spheres: Women in the Western World, 1500 to the Present* (Oxford: Oxford University Press, 1987)
Brand, M. B. von, *Die Frau in der deutschen Landwirtschaft* (Berlin: F. Vahlen, 1939)
Bremme, G., *Die politische Rolle der Frau in Deutschland* (Göttingen: Vandenhoeck & Ruprecht, 1956)
Bridenthal, R., 'Beyond *Kinder, Küche, Kirche*: Weimar Women at Work', *Central European History*, 6:2 (1973), 148–66
Bridenthal, R., 'Class Struggle around the Hearth: Women and Domestic Service in the Weimar Republic', in M. Dobkowski and I. Wallimann (eds), *Towards the Holocaust: The Social and Economic Collapse of the Weimar Republic* (Westport: Greenwood, 1983), pp. 243–64
Bridenthal, R., and C. Koonz, 'Beyond *Kinder, Küche, Kirche*: Weimar Women in Politics and Work', in B. A. Carroll (ed.), *Liberating Women's History* (Chicago: University of Illinois Press, 1976), pp. 301–29
Bridenthal, R., A. Grossmann and M. Kaplan (eds), *When Biology became Destiny: Women in Weimar and Nazi Germany* (New York: Monthly Review Press, 1984)

Brockmann, S., 'Weimar Sexual Cynicism', in T. W. Kniesche and
S. Brockmann (eds), *Dancing on the Volcano: Essays on the Culture of
the Weimar Republic* (Columbia: Camden House, 1994), pp. 165–80
Brocks, C., *Die bunte Welt des Krieges: Bildpostkarten aus dem Ersten
Weltkrieg* (Essen: Klartext, 2008)
Bry, G., *Wages in Germany, 1871–1945* (Princeton: Princeton University
Press, 1960)
Buerkle, D., 'Gendered Spectatorship, Jewish Women and Psychological
Advertising in Weimar Germany', *Women's History Review*, 15:4
(2006), 625–36
Bussemer, H.-U. '"Weit hinter den Schützengräben". Das Kriegserlebnis
der bürgerlichen Frauenbewegung', in Berliner Geschichtswerkstatt e. V.
(ed.), *August 1914: Ein Volk zieht in den Krieg* (Berlin: Nishen, 1989),
pp. 136–46
Büttner, U., *Weimar: Die überforderte Republik 1918–1933* (Stuttgart:
Klett-Cotta, 2008)
Canning, K., *Gender History in Practice: Historical Perspectives on Bodies,
Class and Citizenship* (Ithaca, NY: Cornell University Press, 2006)
Canning, K., 'Sexual Crisis and the Writing of Citizenship: Reflections on
States of Exception in Germany, 1914–1920', in A. Lüdtke and M. Wildt
(eds), *Ausnhamezustand und Polizeigewalt* (Göttingen: Wallstein Verlag,
2008), pp. 168–211
Canning, K., 'Women and the Politics of Gender', in A. McElligott (ed.),
Weimar Germany (Oxford: Oxford University Press, 2009), pp. 146–74
Canning, K., 'Das Geschlecht der Revolution – Stimmrecht und
Staatsbürgertum 1918/19', in A. Gallus (ed.), *Die vergessene Revolution
von 1918/19* (Göttingen: Vandenhoeck & Ruprecht, 2010), 84–116
Canning, K., K. Barndt and K. McGuire (eds), *Weimar Publics / Weimar
Subjects: Rethinking the Political Culture of Germany in the 1920s*
(Oxford: Berghahn, 2010)
Caplan, J., 'The Imaginary Universality of Particular Interests: The
"Tradition" of the Civil Service in German History', *Social History*, 4
(1979), 299–317
Caplan, J., *Government without Administration: State and Civil Service
in Weimar and Nazi Germany* (Oxford: Oxford University Press, 1988)
Carr, G. J., '"The Body Economic" in Contemporary Critiques of First
World War Propaganda', *Forum for Modern Language Studies*, 34:4
(1998), 366–79
Chickering, R., *Imperial Germany and the Great War, 1914–1918*
(Cambridge: Cambridge University Press, 1998)
Chickering, R., *The Great War and Urban Life in Germany: Freiburg,
1914–1918* (Cambridge: Cambridge University Press, 2007)
Chickering, R., and S. Förster (eds) *Great War, Total War: Combat and*

Mobilization on the Western Front, 1914–1918 (Cambridge: Cambridge University Press, 2000)

Childers, T., 'The Social Language of Politics in Germany: The Sociology of Political Discourse in the Weimar Republic', *American Historical Review*, 95:2 (1990), 331–58

Clemens, B., *'Menschenrechte haben kein Geschlecht!' Zum Politikverständnis der bürgerlichen Frauenbewegung* (Pfaffenweiler: Centaurus, 1988)

Crew, D. F., 'German Socialism, the State and Family Policy 1918–1933', *Continuity and Change*, 1 (1986), 235–62

Crew, D. F., *Germans on Welfare: From Weimar to Hitler* (Oxford: Oxford University Press, 1998)

Cullity, J. P., 'The Growth of Governmental Employment in Germany 1882–1950', *Zeitschrift für die gesamte Staatswissenschaft*, 123 (1967), 210–17

Czarnowski, G., 'Women's Crimes, State Crimes: Abortion in Nazi Germany', in M. L. Arnot and C. Usborne (eds), *Gender and Crime in Modern Europe* (London: Routledge, 1999), pp. 238–56

Daniel, U., 'Fiktionen, Friktionen und Fakten – Frauenlohnarbeit im Ersten Weltkrieg', in G. Mai (ed.), *Arbeiterschaft 1914–1918 in Deutschland* (Düsseldorf: Droste, 1985), 277–323

Daniel, U., 'The Politics of Rationing versus the Politics of Subsistence: Working-Class Women in Germany, 1914–1918', in R. Fletcher (ed.), *Bernstein to Brandt: A Short History of German Social Democracy* (London: Edward Arnold, 1987), pp. 89–95

Daniel, U., 'Women's Work in Industry and Family: Germany, 1914–18', in R. Wall and J. Winter (eds), *The Upheaval of War: Family, Work and Welfare in Europe, 1914–1918* (Cambridge: Cambridge University Press, 1988), pp. 267–96

Daniel, U., *The War from Within: German Working-Class Women in the First World War*, trans. Margaret Ries (Oxford and New York: Berg, 1997)

Davis, B., 'Food Scarcity and the Empowerment of the Female Consumer in World War 1 Berlin', in V. De Grazia and E. Furlough (eds), *The Sex of Things: Gender and Consumption in Historical Perspective* (Berkeley: University of California Press, 1996), pp. 287–310

Davis, B., *Home Fires Burning: Food, Politics, and Everyday Life in World War 1 Berlin* (Chapel Hill and London: University of North Carolina Press, 2000)

Davis, B., 'Homefront: Food, Politics and Women's Everyday Life during the First World War', in K. Hagemann and S. Schüler-Springorum (eds), *Home/Front The Military, War and Gender in Twentieth-Century Germany* (Oxford and New York: Berg, 2002), pp. 115–37

Demm, E., 'German Teachers at War', in H. Cecil and P. Liddle (eds), *Facing Armageddon: The First World War Experienced* (London: Pen & Sword Books Ltd, 1996), pp. 709–18

Dickinson, E. R., 'Biopolitics, Fascism, Democracy: Some Reflections on our Discourse about "Modernity"', *Central European History*, 37:1 (2004), 1–48

Dickinson, E. R., 'Policing Sex in Germany, 1882–1982: A Preliminary Statistical Analysis', *Journal of the History of Sexuality*, 16:2 (2007), 204–50

Dobkowski, M. N., and I. Wallmann (eds), *Towards the Holocaust: The Social and Economic Collapse of the Weimar Republic* (London: Greenwood Press, 1983)

Doerner, J., 'Neun Jahrzehnte Frauenbeschäftigung bei der Postverwaltung', *Jahrbuch des Postwesens*, 7 (1956–57), 371–402

Dollard, C., 'Marital Status and the Rhetoric of the Women's Movement in World War 1 Germany', *Women in German Yearbook: Feminist Studies in German Literature and Culture*, 22 (2006), 211–35

Domansky, E., 'Militarization and Reproduction in World War 1 Germany', in G. Eley (ed.), *Society, Culture, and the State in Germany, 1870–1930* (Ann Arbor: University of Michigan Press, 1996), pp. 427–64

Douie, V., *The Professional Position of Women* (London: British Federation of Business and Professional Women, 1947)

Duffy, E., 'Oskar von Miller and the Art of the Electrical Exhibition: Staffing Modernity in Weimar Germany', *German History*, 25:4 (2007), 517–38

Dülffer, J., and G. Krumeich (eds), *Der verlorene Frieden: Politik und Kriegskultur nach 1918* (Essen: Klartext, 2002)

Dyer, R., 'Less and More than Women and Men: Lesbian and Gay Cinema in Weimar Germany', *New German Critique*, 50 (1990), 5–60

Eifert, C., 'Frauenarbeit im Krieg: Die Berliner "Heimatfront" 1914–1918', *Internationale wissenschaftliche Korrespondenz zur Geschichte der deutschen Arbeiterbewegung*, 21:3 (September 1985), 281–95

Eifert, C., 'Coming to Terms with the State: Maternalist Politics and the Development of the Welfare State in Weimar Germany', *Central European History*, 30:1 (1997), 25–47

Eisenberg, C., 'Massensport in der Weimarer Republik', *Archiv für Sozialgeschichte*, 33 (1993), 137–77

Eley, G. (ed.), *Society, Culture, and the State in Germany, 1870–1930* (Ann Arbor: University of Michigan Press, 1996)

Eley, G., and J. Palmowski (eds), *Citizenship and National Identity in Twentieth-Century Germany* (Stanford: Stanford University Press, 2008)

Espinaco-Virseda, A., '"I feel that I belong to you": Subculture, *Die*

Freundin and Lesbian Identities in Weimar Germany', *Spaces of Identity*, 4:1 (2004), 83–113
Evans, R. J., *The Feminist Movement in Germany, 1894–1933* (London: Sage, 1976)
Evans, R. J., 'German Women and the Triumph of Hitler', *Journal of Modern History*, 48:1 (1976), on-demand supplement, pp. 1–53
Evans, R. J., *The Feminists* (London: Croom Helm, 1977)
Evans, R. J., *Sozialdemokratie und Frauenemanzipation im deutschen Kaiserreich* (Berlin: J. H. W. Dietz, 1979)
Evans, R. J., *Comrades and Sisters: Feminism, Socialism and Pacifism in Europe 1870–1945* (Brighton: Wheatsheaf, 1987)
Evans, R. J., *Rituals of Retribution: Capital Punishment in Germany 1600–1987* (Oxford: Oxford University Press, 1996)
Evans, R. J. (ed.), *Society and Politics in Wilhelmine Germany* (London: Croom Helm, 1978)
Evans, R. J., and D. Geary (eds), *The German Unemployed: Experiences and Consequences of Mass Unemployment from the Weimar Republic to the Third Reich* (London: Croom Helm, 1987)
Falter, J., *Hitlers Wähler* (Munich: Beck, 1991)
Falter, J., 'The Social Bases of Political Cleavages in the Weimar Republic', in L. E. Jones and J. Retallack (eds), *Elections, Mass Politics, and Social Change in Modern Germany* (Cambridge: Cambridge University Press, 1992), pp. 371–98
Falter, J., T. Lindenberger and S. Schumann, *Wahlen und Abstimmungen in der Weimarer Republik: Materialien zum Wahlverhalten 1919–1933* (Munich: Beck, 1986)
Feldman, G. D., *The Great Disorder: Politics, Economics and Society in the German Inflation 1914–1924* (Oxford: Oxford University Press, 1993)
Feldman, G. D., *Army, Industry, and Labor in Germany 1914–1918* (Princeton: Princeton University Press, 1966)
Feldman, G. D., C.-L. Holtfrerich, G. A. Ritter and P.-C. Witt (eds), *Die Anpassung an die Inflation* (Berlin and New York: De Gruyter, 1986)
Fell, A. S., and I. Sharp (eds), *The Women's Movement in Wartime: International Perspectives, 1914–1919* (Basingstoke: Palgrave Macmillan, 2007)
Fletcher, R. (ed.), *Bernstein to Brandt: A Short History of German Social Democracy* (London: Edward Arnold, 1987)
Föllmer, M., 'Was Nazism Collectivistic? Redefining the Individual in Berlin, 1930–1945', *Journal of Modern History*, 82:1 (2010), 61–100
Föllmer, M., and R. Graf (eds), *Die 'Krise' der Weimarer Republik: Zur Kritik eines Deutungsmusters* (Frankfurt am Main: Campus 2005)
Förster, B., *Der Königin Luise-Mythos: Mediengeschichte des 'Idealbilds deutscher Weiblichkeit'* (Göttingen: Vandenhoeck & Ruprecht, 2011)

Forschungsgemeinschaft 'Geschichte des Kampfes der Arbeiterklasse um die Befreiung der Frau' (ed.), *Die Frau und die Gesellschaft* (Leipzig: Verlag für die Frau, 1974)

Frame, L., 'Gretchen, Girl, Garçonne? Weimar Science and Popular Culture in Search of the Ideal New Woman', in K. von Ankum (ed.), *Women in the Metropolis: Gender and Modernity in Weimar Culture* (Berkeley: University of California Press, 1997), pp. 12–40

François, A., 'From Street Walking to the Convent: Child Prostitution Cases Judged by the Juvenile Court of Brussels during World War One', in H. Jones, C. O'Brien and C. Schmidt-Supprian (eds), *Untold War: New Perspectives in First World War Studies* (Leiden and Boston: Brill, 2008), pp. 151–77

Franzoi, B., *At the Very Least She Pays the Rent: Women and German Industrialisation, 1871–1914* (London: Greenwood Press, 1985)

Frauengruppe Faschismusforschung (ed.), *Mutterkreuz und Arbeitsbuch: Zur Geschichte der Frauen in der Weimarer Republik und im Nationalsozialismus* (Frankfurt am Main: Fischer, 1988)

Freund-Widder, M., *Frauen unter Kontrolle: Prostitution und ihre staatliche Bekämpfung in Hamburg vom Ende des Kaiserreichs bis zu den Anfängen der Bundesrepublik* (Münster: Lit Verlag, 2003)

Frevert, U., 'Vom Klavier zur Schreibmaschine – weiblicher Arbeitsmarkt und Rollenzuweisungen am Beispiel der weiblichen Angestellten in der Weimarer Republik', in A. Kuhn and G. Schneider (eds), *Frauen in der Geschichte*, vol. 1 (Düsseldorf: Schwann, 1979), pp. 82–112

Frevert, U., 'Traditionale Weiblichkeit und moderne Interessenorganisation: Frauen im Angestelltenberuf 1918–1933', *Geschichte und Gesellschaft*, 7:3–4 (1981), 507–33

Frevert, U., 'Women Workers, Workers' Wives and Social Democracy in Imperial Germany', in R. Fletcher (ed.), *Bernstein to Brandt. A Short History of German Social Democracy* (London: Edward Arnold, 1987), pp. 34–44

Frevert, U., *Women in German History: From Bourgeois Emancipation to Sexual Liberation* (Oxford: Berg, 1989)

Frieden, S., R. W. McCormick, V. P. Petersen and L. M. Vogelsang (eds), *Gender and German Cinema: Feminist Interventions*, vol. 2: *German Film History: German History on Film* (Oxford: Berg, 1993)

Friedrich, O., *Beyond the Deluge: A Portrait of Berlin in the 1920s* (New York: Harper and Row, 1972)

Fritzsche, P., 'Did Weimar Fail?', *Journal of Modern History*, 68:3 (1996), 629–56

Fritzsche, P., *Germans into Nazis* (Cambridge, MA: Harvard University Press, 1998)

Fritzsche, P., 'The Economy of Experience in Weimar Germany', in

K. Canning, K. Barndt and K. McGuire (eds), *Weimar Publics / Weimar Subjects: Rethinking the Political Culture of Germany in the 1920s* (Oxford: Berghahn, 2010), pp. 360–82

Fritzen, F., '"Neuzeitlich Leben": Reformhausbewegung und Moderne, 1925–1933', in M. Föllmer and R. Graf (eds), *Die 'Krise' der Weimarer Republik: Zur Kritik eines Deutungsmusters* (Frankfurt: Campus Verlag, 2005), pp. 165–85

Frohman, L., 'Prevention, Welfare, and Citizenship: The War on Tuberculosis and Infant Mortality in Germany, 1900–1930', *Central European History*, 39:3 (2006), 431–81

Frohman, L., *Poor Relief and Welfare in Germany from the Reformation to World War 1* (Cambridge: Cambridge University Press, 2008)

Fromm, E., *The Working Class in Weimar Germany: A Psychological and Sociological Study* (London: Berg, 1984)

Frye, B. B., *Liberal Democrats in the Weimar Republic: The History of the German Democratic Party and the German State Party* (Carbondale: Southern Illinois University Press, 1985)

Führ, C., 'Schulpolitik im Spannungsfeld zwischen Reich und Ländern: Das Scheitern der Schulreform in der Weimarer Republik', *Aus Politik und Zeitgeschichte*, B 42 (1970), 3–31

Führer, K. C., 'Auf dem Weg zur "Massenkultur"? Kino und Rundfunk in der Weimarer Republik', *Historische Zeitschrift*, 262:3 (1996), 739–81

Führer, K. C., 'A Medium of Modernity? Broadcasting in Weimar Germany, 1923–32', *Journal of Modern History*, 69:4 (1997), 722–53

Führer, K., and C. Ross (eds), *Mass Media, Culture and Society in Twentieth- Century Germany* (Basingstoke: Palgrave Macmillan, 2006)

Fulda, B., 'Industries of Sensationalism: German Tabloids in Weimar Berlin', in in K. Führer and C. Ross (eds), *Mass Media, Culture and Society in Twentieth-Century Germany* (Basingstoke: Palgrave Macmillan, 2006), pp. 183–203

Funke, L. (ed.), *Die Liberalen: Frei sein, um andere frei zu machen* (Stuttgart: Seewald, 1984)

Funkenstein, S. L., 'A Man's Place in a Woman's World: Otto Dix, Social Dancing, and Constructions of Masculinity in Weimar Germany', *Women in German Yearbook: Feminist Studies in German Literature*, 21 (2005), 163–91

Gabriel, N., '"Nichts von diesem Kleinmut, nichts von dieser Angst": Feminismus, Internationalismus und Pazifismus bei Anita Augspurg und Lida Gustava Heymann', *Ariadne*, 24 (November 1993), 60–72

Ganeva, M., 'Fashion Photography and Women's Modernity in Weimar Germany: The Case of Yva', *NWSA Journal*, 15:3 (2003), 1–25

Ganeva, M., *Women in Weimar Fashion: Discourses and Displays in German Culture, 1918–1933* (Rochester: Camden House, 2008)

Gersdorff, U. von, *Frauen im Kriegsdienst, 1914–1945* (Stuttgart: Deutsche Verlagsanstalt, 1969)
Gersdorff, U. von, 'Frauenarbeit und Frauenemanzipation im ersten Weltkrieg', *Francia*, 2 (1974), 502–23
Gilbert, F., *A European Past: Memoirs, 1905–1945* (New York: W. W. Norton Company, 1988)
Glass, D. V., *Population Policies and Movements in Europe* (London: Frank Cass & Co. Ltd, 1967)
Goeschel, C., *Suicide in Nazi Germany* (Oxford: Oxford University Press, 2009)
Götze, D., 'Die organisatorische Vorbereitung für die Schaffung der kommunistischen Frauenbewegung 1919–1921', *Zeitschrift für Geschichtswissenschaft*, 23 (1975), 1165–76
Goodman, K., and R. H. Sanders (eds), *Proceedings of the Second Annual Women in German Symposium* (Oxford, OH: Miami University, 1977)
Graf, R., 'Anticipating the Future in the Present: "New Women" and Other Beings of the Future in Weimar Germany', *Central European History*, 42 (2009), 647–73
Graf, R., 'Either-Or: The narrative of "crisis" in Weimar Germany and its Historiography', *Central European History*, 43 (2010), 592–615
Grayzel, S. R., *Women and the First World War* (Harlow: Pearson, 2002)
Grayzel, S. R., 'The Enemy Within: The Problem of British Women's Sexuality during the First World War', in N. Dombrowski (ed.), *Women and War in the Twentieth Century* (New York: Garland, 1999), pp. 72–89
Grebing, H., *Frauen in der deutschen Revolution 1918/19* (Heidelberg: Stiftung Reichspräsident-Friedrich-Ebert-Gedenkstätte, 1994)
Greiling, W., 'Internationale Frauenliga für Frieden und Freiheit – Deutscher Zweig (IFFF-DZ) 1915–1933', in D. Fricke, W. Fritsch, H. Gottwald, S. Schmidt and M. Weißbecker (eds), *Lexikon zur Parteiengeschichte: Die bürgerlichen und kleinbürgerlichen Parteien und Verbände in Deutschland (1789–1945)*, vol. 3 (Leipzig: Bibliographisches Institut, 1985), pp. 128–37
Greven-Aschoff, B., *Die bürgerliche Frauenbewegung in Deutschland 1894–1933* (Göttingen: Vandenhoeck & Ruprecht, 1981)
Grossmann, A., 'Abortion and Economic Crisis: The 1931 Campaign against §218 in Germany', *New German Critique*, 14 (1978), 119–37
Grossmann, A., 'Crisis, Reaction, and Resistance: Women in Germany in the 1920s and 1930s', in A. Swerdlow and H. Lessinger (eds), *Class, Race, and Sex: The Dynamics of Control* (Boston: G. K. Hall & Co., 1983), pp. 60–74
Grossmann, A., '"Satisfaction is domestic happiness": Mass Working-Class Sex Reform Organisations in the Weimar Republic', in M. Dobkowski

and I. Wallimann (eds), *Towards the Holocaust: The Social and Economic Collapse of the Weimar Republic* (Westport: Greenwood, 1983), pp. 265–93

Grossmann, A., 'The New Woman and the Rationalization of Sexuality in Weimar Germany', in A. Snitow, C. Stansell and S. Thompson (eds), *Desire: The Politics of Sexuality* (London: Virago Press, 1984), pp. 190–208

Grossmann, A., '*Girlkultur* or Thoroughly Rationalised Female: A New Woman in Weimar Germany?', in J. Friedlander, B. W. Cook, A. Kessler-Harris and C. Smith-Rosenberg (eds), *Women in Culture and Politics: A Century of Change* (Bloomington: Indiana University Press, 1986), pp. 62–80

Grossmann, A., 'German Women Doctors from Berlin to New York: Maternity and Modernity in Weimar and in Exile', *Feminist Studies*, 19:1 (1993), 65–88

Grossmann, A., *Reforming Sex: The German Movement for Birth Control and Abortion Reform, 1920–1950* (Oxford: Oxford University Press, 1995)

Grossmann, A., 'German Communism and New Women: Dilemmas and Contradictions', in H. Gruber and P. Graves (eds), *Women and Socialism: Socialism and Women* (Oxford: Berghahn, 1998), pp. 133–68

Gruber, H., and P. Graves (eds), *Women and Socialism: Socialism and Women* (Oxford: Berghahn, 1998)

Guenther, I., *Nazi Chic? Fashioning Women in the Third Reich* (Oxford: Berg, 2004)

Guttsman, W. L., *Workers' Culture in Weimar Germany: Between Tradition and Commitment* (Oxford: Berg, 1990)

Habeth, S., 'Die Freiberuflerin und Beamtin (Ende 19. Jahrhundert bis 1945)', in H. Pohl and W. Treue (eds), *Die Frau in der deutschen Wirtschaft* (Wiesbaden: Franz Steiner Verlag, 1985), pp. 155–70

Hackett, A., 'The German Women's Movement and Suffrage, 1890–1914: A Study of National Feminism', in R. J. Bezucha (ed.), *Modern European Social History* (London: D. C. Heath & Co., 1972), pp. 356–86

Hagemann, K., '"Equal but not the same": The Social Democratic Women's Movement in the Weimar Republic', in R. Fletcher (ed.), *Bernstein to Brandt: A Short History of German Social Democracy* (London: Edward Arnold, 1987), pp. 133–43

Hagemann, K., *Frauenalltag und Männerpolitik: Alltagsleben und gesellschaftliches Handeln von Arbeiterfrauen in der Weimarer Republik* (Bonn: J. H. W. Dietz, 1990)

Hagemann, K., '"... wir werden alt vom Arbeiten": Die soziale Situation alternder Arbeiterfrauen in der Weimarer Republik am Beispiel Hamburgs', *Archiv für Sozialgeschichte*, 30 (1990), 247–95

Hagemann, K., 'Men's Demonstrations and Women's Protest: Gender in Collective Action in the Urban Working-Class Milieu in the Weimar Republic', *Gender and History*, 5 (1993), 101–19

Hagemann, K., 'Of "Old" and "New" Housewives: Everyday Housework and the Limits of Household Rationalisation in the Urban Working-Class Milieu of the Weimar Republic', *International Review of Social History*, 41:3 (1996), 305–30

Hagemann, K., 'Rationalizing Family Work: Municipal Family Welfare and Urban Working-Class Mothers in Germany', *Social Politics*, 4:1 (1997), 19–48

Hagemann, K., '"Jede Kraft wird gebraucht": Militäreinsatz von Frauen im Ersten und Zweiten Weltkrieg', in B. Thoss and H.-E. Volkmann (eds), *Erster Weltkrieg – Zweiter Weltkrieg: Ein Vergleich* (Paderborn: Schöningh, 2002), pp. 79–106

Hagemann, K., and J. Kolossa, *Gleiche Rechte – gleiche Pflichten?* (Hamburg, VSA-Verlag, 1990)

Hagemann, K. (ed.), *Eine Frauensache: Alltagsleben und Geburtenpolitik 1919–1933* (Pfaffenweiler: Centaurus, 1991)

Hagemann, K., and S. Schüler-Springorum (eds), *Home/Front: The Military, War and Gender in Twentieth-Century Germany* (Oxford and New York: Berg, 2002)

Hagenlücke, H., 'The Home Front in Germany', in J. Bourne, P. Liddle and I. Whitehead (eds), *The Great World War, 1914–1945: Who Won? Who Lost?* (London: HarperCollins, 2001), pp. 57–73

Hahn, C., 'Der öffentliche Dienst und die Frauen – Beamtinnen in der Weimarer Republik', in Frauengruppe Faschismusforschung (ed.), *Mutterkreuz und Arbeitsbuch: Zur Geschichte der Frauen in der Weimarer Republik und im Nationalsozialismus* (Frankfurt am Main: Fischer, 1988), pp. 49–78

Hake, S., 'In the Mirror of Fashion', in K. von Ankum (ed.), *Women in the Metropolis: Gender and Modernity in Weimar Culture* (Berkeley: University of California Press, 1997), pp. 185–201

Hales, B., 'Woman as Sexual Criminal: Weimar Constructions of the Criminal Femme Fatale', *Women in German Yearbook: Feminist Studies in German Literature and Culture*, 12 (1996), 101–21

Hamann, B., *Der Erste Weltkrieg: Wahrheit und Lüge in Bildern und Texten* (Munich: Piper Verlag, 2nd edn, 2008)

Hämmerle, C., '"Wirf ihnen alles hin und schau, dass du fort kommst": Die Feldpost eines Paares in der Geschlechter(un)ordnung des Ersten Weltkrieges', *Historische Anthropologie*, 6 (1998), 431–58

Hänger, A., 'Politisch oder vaterländisch? Der vaterländische Frauenverein zwischen Kaiserreich und Weimarer Republik', in E. Schöck-Quinteros and C. Streubel (eds), *Ihrem Volk verantwortlich: Frauen der politischen*

Rechten *(1890–1933)*. *Organisationen – Agitationen – Ideologien* (Berlin: Trafo-Verlag, 2007), pp. 57–86

Hardach, G., *The First World War 1914–1918* (Berkeley: University of California Press, 1977)

Hardt, H., 'Pictures for the Masses: Photography and the Rise of Popular Magazines in the Weimar Republic', *Journal of Communication Inquiry*, 13:1 (1989), 7–30

Harris, V., 'In the Absence of Empire: Feminism, Abolitionism and Social Work in Hamburg (c. 1900–1933)', *Women's History Review*, 17:2 (2008), 279–98

Harris, V., *Selling Sex in the Reich: Prostitutes in German Society, 1914–1945* (Oxford: Oxford University Press, 2010)

Harsch, D., *German Social Democracy and the Rise of Nazism* (Chapel Hill: University of North Carolina Press, 1993)

Harsch, D., 'The Iron Front: Weimar Social Democracy between Tradition and Modernity', in D. E. Barclay and E. D. Weitz (eds), *Between Reform and Revolution: German Socialism and Communism from 1840 to 1990* (Oxford: Berghahn, 1998), pp. 251–73

Harvey, E., 'Private Fantasy and Public Intervention: Girls' Reading in Weimar Germany', in J. Birkett and E. Harvey (eds), *Determined Women: Studies in the Construction of the Female Subject, 1900–1990* (London: Macmillan 1991), pp. 38–67

Harvey, E., 'Serving the Volk, Saving the Nation: Women in the Youth Movement and Public Sphere in Weimar Germany', in L. E. Jones and J. Retallack (eds), *Elections, Mass Politics and Social Change in Modern Germany* (Cambridge: Cambridge University Press, 1992), pp. 201–21

Harvey, E., *Youth and the Welfare State in Weimar Germany* (Oxford: Clarendon Press, 1993)

Harvey, E., 'The Failure of Feminism? Young Women and the Bourgeois Feminist Movement in Weimar Germany 1918–1933', *Central European History*, 28:1 (1995), 1–28

Harvey, E., 'Gender, Generation and Politics: Young Protestant Women in the Final Years of the Weimar Republic', in M. Roseman (ed.), *Generations in Conflict* (Cambridge: Cambridge University Press, 1995), pp. 184–209

Harvey, E., 'Culture and Society in Weimar Germany: The Impact of Modernism and Mass Culture', in M. Fulbrook (ed.), *German History since 1800* (London: Arnold, 1997), pp. 279–97

Harvey, E., 'Pilgrimages to the "Bleeding Border": Gender and Rituals of Nationalist Protest in Germany, 1919–39', *Women's History Review*, 9:2 (2000), 201–29

Harvey, E., 'Visions of the *Volk*: German Women and the Far Right from

Kaiserreich to Third Reich', *Journal of Women's History*, 16:3 (2004), 152–67

Harvey, E., '"Ich war überall": Die NS-Propagandaphotographin Liselotte Purpur', in S. Steinbacher (ed.), *Volksgenossinnen: Frauen in der NS-Volksgemeinschaft* (Göttingen: Hubert & Co., 2007), pp. 138–53

Hau, M., *The Cult of Health and Beauty in Germany: A Social History, 1890–1930* (Chicago: University of Chicago Press, 2003)

Hau, M., 'Sports in the Human Economy: "Leibesübungen", Medicine, Psychology, and Performance Enhancement during the Weimar Republic', *Central European History*, 41:3 (2008), 381–412

Hausen, K., 'Mothers, Sons, and the Sale of Symbols and Goods: The "German Mother's Day" 1923–33', in H. Medick and D. W. Sabean (eds), *Interest and Emotion: Essays on the Study of Family and Kinship* (Cambridge: Cambridge University Press, 1984), pp. 371–413

Hausen, K., 'Unemployment also Hits Women: The New and the Old Woman on the Dark Side of the Golden Twenties in Germany', in P. Stachura (ed.), *Unemployment and the Great Depression in Weimar Germany* (Basingstoke: Macmillan, 1986), pp. 78–120

Hausen, K., 'The German Nation's Obligation to the Heroes' Widows of World War I', in M. R. Higonnet, J. Jenson, S. Michel and M. C. Weitz (eds), *Behind the Lines: Gender and the Two World Wars* (New Haven and London: Yale University Press, 1987), pp. 126–40

Heineman, E. D., *What Difference does a Husband Make? Women and Marital Status in Nazi and Postwar Germany* (Berkeley: University of California Press, 1999)

Heinemann, R., *Familie zwischen Tradition und Emanzipation: Katholische und sozialdemokratische Familienkonzeptionen in der Weimarer Republik* (Munich: Oldenbourg Wissenschaftliches Verlag, 2004)

Heinsohn, K., 'Germany', in K. Passmore (ed.), *Women, Gender and Fascism in Europe, 1919–45* (Manchester: Manchester University Press, 2003), pp. 33–56

Heinsohn, K., 'Kampf um die Wählerinnen: Die Idee der "Volksgemeinschaft" am Ende der Weimarer Republik', in S. Steinbacher (ed.), *Volksgenossinnen: Frauen in der NS-Volksgemeinschaft* (Göttingen: Hubert & Co., 2007), pp. 29–47

Heinsohn, K., *Konservative Parteien in Deutschland 1912 bis 1933* (Düsseldorf: Droste, 2010)

Hellwig, R. (ed.), *Die Christdemokratinnen: Unterwegs zur Partnerschaft* (Stuttgart: Seewald, 1984)

Hering, S., '"Ich ging meinen Weg" – Erinnerungen bürgerlicher Frauenrechtlerinnen an das Jahr 1933', *Ariadne*, 18 (November 1990), 10–17

Hering, S., *Die Kriegsgewinnlerinnen: Praxis und Ideologie der deutschen Frauenbewegung im Ersten Weltkrieg* (Pfaffenweiler: Centaurus, 1990)

Hering, S., 'Die Eroberung des Patriarchats? Frauenbewegung und Staat zwischen 1914 und 1920', *Metis: Zeitschrift für historische Frauenforschung und feministische Praxis*, 1:1 (1992), 28–41

Herrmann, U., 'Social Democratic Women in Germany and the Struggle for Peace Before and During the First World War', in R. R. Pierson (ed.), *Women and Peace* (Beckenham: Croom Helm,1987), pp. 90–102

Herzog, T., *Crime Stories: Criminalistic Fantasy and the Culture of Crisis in Weimar Germany* (Oxford: Berghahn, 2009)

Heymann, L. G., and A. Augspurg, *Erlebtes – Erschautes* (Bodenheim: Athenaeum, 1987)

Hieber, H., '"Mademoiselle Docteur": The Life and Service of Imperial Germany's Only Female Intelligence Officer', *Journal of Intelligence History*, 5:2 (2005), 91–108

Hofmann-Göttig, J., *Emanzipation mit dem Stimmzettel: 70 Jahre Frauenwahlrecht in Deutschland* (Bonn: Verlag Neue Gesellschaft, 1986)

Hong, Y.-S., 'The Contradictions of Modernisation in the German Welfare State: Gender and the Politics of Welfare Reform in First World War Germany', *Social History*, 17:2 (1992), 251–70

Hong, Y.-S., *Welfare, Modernity and the Weimar State, 1919–1933* (Princeton: Princeton University Press, 1998)

Hong, Y.-S., 'The Weimar Welfare System', in A. McElligott (ed.), *Weimar Germany* (Oxford: Oxford University Press, 2009), pp. 175–206

Horan, G., *Mothers, Warriors, Guardians of the Soul: Female Discourse in National Socialism 1924–1934* (Berlin: Walter de Gruyter, 2003)

Horne, J., 'German Atrocities, 1914: Fact, Fantasy or Fabrication', *History Today*, 52:4 (April 2002), 47–53

Horne, J. (ed.), *A Companion to World War 1* (Oxford: Wiley-Blackwell, 2010)

Huber, A. (ed.), *Die Sozialdemokratinnen: Verdient die Nachtigall Lob, wenn sie singt?* (Stuttgart: Seewald Verlag, 1984)

Huerkamp, C., 'Jüdische Akademikerinnen in Deutschland 1900–1938', *Geschichte und Gesellschaft*, 19 (1993), 311–31

Hutton, M. J., *Russian and West European Women, 1860–1939: Dreams, Struggles and Nightmares* (Oxford: Rowman and Littlefield, 2001)

Imhoof, D., 'The Game of Political Change: Sports in Göttingen during the Weimar and Nazi Eras', *German History*, 27:3 (2009), 374–94

James, H., *The German Slump: Politics and Economics 1924–1936* (Oxford: Oxford University Press, 1986)

Janusch, D., *Die plakative Propaganda der Sozialdemokratischen Partei Deutschlands zu den Reichstagswahlen 1928 bis 1932* (Bochum: Brockmeyer, 1989)

Jarausch, K. H., 'The Crisis of German Professions 1918–33', *Journal of Contemporary History*, 20 (1985), 377–98

Jarausch, K., and L. E. Jones (eds), *In Search of a Liberal Germany: Studies in the History of German Liberalism from 1789 to the Present* (Oxford: Berg, 1990)

Jefferies, M., '"For a genuine and noble nakedness"? German Naturism in the Third Reich', *German History*, 24:1 (2006), 62–84

Jensen, E. N., *Body by Weimar: Athletes, Gender, and German Modernity* (Oxford: Oxford University Press, 2010)

Jerram, L., 'Kitchen Sink Dramas: Women, Modernity and Space in Weimar Germany', *Cultural Geographies*, 13 (2006), 538–56

Johnson, J. A., 'German Women in Chemistry, 1895–1925 (Part I)', *NTM: Zeitschrift für Geschichte der Wissenschaften, Technik und Medizin*, 6 (1998), 1–21, and 'German Women in Chemistry, 1925–1945 (Part II)', ibid., pp. 65–90

Jones, L. E., 'Generational Conflict and the Problem of Political Mobilization in the Weimar Republic', in L. E. Jones and J. Retallack (eds), *Elections, Mass Politics and Social Change in Modern Germany* (Cambridge: Cambridge University Press, 1992), pp. 347–70

Jones, E. B., 'The Gendering of the Postwar Agricultural Labour Shortage in Saxony, 1918–1925', *Central European History*, 32:3 (1999), 311–29

Jones, E. B., 'A New Stage of Life? Young Farm Women's Changing Expectations and Aspirations about Work in Weimar Saxony', *German History*, 19 (2001), 549–70

Jones, E. B., 'Pre-and Post-War Generations of Rural Female Youth and the Future of the German nation, 1871–1933', *Continuity and Change*, 19:3 (2004), 347–65

Jones, E. B., *Gender and Rural Modernity: Farm Women and the Politics of Labour in Germany, 1871–1933* (Farnham: Ashgate, 2009)

Jones, H., C. O'Brien and C. Schmidt-Supprian (eds), *Untold War: New Perspectives in First World War Studies* (Leiden and Boston: Brill, 2008)

Jones, L. E., 'German Conservatism at the Crossroads: Count Kuno von Westarp and the Struggle for Control of the DNVP, 1928–1930', *Contemporary European History*, 18:2 (2009), 147–77

Jones, L. E., and J. Retallack (eds), *Elections, Mass Politics, and Social Change in Modern Germany* (Cambridge: Cambridge University Press, 1992)

Kaes, A., M. Jay and E. Dimendberg (eds), *The Weimar Republic Sourcebook* (Berkeley: University of California Press, 1994)

Kampmann, D., '"Zölibat – ohne uns!" – die soziale Situation und politische Einstellung der Lehrerinnen in der Weimarer Republik', in Frauengruppe Faschismusforschung (ed.), *Mutterkreuz und Arbeitsbuch: Zur Geschichte der Frauen in der Weimarer Republik und im Nationalsozialismus* (Frankfurt am Main: Fischer, 1988), pp. 79–104

Kater, M. H., 'Krisis des Frauenstudiums in der Weimarer Republik', *Vierteljahrschrift für Sozial- und Wirtschaftsgeschichte*, 59 (1972), 207–55

Kater, M. H., 'The Work Student: A Socio-Economic Phenomenon of Early Weimar Germany', *Journal of Contemporary History*, 10:1 (1975), 71–94

Kater, M. H., 'Frauen in der NS-Bewegung', *Vierteljahrshefte für Zeitgeschichte*, 31:2 (1983), 202–41

Kater, M. H., 'Professionalization and Socialization of Physicians in Wilhelmine and Weimar Germany', *Journal of Contemporary History*, 20 (1985), 677–701

Kerchner, B., *Beruf und Geschlecht* (Göttingen: Vandenhoeck & Ruprecht, 1992)

Kershaw, I., *Hitler. 1936–45: Nemesis* (London: Allen Lane, 2000)

Kessemeier, G., *Sportlich, sachlich, männlich: Das Bild der 'Neuen Frau' in den zwanziger Jahren* (Dortmund: Edition Ebersbach, 2000)

Kleiber, L., 'Wo ihr seid, da soll die Sonne scheinen!' – Der Frauenarbeitsdienst am Ende der Weimarer Republik und im Nationalsozialismus', in Frauengruppe Faschismusforschung (ed.), *Mutterkreuz und Arbeitsbuch: Zur Geschichte der Frauen in der Weimarer Republik und im Nationalsozialismus* (Frankfurt am Main: Fischer, 1988), pp. 188–214

Kniesche, T. W., and S. Brockmann (eds), *Dancing on the Volcano: Essays on the Culture of the Weimar Republic* (Columbia: Camden House, 1994)

Knodel, J. E., *The Decline of Fertility in Germany, 1871–1939* (Princeton: Princeton University Press, 1974)

Koch, E., 'Jeder tut, was er kann fürs Vaterland: Frauen und Männer an der Heilbronner "Heimatfront"', in G. Hirschfeld, G. Krumeich, D. Langewiesche and H.-P. Ullmann (eds), *Kriegserfahrungen: Studien zur Sozial- und Mentalitätsgeschichte des Ersten Weltkriegs* (Essen: Klartext Verlagsgesellschaft, 1997), pp. 36–52

Kohn, W. S. G., *Women in National Legislatures* (New York: Praeger, 1980)

Kokula, I., 'Freundinnen: Lesbische Frauen in der Weimarer Zeit', in K. von Soden, M. Schmidt, A. Delille and B. Becker (eds), *Hart und Zart: Frauenleben 1920–1970* (Berlin: Elefantenpress, 1990), pp. 128–32

Kontos, S., *Die Partei kämpft wie ein Mann* (Frankfurt am Main: Stroemfeld Verlag, 1979)

Koonz, C., 'Conflicting Allegiances: Political Ideology and Women Legislators in Weimar Germany', *Signs: Journal of Women in Culture and Society*, 1:3 (1976), 663–83

Koonz, C., 'Nazi Women before 1933: Rebels against Emancipation', *Social Science Quarterly*, 56:4 (1976), 553–63

Koonz, C., *Mothers in the Fatherland: Women, the Family and Nazi Politics* (London: Jonathan Cape, 1987)

Kracauer, S., *Die Angestellten* (Frankfurt am Main: Suhrkamp, 2nd edn, 1974)

Kramer, A., *Dynamics of Destruction: Culture and Mass Killing in the First World War* (Oxford: Oxford University Press, 2007)

Kramer, H., 'Frankfurt's Working Women: Scapegoats or Winners in the Great Depression?', in R. J. Evans and D. Geary (eds), *The German Unemployed: Experiences and Consequences of Mass Unemployment from the Weimar Republic to the Third Reich* (London: Croom Helm, 1987), pp. 108–41

Kramer, N., *Volksgenossinnen an der Heimatfront: Mobilisierung, Verhalten, Erinnerung* (Göttingen: Vandenhoeck & Ruprecht, 2011)

Kuczynski, J., *Studien zur Geschichte der Lage der Arbeiterin in Deutschland von 1700 bis zur Gegenwart* (Berlin: Akademie-Verlag, 2nd edn, 1965)

Kuhlman, E., *Reconstructing Patriarchy after the Great War: Women, Gender, and Postwar Reconciliation between Nations* (Basingstoke: Palgrave Macmillan, 2008)

Kuhlman, E., 'The "Women's International League for Peace and Freedom" and Reconciliation after the Great War', in A. S. Fell and I. Sharp (eds), *The Women's Movement in Wartime: International Perspectives, 1914–1919* (Basingstoke: Palgrave Macmillan, 2007), pp. 227–43

Kuhlman, E., 'The Rhineland Horror Campaign and the Aftermath of War', in I. Sharp and M. Stibbe (eds), *Aftermaths of War: Women's Movements and Female Activists, 1918–1923* (Leiden: Brill, 2011), pp. 89–109

Kuhn, A., and G. Schneider (eds), *Frauen in der Geschichte*, vol. 1 (Düsseldorf: Schwann, 1979)

Kundrus, B., *Kriegerfrauen: Familienpolitik und Geschlechterverhältnisse im Ersten und Zweiten Weltkrieg* (Hamburg: Christians, 1995)

Kundrus, B., 'Gender Wars: The First World War and the Construction of Gender Relations in the Weimar Republic', in K. Hagemann and S. Schüler-Springorum (eds), *Home/Front: The Military, War and Gender in Twentieth-Century Germany* (Oxford and New York: Berg, 2002), pp. 159–79

Kunz, A., 'Stand versus Klasse: Beamtenschaft und Gewerkschaften im Konflikt um den Personalabbau 1923/24', *Geschichte und Gesellschaft*, 8 (1982), 55–86

Kunz, A., *Civil Servants and the Politics of Inflation in Germany, 1914–1924* (Berlin and New York: De Gruyter, 1986)

Lacey, K., 'From Plauderei to Propaganda: On Women's Radio in Germany, 1924–1935', *Media, Culture and Society*, 16 (1994), 589–607
Lacey, K., *Feminine Frequencies: Gender, German Radio, and the Public Sphere, 1923–1939* (Ann Arbor: University of Michigan Press, 1996)
Lampela, L., 'Portrait of a Lesbian Couple', *Journal of Gay and Lesbian Issues in Education*, 3:4 (2006), 7–10
Langstrum, J. W., 'The Display Window: Designs and Desires of Weimar Consumerism', *New German Critique*, 76 (1999), 115–60
Lareau, A., 'Lavender Songs: Undermining Gender in Weimar Cabaret and Beyond', *Popular Music and Society*, 28:1 (2005), 15–33
Lauterer, H.-M., 'Republikanerinnen des Herzens: Sozialdemokratinnen und Nation 1914–1933', in U. Planert (ed.), *Nation, Politik und Geschlecht: Frauenbewegungen und Nationalismus in der Moderne* (Frankfurt am Main: Campus, 2000), pp. 275–91
Lauterer, H. M., *Parlamentarierinnen in Deutschland 1918/19–1949* (Königstein: Ulrike Helmer Verlag, 2002)
Lavin, M., 'Androgyny, Spectatorship, and the Weimar Photomontages of Hanna Höch', *New German Critique*, 51 (1990), 62–86
Lavin, M., *Clean New World: Culture, Politics and Graphic Design* (London: MIT Press, 2001)
Lee, W. R., and E. Rosenhaft (eds), *State, Social Policy and Social Change in Germany 1880–1994* (Oxford: Berg, 2nd edn, 1997)
Lewis, B. I., '*Lustmord*: Inside the Windows of the Metropolis', in K. von Ankum (ed.), *Women in the Metropolis: Gender and Modernity in Weimar Culture* (Berkeley: University of California Press, 1997), pp. 202–32
Lilienthal, G., 'The Illegitimacy Question in Germany, 1900–1945. Areas of Tension in Social and Population Policy', *Continuity and Change*, 5:2 (1990), 249–81
Loewenberg, P., 'Germany, the Home Front (1): The Physical and Psychological Consequences of Home Front Hardship', in H. Cecil and P. Liddle (eds), *Facing Armageddon: The First World War Experienced* (London: Pen & Sword Books Ltd, 1996)
Lüders, M.-E., *Fürchte dich nicht: Persönliches und Politisches aus mehr als achtzig Jahren, 1878–1962* (Cologne: Westdeutscher Verlag, 1963)
Lummel, P., 'Food Provisioning in the German Army in the First World War', in I. Zweiniger-Bargielowska, R. Duffett and A. Drouard (eds), *Food and War in Twentieth Century Europe* (Farnham: Ashgate, 2011), pp. 13–25
Lybeck, M. M., 'Gender, Sexuality and Belonging: Female Homosexuality in Germany, 1890–1933', *Bulletin of the German Historical Institute*, 44 (2009), 29–41
Mai, G., 'Arbeitsmarktregulierung oder Sozialpolitik? Die personelle

Demobilmachung in Deutschland 1918 bis 1920/24', in G. D. Feldman, C.-L. Holtferich, G. A. Ritter and P.-C. Witt (eds), *Die Anpassung an die Inflation* (Berlin and New York: De Gruyter, 1986), pp. 202–36

Makela, M., 'The Rise and Fall of the Flapper Dress: Nationalism and Anti-Semitism in Early-Twentieth-Century Discourse in German Fashion', *Journal of Popular Culture*, 34:3 (2000), 183–208

Mason, T., 'Women in Germany, 1925–1940: Family, Welfare and Work', *History Workshop*, 1 (1976), 74–113; 2 (1976), 5–32

Mass, S., 'Von der "schwarzen Schmach" zur "deutschen Heimat"', *WerkstattGeschichte*, 32 (2002), 44–57

Mazon, P. M., *Gender and the Modern Research University: The Admission of Women to German Higher Education, 1865–1914* (Stanford: Stanford University Press, 2003)

McCormick, R. W., *Gender and Sexuality in Weimar Modernity: Film, Literature, and New Objectivity* (Basingstoke: Palgrave, 2001)

McElligott, A. (ed.), *Weimar Germany* (Oxford: Oxford University Press, 2009)

McIntyre, J., 'Women and the Professions in Germany, 1930–1940', in A. Nicholls and E. Matthias (eds) *German Democracy and the Triumph of Hitler* (London: Allen & Unwin, 1971), pp. 175–213

Meier-Scherling, A.-G., 'Die Benachteiligung der Juristin zwischen 1933 und 1945', *Deutsche Richterzeitung*, 53 (1975), 10–13

Mergel, T., *Parlamentarische Kultur in der Weimarer Republik: Politische Kommunikation, symbolische Politik und Öffentlichkeit im Reichstag* (Düsseldorf: Droste Verlag, 2002)

Mergel, T., 'High Expectations – Deep Disappointments: Structures of the public Perception of Politics in the Weimar Republic' in K. Canning, K. Barndt and K. McGuire (eds), *Weimar Publics/Weimar Subjects: Rethinking the Political Culture of Germany in the 1920s* (Oxford: Berghahn, 2010), pp. 192–210

Meskimmon, M., *We Weren't Modern Enough: Women Artists and the Limits of German Modernism* (Berkeley: University of California Press, 1999)

Meskimmon, M., and S. West, *Visions of the Neue Frau: Women and the Visual Arts in Weimar Germany* (Aldershot: Ashgate, 1995)

Michl, S., *Im Dienste des 'Volkskörpers': Deutsche und französische Ärzte im Ersten Weltkrieg* (Göttingen: Vandenhoeck & Ruprecht, 2007)

Mogulof, M., *Foiled, Hitler's Jewish Olympian: The Helene Mayer Story* (Oakland: RDR Books, 2002)

Morsey, R., *Die Protokolle der Reichstagsfraktion und des Fraktionsvorstandes der deutschen Zentrumspartei, 1926–1933* (Mainz: Matthias-Grünewald-Verlag, 1969)

Mouton, M., 'Rescuing Children and Policing Families: Adoption Policy in Weimar and Nazi Germany', *Central European History*, 38:4 (2005), 545–71

Mouton, M., *From Nurturing the Nation to Purifying the Volk: Weimar and Nazi Family Policy, 1918–1945* (Cambridge: Cambridge University Press, 2007)

Mühlberger, D., *Hitler's Voice: The Völkischer Beobachter, 1920–1933*, vol. 2: *Nazi Ideology and Propaganda* (Oxford: Peter Lang, 2004)

Murray, B., 'The Role of the Vamp in Weimar Cinema: An Analysis of Karl Grune's *The Street (Die Straße)*', in S. Frieden, R. W. McCormick, V. P. Petersen and L. M. Vogelsang (eds), *Gender and German Cinema: Feminist Interventions*, vol. 2: *German Film History: German History on Film* (Oxford: Berg, 1993), pp. 33–41

Nelson, R. L., 'German Comrades – Slavic Whores: Gender Images in the German Soldier Newspapers of the First World War', in K. Hagemann and S. Schüler-Springorum (eds), *Home/Front: The Military, War and Gender in Twentieth-Century Germany* (Oxford and New York: Berg, 2002), pp. 69–85

Nettl, J. P., *Rosa Luxemburg* (Oxford: Oxford University Press, 1966)

Niehuss, M., 'Lebensweise und Familie in der Inflationszeit', in G. D. Feldman et al. (eds), *Die Anpassung an die Inflation* (Berlin and New York: De Gruyter, 1986), pp. 237–65

Nienhaus, U., 'Weibliche Angestellte in den USA, Frankreich und Grossbritannien 1850 bis 1930 – Arbeitsmarkt, Arbeitsplatzsituation, soziale Lage, Organisation: Ein Literaturbericht', *Internationale wissenschaftliche Korrespondenz zur Geschichte der deutschen Arbeiterbewegung*, 21:3 (1985), 330–53

Nienhaus, U., 'Frauen, Männer und Arbeitgeber Staat – das Beispiel der deutschen Post', *Sozialwissenschaftliche Informationen*, 4 (1989), pp. 237–48

Nienhaus, U., *Vater Staat und seine Gehilfinnen: Die Politik mit der Frauenarbeit bei der deutschen Post (1864–1945)* (Frankfurt am Main: Campus Verlag, 1995)

Nienhaus, U., *Nicht für eine Führungsposition geeignet: Josephine Erkens und die Anfänge weiblicher Polizei in Deutschland, 1923–1933* (Münster: Westphälisches Dampfboot, 1999)

Nolan, M., '"Housework made easy": The Taylorized Housewife in Weimar Germany's Rationalised Economy', *Feminist Studies*, 16:3 (1990), 549–77

Orfali, S., *A Jewish Girl in the Weimar Republic* (Berkeley: Ronin Publishing, 1987)

Paul, G., *Aufstand der Bilder: Die NS-Propaganda vor 1933* (Bonn: Dietz, 1990)

Pauwels, J. R., *Women, Nazis, and Universities: Female University Students in the Third Reich* (Westport: Greenwood Press, 1984)

Peach, M., '"Der Architekt denkt, die Hausfrau lenkt": German Modern Architecture and the Modern Woman', *German Studies Review*, 18:3 (1995), 441–63
Peterson, B., 'The Politics of Working-Class Women in the Weimar Republic', *Central European History*, 10:2 (1977), 87–111
Petersen, V. R., *Women and Modernity in Weimar Germany: Reality and its Representation in Popular Fiction* (Oxford: Berghahn, 2001)
Petro, P., *Joyless Streets: Women and Melodramatic Representation in Weimar Germany* (Princeton: Princeton University Press, 1989)
Peukert, D., *Inside Nazi Germany: Conformity, Opposition, and Racism in Everyday Life*, trans. R. Deveson (London: Yale University Press, 1987)
Peukert, D., 'The Weimar Republic – Old and New Perspectives', *German History*, 6:2 (1988), 133–44
Peukert, D., *The Weimar Republic: The Crisis of Classical Modernity*, trans. R. Deveson (London: Allen Lane, 1991)
Pfister, G., 'Demands, Realities and Ambivalences – Women in the Proletarian Sports Movement in Germany (1893–1933)', *Women in Sport and Physical Activity Journal*, 3:2 (1994), 39–68
Pfister, G., 'Sport for Women', in R. Naul and K. Hardman (eds), *Sport and Physical Education in Germany* (London: Routledge, 2002), pp. 165–90
Phillips Shively, W., 'Party identification, Party Choice, and Voting Stability: The Weimar Case', *American Political Science Review*, 66:4 (December 1972), 1203–25
Pine, L., *Education in Nazi Germany* (Oxford: Berg, 2010)
Planert, U., *Antifeminismus im Kaiserreich: Diskurs, soziale Formation und politische Mentalität* (Göttingen: Vandenhoeck and Ruprecht, 1998)
Planert, U. (ed.), *Nation, Politik und Geschlecht: Frauenbewegungen und Nationalismus in der Moderne* (Frankfurt am Main: Campus, 2000)
Planert, U., 'Mutter und Volk', in E. Schöck-Quinteros and C. Streubel (eds), *Ihrem Volk verantwortlich: Frauen der politischen Rechten (1890–1933). Organisationen – Agitationen – Ideologien* (Berlin: Trafo-Verlag, 2007), pp. 109–30
Pohl, H., and W. Treue (eds), *Die Frau in der deutschen Wirtschaft* (Wiesbaden: Franz Steiner Verlag, 1985)
Pore, R., *A Conflict of Interest: Women in German Social Democracy 1919–1933* (London: Greenwood Press, 1981)
Preller, L., *Sozialpolitik in der Weimarer Republik* (Düsseldorf: Athenäum-Droste, 1978)
Prestel, C., 'The "New Jewish Woman" in Weimar Germany', in W. Benz, A. Paucker and P. Pulzer (eds) *Jüdisches Leben in der Weimarer Republik / Jews in the Weimar Republic* (Tübingen: Mohr Siebeck, 1998), pp. 135–58
Quataert, J. H., 'Women's Work and Worth: The Persistence of Stereotype

Attitudes in the German Free Trade Unions, 1890–1929', in N. C. Soldon (ed.), *The World of Women's Trade Unionism* (Westport: Greenwood Press, 1985), pp. 93–124

Quataert, J. H., 'Women's Wartime Services under the Cross: Patriotic Communities in Germany, 1912–1918', in R. Chickering and S. Förster (eds), *Great War, Total War: Combat and Mobilization on the Western Front, 1914–1918* (Cambridge: Cambridge University Press, 2000), pp. 453–83

Quataert, J. H., *Staging Philanthropy: Patriotic Women and the National Imagination in Dynastic Germany, 1813–1916* (Ann Arbor: University of Michigan Press, 2001)

Ras, M. E. P. de, *Body, Femininity and Nationalism: Girls in the German Youth Movement, 1900–1934* (London: Routledge, 2008)

Ray, K. R., 'Bauhaus Hausfraus: Gender Formation in Design Education', *Journal of Architectural Education*, 55:2 (2001), 73–80

Reagin, N. R., *A German Women's Movement: Class and Gender in Hanover, 1880–1933* (Chapel Hill and London: University of North Carolina Press, 1995)

Reagin, N. R., *Sweeping the German Nation: Domesticity and National Identity, 1870–1945* (Cambridge: Cambridge University Press, 2007)

Reese, D., *Growing Up Female in Nazi Germany* (Ann Arbor: University of Michigan Press, 2006)

Reuveni, G., 'Reading, Advertising and Consumer Culture in the Weimar Period', in K. Führer and C. Ross (eds), *Mass Media, Culture and Society in Twentieth-Century Germany* (Basingstoke: Palgrave Macmillan, 2006), pp. 204–16

Reuveni, G., *Reading Germany: Literature and Consumer Culture in Germany before 1933* (Oxford: Berghahn, 2006)

Rich, B. B., 'From Repressive Tolerance to Erotic Liberation: *Girls in Uniform* (*Mädchen in Uniform*)', in S. Frieden, R. W. McCormick, V. P. Petersen and L. M. Vogelsang (eds), *Gender and German Cinema: Feminist Interventions*, vol. 2: *German Film History: German History on Film* (Oxford: Berg, 1993), pp. 61–96

Rigby, I. K., 'German Expressionist Political Posters 1918–1919 – Art and Politics: A Failed Alliance', *Art Journal*, 44:1 (1984), 33–9

Roos, J., 'Backlash against Prostitutes' Rights: Origins and Dynamics of Nazi Prostitution Policies', in D. Herzog (ed.), *Sexuality and German Fascism* (Oxford: Berghahn, 2005), pp. 67–94

Roos, J., 'Women's Rights, Nationalist Anxiety and the "Moral" Agenda in the Early Weimar Republic: Revisiting the "Black Horror" Campaign against France's African Occupation Troops', *Central European History*, 42:3 (2009), 473–508

Roos, J., *Weimar through the Lens of Gender: Prostitution Reform,*

Women's Emancipation, and German Democracy, 1919–33 (Ann Arbor: University of Michigan Press, 2010)

Roos, J., 'Nationalism, Racism and Propaganda in Early Weimar Germany: Contradictions in the Campaign against the "Black Horror on the Rhine"', *German History*, 30:1 (2012), 45–74

Roseman, M. (ed.), *Generations in Conflict: Youth Revolt and Generation Formation in Germany 1770–1968* (Cambridge: Cambridge University Press, 1995)

Rosenhaft, E., 'Women, Gender, and the Limits of Political History in the Age of "Mass" Politics', in L. E. Jones and J. Retallack (eds), *Elections, Mass Politics and Social Change in Modern Germany* (Cambridge: Cambridge University Press, 1992), pp. 149–73

Rosenhaft, E., 'Restoring Moral Order on the Home Front. Compulsory Savings Plans for Young Workers in Germany, 1916–19', in F. Coetzee and M. Sherin-Coetzee, *Authority, Identity and the Social History of the Great War* (Oxford: Berghahn, 1995), pp. 81–112

Ross, C., 'Visions of Prosperity: The Americanisation of Advertising in Interwar Germany', in P. E. Swett, S. J. Wiesen and J. R. Zatlin (eds), *Selling Modernity: Advertising in Twentieth-Century Germany* (London: Duke University Press, 2007), pp. 52–77

Ross, C., *Media and the Making of Modern Germany* (Oxford: Oxford University Press, 2008)

Ross, C., 'Cinema, Radio, and "Mass Culture" in the Weimar Republic: Between Shared Experience and Social Division', in J. A. Williams (ed.), *Weimar Culture Revisited* (Basingstoke: Palgrave Macmillan, 2011), pp. 23–48

Rouette, S., '"Gleichberechtigung" ohne "Recht auf Arbeit": Demobilmachung der Frauenarbeit nach dem Ersten Weltkrieg', in C. Eifert and S. Rouette (eds), *Unter allen Umständen: Frauengeschichte(n) in Berlin* (Berlin: Rotation, 1986), pp. 159–82

Rouette, S., *Sozialpolitik als Geschlechterpolitik: Die Regulierung der Frauenarbeit nach dem Ersten Weltkrieg* (Frankfurt am Main: Campus Verlag, 1993)

Rouette, S., 'Mothers and Citizens: Gender and Social Policy in Germany after the First World War', *Central European History*, 30:1 (1997), 48–66

Rowold, K., *The Educated Woman: Minds, Bodies, and Women's Higher Education in Britain, Germany, and Spain, 1865–1914* (London: Routledge, 2010)

Rowe, D., *Representing Berlin: Sexuality and the City in Imperial and Weimar Germany* (Aldershot: Ashgate, 2003)

Rupp, L., 'Constructing Internationalism: The Case of Transnational Women's Organisations, 1888–1945', *American Historical Review*, 99:5 (December 1994), 1571–1600

Sachsse, C., 'Social Mothers: The Bourgeois Women's Movement and German Welfare-State Formation, 1890–1929', in S. Koven and S. Michel (eds), *Mothers of a New World: Maternalist Politics and the Origins of Welfare States* (London: Routledge, 1993), pp. 136–58
Sack, B., 'Katholismus und Nation: Der katholische Frauenbund', in U. Planert (ed.), *Nation, Politik und Geschlecht: Frauenbewegungen und Nationalismus in der Moderne* (Frankfurt am Main: Campus, 2000), pp. 292–308
Saldern, A. von, 'Social Rationalization of Living and Housework in Germany and the United States in the 1920s', *History of the Family*, 2:1 (1997), 73–93
Saldern, A. von, 'Modernization as Challenge: Perceptions and Reactions of German Social Democratic Women', in H. Gruber and P. Graves (eds), *Women and Socialism: Socialism and Women* (Oxford: Berghahn, 1998), pp. 95–134
Saldern, A. von, *The Challenge of Modernity: German Social and Cultural Studies, 1890–1960* (Ann Arbor: University of Michigan Press, 2002)
Saldern, A. von, '"Neues Wohnen": Housing and Reform', in A. McElligott (ed.), *Weimar Germany* (Oxford: Oxford University Press, 2009), pp. 207–33
Sauerteig, L. D. H., '"The Fatherland is in danger, save the Fatherland": Venereal Disease, Sexuality and Gender in Imperial and Weimar Germany', in R. Davidson and L. A. Hall (eds), *Sex, Sin and Suffering: Venereal Disease and European Society since 1870* (London: Routledge, 2001), pp. 76–92
Sawahn, A., *Die Frauenlobby vom Land: Die Landfrauenbewegung in Deutschland und ihre Funktionärinnen 1898 bis 1948* (Frankfurt am Main: DLG Verlag, 2009)
Schaser, A., 'Bürgerliche Frauen auf dem Weg in die linksliberalen Parteien (1908–1933)', *Historische Zeitschrift*, 263:3 (1996), 641–80
Schaser, A., *Helene Lange und Gertrud Bäumer: Eine politische Lebensgemeinschaft* (Cologne: Böhlau Verlag, 2000)
Schaser, A., 'Women in a Nation of Men: The Politics of the League of German Women's Associations (BDF) in Imperial Germany', in I. Blom, K. Hagemann and C. Hall (eds), *Gendered Nations: Nationalisms and Gender Order in the Long Nineteenth Century* (Oxford: Berg, 2000), pp. 249–68
Scheck, R., 'German Conservatism and Female Political Activism in the Early Weimar Republic', *German History*, 15:1 (1997), 34–55
Scheck, R., 'Women against Versailles: Maternalism and Nationalism of Female Bourgeois Politicians in the Early Weimar Republic', *German Studies Review*, 2:1 (February 1999), 21–42
Scheck, R., 'Zwischen Volksgemeinschaft und Frauenrechten: Das

Verhältnis rechtsbürgerlicher Politikerinnen zur NSDAP 1930–1933', in U. Planert (ed.) *Nation, Politik und Geschlecht: Frauenbewegungen und Nationalismus in der Moderne* (Frankfurt am Main: Campus, 2000), pp. 234–53

Scheck, R., 'Women on the Weimar Right: The Role of Female Politicians in the Deutschnationale Volkspartei (DNVP)', *Journal of Contemporary History*, 36:4 (2001), 547–60

Scheck, R., 'Wahrung des Burgfriedens: Die Wirkung des Ersten Weltkrieges auf die bürgerliche Frauenbewegung der Weimarer Republik', in J. Dülffer and G. Krumeich (eds), *Der verlorene Frieden. Politik und Kriegskultur nach 1918* (Essen: Klartext, 2002), pp. 215–28

Scheck, R., 'Women in the Non-Nazi Right during the Weimar Republic: The German Nationalist People's Party (DNVP)', in P. Bacchetta and M. Power (eds), *Right-Wing Women: From Conservatives to Extremists around the World* (London: Routledge, 2002), pp. 141–53

Scheck, R., *Mothers of the Nation: Right-Wing Women in Weimar Germany* (Oxford: Berg, 2004)

Scheck, R., 'Die Partei als Heim und Familie. Frauen in den Ortsvereinen der Deutschnationalen Volkspartei und der Deutschen Volkspartei in der Weimarer Republik', in E. Schöck-Quinteros and C. Streubel (eds), *Ihrem Volk verantwortlich: Frauen der politischen Rechten (1890–1933). Organisationen – Agitationen – Ideologien* (Berlin: Trafo-Verlag, 2007), pp. 153–75

Schöck-Quinteros, E., 'Der Bund Königin Luise: "Unser Kampfplatz ist die Familie"', in E. Schöck-Quinteros and C. Streubel (eds), *Ihrem Volk verantwortlich: Frauen der politischen Rechten (1890–1933). Organisationen – Agitationen – Ideologien* (Berlin: Trafo-Verlag, 2007), pp. 231–70

Schöck-Quinteros, E., and C. Streubel (eds), *Ihrem Volk verantwortlich: Frauen der politischen Rechten (1890–1933). Organisationen – Agitationen – Ideologien* (Berlin: Trafo-Verlag, 2007)

Schoenbaum, D., *Hitler's Social Revolution: Class and Status in Nazi Germany 1933–1939* (London: Weidenfeld and Nicolson, 1967)

Schönberger, B., 'Motherly Heroines and Adventurous Girls: Red Cross Nurses and Women Army Auxiliaries in the First World War', in K. Hagemann and S. Schüler-Springorum (eds), *Home/Front: The Military, War and Gender in Twentieth-Century Germany* (Oxford and New York: Berg, 2002), pp. 87–113

Schoppmann, C., *Days of Masquerade: Life Stories of Lesbians during the Third Reich*, trans. A. Brown (New York: Columbia University Press, 1996)

Schulte, R., 'The Sick Warrior's Sister: Nursing during the First World War', in L. Abrams and E. Harvey (eds), *Gender Relations in German*

History: Power, Agency and Experience from the Sixteenth Century to the Twentieth (London: UCL Press, 1996), pp. 121–41

Schulz, G., 'Die weiblichen Angestellten vom 19. Jahrhundert bis 1945', in H. Pohl and W. Treue (eds), *Die Frau in der deutschen Wirtschaft* (Wiesbaden: Franz Steiner Verlag,1985), pp. 179–215

Schwarz, M., MdR. *Biographisches Handbuch der Reichstage* (Hanover: Verlag für Literatur und Zeitgeschehen, 1965)

Seipp, A. R., *The Ordeal of Peace: Demobilisation and the Urban Experience in Britain and Germany, 1917–1921* (Farnham: Ashgate, 2009)

Sender, T., *The Autobiography of a German Rebel* (London: Labour Book Service, 1940)

Sharp, I., 'Riding the Tiger: Ambivalent Images of the New Woman in the Popular Press of the Weimar Republic', in A. Heilmann and M. Beetham (eds), *New Woman Hybridities: Femininity, Feminism and International Consumer Culture, 1880–1930* (London: Routledge, 2004), pp. 118–41

Sharp, I., 'Blaming the Women: Women's "Responsibility" for the First World War', in A. S. Fell and I. Sharp (eds), *The Women's Movement in Wartime: International Perspectives, 1914–1919* (Basingstoke: Palgrave Macmillan, 2007), pp. 67–87

Sharp, I., 'The Disappearing Surplus: The Spinster in the Post-War Debate in Weimar Germany, 1918–1920', in Sharp I. and M. Stibbe (eds) *Aftermaths of War: Women's Movements and Female Activists, 1918–1923* (Leiden: Brill, 2011), pp. 135–57

Sharp I., and M. Stibbe (eds), *Aftermaths of War: Women's Movements and Female Activists, 1918–1923* (Leiden: Brill, 2011)

Siebrecht, C., 'Martial Spirit and Mobilisation Myths: Bourgeois Women and the "Ideas of 1914" in Germany', in A. S. Fell and I. Sharp (eds), *The Women's Movement in Wartime: International Perspectives, 1914–1919* (Basingstoke: Palgrave Macmillan, 2007), pp. 38–52

Siebrecht, C., 'The *Mater Dolorosa* on the Battlefield – Mourning Mothers in German Women's Art of the First World War', in H. Jones, C. O'Brien and C. Schmidt-Supprian (eds), *Untold War: New Perspectives in First World War Studies* (Leiden and Boston: Brill, 2008), pp. 259–91

Siemens, D., 'Explaining Crime: Berlin Newspapers and the Construction of the Criminal in Weimar Germany', *Journal of European Studies*, 39:3 (2009), 336–52

Smaldone, W., *Confronting Hitler: German Social Democrats in Defense of the Weimar Republic, 1929–1933* (Lanham: Lexington Books, 2010)

Smith, J. S., 'Working Girls: White-Collar Workers and Prostitutes in late Weimar fiction', *German Quarterly*, 81:4 (2008), 449–70

Sneeringer, J., *Winning Women's Votes: Propaganda and Politics in*

Weimar Germany (Chapel Hill: University of North Carolina Press, 2002)

Sneeringer, J., 'The Shopper as Voter: Women, Advertising, and Politics in Post-Inflation Germany', *German Studies Review*, 27:3 (2004), 475–501

Sneeringer, J., '"Frauen an die Front!" The Language of "Kampf" in DNVP Women's Propaganda 1918–33', in E. Schöck-Quinteros and C. Streubel (eds), *Ihrem Volk verantwortlich: Frauen der politischen Rechten (1890–1933). Organisationen – Agitationen – Ideologien* (Berlin: Trafo-Verlag, 2007), pp. 177–98

Soden, K. von, *Die Sexualberatungsstellen der Weimarer Republik, 1919–1933* (Berlin: Druckhaus Hentrich Verlag, 1988)

Soden, K. von, and G. Zipfel, *Siebzig Jahre Frauenstudium: Frauen in der Wissenschaft* (Cologne: Pahl-Rugenstein, 1979)

Soden, K. von, M. Schmidt, A. Delille and B. Becker (eds), *Hart und Zart: Frauenleben 1920–1970* (Berlin: Elefantenpress, 1990)

Søland, B., *Becoming Modern: Young Women and the Reconstruction of Womanhood in the 1920s* (Princeton: Princeton University Press, 2000)

Stachura, P. (ed.), *Unemployment and the Great Depression in Weimar Germany* (Basingstoke: Macmillan, 1986)

Stahl, G., 'Von der Hauswirtschaft zum Haushalt oder wie man vom Haus zur Wohnung kommt', in Neue Gesellschaft für Bildende Kunst (ed.), *Wem gehört die Welt: Kunst und Gesellschaft in der Weimarer Republik* (Berlin: Neue Gesellschaft für Bildende Kunst, 1977), pp. 87–108

Stanley, A. C., *Modernising Tradition: Gender and Consumerism in Interwar France and Germany* (Baton Rouge: Louisiana State University Press, 2008)

Statistisches Bundesamt (ed.), *Statistisches Jahrbuch für die Bundesrepublik Deutschland 1972* (Stuttgart: W. Kohlhammer GmbH, 1973)

Statistisches Bundesamt (ed.) *Statistisches Jahrbuch 1981 für die Bundesrepublik Deutschland* (Stuttgart: W. Kohlhammer GmbH, 1981)

Steinbacher, S., 'Differenz der Geschlechter? Chancen und Schranken für die "Volksgenossinnen"', in F. Bajohr and M. Wildt (eds), *Volksgemeinschaft: Neue Forschungen zur Gesellschaft des Nationalsozialismus* (Frankfurt am Main: S. Fischer Verlag, 2009), 94–104

Steinbacher, S. (ed.), *Volksgenossinen: Frauen in der NS-Volksgemeinschaft* (Göttingen: Hubert & Co., 2007)

Stephenson, J., 'Girls' Higher Education in Germany in the 1930s', *Journal of Contemporary History*, 10:1 (1975), 41–69

Stephenson, J., *Women in Nazi Society* (London: Croom Helm, 1975)

Stephenson, J., *The Nazi Organisation of Women* (London: Croom Helm, 1981)

Stephenson, J., 'National Socialism and Women before 1933', in P. D. Stachura (ed.), *The Nazi Machtergreifung* (London: Allen and Unwin, 1983), pp. 33–48

Stephenson, J., 'Women and the Professions in Germany, 1900–1945', in G. Cocks and K. H. Jarausch (eds), *German Professions, 1800–1950* (Oxford: Oxford University Press, 1990), pp. 270–88

Stephenson, J., 'Modernization, Emancipation, Mobilization: Nazi Society Reconsidered', in L. E. Jones and J. Retallack (eds), *Elections, Mass Politics and Social Change in Modern Germany* (Cambridge: Cambridge University Press, 1992), pp. 223–43

Stephenson, J., *Women in Nazi Germany* (Harlow: Longman, 2001)

Sternsdorf-Hauck, C., *Brotmarken und rote Fahnen: Frauen in der bayerischen Revolution und Räterepublik 1918/19* (Cologne: Neuer ISP Verlag, 2008)

Stibbe, M., 'Anti-Feminism, Nationalism and the German Right, 1914–1920: A Re-Appraisal', *German History*, 20:2 (2002), 185–210

Stibbe, M., *Women in the Third Reich* (London: Arnold, 2003)

Stibbe, M., *Germany 1914–1933: Politics, Society and Culture* (Harlow: Pearson, 2010)

Stöckel, S., 'Infant Mortality and Concepts of Hygiene: Strategies and Consequences in the Kaiserreich and the Weimar Republic. The Example of Berlin', *History of the Family*, 7 (2002), 601–16

Stokes, P. R., 'Pathology, Danger and Power: Women's and Physicians' Views of Pregnancy and Childbirth in Weimar Germany', *Social History of Medicine*, 13:3 (2000), 359–80

Storer, C., 'Weimar Germany as Seen by an Englishwoman: British Women Writers and the Weimar Republic', *German Studies Review*, 32:1 (2009), 129–47

Stratigakos, D., 'The Professional Spoils of War: German Women Architects and World War 1', *Journal of the Society of Architectural Historians*, 66:4 (2007), 464–75

Streubel, C., 'Frauen der politischen Rechten in Kaiserreich und Republik', *Historical Social Research*, 28:4 (2003), 103–66

Streubel, C., *Radikale Nationalistinnen: Agitation und Programmatik rechter Frauen in der Weimarer Republik* (Frankfurt am Main: Campus Verlag, 2006)

Streubel, C., '"Meine Herren und Damen!" Rednerinnen der deutschnationalen Fraktion im Parlament der Weimarer Republik', in D. Boschoff and M. Wanger-Egelhaaf (eds), *Mitsprache, Rederecht, Stimmgewalt: Genderkritische Strategien und Transformationen der Rhetorik* (Heidelberg: Universitätsverlag Winter, 2006), pp. 113–42

Streubel, C., 'Forschungen zur politischen Rechten', in E. Schöck-Quinteros and C. Streubel (eds), *Ihrem Volk verantwortlich: Frauen der politischen*

Rechten (1890–1933). Organisationen – Agitationen – Ideologien (Berlin: Trafo-Verlag, 2007), pp. 9–95

Streubel, C., 'Raps across the Knuckles: The Extension of War Culture by Radical Nationalist Women Journalists in Post-1918 Germany', in I. Sharp and M. Stibbe (eds), *Aftermaths of War: Women's Movements and Female Activists, 1918–1923* (Leiden: Brill, 2011), pp. 69–88

Süchting-Hänger, A., 'Die Anti-Versailles-Propaganda konservativer Frauen in der Weimarer Republik – eine weibliche Dankschuld?', in G. Krumeich (ed.), *Versailles 1919: Ziele – Wirkung – Wahrnehmung* (Essen: Klartext Verlag, 2001), pp. 302–13

Süchting-Hänger, A., *Das 'Gewissen der Nation': Nationales Engagement und politisches Handeln konservativer Frauenorganisationen 1900 bis 1937* (Düsseldorf: Droste Verlag, 2002)

Sutton, K., 'The Masculinized Female Athlete in Weimar Germany', *German Politics and Society*, 27:3 (2009), 28–49

Sutton, K., *The Masculine Woman in Weimar Germany* (Oxford: Berghahn, 2011)

Swett, P. E., *Neighbors and Enemies: The Culture of Radicalism in Berlin, 1929–1933* (Cambridge: Cambridge University Press, 2004)

Tamagne, F., *A History of Homosexuality in Europe: Berlin, London, Paris 1919–1939*, vol. 1 (New York: Algora Publishing, 2004)

Tatar, M., *Lustmord: Sexual Murder in Weimar Germany* (Princeton: Princeton University Press, 1995)

Teuteberg, H.-J., 'Food Provisioning on the German Home Front, 1914–1918', in I. Zweiniger-Bargielowska, R. Duffett and A. Drouard (eds), *Food and War in Twentieth Century Europe* (Farnham: Ashgate, 2011), pp. 59–72

Thönnessen, W., *The Emancipation of Women: Germany 1863–1933* (London: Pluto Press, 1973)

Timm, A. F., *The Politics of Fertility in Twentieth-Century Berlin* (Cambridge: Cambridge University Press, 2010)

Tingsten, H., *Political Behaviour: Studies in Election Statistics* (London: P. S. King & Son, 1937)

Tobin, E. H., 'War and the Working Class: The Case of Düsseldorf 1914–1918', *Central European History*, 13:3–4 (1985), 257–98

Todd, L. M., '"The Soldier's Wife who Ran away with the Russian": Sexual Infidelities in World War 1 Germany', *Central European History*, 44 (2011), 257–78

Usborne, C., 'Abtreibung: Mord, Therapie oder weibliches Selbstbestimmungsrecht? Der §218 im medizinischen Diskurs der Weimarer Republik', in J. Geyer-Kordesch and A. Kuhn (eds), *Frauenkörper, Medizin, Sexualität* (Düsseldorf: Patmos, 1986), pp. 192–236

Usborne, C., 'The Christian Churches and the Regulation of Sexuality in Weimar Germany', in J. Obelkevich, L. Roper and R. Samuel (eds), *Disciplines of Faith: Studies in Religion, Politics and Patriarchy* (London: Routledge and Kegan Paul, 1987), pp. 99–112

Usborne, C., 'Pregnancy is the Woman's Active Service: Pronatalism in Germany during the First World War', in R. Wall and J. Winter (eds), *The Upheaval of War: Family, Work and Welfare in Europe, 1914–1918* (Cambridge: Cambridge University Press, 1988), pp. 389–416

Usborne, C., 'Abortion in Weimar Germany – the Debate amongst the Medical Profession', *Continuity and Change*, 5:2 (1990), 199–224

Usborne, C., *The Politics of the Body in Weimar Germany* (Basingstoke: Macmillan, 1992)

Usborne, C., 'The New Woman and Generational Conflict: Perceptions of Young Women's Sexual Mores in the Weimar Republic', in M. Roseman (ed.), *Generations in Conflict: Youth Revolt and Generation Formation in Germany 1770–1968* (Cambridge: Cambridge University Press, 1995), pp. 137–63

Usborne, C., 'Rhetoric and Resistance: Rationalisation of Reproduction in Weimar Germany', *Social Politics*, 4:1 (1997), 65–89

Usborne, C., 'Abortion for Sale! The Competition between Quacks and Doctors in Weimar Germany', in M. Gijswijt-Hofstra, H. Marland and H. De Wardt (eds), *Illness and Healing Alternatives in Western Europe* (London: Routledge, 1997), pp. 183–204

Usborne, C., 'Representation of Abortion in Popular Culture in Weimar Germany', in P. Pasteur, N. Niederacher and M. Mesner (eds), *Sexualität, Unterschichtenmilieus und ArbeiterInnenbewegung* (Leipzig: Akademische Verlagsanstalt, 2003), pp. 81–92

Usborne, C., 'Rebellious Girls and Pitiable Women: Abortion Narratives in Weimar Popular Culture', *German History*, 23 (2005), 321–38

Usborne, C., *Cultures of Abortion in Weimar Germany* (Oxford: Berghahn, 2007)

Usborne, C., 'Body Biological to Body Politic', in G. Eley and J. Palmowski (eds), *Citizenship and National Identity in Twentieth-Century Germany* (Stanford: Stanford University Press, 2008), pp. 129–45

Vaizey, H., *Surviving Hitler's War: Family Life in Germany, 1939–48* (London: Palgrave Macmillan, 2010)

Verhey, J., *The Spirit of 1914: Militarism, Myth and Mobilization in Germany* (Cambridge: Cambridge University Press, 2000)

Wall, R., and J. Winter (eds), *The Upheaval of War: Family, Work and Welfare in Europe, 1914–1918* (Cambridge: Cambridge University Press, 1988)

Walle, M., 'Die Heimatchronik Gertrud Bäumers als weibliches Nationalepos', *Ariadne*, 24 (1993), 17–21

Ward, J., *Weimar Surfaces: Urban Visual Culture in 1920s Germany* (Berkeley: University of California Press, 2001)
Watson, A., *Enduring the Great War: Combat, Morale and Collapse in the German and British Armies, 1914–1918* (Cambridge: Cambridge University Press, 2008)
Weber, H., Die *Wandlung des deutschen Kommunismus* (Frankfurt am Main: Europäische Verlagsanstalt, 1969)
Weberling, A., *Zwischen Räten und Parteien: Frauenbewegung in Deutschland 1918/1919* (Centaurus, Pfaffenweiler, 1994)
Wehler, H.-U., *The German Empire 1871–1918* (Leamington Spa: Berg, 1985)
Weill, C., 'Women in the German Revolution: Rosa Luxemburg and the Workers' Councils', in C. Fauré (ed.), *Political and Historical Encyclopaedia of Women* (London: Fitzroy Dearborn, 2003), pp. 412–23
Weindling, P., 'The Medical Profession, Social Hygiene and the Birth Rate in Germany, 1914–1918', in R. Wall and J. Winter (eds), *The Upheaval of War: Family, Work and Welfare in Europe, 1914–1918* (Cambridge: Cambridge University Press, 1988), pp. 417–37
Weindling, P., *Health, Race and German Politics between National Unification and Nazism, 1870–1945* (Cambridge: Cambridge University Press, 1989)
Weindling, P., 'Eugenics and the Welfare State during the Weimar Republic', in W. R. Lee and E. Rosenhaft (eds), *State, Social Policy and Social Change in Germany 1880–1994* (Oxford: Berg, 2nd edn, 1997), pp. 134–63
Weitz, E. D., *Creating German Communism, 1890–1990: From Popular Protests to Socialist State* (Princeton: Princeton University Press, 1996)
Weitz, E. D., 'The Heroic Man and the Ever-Changing Woman: Gender and Politics in European Communism, 1917–1950', in L. L. Frader and S. O. Rose (eds), *Gender and Class in Modern Europe* (Ithaca: Cornell University Press, 1996), pp. 311–52
Weitz, E. D., *Weimar Germany: Promise and Tragedy* (Princeton: Princeton University Press, 2007)
Weitz, E. D., 'Weimar Germany and the Dilemmas of Liberty', in J. C. Friedman (ed.), *The Routledge History of the Holocaust* (London: Routledge, 2010), pp. 59–68
Welch, D., *Germany, Propaganda and Total War 1914–1918* (London: Athlone Press, 2000)
Welch, D., *The Third Reich: Politics and Propaganda* (London: Routledge, 2nd edn, 2002)
Wellner, G., 'Industriearbeiterinnen in der Weimarer Republik: Arbeitsmarkt, Arbeit und Privatleben 1919–1933', *Geschichte und Gesellschaft*, 7 (1981), 534–54

Wenzel, G., 'Schöneberg voran! An der Front der Tod, in der Heimat die Not', in Berliner Gewerkstatt e.V. (ed.), *August 1914: Ein Volk zieht in den Krieg* (Berlin: Nishen, 1989), pp. 158–71

Weyrather, I., *Mutterkreuz und Muttertag: Der Kult um die 'deutsche Mutter' im Nationalsozialismus* (Frankfurt am Main: Fischer Taschenbuch Verlag, 1993)

Whalen, R., *Bitter Wounds: German Victims of the Great War, 1914–1939* (Ithaca, NY: Cornell University Press, 1984)

Wheeler, R. F., 'German Women and the Communist International: The Case of the Independent Social Democrats', *Central European History*, 8:2 (1975), 113–39

Wickert, C., B. Hamburger and M. Lienau, 'Helene Stöcker and the Bund für Mutterschutz', *Women's Studies International Forum*, 5:6 (1982), 611–18

Widdig, B., *Culture and Inflation in Weimar Germany* (Berkeley: University of California Press, 2001)

Wigger, I., '"Black Shame" – the Campaign against "Racial Degeneration" and Female Degradation in Interwar Europe', *Race and Class*, 51:3 (2010), 33–46

Williams, J. A. (ed.), *Weimar Culture Revisited* (Basingstoke: Palgrave Macmillan, 2011)

Winter, J., 'Demography', in J. Horne (ed.), *A Companion to World War 1* (Oxford: Wiley-Blackwell, 2010), pp. 248–62

Winter, J., and J.-L. Robert (eds), *Capital Cities at War: Paris, London, Berlin 1914–1919* (Cambridge: Cambridge University Press, 1997)

Winter, J., and J. Cole, 'Fluctuations in Infant Mortality Rates in Berlin During and After the First World War', *European Journal of Population*, 9 (1993), 235–63

Wittmann, I., '"Echte Weiblichkeit ist ein Dienen" – die Hausgehilfin in der Weimarer Republik und im Nationalsozialismus', in Frauengruppe Faschismusforschung (ed.), *Mutterkreuz und Arbeitsbuch: Zur Geschichte der Frauen in der Weimarer Republik und im Nationalsozialismus* (Frankfurt am Main: Fischer, 1988), pp. 15–48

Wittmann, R., *Geschichte des deutschen Buchhandels* (Munich: Verlag C. H. Beck, 1999)

Woodfin, C. G., 'Reluctant Democrats: The Protestant Women's Auxiliary and the German National Assembly Election of 1919', *Journal of the Historical Society*, 4:1 (2004), 71–112

Woycke, J., *Birth Control in Germany 1871–1933* (London: Routledge, 1988)

Wurms, R., '"Krieg dem Krieg" – "Dienst am Vaterland": Frauenbewegung im Ersten Weltkrieg', in F. Herve (ed.), *Geschichte der deutschen Frauenbewegung* (Bonn: Pahl-Rugenstein, 1982), pp. 84–118

Zagula, J. T., 'Saints, Sinners and Society: Images of Woman in Film and Drama, from Weimar to Hitler', *Women's Studies*, 19 (1991), 55–77
Zahn-Harnack, A., von, *Schriften und Reden* (Tübingen: Hopfer, 1964)
Ziemann, B., 'Germany after the First World War – a Violent Society? Results and Implications of Recent Research on Weimar Germany', *Journal of Modern European History*, 1 (2003), 580–95
Ziemann, B., 'Geschlechterbeziehungen in deutschen Feldpostbriefen des Ersten Weltkreiges', in C. Hämmerle and E. Saurer (eds), *Briefkulturen und ihr Geschlecht: Zur Geschichte der privaten Korrespondenz vom 16. Jahrhundert bis heute* (Vienna: Böhlau Verlag, 2003), pp. 261–82
Ziemann, B., *War Experiences in Rural Germany, 1914–1923* (Oxford: Berg, 2007)
Ziemann, B., 'Weimar was Weimar: Politics, Culture and the Emplotment of the German Republic', *German History*, 28:4 (2010), 542–71
Ziemann, B., 'Germany 1914–1918: Total War as a Catalyst of Change', in H. W. Smith (ed.), *The Oxford Handbook of Modern German History* (Oxford: Oxford University Press, 2011), pp. 378–99
Zimmeck, M., 'Strategies and Stratagems for the Employment of Women in the British Civil Service, 1919–1931', *Historical Journal*, 27 (1984), 901–24
Zweiniger-Bargielowska, I., R. Duffett and A. Drouard (eds), *Food and War in Twentieth Century Europe* (Farnham: Ashgate, 2011)

Dissertations

Baldauf, E., 'Die Frauenarbeit in der Landwirtschaft' (PhD dissertation, University of Kiel, 1929)
Boyd, C. E., '"Nationaler Frauendienst": German Middle-Class Women in Service to the Fatherland, 1914–1918' (PhD dissertation, University of Georgia, 1979)
Disko, S., 'Men, Motorcycles and Modernity: Motorisation during the Weimar Republic' (PhD dissertation, New York University, 2008)
Fessenden, P. L., 'The Role of Women Deputies in the German National Constituent Assembly and the Reichstag, 1919–1933' (PhD dissertation, Ohio State University, 1976)
Hackett, A. K., 'The Politics of Feminism in Wilhelmine Germany, 1890–1918' (PhD dissertation, Columbia University, 1976)
Honeycutt, K., 'Clara Zetkin: A Left-Wing Socialist and Feminist in Wilhelmian Germany' (PhD dissertation, Columbia University, 1975)
Jehle, W., 'Die Arbeiterlöhne in der Badischen Textilindustrie seit der Stabilisierung der Mark (1923–1933)' (PhD dissertation, University of Heidelberg, 1935)
Koch, S. H., 'Militärpolitik im "Jahr der Frau": Die Öffnung der

Bundeswehr für weibliche Sanitätsoffiziere und ihre Folgen' (PhD dissertation, University of Brunswick, 2008)

Lowitsch, V., 'Die Frau als Richter' (PhD dissertation, University of Freiburg im Breisgau, 1933)

Lynn, J. M., 'Contesting Images: Representations of the Modern Woman in the German Illustrated Press, 1924–1933' (MA dissertation, University of North Carolina, 2008)

Neunsinger, S., 'Die Arbeit der Frauen – die Krise der Männer: Die Erwerbstätigkeit verheirateter Frauen in Deutschland und Schweden 1919–1939' (PhD dissertation, University of Uppsala, 2001)

Quataert, J. H., 'The German Socialist Women's Movement 1890–1918: Issues, Internal Conflicts, and the Main Personages (PhD dissertation, University of California, Los Angeles, 1974)

Roos, J., 'Weimar's Crisis through the Lens of Gender: The Case of Prostitution' (PhD dissertation, Carnegie Mellon University, 2001)

Sach, L., '"Gedenke, daß du eine deutsche Frau bist!" Die Ärtzin und Bevölkerungspolitikerin Ilse Szagunn (1887–1971) in der Weimarer Republik und im Nationalsozialismus' (PhD dissertation, University of Berlin, 2006)

Sneeringer, J., 'The Political Mobilisation of Women in Weimar Germany, 1918–1932' (PhD dissertation, University of Pennsylvania, 1995)

Stokes, P. R., 'Contested Conceptions: Experiences and Discourses of Pregnancy and Childbirth in Germany, 1914–1933' (PhD dissertation, Cornell University, 2003)

Todd, L. M., 'Sexual Treason: State Surveillance of Immorality and Infidelity in World War One Germany' (PhD dissertation, University of Toronto, 2005)

Wack, A., 'Frauenarbeit in der Kriegsfürsorge in München' (PhD dissertation, University of Munich, 1918)

Walmsley, J., 'The Political Role of Catholic Women during the Weimar Republic, 1918–1933' (PhD dissertation, University of California Riverside, 2000)

Woodfin, C. G., 'Reluctant Democrats: Women of the Protestant *Frauenhilfe* and Weimar Politics 1918–1933' (PhD dissertation, University of Nashville, 1997)

Internet sources

'Gleicher Lohn für gleiche Arbeit: Eckpunkte für geseztliche Regelung', *Fraktion Intern*, 3 (11 April 2011), 11, www.spdfraktion.de/cnt/rs/rs_datei/0,,14434,00.pdf (accessed 21 April 2012)

Göttingen chronicle for 15 March 1915, www.stadtarchiv.goettingen.de/chronik/1915__03htm (accessed 19 July 2007)

Hertling, A., 'Representing Gender: Automobility in Discourse of

Femininity in the Weimar Republic' (2004), 4–6, www.carstudies.de/gender/repr_gender/representinggender.pdf (accessed 26 March 2012)

Hessler, M., '"Do companies know what women want?" The Introduction of Electrical Domestic Appliances during the Weimar Republic', *Technology/Technologies*, 13 (1998–99), http://hdl.handle.net/2027/spo.ark5583.0013.002 (accessed 19 November 2011)

Schoppmann, C., 'Anna Elisabet Weirach (1887–1970)', www.lesbengeschichte.de/bio_weirauch_d.html (accessed 25 July 2012)

Schröder, W. H., W. Weege and M. Zech, *Kollektive Biographie der Landtagsabgeordneten der Weimarer Republik 1918–1933* (Cologne: Quantum, 2004), http://biosop.zhsf.uni-koeln.de/ParlamentarierPortal/bioweil.htm (accessed 5 August 2011)

'Vor 80 Jahren um die Welt', *Welt Online* (3 March 2007), www.welt.de/welt_print/article743782/Vor_80_Jahren_um_die_Welt.html (accessed 18 February 2012)

Index

Note: page numbers in italics refer to illustrations.

Aachen 26
abortion 31–2, 71, 88, 99, 200,
    210–15, 235, 296
    see also Criminal Code, Articles
    218–20
ADLV *see* General German Women
    Teachers' Association
adoption 221
advertising 3, 233, 255, 259–60,
    266–7, 269, 277, 279, 280
agriculture 16, 18, 20–1, 137,
    140, 143–4, 148, 170, 293,
    295
Allen, Ann Taylor 18
Allen, Keith 25
Altmann-Gottheiner, Elisabeth 18,
    159
Altona 19
amenorrhoea 32
Amsterdam 106, 263
Anhalt 160
Ankum, Katharina von 255
Antwerp 20
apprentices/ apprenticeships 146,
    150, 153, 166
Arbeiterwohlfahrt see Workers'
    Welfare Organisation
Arras 106
Association of Catholic Women
    Teachers 160
Association of German Doctors
    156, 212

Association of German Female
    Reich Postal and Telegraph
    Civil Servants (VRT) 163, 169,
    294
Association of German Female
    University Lecturers 158
Augspurg, Anita 35, 66, 106
Aussem, Cilly 263
Austria 98, 101
Auxiliary Service Law 17–19

Baden 20, 35, 83, 90–1, 104, 136,
    148, 154, 157–8, 160, 162,
    167, 209
    Education Ministry 159
    Superior Court 168
    Welfare Ministry 162
Baden, Max von 37
Baden-Baden 160
Bang, Nina 98
Baranowski, Shelley 266
Bauhaus 277
Baum, Marie 88, 162
Baum, Vicki, 259, 262, 278
    Menschen im Hotel 276
    Stud. Chem. Helene Willfüer
    259, 276
Bäumer, Gertrud 14, 18, 23, 33–4,
    69, 84, 88, 93, 96–7, 102,
    107–8, 161–2, 169, 206, 259
Bavaria 16, 20–1, 35, 71, 81, 89,
    106, 158, 163, 260, 263–4, 292

Bavarian People's Party (BVP) 79–80, 93, 222, 224
BdÄ see Federation of German Women Physicians
BdF see Federation of German Women's Associations
BdM see League for the Protection of German Mothers
beauty contests 267
beauty products 267, 273, 277
Beckmann, Emmy 169
Behm, Margarete 93, 97, 99
Beinhorn, Elly 265
Belgium 19
Bergmann, Gretel 265
Berlin 3, 6, 14–15, 18, 23–8, 32, 34, 37, 64–9, 83, 103, 107, 135, 137, 150, 152, 155–6, 160, 162, 164, 167–8, 203, 205, 206, 208–9, 211, 214, 217, 222, 225, 227, 231, 233–4, 254, 257, 261, 264, 265, 267–8, 272, 274–8
Berliner Illustrirte Zeitung 258–9, 269, 270–1
Bessel, Richard 15, 18, 22, 31, 136–7
BfM see League for the Protection of German Mothers
birth control 3–5, 31, 200, 208–10, 213, 234
  birth control clinics 206, 210
birth rate 30–2, 38, 138, 165, 200, 203, 209–10, 216, 234, 272, 295
'black shame' 100–1
blockade 25, 99
Blücher, Evelyn, Princess von 28, 64
Bluhm, Agnes 213
Bondfield, Margaret 98
Bosch 22, 136
Bott, Hilde 157
Boyd, Catherine 21
Brandenburg 36, 144
Brauns Commission 167
Bremen 82, 91, 222
Bremme, Gabriele 5

Bridenthal, Renate 4, 6, 134, 171
Brockmann, Stephen 273–4
Brunswick 15, 66, 160, 230
Brussels 17, 20
Bubikopf 2, 151, 268–9, 280, 295
Burgdörfer, Friedrich 209
BVP see Bavarian People's Party

cabaret 275, 277
Canning, Kathleen 13, 146
Caritas 229
Casti Connubii 167, 210, 214
Catholic Church 210, 212, 222, 224, 228, 235, 263, 294
Catholic Women's League (KFB) 23, 30, 76, 86, 88–9, 101, 105, 109, 216, 224, 267
Cecilie, Crown Princess 104
Central Union of White-Collar Workers (ZdA) 153
Centre Party (Z) 37, 70–1, 76, 79–80, 82, 84, 88, 89, 91, 93, 99, 109, 167, 212, 220–2, 224
  Women's Advisory Committee 86, 278
childbed fever 226–7
childbirth 148, 226–7
Childers, Thomas 70–1
cinema 255–8, 265, 268, 278
Civil Code 106, 138, 205, 220, 222, 224, 294
civil servants/ service 16–17, 137, 139, 142, 150, 152, 154, 159–69, 171, 23
  Remuneration Law (1920) 232
coitus interruptus 32, 40, 209
Cologne 2, 26, 86, 91, 217
Communist International 65
Constitution see Weimar Constitution
contraception 4, 32, 206–10, 212–13, 219, 234–5, 295
Cooper, Ethel 26
Cottbus 104
Council of People's Delegates 37, 63–4, 278
Courths-Mahler, Hedwig 256

Crew, David 221, 225, 227, 235
crime 274–5
Criminal Code 213–14
　Article 175 233
　Article 184 209
　Articles 218–220 78, 212–14, 230
Crowdy, Rachel 107

DAB *see* German Federation of Female Academics
Daniel, Ute 14, 26, 38
Darmstadt 136
Davis, Belinda 25, 33
DDP *see* German Democratic Party
death penalty 106, 215, 275
DEF *see* German Protestant Women's League
demobilisation 22, 66, 134–7, 145, 147, 154, 166, 216
Denmark 100, 296
department store 150, 152, 255, 267, 272
Depression 105, 134, 138, 144, 147, 154–5, 157, 161, 164–71, 203–4, 206, 210, 226–8, 231, 276, 293–4
deputy commanding generals 25, 30
Der Weg der Frau 70, 262
Detmold 135
Dickinson, Edward Ross 1
Die Dame 258–9
Die deutsche Frau 103
Die Frau 19
Die Frau im Staat 106
Die Frauenwelt 70
Die Freundin 233
Die Genossin 86
Die Gleichheit 63
Die Kämpferin 88
Diehl, Guida 104–5
Dietrich, Marlene 262, 275, 278
disarmament 105–6
divorce 71, 99, 201, 221–5, 235, 294
Dix, Otto 273

DNHV *see* German National Commercial Employees' Association
DNVP *see* German National People's Party
domestic servants/ service 15–16, 78, 135–7, 139–44, 148, 170, 231, 293
Doppelverdiener 164, 166–7, 169
Dransfeld, Hedwig 76, 101–2
Dresden 170
DStP *see* German State Party
Düncker, Käte 65
Düsseldorf 278
DVP *see* German People's Party

East Prussia 13, 33
Economics Party 224
education 66, 71, 90, 98, 106, 154, 160, 171, 221, 230, 258, 261
　further education 138, 150, 153–4, 229, 257, 293
Eifert, Christiane 87
eight-hour day 22, 147, 279
Eisner, Kurt 37
Elegante Welt 259
Empress Auguste Victoria 13, 28, 34, 228
Enabling Act (1923) 163
Ender, Emma 96
Erfurt 135
eugenics 200, 206–7, 212–13, 235
Erkens, Josephine 234
Evans, Richard 63

Falkenhausen, Marga von 19
Falter, Jürgen 79
family helper 137–8, 140–1, 144
Family Maternity Benefit 226
Family War Benefit 16, 18, 28, 39, 220
fashion 257, 271
Federal Republic *see* West Germany
Federation of German Women Physicians (BdÄ) 156, 158, 214

Federation of German Women's Associations (BdF) 14, 23, 30–4, 36–7, 67, 84, 88–9, 93, 96, 100–2, 105–6, 109, 157–8, 169, 213, 216, 218, 224, 267, 294
First World War 13–40, 64, 101, 142, 145, 165, 201, 261, 267–9, 273, 293, 297
Fleischer, Tilly 265
food shortages 25–7
Föllmer, Moritz 278
Förster, Hedwig 170
fostering 221
Frame, Lynne 279
France 20, 100, 106, 295
Frankfurt am Main 35, 66, 226, 232, 262, 265
Franzoi, Barbara 15
Frauenfront 1932 96
Free Trade Unions 147, 154
Freiburg 154–5
Freikorps 65, 473
Freund-Widder, Michaela 217
Frevert, Ute 165
Fritzsche, Peter 2
Frohman, Larry 228–9
Fromm, Erich 218, 267, 269

Gaebel, Käthe, 156, 159, 162, 169
Ganeva, Mila, 269, 272
Gärtner, Margarete 100
GdA *see* Trade Union of White-Collar Workers
General German Women Teachers' Association (ADLV) 160, 169
Geneva 105
German Communist Party (KPD) 5, 65, 69–71, 74, 80–2, 87–90, 93, 97, 99, 100, 108, 204, 208, 212–14, 224, 234, 297
German Democratic Party (DDP) 5, 69, 71, 75, 80, 84–6, 89, 93, 103, 109, 212, 224
German Fatherland Party 36
German Federation of Female Academics (DAB) 96, 158

German Florists' League 229
German Friendship Association 233
German National Commercial Employees' Association (DNHV) 167
German National People's Party (DNVP) 5, 70–1, 72, 79–81, 84–5, 88–9, 91, 93, 97, 99, 102, 104, 107, 212, 220–1, 224
German People's Party (DVP) 5, 70–1, 80, 84–5, 88, 91, 93, 96–7, 99, 103, 109, 212, 224
German Protestant Women's League (DEF) 37–8, 85, 88–9, 97, 100–1, 216, 218, 224, 267
German Social Democratic Party (SPD) 5, 24, 63, 65–6, 69–71, 73, 79–80, 82, 86–7, 90–1, 99, 109, 208, 212–13, 218, 224, 276, 297
German State Party (DStP) 80, 83, 93, 97
German Textile Workers' Union 148
German Women's Committee to Combat the War Guilt Lie 102, 107
German Women's Fighting League 104
German Women's Order 83
Gesindeordnung 137, 144
Gierke, Anna von 98
Gotha 24
Graf, Rüdiger 1
Great Britain 98, 169, 211, 295
Grossmann, Atina 2, 4, 5, 206, 208, 234, 219
Grosz, Georg 273–4

Hadeln, Charlotte von 104
Haensgen-Dingkuhn, Elsa 274
Hagemann, Karen, 69–70, 206, 209–10, 221, 227–30
Halle 103
Hallgarten, Constanze 35

Hamburg 18, 24, 26, 37, 91, 107, 155, 158, 166, 169, 203–4, 206, 209, 216, 221–2, 226–9, 234, 277
Hanover 19, 34, 135, 231
Harris, Victoria 215, 217
Harvey, Elizabeth 2, 104–5
Heidelberg 22, 154–5
Heineman, Elisabeth 205–6
Heinemann, Rebecca 32
Heinsohn, Kirsten 87, 97, 104
Heiser, Paul 211
Hermann, Else 292, 295
Hesse 160, 168
Hessen-Offenbach 86
Heymann, Lida Gustava 35, 66, 106
Hindenberg-Delbrück, Bertha 107
Hindenburg, Paul von 17, 20, 24, 34, 82
Hindenburg Programme *see* Auxiliary Service Law
Hirschfeld, Magnus 208
Hitler, Adolf 76, 81, 104, 109–10, 265, 273, 297
Holland 100–1, 169
homework/homeworkers 99, 141, 148, *149*, 268, 277
housewives 27, 39, 66, 70, 76, 138, 230–2, 266, 279
housewives' associations 85, 88, 103, 107, 203, *204*, 231, 259
housework 144, 166, 230–2, 235, 258
housing 16, 66, 227, 230–2, 234–5
Hugenberg, Alfred 85, 97
Hutton, Marcelline 110
hyperinflation 134, 144, 147, 154, 166, 203, 208, 219, 221, 226–7, 232, 274, 280, 293

ICW *see* International Council of Women
IFFF *see* International Women's League for Peace and Freedom
illegitimate children 99, 206, 219–21, 235, 294

Imperial Post and Telegraph Service 16–17
India 265
industry 15–16, 19–21, 134, 137, 139, 142, 144–7, 165, 168, 170–1, 234, 293, 295
infant mortality 220, 227–8, 235, 296
International Council of Women (ICW) 106–7
International Women's League for Peace and Freedom (IFFF) 105–6, 214
Iron Front 71, 109

Jannasch, Lilli 35, 101
Jena 66, 158
Jensen, Erik 265
Jews 71, 103, 278–9, 298
Jones, Elizabeth Bright 4, 18, 137, 144, 165
Jovanowitsch, Sonja 267
Juchacz, Marie 65, 86–8, 110
Jürgens, Grete 279
Jus Suffragii 19

Kaiser 14, 36–7
Kampmann, Doris 4
Karlsruhe 18, 83, 148, 222
Kästner, Erich *Fabian* 275
Kessemeier, Gesa 272
Keun, Irmgard 275–6, 278
 Das kunstseidene Mädchen 275–6
 Gilgi, eine von uns 276
KFB *see* Catholic Women's League
Kiel 64, 230
Kienle, Else 214
Kirchhoff, Auguste 31, 35, 109
Klein, Ella 275
Klink, Getrud 83
Knobelsdorff, Elisabeth von 20, 164
Köhler, Hanni 265
Kollwitz, Käthe 277, 279
KPD *see* German Communist Party

Kracauer, Siegfried 258, 280
Krahwinkel, Hilde 263
Kramer, Helgard 143, 165
Kuczynski, Jürgen 21
Kuhr, Piete 27
Kundrus, Birthe 3
labour service 156, 166
Lacey, Kate 69, 260
Lang-Brumann, Thusnelda 93, 96, 98
Lange, Helene 21–2, 88, 102, 169, 298
Laserstein, Lotte 279
Law Concerning the Employment of Women before and after Childbirth (1927) 99, 226
Law to Prevent Hereditarily Diseased Offspring (1933) 213
Law to Protect Young People from Trashy and Smutty Literature 99, 233
League against Women's Emancipation 36
League for Human Rights 233
League for the Protection of German Mothers (BfM) 31, 35, 101, 205–6, 208, 214, 225
League of Jewish Women 101
League of Nations 34, 101, 107
League of Rhenish Women 100
Leipzig 26, 29, 82, 92, 156, 212, 216, 225, 256, 260, 265
leisure 153, 255–66, 272, 279, 292, 295, 297
lesbian(s) 2, 200, 233–4, 235, 275
Lewis, Beth Irwin 272
Lex-Nerlinger, Alice 279
Lübeck 222
Lüders, Else 162, 169
Lüders, Marie-Elisabeth 15, 17–18, 21, 88, 97–8, 158–9, 162, 224, 259
Lustmord 273
Luxemburg, Rosa 64–5

Magdeburg 19, 82, 86, 154, 203
Magnus-Hausen, Frances 84
malnutrition 21, 32
Mammen, Jeanne 233
Mann, Erika 265
Mannheim 90, 216
manual work/workers 21, 136–7, 141–9, 153–4, 163, 165–6, 170, 221, 258, 293
marriage 4, 5, 17, 22, 40, 70, 138, 162–3, 200–1, 204–9, 218–19, 222–5, 231, 234, 294, 296
health certificates for 206
marriage guidance clinics 206–7
married women 16, 28, 37–8, 78, 138, 144–7, 152, 166–70, 201, 226, 294
masculinity 3, 39
masculinisation 16, 108, 263, 269, 272, 274, 296
maternal mortality 227, 235
Maternity Benefit 226
maternity benefits 32, 148
Maternity Welfare 226
Mauermeyer, Gisela 265
Mayer, Helene 265
McCormick, Richard 6, 275, 296–7
Mecklenburg 145, 154
Mende, Clara 102, 107
midwife 32, 211, 225–6
Miss Germany 267
modernity 1–2, 165, 171, 200, 272–3, 295–6
Mother's Day 229–30
motherhood 4, 83, 206, 225–30, 266, 276, 296
unmarried 206, 219–21, 226, 235, 276, 296
Mouton, Michelle 200, 220–2, 224
Mueller-Otfried, Paula 38, 63, 97–9, 102, 216
Munich 37, 66, 106, 155, 231, 263
Munk, Marie 157
Münster 19, 26, 217, 228, 230

National Assembly 65–6, 88–9, 94, 97–9, 136, 212, 216
  elections to 69, 76, 79, 108
National Congress of Workers' and Soldiers' Councils 66
National Day of German Women 33
National Socialist German Workers' Party (NSDAP) 1, 5–6, 63, 69, 77, *84*, 85, 90, 96–7, 104–5, 110, 169–70, 200, 204, 207, 210, 213–14, 218, 221, 225, 232, 234–6, 265, 272, 278, 296, 298
  attitudes to women 70, 76, 80–3, 90, 96, 104, 108–9, 170, 297
National Socialist Women's Organisation (NSF) 82–3
National Women's Committee to Combat Versailles 102
National Women's Service (NFD) 23–5
Nebbe, Margarete 275
Neher, Carola 262
Nelson, Robert 16, 39
Neulussheim 104
New Land Movement 104–5
'new woman' 2–4, 6, 76, 134, 150, 200–1, 203, 230, 254, 257, 266–9, 272, 276, 280, 292, 295
New York 259, 265, 275
Nienhaus, Ursula 4
NSDAP *see* National Socialist German Workers' Party
NSF *see* National Socialist Women's Organisation
Nuremberg 26, 264
nurses 19, 150

Offenburg 213
Oldenburg 145, 158, 201
Opferdienst der deutschen Frau 83
Orfali, Steffi 264
Oslo 106
Ostwald, Hans 219, 227
Overbeck, Gerta 274

pacifism/pacifists 34–5, 64, 83, 101, 106, 109–10
Papen, Fritz von 218
Paris 263, 267
Patriotic Women's Association 23
peace 14, 22, 26, 33–6, *68*, *73*, 100
Personnel Reduction Decree 163–4, 169
Peterson, Brian 80
Petro, Patrice 3, 296
Peukert, Detlev 1, 171, 200, 257
Pfülf, Toni 110
Pine, Lisa 265
Poland 19
Pomerania 144, 292
Pope Benedict 34
Pope Pius XI 167, 210
population policy 4, 31, 98, 100, 200, 207, 212, 216, 234–6
pregnancy 32–3, 147–8, 204, 206, 208–9, 211–13, 225–6, 235, 277
Prilipp, Beda 102, 107
prisoners of war 13, 22, 29, 32, 99
professions 137, 154, 157, 170–1, 293
  architects 17, 20, 158, 164, 232
  dentists 157
  lawyers 155, 157–8, 170–1, 293, 297
  pharmacists 155, 157
  physicians 17, 20, 155–7, 170–1, 219
  teachers 17, 154–61, 163–4, 167–71
  veterinary surgeons 158
propaganda 27, 29, 36, 39, 106, 218, 258, 265
  party-political 3, 5, 7, 63, 69–71, 76, 83, 109, 255
prostitutes/prostitution 5, 22, 30–1, 143, 200, 215–18, 235–6, 255, 267, 274, 276, 278, 296
  system of regulation 30, 215–16
Protestant Church 67, 158, 210, 212, 228

Protestant Women's Aid 104, 229
Prussia 1, 19, 22, 103, 157–8,
  160–4, 168, 206–9, 218, 222,
  225, 228, 230, 263, 275
  Academy of Arts 277, 279
  Diet 37
  Education Ministry 170
  Justice Ministry 157
  Landtag 76, 91–2
  Law of Siege 25, 29–30
  Welfare Ministry 162, 206, 225
Purpur, Liselotte 278

Quadragesimo Anno 167
Quandt, Hildegard 267
Queen Luise League 103–5

radio 69, 259, 260, 277
Radke-Batschauer, Lina 263
Radusch, Hilde 234, 275
rationalisation 134, 146, 170, 232,
  234, 293
  household 229, 232
rationing 24–7, 32–3, 227
Rauschning, Hermann 63
Red Cross 14, 19, 23, 27
Red Women's and Girls' League
  (RFMB) 87
Reese, Dagmar 262
Reich Association of Married
  Women Teachers 164
Reich Finance Ministry 162
Reich Health Council 206
Reich Interior Ministry 162–3,
  170, 206, 278
Reich Justice Ministry 162, 224
Reich Postal Service 161–3, 167
Reichsfrauenausschuss 84–6, 101,
  105
Reichstag 5, 16, 67, 70–1, 91, 93,
  97, 99, 163, 167, 212, 214,
  216, 220, 224
  elections 76, 78–84, 93, 96, 106
  population policy committee 31,
  212
  suffrage and 23, 37
  women in 89, 91, 93–4, 96, 98–9

Reitsch, Hanna 265
Reuveni, Gideon 259
revolution 6, 31, 37, 40, 63–4, 66,
  71, 146, 159, 292, 295–7
RFMB *see* Red Women's and Girls'
  League
Rich, B Ruby 275
Riefenstahl, Leni 278
Ring of National Women (RNF)
  101–5
Romania 17
Roos, Julia 5, 209, 215, 217
Rosemeyer, Bernd 265
Rosenhaft, Eve 5
Ross, Corey 255
Rouette, Susanne 137
Rowe, Dorothy 272
Rudel-Zeynek, Olga 98

Saldern, Adelheid von 230, 232
Salomon, Alice 18, 64, 107
Sawahn, Anke 26–7
Saxony 4, 29, 91, 144, 160, 162
Schaser, Angelika 13
Scheck, Raffael 5, 34, 85, 91, 97
Schirmacher, Käthe 36, 101
Schleswig-Holstein 201
Schmitz, Marie 99
Schöck-Quinteros, Eva von 104
Schoenbaum, David 134, 171
Schragmüller, Elisabeth 20
Schreiber-Krieger, Adele 98
Second World War 140, 170, 297
Seipp, Adam 18, 29
Sender, Toni 26, 65–6, 97–9, 110
Sennewald, Else 103
sex education 5, 207, 218–19,
  276
sex reform 4, 200, 207–8, 210,
  213–14, 234
sexuality 30, 200, 207, 218–19,
  233–4, 271, 273–6, 278, 295
Siber, Paula 170
sickness insurance funds 148, 165,
  179, 209, 225
Siebrecht, Claudia 33
Sneeringer, Julia 3, 5, 69–71, 80

social work/workers 17, 23, 134, 225–9, 236
Søland, Brigitte 296
soldiers' and workers' councils 64–6
soldiers' wives 16, 18, 24, 28–30, 32
Spartacus League 64–5
SPD *see* German Social Democratic Party
sport 255–7, 261–7, 279–80
Stahlhelm 103–4
Steinbacher, Sybille 110
Stephenson, Jill 4, 109
sterilisation 31, 213, 215, 221
Stibbe, Matthew 27, 35–6, 296
Stinnes, Clärenore 265
Stöcker, Helene 35, 205
Stokes, Patricia 32, 220, 225
Stratigakos, Despina 20
Strauss, Rahel 218
Streubel, Christiane 97
Stritt, Marie 63, 66, 88, 108
students 20, 145, 154–6, 159, 276–7
Sturmabteilung (SA) 83, 272
Stuttgart 214
Süchting-Hänger, Andrea 85, 100, 102, 104
suffrage 4, 23, 36–8, 63, 69, 76, 79–80, 97, 107, 109–10, 295, 297
surplus of women 40, 200–3
Sweden 100–1
Swett, Pamela 208, 255
Switzerland 35, 100, 154

Tatar, Maria 273
Tergit, Gabriele 274
Thälmann, Ernst 81
The Hague International Women's Congress 33, 35
Theweleit, Klaus 273
Thuringia 158, 160, 168, 264
Tiller girls 277–8
Timm, Annette 218
Tingsten, Herbert, 80–2

Todd, Lisa 29–30
town councillors 89–90, 216
Trade Union of White-Collar Workers (GDA) 153
trade unions 6, 37, 147, 154, 293
Treaty of Versailles 38, 99–2, 104–5, 107, 296
Tübingen 22

Ulich-Beil, Else 169
Ullstein 259, 268
unemployment 15, 22, 24, 71, 109, 135–8, 161, 165–9, 204, 217, 228, 297
unemployment benefit 71, 136–7, 166
Union of Female Commercial and Office Personnel 154
Union of German Employers' Associations 166
Union of German Protestant Women's Organisations (VEFD) 67, 85, 100–1, 105
United States of America 211, 268–9, 272, 295
university/universities 20, 22, 154–8, 170–1, 292
Upper Silesia 101
Usborne, Cornelie 2, 31–2, 203, 207–8, 210–13
USPD *see* German Independent Social Democratic Party

Vaerting, Mathilde 158
VEFD *see* Union of German Protestant Women's Organisations
Velde, Theodor van de 208
The Ideal Marriage 208
Velsen, Dorothee von 18, 84
venereal disease 30–1, 38, 143, 206, 215–19, 235–6, 278
Law for Combating 5, 99, 209, 215–18
Verdun 17, 107
Vertrauensfrauen 85–6
Vienna 107

354 Index

Vorwärts 276
Vossische Zeitung 258
voters/voting 67, 70, 76–9, 81
VRT see Association of German Female Reich Postal and Telegraph Civil Servants
wages 18, 35, 144–50, 153, 165, 226, 293
Walmsley, Janet 93, 99
Walter, Hilde 294
war auxiliaries 19, 38
War Office 17–18
Washington 107
Washington Convention 148
Weber, Helene 99–100, 162, 169, 272
Weber, Marianne 88
Weimar Constitution 40, 106, 159, 169, 171, 209, 216, 292–4, 296–7
Article 48 106
Article 109 4
Article 118 278
Article 119 205, 224
Article 121 220
Article 128 157, 162–3, 167–8
Article 145 138, 293
Article 155 230, 232
Weindling, Paul 207
Weirauch, Anna 275, 278
Der Skorpion 275, 278
Weitz, Eric 2–4, 207, 292, 296
welfare 65–6, 83, 87, 90, 98, 100, 108, 138, 150, 154, 156, 200, 203–4, 212, 214, 216, 225, 227–8, 235–6, 292
First World War 13, 15, 17–19, 23–4, 28, 32–3, 36–9
office 32, 143, 166, 203, 217, 220–1
West Germany 78, 138, 143, 146, 165, 210, 294
Westphalia 201, 229
Weyrather, Irmgard 230
Wheeler, Robert 65
white-collar worker(s) 2, 16, 28, 38, 135–7, 141–3, 148, 150–4, 165, 170, 221, 231, 258, 268, 293–5
Widdig, Bernd 274
widows 16, 40, 136, 138, 152, 203, 232
Wiesbaden 82, 201
Wilhelmshaven 64
Wilson, Woodrow 34
Fourteen Points 100
Winter, Jay 201
Wolf, Friedrich 214
Cyankali 214
Women's League of the German Peace Society 14
women's movement 33–8, 89, 105, 107, 159, 295
middle-class 4, 15, 18, 22–4, 33, 67, 69, 83, 88, 96, 105, 108, 110
social democratic 24, 37, 65, 69, 86–7, 100, 257
Women's Suffrage League 34
worker protection laws 21–2, 142–3, 148, 296
Workers' Gymnastics and Sports Association 262
Workers' Welfare Organisation 87, 236
Working Group for the Recovery of the Volk 229–30
working hours 21, 142, 144, 147
World Congress against War 106
Wulffen Erich, 274
Woman as Sexual Criminal 274
Württemberg 145, 160, 164

Young Plan, referendum on 102–3
youth 29, 153, 218
youth groups 105, 219, 256–7, 264–5, 295
youth welfare 162, 200
Youth Welfare Law 99, 220–1

Z *see* Centre Party
Zander, Elsbeth 83

ZdA *see* Central Union of White-
    Collar Workers
Zetkin, Clara 35, 65–6, 87, 97
Ziemann, Benjamin 14, 21, 39, 64
Zietz, Luise 65, 98
Zimmeck, Meta 169
Zirkel, Helene 64
Zweig, Stefan 255